Date Due

Communication and Education
for
Health Promotion and Population Regulation

A Global Perspective

Communication and Education
for
Health Promotion and Population Regulation

A Global Perspective

Edited by

Kuttan Mahadevan

Co-editors

Gao Ersheng
K.A. Pisharoti
Vijayan K. Pillai
Iqbal Shah
Lory Laing
S.L.N. Rao

Kausalya Devi
K.V. Ranganathan
P. Rajaram
Guang Zhen Wang
N. Murugesan
V.M. Sandeep

B.R. Publishing Corporation

[A Division of BRPC (India) Ltd.]

Delhi-110052

Communication and Education

for

Health Promotion and Population Regulation

A Global Perspective

Kuttan Mahadevan

First Published : 2005

ISBN 81-7646-457-0

Rs. 1000

Printed & Published by :
B.R. Publishing Corporation
[A Division of BRPC (India) Ltd.]
425, Nimri Colony,
Ashok Vihar, Phase IV
Delhi – 110052
E-Mail : *brpcltd@del2.vsnl.net.in*

Printed In India

Contents

Abbrevations

AFLA	Adolescent Family Life Act
AIDS	Acquired Immuno Deficiency Syndrome
AIDSVAX	Acquired Immuno Deficiency Syndrome Vaccine
ARC	AIDS Related Condition
ARI	Acute Respiratory Infection
ASB	Antenuptial Sexual Behaviour
AZT	Azidothymidine (Drug for HIV/AIDS)
BRAC	Bangladesh Rural Advancement Committee
CD	Community Development
CDC	Centre for Disease Control
CDCP	Centre for Disease Control and Prevention
CSWs	Commercial Sex Workers
DALY	Disability Adjusted Life Years
DANLEP	Danish Assistance to NLEP
DNA	Deoxyribonucleic Acid
DPT	Diphtheria, Patois and Tetanus
DST	Department of Science and Technology
DWCRA	Development of Women and Children in Rural Areas
EC	Emergency Contracaptive
ELISA	Enzyme Linked Immonosorbent Assay
ESCAP	Economic & Social Communism for Asia & Pacific
FDA	Food and Drug Administration
FSCs	Farm Science Clubs
FWT	Family Warfare Training
GLCUs	Government Leprosy Control Units
GOI	Government of India

GRH	The Ganhigram Institute for Rural Health
GRI	Gandhigram Rural Institute
HAART	Highly Active Anti-Retro Virus Therapy
HCs	Health Centres
HERT	Heardened Electronic and Radiation Technology
HEART	Healing and Early Afterload Reduction Therapy
HFA	Health Family Planning Agency
HIV	Human Immuno Virus
HRD	Human Resource Development
HRT	Harmonal Replacement Therapy
HSC	Hutington Society of Canada
HSC	Health Sciences Centre
HSV	Herpes Simplex Virus
ICDC	Intensive Health Education Cum Leprosy Case Detection Campaign
ICDS	Integrated Child Development Services
ICPD	International Conference on Population and Development
IDUs	Injecting Drug Users
IEC	Information, Education and Communication
IET	Independent Evaluation Team
IMR	Inter Medical Research
IUD	Intra Uterine Device
JIPMER	Jawaharlal Institute for Post-Graduate Medical Education and Research
KAP	Knowledge, Attitude and Practice
KVK	Krishi Vigyan Kendra
LEC	Leprosy Elimination Campaign
MB	Multi Bacillary
MCH	Maternal and Child Health
MDT	Multi Drug Treatment
MLEC	Modified Leprosy Elimination Campaign
MSM	Men Sex Men
MTCT	Mother to Child Transmission
MTP	Medical Termination of Pregnancy

NACO	National Aids Control Organization
NCAPC	National Centre for AIDS Prevention and Control
NCDR	New Case Detection Rate
NDRHS	National Demography and Reproductive Health Survey
NGOs	Non-Government Organizations
NHEI	National Health Education Institute
NLEP	National Leprosy Eradication Programme
NNRTIs	Non-Nucleoside Reverse Transcriptase Inhibitors
NYK	Nehru Yuvak Kendra
PA	Proportion of Agreement
PB	Pauci Bacillary
PCR	Polymerase Chain Reaction
PGL	Persistent Glandular Lymphadenopathy
PHC	Primary Health Care
PHCs	Public Health Centres
PID	Pelvic Inflammatory Disease
PMTCT	Prevention of Mother to Child Transmission
PPTCT	Prevention of Parent to Child Transmission
PRA	Participatory Rural Appraisal
PRC	Population Research Centre
QOC	Quality of care on Contraception
RDA	Recommended Dietary Allowances
RHR	Reproductive Health and Research
RHR	Retail Human Resources
	Rattis for Human Rights
	Rohner, Hibler & Replogle
	Reproductive Health & Research
RNA	Ribonucleic Acid
RTI	Reproductive Tract Infections
SAFE	Surgery for Trichiasis, Antibiotics, Facial Cleanliness
SARS	Severe Acute Respiratory Syndrome
SEWA	Self-Employed Women's Association

SFPC	State Family Planning Commission
SHGs	Self-Help Groups
SIDA	Swedish International Development Association
SSAU	Sample Survey and Assessment Units
STD	Sexually Transmitted Diseases
STIs	Sexually Transmitted Infections
SVIMS	Sri Venkateswara Institute of Medical Sciences
TB	Tuberculosis
TRY	Tap and Reposition Youth
TTK	T.T. Krishnamachari (former Minister)
TVT	Trans Vaginal Tubectomy
UGC	University Grants Commission
ULCs	Urban Leprosy Centres
UNAIDS	United Nations Programme on HIV/AIDS
UNESCAP	United Nations Economic and Social Commission for Asia and the Pacific
UNESCO	United Nations Economic, Social & Cultural Organization
UNFPA	United Nations Population Funds
UNICEF	United Nations International Children Emergency Fund
USDA	US Department of Agriculture
UTI	Urinary Tract Infection
VHN	Village Health Nurse
VHS	Voluntary Health Services
WHO	World Health Organization
YZ	Youth Zone

Introduction

The present book, "Health and Population Education and Communication" was prompted by the deep desire to honour the nonagenarian scholar, Dr. V. Ramakrishna, the doyan of Indian Health Education. For lives to have more productive, healthy and academically valuable contributions in our country, such eminent scholars as Dr. Ramakrishna must be honoured and their achievements their contributions made widely known at home and abroad to serve as role models for posterity for emulation. Therefore, the chief editor of the present book has also published similarly another book on Health Education to honour posthumously the late Dr. D. Jagannatha Reddy, one of the most experienced and respected faculty of the Indian Medical Science and a renowned Institution builder. Owing to the general academic pre-occupations of the editor, the bringing out of this festschrift to Dr. Ramakrishna has been delayed inordinately. However, there is some comfort that though belatedly, we are able to bring out this book in his honour.

This book is international in scope and a valuable contribution to the existing literature on Health Education. Unfortunately as yet there are only very few valuable books, on Health-Education in India. Further, the field is very vast and a single volume cannot hope to cover all the essential aspects. Therefore, whatever themes that could not accommodate in the present volume have been covered in three other book's. They are

1. "Reproductive Health of Humankind in Asia and Africa",
2. "Communication, Modernization and Social Development" and

3. "Health Education for Quality of Life". The present book focuses on

   (i) International policy aspects,
   (ii) Reproductive health,
   (iii) Sexual behaviour,
   (iv) Population dynamics,
   (v) Communication strategies, and
   (vi) Ayurveda and health.

It also provides a synopsis of the phenomenal contributions made by Dr. V. Ramakrishna to Health Education.

The major thrust of this book is on Reproductive Health and related aspects like, Human Sexuality and provides wide coverage to HIV/AIDS in the world in general the USA, China and India. in particular. There are seven articles by Chinese scholars, who focus on most of these aspects with particular reference to their country. As Reproductive Health is very much determined by sexual behaviour, on Human Sexuality, Sexuality and Health, frequency of sex, sexual behaviour and sex education in China and India have been presented in great detail in this volume.

In the area of population dynamics, the inter-relationship between ecology, population and health has been carefully documented using the systems model for a proper understanding of the issues involved. The threat held out by the recent (2003) epidemic of SARS in the Asian countries and Canada, emphasises that ecology has very great relevance for health and human survival. Therefore, the opening chapter under the section on Population Dynamics, very rightly focuses on ecology and health. As a result of unprecedented ecological change, heat waves struck severely in Paris and the other parts of France in August 2003, and 10,000 people are reported to have died for the first time in human history. This traumatic experience should alert everyone to protect the ecosystem throughout the world. Another serious threat to Humanity is posed by pesticides and chemical fertilisers. Their residues reach children and adults through the fodder eaten by cows and buffaloes and subsequently from their milk. Of course infected animal meat also endangers life because of the risk of cancer, the chemicals may cause. Unfortunately people have not been made sufficiently aware of this dangerous risk to humanity through Health Education. In order to prevent such danger, the use of bio-fertilisers and neem as pesticide has to be promoted expeditiously and the process has to be continued without any letup. There are in this volume chapters on successful family planning education and management and replacement of induced abortion with emergency contraception accomplished in China. They are the need of the hour in India too. Therefore, the opening chapter on Ecology, Population and Health Education calls for the higher priority to be given to the implication of ecology in Health Education. Of course, when bio-fertiliser replaces chemical fertiliser the yield of agricultural products per hectare may reduce drastically. If population growth is not controlled, at the same time, the abrupt discontinuation of chemical fertiliser, which helps better and quick yield may not be feasible. However, neem as pesticide must be adopted as soon as possible and extended to as many fields as possible.

Effective communication is the principal strategy of Health Education. However, effective communication strategies are not often adopted in Health Education Programmes. In a backward and illiterate society, ordinary communication will not deliver the goods. Therefore, two effective communication strategies which have been proved to be very successful are presented here.

(i) Communication through satisfied adopters and
(ii) Repeated and multiple communication successfully adopted at the women's group meetings (Self-Help Group/DWCRA).

These methods of communication deserve to be adopted by all health educators for the success of Health Education. The role of communication in preventing the risk of HIV/AIDS in the USA, importance of counselling in communication adopted in China and successful communication through a Communication networking in Leprosy eradication programme, which is a landmark achievement, have also been lucidly presented in this book.

Life Style and Health

Life-style is the way in which a person or group of people lives and works. It includes their habits, customs, exercises pertaining to their region and the other related aspects of everyday life, which affect their health, and deserves to be given high priority. Since a number of articles on this topic have already been presented in our first Health Education book it is not repeated here. However, we emphasize here the highest priority to be given under health education to life-style for the prevention of several diseases. For instance, very often conventional advice given by doctors to patients is that they should go for a walk everyday. This general advice has to be suitably modified for the practical benefit of people. Walking, though good, is not a panacea for all bodily ills; it is essential for one and all to *follow organ-specific and morbidity-preventing exercise* rather than mere going for a walk. For example, such exercises for the whole body as swimming and cycling; play like shuttle cock or badminton and yoga like suryanamaskaram may be followed according to one's age. Further to strengthen oneself, pranayama and bastrika may be daily practised. Since diabetic mellitus is on the increase every body should practice daily Navasana and Dhanurasana to revitalise the pancreas, instead of depending on walking, which would not give exercise to the pancreas. In addition, cardiac and cerebral problems are on the increase now-a-days. In order to prevent both of them, appropriate physical exercise and suitable food and meditation are required. For example, exercise for the chest and neck must be given daily. Further, food with less fat, salt and carbohydrates and with more fibre and leafy vegetables, must be used. It is worth knowing that the Chinese in general have less risk of diabetics because their intake of rice is only ¼ or even less than that of the quantity of rice most Indians consume. Therefore, scientific food habits, those which promote bodily and mental health and appropriate physical exercises are to be together followed daily by everybody for maintaining good health and to prevent those diseases that are on the increase in both the developed and developing countries. Therefore, Health Education which has a very significant role to play, must focus on these aspects of health through the multiple communication channels and media by reducing the over emphasis on mere entertainment especially in the electronic channel, which promotes only mental and physical inertia. The enormity of the damage being done to millions of television watchers in our country, especially to the health of their body and mind, has not been realised.

A valuable addition to this book is a paper on the significance and efficacy of Ayurveda, the indigenous system of medicine, which has suffered enormous damage because of neglect, prejudice, and false propaganda by vested intersects against it. It is only now some attention is being given to it and grudgingly its value recognised. Several diseases, which have not registered cure by the other system of medicine, notably Allopathy, can be curved by this system without side effects. Eminent Ayurvedic Physician's Dr. Ravindranath, has demonstrated that their therapy can successfully treat retinites and prevent its recurrence which was not possible through Allopathy. Similarly degenerative discuses like Arthritis, sodalities, chronic backache, sexual and the other degeneration, can be successfully treated by Ayurveda, which is within the means of an average man, and free from side effects. It is time that this system of medicine of centuries' standing is properly understood and popularised, and freed from prejudice and hangover of colonial past, what is most important is that to promote sound health for all, any system of medicine, which has a rational and scientific basis and proved its efficacy should be gladly welcomed.

Importance of Exercise

According to Dr. John J. Ratey, Harward Professor of Clinical Psychiatry, who is the author of "A user's guide to the Brain" "Physical movements call upon writing and match" and that "Physically active people reported an increase in academic abilities, memory retrieval and cognitive abilities". Formerly scientists believed that individuals as they aged lost the function of the brain due to outright loss of cells. Today, research indicates that memory lapses are more likely due to breakdown in the synapses or connections between nerves. Similarly researchers from the University of California at Irvine have found that a healthy brain continues to grow new neurons indefinitely, which can actually slow the brain's ageing process and even reverse the existing damage. In fact, a healthy brain is the product of a well-organised and balanced LIFESTYLE that includes proper nutrition, stress management and mental and physical exercise. For example, at University of Illinois, people who moved from a sedentary to active lifestyle (45-minute aerobic workouts per week) improved their mental performance by as much as 25 per cent in six months. In addition, individuals whose diets included vitamins CEB, and beta-carotene scored higher in memory tests and maintained mental functions better. Judi Sheppard Missett Lats concludes in her article that physical exercise has a positive influence on everything from weight control to cancer and heart disease risk. Mentally and emotionally, exercise is a natural stress reducer, self-esteem booster and anti-depressant (*The Hindu*, Aug 17, 2003).

The last section of the present book highlights on the valuable contributions of Dr. V. Ramakrishna and presents his unique profile, so that present and future generation may be inspired by his example. Therefore, this book will be a source of inspiration for all health educators. It would be found valuable as a text for M.P.H. course, Masters in Population Studies and social workers. It would be equally useful to all those who are engaged in community medicine, Rural Development, Women's Studies, Home Science, Communication, Management and Behavioural Sciences. Thus, we present it for the benefit of all Universities, International agencies and Institutions, concerned with health, health education, and better quality of life for inspiring the posterity.

Prof. Dr. Kuttan Mahadevan

Part - I

POLICY PERSPECTIVES

1

World Health Organization and Health Education

Ronald Swatzyna

The World Health Organization utilizes education as an integral component of their prevention program. Raising awareness through provision of information, in theory, will enable people to change their behaviour and reduce health risks (EB105/12). This paper delineates the World Health Organization's approach to health within the framework of the role of health education in prevention of health risks and disease.

"Worldwide, health life expectancy can be increased by 5 to 10 years if governments and individuals work together to reduce major health risk in each region" (WHO, 2002, para. 3). The World Health Organization's 110th Session (5-2002) identifies the top ten preventable health risks; childhood and maternal underweight; unsafe sex; high blood pressure; tobacco; alcohol; unsafe water; sanitation and hygiene; high cholesterol; indoor smoke from solid fuels; iron deficiency; and overweight/obesity. These preventable health risks account for approximately 22 million of the 56 million deaths that occur globally each year (Press Release WHO, 30 October, 2002). Additionally, these health risks contribute to susceptibility to communicable disease (e.g. malaria, tuberculosis, polio and HIV/AIDS), non-communicable disease (cardiovascular diseases, diabetes, cancer and lung diseases) and mental illness (EB110/11). To meet this challenge, the World Health Organization is dedicating its efforts to improve health globally by the year 2005. Accomplishment of this monumental task requires a multifaceted strategic approach specifically involving monitoring and evaluation, education and prevention, treatment and technology.

Organizational Structure and Priorities

The World Health Organization's health focus (Programme budget 2000-2001) identifies four strategic directions and provides a technical framework for operation:

1. Reducing excess mortality, morbidity, and disability, especially in poor and marginalized population
2. Promoting health lifestyles and reducing risk factors to human health that arises from environmental, economic, social and behavioural causes
3. Developing health systems that equitably improve health outcomes, respond to people's legitimate demands, and are financially fair
4. Framing and enabling policy and creating an institutional environment for the health sector, and promoting an effective health dimension to socio, economic, environmental and developmental policy.

(EB110/11, 2002, p. 2)

The work of the World Health Organization is further organized into nine broad themes reflecting their strategic emphases linking strategy, organizational structure, budget and accountability (EB110/11). These broad themes include: communicable diseases, non-communicable diseases, family and community health, sustainable development and healthy environments, social change and mental health, health technology and pharmaceuticals, evidence and information for policy, external relations and governing bodies, and general management. Furthermore, the World Health Organization has five priority areas: malaria, tuberculosis, HIV/AIDS, mental health, and strengthening of health systems. Innovatively, in 2000-2001, the World Health Organization established three cabinet projects: Roll Back Malaria, the Tobacco Free Initiative and Partnerships for Health Sector Development. The hope is that establishment of such projects will perpetuate visibility and impact in these areas of high health risk and create a 'unity of purpose' throughout World Health Organization.

Of the nine organizational themes, communicable diseases, non-communicable diseases, family and community health, sustainable development and healthy environments, and social change and mental health, use education at the micro (individual/family) level, meso (community/organizational) and macro (societal/policy) level. This paper is organized around these five themes discussing the World Health Organization's educational integration.

Communicable Diseases

With approximately 11 million people killed annually due to communicable diseases, the World Health Organization has "intensified global and country level efforts for disease control by catalyzing global partnerships between governments, international organizations, donor agencies, foundations, non-governmental organizations and private entities" (EB110/11, p. 2). The primary goals of these partnerships are to "roll back malaria," and to "stop tuberculosis" by providing the necessary medical supplies to governments and non-governmental organizations working in developing countries. Specific to Africa, partnerships with pharmaceutical companies are helping the fight against trypanosomiasis and lymphatic filariasis.

A joint report by UNAIDS, UNICEF, and the World Health Organization released on 22 April, 2002 states that the right intervention at the right time can prevent AIDS, TB, and Malaria. "Any effective effort to reduce the burden of disease faced by the world's poorest people must concentrate on AIDS, TB and malaria" (Press Release WHO, 22 April, 2002, para. 6). The main points of this report are:

- Young people account for half of all new HIV infections;
- The most rapid spread of HIV/AIDS is in Eastern Europe and Central Asia;
- HIV and tuberculosis form a lethal combination;
- Malaria places 40% of the world's population at risk;
- The most effective interventions against all three diseases is prevention and treatment;

- Young people in developing countries still have far too little knowledge about HIV/AIDS and how it is transmitted;
- Fewer than 5% of people who need treatment for AIDS in the developing world have access to the medicines they need;
- Only one fifth of all TB cases globally receive high-quality treatment;
- In 28 African countries, 50% of the antimalarial medicines available are ineffective due to bad quality or drug resistance.

Although there are many more communicable diseases in the world, AIDS, TB, and malaria pose the gravest threat to humanity. Providing health education to families, communities and governments about prevention and intervention of these three world health threats will also reduce other communicable diseases, for instance, other sexually transmitted diseases.

Non-communicable Diseases

Cardiovascular disease, diabetes, cancer and chronic lung diseases share common risk factors. These common risk factors made it possible for the World Health Organization to develop a standardized surveillance "tool" for non-communicable diseases. "The tool defines core variables for surveys, surveillance and monitoring, and offers guidance for low- and middle-income countries on initiation of control of non-communicable diseases" (EB110/ 11, p. 3). Additionally, the World Health Organization developed management tools for tracking chronic lung disease, diabetes, cardiovascular disease, and cancer and, most importantly, guidelines for prevention and clinical management of non-communicable diseases. Worldwide, physical inactivity, increasing tobacco use and poor diet and nutrition are causing a rapid rise in cardiovascular diseases, diabetes and obesity and has increased the risk of colon cancer, high blood pressure, osteoporosis, lipid disorders, depression and anxiety (Press Release WHO, 4 April, 2002).

Cardiovascular disease and strokes kill more than 12 million people per year worldwide. WHO says that the major risk factors are high blood pressure, high cholesterol, obesity and smoking (Press Release WHO, 17 October, 2002). The World Health Organization predicts that by 2020, 25 per cent more healthy years will be lost if cardiovascular disease is allowed to progress. The World Health Report 2002 urges countries to "adopt policies and programmes to promote population-wide interventions like reducing salt in processed foods, cutting dietary fat, encouraging exercise and higher consumption of fruits and vegetables and lowering smoking" (para. 13). In regard to physical inactivity, WHO recommends that governments enact transportation policies that promote walking and riding bicycles, legislating tobacco-free policies for public spaces, build parks, playgrounds and community centres, promote physical activity programmes in schools and communities (Press Release WHO, 4 April, 2002).

Family and Community Health

The World Health Organization has focused its efforts in three areas of family and community health; childhood illness, pregnancy, and HIV/AIDS.

Childhood illness

Every year, 11 million children die from preventable and treatable causes (WHO/18, 12 March, 2002). Of the 11 million, 1.5 million are adolescents and 8 million are babies (half of which are less than one month old). The predominant causes of adolescent deaths are substance abuse, reproductive ill health, suicide, injuries and violence, while the main killers of children are pneumonia, diarrhoea, malaria, measles, HIV/AIDS, and malnutrition. Malnutrition affects 150 million children and undermines their immune system. As a result, 1.9 million children die annually from bacterial polluted food and water (Press Release WHO, 9 May, 2002).

Ninety per cent of the 11 million children that die each year die at home. The Executive Director of UNICEF, Carol Bellamy, posits that children's survival is dependent upon the care they receive in the home. The parents and caregivers need learn the basic skills about child rearing and have access to the necessary and commodities to save their children's lives (Press Release WHO/18, 12 March, 2002).

The approach that the World Health Organization and UNICEF uses is to strengthen health services and, more importantly, to educate communities, families and individuals. This empowering approach focuses on bringing services to the people instead of bringing people to the services (Press Release WHO/18, 12 March, 2002). The year 1997 marked the beginning of an integrated care approach for children and moved away from support of single childhood disease programmes within the World Health Organization (AF/INF.DOC./2, 1999). The Integrated Management of Childhood Illness has now been implemented or at least introduced in over 100 countries (EB110/11).

Pregnancy

Ten countries have begun work on the initiative "Making Pregnancy Safer." The goals of this program are to increase access to health services for mothers and newborns, and to improve that quality of care (EB110/11). To assure success of this initiative, the World Health Organization researched maternal health, family planning, reproductive tract infections, and sexually transmitted infections. This information provided the basis for needed reproductive health services and the development guidelines for integrated management of pregnancy.

Women's right to safe sexuality and to autonomy in all decisions relating to sexuality is respected almost nowhere... By and large, most men, however poor, can choose when, with whom and with what protection if any, to have sex. Most women cannot" (Fact Sheet No 247, 2000). World Health Organization has "scaled up" its efforts to combat HIV/AIDS via both prevention and care with particular attention to the sub-Saharan, Africa (EB110/11). In an effort to bring attention to the AIDS epidemic, the World Health Organization educates the world through Fact Sheets published online at *www.World Health Organization.int/inf-fs/en/fact.html.*

HIV/AIDS

In June of 2000, the World Health Organization reported that of the 33.6 million people who are living with HIV/AIDS, 22 million are located in sub-Saharan Africa and 14.8 million are women. "Studies conducted in nine countries in sub-Saharan Africa suggest that prevalence among women is now higher than among men, with 12 to 13 women currently infected for every 10 men" (EB105/12, 1999, p. 1).

Human rights and women with HIV/AIDS is a topical subject with the World Health Organization because women are more vulnerable to infection biologically, economically, socially and culturally. The World Health Organization has developed gender-based response based on three main reasons:

1. The AIDS epidemic is being driven by unequal gender relations in the areas of socio, economic, and power distribution.
2. Women are disproportionately affected by the epidemic because they are physically more vulnerable to infections via their reproductive systems, they are the primary AIDS caregivers regardless of their health, and they are often blamed for spreading the infection.
3. Finally, women's clinical management has always been based on research undertaken by men.

Women must have clinical management tailored to their particular symptomatology and disease progression to combat HIV/AIDS effectively.

The major issues of women and human rights as cited by the World Health Organization (2000) are that women:

- Have lack of control over sexuality and sexual relationships.
- Have poor reproductive and sexual health, leading to serious morbidity and mortality.
- Experience neglect in areas of health needs, nutrition and medical care.
- Are subject to clinical management based on research on men.

- Are subjected to all forms of coerced sex—violent rape to cultural and economic obligations.
- Suffer harmful cultural practices: from genital mutilation to practices such as "dry" sex.
- Are stigmatized and experience discrimination with regard to AIDS and all STIs.
- Adolescents lack access to education for prevention, condoms, reproductive rights, and health services before and after they are sexually active.
- Are finding their children infected with HIV due to sexual abuse.
- Are experiencing negative consequences when they disclose their HIV status to their partner/husband (WHO) infected them.
- Find that after disclosing their HIV status, it is more difficult to enlist care and support.

Mother to Child Transmission

Half a million under the age of 15 suffer infections. Most of these infections have been transmitted from mother to child (Fact Sheet 242, 2000). World Health Organization's educational approach to prevent mother to child transmission (MTCT) of HIV/AIDS, begins with informed consent: informed consent in regard to testing mothers during pregnancy, informed consent to the intervention and informed consent as to the mothers' options of termination or continuation with the pregnancy (Fact Sheet No. 242).

The informed consent program includes a health education approach, which involves the husband/partner at all stages. In addition to the intervention itself, the program provides provisions for counselling in a variety of areas (pre-test, pre-intervention, infant feeding and contraceptive advice) and provisions of family planning and support services.

Prevention

"Where effective prevention strategies have been systematically implemented, the incidents of HIV infection have been reduced. Where they have not, HIV continues to spread with great speed in some countries" (EB105/12, 1999, p. 2). A major United Nations study finds an alarming lack of knowledge about HIV/AIDS among young people. This ignorance contributes significantly to the infection of 6000 young people per day (Press Release WHO, 2 July, 2002). In a report given at the 105th Session (1999) the Director-General stated that health education was a key proven intervention which includes; raising and promoting safer awareness; promoting safer sex through information; providing life-skills education for young people (in and out of school); providing protection methods such as male and female condoms, so that young people may opt to change their behaviour reducing the transmission of infection; and finally, targeting young people (in the schools) before they become sexually active (EB105/12, 1999).

Sustainable Development and Healthy Environments

Sustainable development requires a healthy nutritional environment relatively free from toxins. Malnutrition and high-risk pollutants, common to many developing countries, have a high human and economic cost inhibiting social development. The World Health Organization's educational approach to malnutrition has been to develop normative standards and guidelines for "nutrition, energy requirements of all age groups, vitamin and mineral requirements, management of nutrition in major emergencies, and safe levels of vitamin A in pregnant women and children" (EB110/11, 2002, p. 4). In addition, the World Health Organization has prepared a global strategy for feeding infants and young children. Nutrition, although vital, cannot solely protect against high-risk pollutants.

The World Health Organization is committed to protect the human environment and has recently evaluated and published findings on 250 specific chemical and other high-risk pollutants (EB110/11, 2002). Additionally, Worl Health Organization's drinking water guidelines were amer global and regional guidelines for air quality wer Member States are now developing national r instruments to improve their environments us guidelines.

Social Change and Mental Health

How humans treat themselves intentionally or unintentionally due to lack of education are of high priority to the World Health Organization. This is identified in five primary areas of social change: diet and physical activity, substance abuse, traffic injury, blindness, and school health programms. The theme for World Health Day 2001 was "Move for Health" and the focus was on diet and physical activity to prevent non-communicable diseases (EB110/11, 2002). At the United Nations Second Assembly (2002) the World Health Organization presented their work on healthy aging. The World Health Organization promotes health lifestyle changes through these types of forums so that an impact for social change can be accomplished at the micro or individual/ family level.

To promote social change in regard to substance abuse, the World Health Organization "compiled and disseminated a global database on alcohol consumption, prepared a multinational study on drug injecting and on use of amphetamine-type stimulants, and launched a global initiative on the primary prevention of substance abuse" (EB110/11, 2002, p. 4). The creation of this database provides unfounded opportunity for empirically based research on a global scale. Although the world's population is very diverse, when it comes to substance abuse, the effect upon our human bodies is the common to all.

The automobile technology is now global and has a paradoxical effect upon developing societies. Traffic injuries have come to the forefront of concern for social change. World Health Organization's first strategy for reducing these injuries began with a proposed five-year investigation into the epidemiology and prevention of traffic-injury.

WHO estimates that 180 million people worldwide are visually disabled. Forty to forty-five million of those are blind, and over seven million go blind each year (Press Release WHO, 10 October, 2002). Poverty and lack of access to eye care are most frequently associated with preventable blindness. "Despite the progress made in controlling blinding conditions such as zerophthalmia and onchocerciasis, there evidence that the overall number of blind persons continues to increase, particularly in the African and South-East Asia Regions" (A55/INF.DOC./2, 1999, p. 12). The programme for the prevention of blindness includes recommending the SAFE strategy (Surgery for trichiasis, Antibiotics, Facial cleanliness and Environmental improvement) (EB110/11, 2002). Thus far, 17 countries have implemented this strategy. The World Health Organization wants to draw attention to the 'right to sight' and get governments to pledge to increase access to quality eye care for prevention and treatment of eye conditions.

"The XVII World Conference on Health Promotion and Health Education (Paris, 2001) launched a global forum for health promotion dialogue with the International Union for Health Promotion and Education and other partners" (EB110/11, 2002, p. 5). World Health Organization, jointly with UNESCO, UNICEF, and the World Bank, continue to foster effective social programmes. The promotion of, and indoctrination into health behaviours, begins in the "formative years." The World Health Organization recognizes the school as a forum of educational opportunity for social change.

The year 2001 was declared as the year of mental health and for the first time since the inception of the World Health Organization, mental health has become a priority (EB110/11, 2002).

Mental Health

The World Health Organization launched a mental health campaign in January 2001, asking governments, health professionals and people throughout the world to acknowledge and attune to the difficulties posed by mental and brain disorders (Press Release WHO/01, 10 January, 2001). WHO estimates 400 million people "suffer from mental or neurological disorders or from psychosocial problems such as those related to alcohol or drug abuse" (para. 3).

The biggest obstacle to treatment is the stigma attached to those with mental illness and the subsequent discrimination and stigmatization. Ultimately, it is shame and fear that prevents nearly two-thirds of those, with a known mental disorder, not to seek help (Press Release

WHO/42, 28 September, 2001). "Stop exclusion—Dare to care," was the slogan for World Health Day, 2001. This was an opportunity for the World Health Organization to raise awareness about the barriers to mental health services and efficacious treatment available for mental and brain disorders.

The fact that many of the WHO Member States lack a mental health programme appears to be the biggest barrier to mental health treatment (Press Release WHO/18, 6 April, 2002). "Seventy-eight countries (43%) have no mental health policy at all, 37 countries (23%) have no community care facilities and in 73 countries-41%-treatment of severe mental disorders is unavailable in primary health care" (Press Release WHO/18, 6 April, 2001, para. 2).

The World Health Organization predicts a continued worldwide rise in mental and neurological disorders and many countries are do not have programmes nor policies necessary to respond to this need. A global survey by WHO found that 11 per cent of the world's disease burden stems from mental and neurological disorders and predicts an increase to 14.6 per cent by the 2020 (Press Release WHO/18, 6 April, 2001). "A lack of urgency, misinformation and competing demands are blinding policy-makers from taking stock of a situation where mental disorders figure among the leading causes of disease and disability in the world, says WHO" (Press Release WHO/42, 28 September, 2001, para. 5). The World Health Organization's approach is to enlighten all countries to the fact that mental and neurological illness must no longer be ignored, the stigma and discrimination must be eliminated and that these countries bear the responsibility to improve the mental health of their people.

Cabinet Projects

During 2001-2002, the World Health Organization created two educational cabinet projects: Roll Back Malaria and the Tobacco Free Initiative. These projects are key issues on the Director-General's agenda. Bringing attention to these key issues is seen as a way to rapidly create visibility and impact throughout the World Health Organization and educate the world in the process.

Roll Back Malaria

The United Nations General Assembly proclaimed 2001-2010 as the decade to Roll Back Malaria in developing countries, particularly in Africa (United Nations General Assembly Resolution 55/284). "The main benefit of designating Roll Back Malaria as a cabinet project was that it fostered a greater understanding in WHO of the problem of malaria, and led to an agreement on the actions needed to make an effective impact" (EB110/11, 2002, p. 8). The World Health Organization's strategy includes "prompt access to treatment, prevention with insecticide-treated nets, epidemic prediction and response, and malaria in pregnancy" (p. 8).

Parasite resistant strains of malaria can render certain antimalarial drug treatments ineffective. In developing countries, the inability to monitor and identify these strains results in not only ineffective treatment, but also delays treatment with effective and available antimalarial medications. The World Health Organization uses this greater understanding of the problem of malaria to encourage governments to monitor the development of parasite resistance to antimalarial medications and to replace drugs that are no longer effective (EB110/11, 2000). In the case of Malaria, education is targeted at the macro level working with governments and other partnerships dedicated to Roll Back Malaria.

Tobacco Free Initiative

Tobacco's impact on world health is documented globally. WHO reports tobacco kills 560 people per hour, which is 13,400 people per day or 4.9 million people annually. They estimate that by the year 2020 tobacco will kill 8.4 million per year (Press Release WHO, 15 October, 2002) with over 70% of these deaths occurring in developing countries (Press Release WHO, 30 July, 2002). Although tobacco is neither a disease (communicable or non-communicable) nor an environmental toxin, it is as deadly.

The World Health Organization's Press Release on May 4, 2001 proposed that tobacco poses a major obstacle to children's rights and later that month (May 30) urged all countries to prevent a tobacco epidemic among women and girls. There are nearly 700 million children in the world and sadly, almost half of them are forced to breathe second-hand smoke (Press Release WHO 27, 30 May, 2001). Children's rights to basic health and welfare are gravely jeopardized when exposed to second-hand smoke. Additionally, "new evidence shows that prenatal smoking contributes to higher rates of Sudden Infant Death Syndrome as well as asthma, bronchitis, colds and pneumonia in children" (para. 4). In the United States, more women die from lung cancer, now surpassing breast cancer. "In addition to lung cancer, women who smoke have markedly increased risks of cancers of the mouth and pharynx, oesophagus, larynx, bladder, pancreas, kidney, and cervix" (Press Release WHO 27, 30 May, 2001, para. 9). Additionally, pregnant women who smoke, or are exposed to second-hand smoke, are more likely to miscarry and bear low-weight babies.

"The Tobacco Free Initiative was launched as a cabinet project to provide global leadership and to mobilize national and international action for preventing and reducing tobacco use" (EB110/11, 2002, p. 8). In an attempt to acknowledge tobacco's impact on health, and begin to educate the world, the World Health Organization organized the first public hearing in 2000 at the United Nations. An interagency Task Force on Tobacco was formed (chaired by WHO) and studies were initiated. The studies focused not on the health implications of tobacco usage, but on the economic implications of tobacco reduction in the areas of employment issues, smoke-free policies, smuggling, trade issues, economic analysis of tobacco control, and illicit trade (not an all inclusive list).

Feeling pressure from the tobacco industry, "the Director-General appointed a committee of experts to review and report on the tactics used by tobacco companies in targeting United Nations activities" (EB110/11, 2002, p. 9). Working with the global media network, the Tobacco Free Initiative has been able to disseminate the World Health

Organization's message on tobacco control. The 'Tobacco kills, don't be duped' media advocacy project is currently active in over 20 countries. Activity related to "World No Tobacco Day" continues to be one of the major annual public health events.

Summary

The World Health Organization utilizes health education primarily to raise awareness of individuals and families (micro level), communities and organizations (meso level) and societies and governments (macro level) in order to reduce health risk and disease. Changing behaviour globally, at these three levels of intervention, is a monumental task given that it is human nature to resist change. The promotion of, and indoctrination into societal health behaviours, begins in the "formative years" with children, because they are naturally less resistant to change. Providing health education to families, via their children has the greatest potential to reduce disease and increase societal health. The WHO finds that where health educational prevention strategies have been systematically implemented, health has improved. Although modern medicine is very effective, without societal behavioural change, success is limited.

Worldwide, we have become an unhealthy species. Physical inactivity, increasing tobacco use and poor diet and nutrition are causing a rapid rise in cardiovascular diseases, diabetes and obesity. In the developing world, many countries have degraded their environment through depletion of resources and pollution, in the process of modernization. Rapid urbanization increases a developing country's population density into areas that are toxic, bacterially infected and void of clean water and sanitation. When you combine marginalized uneducated people wit
environment, and add the pandemic of HIV/AI
are catastrophic. Reversing the global tren
behaviour begins and ends with education. Th
Organization is dedicating its efforts to imp
the year 2005 and is using health education, a
weapon against disease and ignorance.

References

1. World Health Organization (1999, April 21). *Proposed Program Budget for 2000-2001: Implementation of Resolution EB103.R6* (A52/INF.DOC./2). Geneva: Fifty-Second World Health Assembly.
2. World Health Organization (1999, December 22). *HIV/AIDS: Confronting the Epidemic* (EB105/12). Geneva: Executive Board.
3. World Health Organization (2000, June). Human Rights, Women and HIV/AIDS. *Fact Sheet 247.* Retrieved November 2, 2002 from http://www.who.int/inf-fs/en/fact247.html.
4. World Health Organization (2001, January 10). WHO launches Mental Health 2001 Campaign. *Press Release.* Retrieved December 8, 2002 from http://www.who.int/inf-pr2001/en/pr2001-01.html.
5. World Health Organization (2001, April 6). As a burden of Mental Disorders looms large, Countries report lack of Mental Health Programmes. *Press Release.* Retrieved December 8, 2002 from http://www.who.int/inf-pr-2001/en/pr2001-18.html.
6. World Health Organization (2001, May 30). WHO urges countries to prevent a Tobacco Epidemic among Women and Girls. *Press Release.* Retrieved December 8, 2002 from http://www.who.int/inf-pr-2001-27.html.
7. World Health Organization (2001, September 28). Mental Disorders affect one in four People. *Press Release.* Retrieved December 2, 2002 from http://www.who.int/inf-pr-2001-42.html.
8. World Health Organization (2002, March 12). Unfinished Business: Global push to save 11 million Children. *Press Release.* Retrieved December 8, 2002 from http://www.who.int/inf/en/pr-2002-18.html.
9. World Health Organization (2002, April 4). Physical Inactivity a leading cause of Disease and Disability, warns WHO. *Press Release.* Retrieved December 8, 2002 from http://www.who.int/mediacentre/releases/release23/en/print.html.
10. World Health Organization (2002, April 22). We can beat AIDS, TB and Malaria, UN Agencies says. *Press Release.* Retrieved December 8, 2002 from http://www.who.int/mediacentre/releases/release29/en/print.html.
11. World Health Organization (2002, May 9). Pollution-related Diseases kill millions of Children a Year. *Press Release.* Retrieved December 8, 2002 from http://www.who.int/mediacentre/releases/release36/en/print.html.
12. World Health Organization (2002, May 17). *WHO Programmes 2000-2001: Report by the Secretariat* (EB110/11). Geneva: Executive Board.

13. World Health Organization (2002, July 2). Major UN Study finds alarming lack of knowledge about HIV/AIDS among young People. *Press Release.* Retrieved December 8, 2002 from http://www.who.int/mediacentre/releases/release56/en/print.html.

14. World Health Organization (2002, October 10). Eighty per cent of all cases of Blindness can be prevented or treated; the right to sight can and must be fulfilled. *Press Release.* Retrieved December 8, 2002 from http://www.who.int/mediacentre/releases/pr79/en/print.html.

15. World Health Organization (2002, October 15). WHO Atlas Maps Global Tobacco Epidemic. *Press Release.* Retrieved December 8, 2002 from http://www.who.int/mediacentre/releases/pr82/en/print.html.

16. World Health Organization (2002, October 17). Cardiovascular Death and Disability can be reduced more than 50 per cent. *Press Release.* Retrieved December 8, 2002 from http://www.who.int/mediacentre/releases/pr83/en/print.html.

17. World Health Organization (2002, October 30). Years of Healthy Life can be increased 5-10 Years, WHO says. *Press Release.* Retrieved December 8, 2002 from http://www.who.int/mediacentre/releases/pr84/en/print.html.

2

Health Education Program in China

Gao Ersheng and Lin Xia

Introduction of Chinese Health Education

In China the general concept and objectives of health education follow the WHO definition: the aims of health education is "to further healthy habits, to promote the full use of health care services, and support people in their efforts to influence the decision-making process for the improvement of health". Health education is to garner the political will and the people's know-how to get that knowledge applied, which is the process of enabling people to increase control over, and to improve, their health. To reach health, a state of complete physical, mental and social well-being, an individual or group must be able to identify and to realize aspirations, to satisfy needs, and to change or cope with the environment around. Therefore, health education is not just the responsibility of the health sector, but goes beyond healthy life-styles to well being.

China has a long history, which dated back to two thousand years ago. At that time there are records of preserving one's health and health care. At the very beginning of 1920's, scientific theory of health education was introduced to China for the first time, indicating the spring of health education in China. From 1930's through 1940's, many scholars studied and discussed health education in definition, goal, mission and training, etc. At that time, Chinese Society of Health Education and Chinese Health Education Seminar were founded in 1935, which play a positive role for development of health education of the time.[1]

In 1950 before long the foundation of P.R China, the importance of health education has been stressed in the first national sanitary conference. It advanced teaching general people how to fight against diseases and let people know how to do and do it by themselves and to solve problem. As for construction of the organization, many propagandistic health organizations have been constructed throughout the country. Since 1978, new advanced international conception and theory about health education has been increasingly taken in and the word "health education" has been formally cited.[1] During more than two decades the emphasis has been moved from diseases prevention to health promotion and from focusing on individual lifestyle to monitoring social factors. Now there're lots of international cooperative projects to strengthen health promotion on control of tobacco use, hypertension, TB, endemic, maternal and child health, etc.

Framework of Health Education in China

The most important national bodies of health education are Health Education Association of China and the National Health Education Institute. However, there're many other provincial and civic health education institutes all over the country contributing conceptually and materially to health education.[1]

Health Education Association of China

Health Education Association of China, founded in 1984, is a non-governmental organization and academic society consisting of health education and health-promoting workers nation-wide. The goal of the association is to unite health education and health promotion workers nation-wide, to promote the undertaking of health education and health promotion in China, to increase knowledge level of health and science among Chinese people, to develop healthy behaviours and life-style, and to develop the construction of social, material and cultural civilization.

Health Education Association of China now has approximately 500 organization members and 10000 individual members. Under its leadership there are many professional commissions, such as Social Health Education Commission, Health Periodical Commission, Health Fine Arts Commission, Health TV and Film Commission, School Health Education Commission, Human Resource Development Commission, Enterprise Health Education Commission, Hospital Health Education Commission, and International Exchange Commission. It publishes a monthly magazine—*Chinese Journal of Health Education* and a quarterly—*Newsletter of Health Education Association of China.* This association and its professional commissions hold many activities annually, such as symposium, essay solicitation, and workshop, thus playing an important and positive role in the development of health education and health promotion in China.

National Heath Education Institute

In 1986, with approval of the State Council, the National Heath Education Institute (NHEI) was founded as a national specialized institution for health education and health promotion under the Ministry of Health. It serves as a scientific research and technical guidance centre in Health education and health promotion for the whole country.

NHEI has held so many health education programms in China. The main areas of research are as follows:

- 900 million Farmers Health Promotion Project.
- The Project of Health-Promoting School
- The Activity of Healthy Life Style Exhibit.
- Health Education about Tobacco Control among Adolescents.
- Health Education on AIDS Prevention and Control.
- China/WHO Community Comprehensive Prevention and Intervention on Dysthymia.

Dimensions of Health Education

School Health Instruction

Students' health and their ability to learn are inextricably linked to health education. It is foreseen that population of children younger than 25 years old would account for half of the population of the world after several years. Now in our country the population of children in primary and middle schools is more than two hundred million.[2] If students are healthy, they are more likely to succeed in school. Health education works with schools around the country to address all aspects of school life that can improve the health of students and staff. Key components include policy, curriculum, health and nutrition services, the psychosocial environment of the school, and health promotion for staff.

Development of international health education mostly begins with school, and then expands to all the society. WHO advocated a new work model of school health promotion, according to integrating health instruction with health promotion increasingly closely, health-promoting schools, at beginning of 1990's. In 1994, Western Pacific Area of WHO began promoting this program, and in 1995 this program was formally started in China. At present there're more than 300 health-promoting schools in our country.

School Health Instruction Includes Three Aspects:

Health Curriculum Teaching

Today health education is included in the official curriculum for many primary and secondary schools. For instance, in Shanghai, since 1991 primary and secondary schools have already had their teaching material for health education.[3] However, in other schools whose curricula hasn't included health education, many topics included in those regular curricula are connected with health education, for example, 'social studies', 'road safety', 'moral education', etc. Since 1995, under technical support and financial aids from WHO, Chinese National Institute for Health Education has developed more than one hundred health-promotion schools including primary and secondary schools, in sixteen provinces/cities like Beijing, Shanghai, Shandong etc.[4,5] Now a great deal of primary and secondary schools has put health education into formal curricula. In some higher schools, health curriculum has already become an elective. Today health curriculum covers such topics as preventing worm infection, oral hygiene, fitness, communication, eating well, obesity, feelings and stresses, friendship, tobacco use prevention and so on. The curriculum is supplemented by teacher's guides and trainings. It is implemented in accordance with some special programms of health education for school-children, which is an essential part of the learning process. Some programms have developed numerous other curricula including middle school curriculum, such as sedentary lifestyles, combating prejudice, violence, alcohol and drug abuse, preventing accidental injury, preventing AIDS, sexuality and reproductive health education, etc.[6] The health education curriculum was organized around health topic areas, taught as multiple independent instructional units, designed to increase knowledge. Now the emerging model of health education emphasizes the ability to use essential knowledge and skills necessary to adopt, practise, and maintain healthy behaviours.

Health Activity

The goal of health activity is to strengthen impressions and promote effectiveness through school-children's practice in person. Schools can select proper activity according to age. There're a variety of health activities, such as training red-cross youth, participating social health service, organizing health focused summer camp, health knowledge oriented contest, and so on.[7]

Health Counselling

Health counseling is one kind of health education, in which school-children or parents contact certified health education counsellors, for example, teachers, doctors, nurses and other related personnel, face to face and to discuss some health issue.[8] Of course, mental health counselling account for a very important part of health counselling. Now most of Chinese high schools have their own mental health counsellor association. Contents of mental health counselling include: counselling for mental health of learning, counselling for social mental health, counselling for occupational selection and mental health.

Health education is the school's instructional program that provides the opportunity for all students to understand

and practise concepts related to health promotion and disease prevention. The project of Health-Promoting School,[9] which started in 1995, has held lots of health instruction programms, which played a critical role in school health instruction, and got significant effect. The main programms about health instruction based on schools include:

Establish and develop "non-smoking schools" activity. Now most provinces have practised this activity and the number of "no smoking schools" is more than ten thousand.[10]

In 1988-1993, entrance education, as an entry point, has given a course of combating smoke and implemented method of "prevention smoking in a group".[11]

In 1996, the China/UNICEF Project "Research of new instructional model with Tobacco use prevention in schools" succeeded in 35 schools of 17 provinces and developed to 400 schools.[12]

According to WHO document-Tobacco use prevention: an important entry point for the development of health-promoting schools, comprehensive interventions of the development of health-promoting schools were implemented in Jiaxing city, Zhejiang province and Jinan city, Shandong province during October 1998 to July 2000.[13]

At present, the project of "health-promoting schools with tobacco use prevention" has been practised in five provinces.[14,15]

In addition, project of health-promoting schools supported by World Bank in eight cities have implemented many health-promoting activities including controlling tobacco use, nutritional unbalance, hypertension, lack of exercise, accidental injury and unsafe sexual behaviour since 1996.[16]

The China/WHO Project "Development of Health-Promoting Schools with STD/AIDS Prevention as an Entry Point" was implemented in 1997.[17]

In a word, health-promoting schools have been developing in an impressible trend.

Community Health Education

Community health education is one kind of health education activity and process that increases the awareness and favourably influences the attitudes and knowledge relating to the improvement of health on a community basis. Preventing and managing diseases such as diabetes, arthritis, hypertension, heart disease, cancer, STD and HIV have long presented special challenges to health sectors, education sectors and social service agencies, especially to community health education sectors.[18]

The goal is to guide community people:

- to care about health issue of themselves, family and community;
- to participate actively in community health education activities;
- to develop good healthy behaviour and life style;
- to promote self-care and public health standard.

Community health education in China started from the beginning of 1980's.[19] As a basal content of community-based health service, community health education develops rapidly in some cities, such as Jilin, Anshan, Chifeng, Ningbo, etc. For the moment, more than 90% of community health service centres have developed various kinds of health education activities through diversified modes, which may include health education lecture, health education materials (videos, slide, booklet, pamphlet, fact sheet, etc.), health education exhibit (board, foldout), etc.[20, 21]

Health Education in Urban Community

Contents of health education in urban community include following parts:

- Prevention and treatment of chronic diseases in community such as hypertension, diabetes, cardiovascular and cerebral disease, etc.;
- Prevention of infectious disease;
- Avoidance of accidental injury;
- Family health education including life style, emergency treatment and nursing, health knowledge about house and environment, reproductive health education and health education of family mental;

- Promotion and advocacy of health city;
- Instruction on social virtue of public health and laws and regulations.

In 2001, in an effort to advocate healthy lifestyle and enhance awareness of preventing and controlling diseases among general population, the National Health Education Institute conducted large-scale exhibition of "healthy lifestyle in 21st century" in five provinces, for instance, Beijing, Shandong, Hainan, etc. The content of exhibition include: healthy lifestyle, mental health, prevention and control of some common diseases including hypertension, diabetes, hepatitis, tuberculosis, AIDS, *et al.*, children's care, reproductive health, environment and health, emergency treatment in family, and so on.

Community Health Education in Rural Area

In the vast countryside of China, especially in the poor and remote areas, many farmers continue to have comparatively feudal and ignorant thinking ways, unhealthy customs and habits that feature their lifestyles in general. They lack basic health care knowledge. They have inadequate ability to properly use the existing health-care resources. Improvement on the health of rural residents and on the quality of their environment is vital to a civilized and healthy lifestyle of the 900 million Chinese farmers. Health education provides the basic work of health care in the rural areas. It is also an important part of spiritual civilization among rural citizens. In rural area, health education is mainly based on three-level prevention and care network, and this network, with many organizations' help, has been operating weightily in health campaign and health propaganda and education.

During 1990-1996, The China/UNICEF Project has disseminated maternal and child health care related to "life knowledge" to rural women among 60 counties, 18 provinces.

With assistance from some international organizations' like WHO, UNICEF, health education, as a supporting activity to some projects on control of maternal and child health, infectious disease, chronic disease, endemics, etc., has developed in many rural areas.

The campaign of "900 Million Farmers Health Promotion Project" was jointly launched in 1994 with its aim at attacking major health problems of the rural areas. Four Chinese Ministries, National Committee for Patriotic Health Campaign, Ministry of Public Health, Ministry of Agriculture and Ministry of Broadcasting and Television, joined the effort. With its basic strategy of incorporating mass communication and education, the program has been warmly welcomed widely by the farmers. It has helped to popularize health knowledge, enhance the individual health-care awareness, change the bad and unhealthy customs and habits, and improve the construction of material and spiritual civilizations, resulting in improved health level for the farmers. Today it has been spread to 2000 counties, 35 provinces since 1997. In the 21st century, the 900 Million Farmers Health Promotion Programme will develop in a sustainable manner and is likely to become a famous brand for health education in rural China.

Above all, one of the key lessons learned in the last few decades of public health research is the importance of understanding the subtle, unique characteristics of the communities in which people live and work. To improve health education within community, it is critical to know different prevention strategies in every community. According to experiences of decade in this aspect, community health education must get support from local leaders and organizations, who work with related personnel to shape programms and interventions to fit the needs of their communities—including schools, rural villages, urban neighbourhoods, and colleges/universities.

Hospital Health Education

Hospital health education, also called patient health education or clinical health education, is a process of teaching or training of patients to concern their own health needs.

As an essential part among Chinese health education, hospitals are places to provide prevention of diseases, treatment service and community health care rather than only to provide clinical services. Hospital health education began with 1980's. In 1992, National Committee for Patriotic Health Campaign put hospital health education into the criterion of national health city, and then hospital health education is promoted through government's behaviour and administrative intervention. Hospital Health Educational Science Association, Chinese Health Education Association was founded in 1997, which indicated the Chinese hospital health educational net came into being.

There're three forms of hospital health education, namely, health education of clinical approach, education oriented admission and education based on follow-up. Hospital health education has its own advantages, for example, strong pertinence, intensive technology and more centralized patients. The main methods of hospital health education used in China are lingual education, literal education and visualized education. Now many hospitals held varies of health education activities through proper form according to their own features, like wall chart on health, instruction during pre-and post-operation, lecture to patients. In short, hospital health education has been increasingly displayed its vital role in Chinese health education.

Workplace Health Education

Workplace health education is of growing interest to health professionals, community health agencies, academic institutions, government departments, unions, employers and employees. Early programs gave emphasis to exercise components but a broader, multi-faceted approach is now evident. With this growth the need to develop training and in-service program suitable for health professionals specializing in the workplace has emerged. It works with workplaces and community organizations to promote the knowledge and skills to add healthy years to the lives of their employees.

The content of health education in workplace is to impart general health education and occupational health knowledge and defending skills for workers, which include prevention of occupational disease coming on, work-related disease prevention, physical and psychological disease prevention and women's occupational health issue. The Code of Occupational Disease Prevention of PRC, which is to implement regulations education within workplaces, was promulgated for enforcement from May 1, 2002. Collaborating with occupational health department, health education within workplace has been promoted greatly. Lots of industrial departments such as civil airline, railway, labour, metallurgy, mines and factories, etc., have formulated their own health education requirement.

Prospect of Health Education in China

Now pattern of health education has transformed into education handling together with health promotion. With social support, health education in China has applied varied forms and got varied degrees of success. Nevertheless, much remains to be done. Further development of health education in China should take account of a number of areas of need. Health education should heighten the interest of policy-makers and the public on health, ensure that people indeed have the knowledge and skills to act for individual and community health and mobilize social forces to accelerate progress in health development.

The main future challenges are presented below:

- The focus should be on strengthening advocacy for health, improving efforts to empower people, and influencing social groups at all levels to support health education. Some issues crucial to health education are future challenges for health promotion.
- Public attention must be mobilized, national policy strengthened, political commitment made favourable to health and adequate resources obtained.
- Strength of governmental function and substantial fund from government is not enough for health promotion.
- Professional actual abilities must be further cultured and enhanced.
- Efforts to empower people for health action must be further improved.

- Political action and health-supportive public policies must safeguard health in the context of rural areas.
- Partnerships must be built and strengthened between organizations, instructions and workplaces that can be influential for health promotion.
- True intersectional collaboration must be achieved in order to generate community interest and social support for health.

References

1. Lü Zizhi. Health Education and Health Promotion (second edition), Beijing: Publishing Company of Beijing Medical University. 2002.
2. Zhou Weiping. Model of Health-Promotion School in Shanghai. Chinese Journal of Health Education. 1999,15(12): 50-51.
3. Ma Hongliang, Geng Li, Xia Shichang, etc. Effectiveness of Evaluation of the China/WHO Project "Development of Health-Promoting Schools with Tobacco Use Prevention as an Entry Point". Chinese Journal of Health Education, 2002, 18(7): 414-417.
4. Lü Shuhong, Zhou Wei. Anti-smoking Program for Youngersters. Chinese Journal of Health Education. 2002, 18(3): 165-167.
5. Gao Ersheng, Lou Chaohua, Wu Junqing, etc. Academic Report on the International Symposium on Reproductive Health Research and Policy Issues of Adolescents and Unmarried Young Adults. Reproductive Health of Adolescents and Unmarried Youth: Status, Perspectives and Strategies. Shanghai: 2003.
6. Tian Benchun, An Jiaao, Ren Xuefeng, etc. Study on New Model of School-based Smoking Prevention. Chinese Journal of Health Education.1999,15(11): 38-40.
7. Hu Changfeng, Li Hong, Ma Yinghua, etc. Evaluation on Effectiveness of Five Years of Behavioural Group Intervention on Medical Students. Chinese Journal of Health Education. 2000, 16(5): 261-264.
8. Ma Hongliang. Health-promotion School, an Effective Means of Tobacco Control among Young Students. Chinese Journal of Health Education. 2002,18(4): 232-233.
9. Chen Zhongwen, Yu Huifang. On the Working Model of Health-Promoting School. Chinese Journal of Health Education, 2002,18(6): 380-382.
10. Xu Tao, Hu Junfeng, Hou Peisen. Progress in Research on Health Education of AIDS. 2002, 18(2): 111-114.
11. Shao Liwen, Wang Weidong. Strategies of Community Health Education and Health Promotion. Chinese Journal of Health Education. 2002,18(5): 322-323.

12. Du Ping, Wang Fang, Bei Shiguang, etc. Four Years of WHO/ Anshan Community, China Health Education Cooperative Program. Chinese Journal of Health Education. 2001,17(4): 224-226.

13. An Jiaao, Ren Xuefeng, Zhou Wei. Health Problems in Rural Areas in China and Relevant Health Education/Health Promotion Strategies. Chinese Journal of Health Education. 2001,17(1): 56-59.

14. Zhang Dongmei, Chen Feihu. Problems of Chinese Rural Health Education and Relevant Strategy. Healthcare System Administration in Rural China. 2002, 22(5): 29-30.

15. Jiang Chunqing. Status quo and Perspective of Hospital Health Education in China. Anthology of Medicine. 2000,19 sup: 154-157.

16. Zhang Yue, Wu Guangyu, Sun Yue-gang. The Origins, Status quo and Perspectives of Patient Education. Chinese Journal of Nursing. 2000, 35(6): 366-369.

17. Fan Jianhua. Reflection on the Construction of Health Education within Hospitals. Chinese Journal of Hospital Administration. 1999,15(11): 667-669.

18. Yin Dakui. Active Promotion of "Promotion Project of Health Education among Industrial and Mining Enterprise" for New Situation of Health Education among Industrial and Mining Enterprise. Chinese Journal of Health Education. 1998,14(1): 4-5.

19. Yu Shuming. Several Problems of Health Education in Mines and Factories. Chinese Journal of Health Education. 2002,18(2): 98-99.

20. Zhang Yanxia, Jin Shui-gao. Health Education in China, Review and Relevant Suggestions. Chinese Journal of Health Education. 2002,18(11): 711-713.

21. Wang Ying, Li Chunhua, Liu Qimin, etc. Development Trend of Health Education in 21st Century. Chinese Journal of Hospital Administration. 2000, 20(5): 20.

3

Health Achievement—Millennium Challenges

Dr. K.A. Pisharoti and S.H. Hasan

Introduction

Since independence (1947) the Nation, India, has launched largescale efforts in planning and development to raise the standard of living of its people and to improve their health. The progress achieved is reflected in increased life expectancy from 32 (1947) to 64 years (2000); decrease in infant mortality from 144 (1960) to 66 (2000); reduction in crude death rate from 37 (1971) to 9.0 (1995); and reduction in total fertility from 4.6 (1982) to 3 (2000).

Morbidity and mortality from a number of communicable diseases have come down. Smallpox has been eradicated. Epidemics like cholera have become rare events. The number of deaths from malaria has come down from 1 million (1950) to 421 (1991). There has been considerable decline in vaccine preventable diseases among children. As for nutrition related problems severe protein energy malnutrition has declined from 15% to 7% among children of 1-5 years old and steep decline in Vit. A deficiency and a modest increase in mean height and weight of all age groups are observed. While these are encouraging signs on one hand, on the other new diseases have surfaced, one of the most serious being HIV/AIDS. Alcoholism and drug abuse are also on the increase. Similarly there has been higher incidence of non-communicable diseases.

In spite of the many sided improvements in the country's health status over the past five decades, India continues to bear a major burden of diseases in the world, exceeded only by sub-Saharan Africa. According to World Health Report (World Bank, 1990), the disability adjusted life years lost (DALY) per 1000 population in India is 344 compared with 575 in sub-Saharan Africa. The corresponding figure for China is 198. Of this (i.e. 344) 50.7% is attributable to communicable diseases, 40.4% to non-communicable disease and 9.1% to injuries. Another important point is that diseases associated with poor household environment account for 30% of the total burden of diseases. Household environment includes water supply sanitation and indoor air pollution. It is possible that the pattern may undergo changes in the next 2-3 decades with the percentage of DALY lost from communicable diseases going down and from non-communicable diseases going up.

Projected Health Scenario in the Future

The health scenario in the early part of the new millennium as can be foreseen now will be as under:

1. Control of communicable diseases will still call for major attention. Of these tuberculosis will be a major area. HIV/AIDS has already emerged as a challenge. It was estimated by WHO that, as of July 1997, an estimated 2.5 million HIV infected cases would be there in India (262 per 100,000 population). The figure is increasing gradually. Eradication of leprosy calls for greater efforts. While mortality from diarrhoea has come down. The morbidity level is high. So too ARI among children. Though the overall incidence of malaria has come down, there are still pockets in the country where its incidence is high providing the foci from where the disease can spread.
2. Among non-communicable diseases, major problem areas are cardiovascular diseases, diabetes and cancer. Most of the risk factors associated with non-communicable diseases like hypertension, obesity, smoking, hypocholestromia and sedentary habits, are widely prevalent. Cancer of the respiratory tract is the commonest, so too cancer of the cervix. Out of every seven persons with diabetes in the world, one is from India.

Nutritional disorders: These are major problems to be tackled which arise out of micro nutrient deficiencies. Anaemia among women and particularly among pregnant women continues to evade rapid solution. The problems of stunting and wasting are high - 52% (stunting) and 17.57% (wasting) [<2.SD (%)]. Both food and nutritional insecurity persist among the vast population, in spite of commendable increase in food production.

Diseases associated with pregnancy and child-birth are another area to be tackled. While infant mortality has come down, it is still high and 2/3 of all infant deaths take place within the first four weeks after delivery. India ranks second in the world in maternal mortality at 400 per 100,000 live births. Of all the babies born, 25% are of low birth weight. Mental health problems are also of serious concern. Another emerging area is that of the health of the aged and elderly. The percentage of elderly population is about 10% of the total population and it is on the increase. Health problems of this group are different from those of the general population calling for a differential approach.

The above scenario poses serious challenges to us. The challenge is to tackle simultaneously a host of problems related to communicable deseases, non-communicable diseases, and those of the elderly. For a developing country, the challenge is indeed serious and formidable.

Health in Broader Perspective—Determinants of Health

There is increasing realization, supported by scientific evidence, that neither the individual nor the nation can achieve optimal health until we tackle, what are commonly known as the determinants of health. What are these determinants? One way of looking at the problem is to analyse health within the context of its environment. In the beginning of the medical era, value was attached to both biological and physical environment, the latter to include soil, water and air. As we gained further knowledge, it was recognized that health was impaired by social and cultural environment too. The concept of environment began to change with the opening of new frontiers of knowledge and environment is now looked at in its totality to include physical, social, cultural, political, economic and even ecological dimensions. The new approach will enable us to move away from a narrow life-style perspective to an enabling and promotional approach. It will also help us to build bridges between various sectors, professions, between theoretical concerns and practical action.

While the above provide a framework to look at health and its determinants, it is essential that every country looks at those components of environment that are of importance to it at any point of time. Looking at India and many other developing nations the major components that need attention are:

a. Inequality in health

b. Environmental degradation

c. Population pressure, gender inequalities and globalization.

The inequalities result mainly from poverty, lack of education, urban-rural differences, differential in development within the nation and between nations, differences among socio-economic groups and many other factors. Without going to details some of these determinants and their impacts are discussed below one after the other.

Poverty

Poverty is one of the major determinants of ill health. Poverty and ill health are interrelated. Poverty leads to deprivation, in that poor people are forced to live in insanitary conditions, without sufficient food to eat and are not able to utilize health services for fear of loss of wage for the day. They have no control over the reproductive process for lack of education. In fact, poverty confines people to poor health and exercises its influence at every stage of human life, from womb to tomb. When poor people fall ill, it exacerbates both poverty and ill health.

The relationship between poverty and health is well established. At the macro level, child mortality in sub-Saharan Africa was 175 in 1990 compared with 11 (1990) in the countries covered by the market economy. Studies in India have shown that infant mortality varies from 76.1 to

33.0 (1998-99) across population, where the standard of living varies from low to high income groups.

Lack of Education

Another major determinant of health is education. The literacy rate, particularly of women, is critical to health development, since health within the family is so much in the hands of women, who buy and prepare food, maintain cleanliness at home, care for children and the elderly, and initiate contact with the health system. Studies have also shown that a horizontal system of education providing for a high minimum standard of schooling for all is cost-effective way of improving health.

Regarding the quantitative relationship between health and education the data from Indian studies show that the overall infant mortality rate declines sharply with education of the mother, ranging from a high of 87 per cent 1000 for illiterate mothers to a low of 33 for mothers who have completed high school education. While the total literacy rate has increased from 18 (1951) to 52 (1992-93) in India, there is considerable difference between male (69) and female literacy (43) (1992-93). India still harbours the maximum number of illiterates in the world.

Demographic Transition

The demographic transition through which the country is passing, has increased population pressure on the nation leading to undesirable consequence to health, development, environmental degradation and others. According to the current estimates, the country's population reached 1000 million by 2000 and is expected to reach 1.3 billion by 2021 and stabilize at 1.6 to 1.8 billion between 2050. Simultaneously, the world population is also expected to stabilize at about 10 billion during 2050-2100.

A major consequence of the increase in population will be reflected in urbanisation of the country. Urban population has already reached 1/3 of country's total population and will be growing still. This massive and uncontrolled urbanisation is putting an enormous strain on essential services in cities particularly of safe water supply, sewage, housing, transport, communication, etc. noise and air pollution are increasing day by day. Simultaneously the cities financial resources are also badly hit. The health effects of such massive urbanisation are being increasingly felt.

Another consequence of population growth is the increase in the population of the aged. The percentage of population over 65 years of age has increased to 10%. The health requirements of the elderly are different and belong to the category of non-communicable disease and mental health problems. The health system has to be geared to meet their needs also.

Population pressure is eroding the gains made in health services coverage, while the percentage of coverage has increased, the actual number of people without coverage also continues to increase. It has affected our developmental efforts. While the developmental inputs have increased over the years, their effect on the population has not correspondingly risen. For example, the net national product rose five-fold between 1950-51 and 1993-94 at constant (1980-81) prices, while the per capita national product could only be doubled as major part of the growth was nullified by the increase in population. Population growth has exercised undue pressure on deforestation, overgrazing, urbanization, poverty, climatic change and pollution. These have contributed to accentuating the health problems.

Women, Health and Gender Inequality

Discrimination against women in health care for them is rampant in the countries of the region. It is an evidence in the lower health status of the girl child and women and also in the declining female-male ratio in the country. Among the main reasons for gender inequality are the discriminative practices directed against girl children and women. The discrimination often takes the form of delay in seeking health care in the case of a girl child, unequal food sharing practices at home; priority to the male child in education; female infanticide practices, etc.

Excessive female mortality can be observed in many developing countries in early childhood and reproductive years. This is partly due to low value attached to female children, and partly due to lack of adequate maternity and family planning care. Nearly half of the women of child bearing age and 60% of pregnant women suffer from nutritional anaemia. Sex preference for sons is one of the main reasons for the declining male-female ratio. The all India sex ratio declined from 972 to 927 during 1990-91.

Environmental Factors

Significant differences exist between the environmental problems of rural and urban areas. In rural areas, unsafe drinking water, lack of facilities for proper disposal of excreta and solid wastes, waste water stagnation, food contamination and smoke filled houses are among the problems and they are responsible for a majority of illnesses of rural people.

The problems in urban areas are heavy migration arising out of population pressure, massive industrialization and social unrest due to population pressure, etc. Studies have shown the percentage of population served by protected water supply in urban area is 85%, while it is 8.6% in rural areas. Houses that have access to sanitation ranges from 70% (urban) to 25% (rural). The mushroom growth of slums in urban areas constitutes a big problem. The percentage of slum-dwellers in 1981 in the major cities was 31.4% in Delhi, 32.1% in Madras, 32.89% in Calcutta, and 34.3% in Bombay. These percentages obviously have increased since then. This has both health and social consequences.

Priority Action to Meet Millennium Challenges

Building Partnership

The Jakarta Declaration on Health Promotion identifies the new challenges that we must face to make every individual, family, community and nation enjoy optimum health. The prerequisites for health identified are many, and some of the more important ones like poverty, literacy, food intake, empowerment of women have been dealt with earlier in this paper. To address these and newly emerged and emerging threats like globalization, new forms of action are needed. The case for partnership in health arises out of the need for such action. The challenges in the coming years will be to unlock the potential for health promotion inherent in many sectors of society, among local communities and within families. Health should be the responsibility of all.

There is a clear need to break through traditional boundaries within governmental sectors, between government and non-governmental sectors and between public and private sectors. Cooperation is essential specifically, this requires the creation of new partnerships for health, on equal ground, between the different sectors at all levels within government and societies.

In this connection, a special mention has to be made of the vast opportunities in India to build such partnership at the grassroots level. The local bodies with 33.3% membership for women are vested with the responsibility for health, family welfare and nutrition, and they can provide the community base for building partnership. The partnership between elected bodies, the NGOs, social groups operating in the community and governmental workers at that level can join hands and provide a nodal group for planning and implementing a decentralized health programme. They can also bring in others wherever other health determinants have to be addressed. They can also play an effective role in the advocacy for health.

Healthy Public Policies

Even since independence, we have concentrated on evolving effective health policies and their implementation. Considerable success has been achieved in this regard. But we have not paid sufficient attention to see that public policies, especially those related to agriculture, education, industries, social welfare, rural development, communication etc., are made health friendly. There are evidences to show that both food and nutrition security has to be ensured for the promotion and maintenance of health. This cannot be achieved unless the policies of the agriculture sector are oriented towards this end. So too girls education, as a priority, will have to find a prominent place in the education sector policies. Poverty alleviation will have to have a central place cutting across many sectors. In some instances policies also are found to contradict each other. Specifically, the one relating to tobacco cultivation may be mentioned. Health agencies should henceforth take up the lead to see that policies of related sectors are made health-friendly. To enable this to happen, the health sector should develop or promote the capacity to study on a continuous basis the relationship between health and its determinants, develop the capacity to analyse public policies at the stage of their formulation itself and make imputs to see that the policies reflect health orientation. Advocacy for health should be planned and implemented.

Community Involvement

It is now well recognized that community involvement should be the foundation for planning and implementing all programmes related to health, family welfare and nutrition. Analysis of experiences in India and abroad has clearly demonstrated that the demand for and utilization of health services would be much better when people, through their representatives are involved in the identification of their health needs, setting priorities, planning, implementing and monitoring the interventions agreed upon to meet the priority needs, the same has been found to be true in agriculture and other sectors. It has also been found that community involvement provides a solid base to bring about intersectorial coordination at the grass-roots level. The basic concept of community involvement is transfer of responsibility. Translation of this concept into practice is not so easy in view of the prevailing attitudes both within the community and among service providers. The community feels that health care is someone else's responsibility and every thing should be done by the government. The service providers feel that the community is not in a position to take the responsibility. Both attitudes need to be changed. It should be mentioned that the decentralized set up existing in India upto the villages level should be able to make the process of community involvement function successfully.

Involvement of Women

Evidences accumulated over the last 2-3 decades demonstrate that involvement of women in health care delivery is crucial to the success of the programme. Women are the key to primary health care and the general welfare of the communities in all developing countries. A recent study of woman and health, prepared for the Aga Khan foundation and the UNICEF by the World Federation of Public Health Association presents a useful overview of women's different roles as beneficiaries and caretakers in primary health care. The overview highlights the role of women in education at home, in a charge of nutrition, water and basic sanitation management, use and promotion of immunization, decision making in material and child health and family planning and control of locally prevailing diseases. So far women were addressed as recipients of services, but recent experience has shown that they can play an important role in the programms aimed at women in an integrated manner, the issues of health, nonformal education and income generating activities. This will call for intersectoral efforts.

Improvement of Infrastructure

Over the years, a vast infrastructure for the delivery of health, family welfare and nutrition services has been built up in India. A developing country like India can be proud of the infrastructure. It consists of health sub-centres for every 5000 population, one primary health centre for every 25,000 population, one community health centre for every three primary health centre and referral services at taluk and district headquarters. While the infrastructure exists, many studies have shown that their performances needs to be vastly improved. Once fully established and staffed, the infrastructure can cater to the existing and emerging needs of the health sector. In order that the full potential of the infrastructure is achieved, the following actions are proposed.

1. Early completion of all physical facilities, providing necessary equipment and filling up staff vacancies.
2. There is one ICDS centre for every 1000 population in most parts of the country. Even the uncovered areas are being covered at present in a phased manner. The centre run by the social welfare department caters to child care, nutrition, pre-school education and essential

maternal services. In order to bring about better coordination with the health service, it is recommended that the ICDS centres are made satellite centres of the health sub-centres. Joint programming between the ICDS worker and the Village Health Nurse (VHN) for many activities are not only feasible but also desirable.

3. Steps have to be taken to make decentralized planning truly functional. As of today, there is a considerable differential in development, health indices, epidemiological patterns, fertility levels among districts in India and as such centralized planning is redundant. The partnership approach suggested earlier will be a suitable at the Health Sub-Centre (HSC) level together with services rendered at the HSC. Similar aggregation can be done at PHC level and district level. The district level administration should be strengthened to cater to the planning needs.
4. Improvement in managerial practices at various levels to include, decentralized planning and implementation, supportive supervision, inter-sectoral coordination, logistics and supplies, improved management information systems and its utilization for making correctives and better planning of outreach services.
5. All vertical programmes have to be integrated with the primary health centre.
6. A well designed and executed programme of human resource development is necessary.

The success in the field of health development will, to a large extent, be determined by those who maintain the health system. They have to have the capability to lead, plan, staff, implement, and monitor and evaluate health related services and programmes. Commitment to serve the people, commitment to efficiently maintain the health services and commitment to quality should be embedded in the educational process. The new processes outlined in this paper will call for relevant skills among the health personnel to build up and maintain partnership, promote social action for health, provide leadership to the health team, making the system respond to the health needs of the population, provide supportive supervision, inter-and intra-sectoral coordination and many others. The programmes of the HRD should consider the above factors, in addition to upgradation of technical skills.

Involving Private Sector

Of late, there has been an increasing reliance by people on the market sector for health care. This sector involves a broad range of private practitioners, private hospitals in urban areas, private traditional medicine practitioners, and non-governmental organizations. This trend has to be encouraged, as the government alone cannot cater to the entire health needs of the population. However market forces may steer the services more towards profit than quality. It is therefore the duty of the government to formulate polices on privatization that encourage quality of services in general. At the same time they should ensure that the poor are not left out of reach of the services.

Science and Technology

Science and Technology should address to meet (a) existing gaps in knowledge and (b) the needs of emerging health problems. Technology developed outside the country should also be imported at reasonable cost and adapted to our environment. However, there is a major problem, as of now, of a wide gap between what is known and what is utilized. Dissemination of available knowledge should receive priority, so that the gaps between research, policy and programme are reduced.

Advocacy

There is a recognition of the increasing role that advocacy can play in health promotion, particularly in influencing policies, programmes and environments and mobilization of resources and opinions to support them. Many target audience like policy makers, programmes administrators and social and community groups, media have to be addressed. What is specific to advocacy is the objective and target audience. Promotion of advocacy can take many forms like working with the media, promoting coalition with various groups, working with community, professionals and others.

A major advocacy programme has to be directed to place health on the political agendas. Eventhough considerable progress has been made in this respect, health still continues to retain a low priority in developmental planning and resources allocation. For health to take a central place, there is a need to continue and strengthen the advocacy programme. A second major area for advocacy is to make public policies health friendly. The target audience will be health related sectors. Advocacy of factors that promote equity in health, conservation of natural resources, protection of environment, prevention of newly emerging diseases are the other areas of priority.

Surveillance System

For control of communicable diseases, the surveillance system needs to be strengthened with an early warning system and a rapid response mechanism. The health system should have the responsibility and resources to initiate control measures soon after notification is received.

Indigenous System of Medicine

The indigenous systems of medicine make use of locally available resources relying on the local flora, fauna, and minerals, Ayurveds, Unani and Siddha system are more compatible with the local health traditions, however, patronage for the systems has to be increased and should be integrated with the regular health care system wherever possible. National guidelines to ensure efficiency, standardization, safety of drugs should be drawn up. A nationally coordinated and collaborative research programme will also help. The policy should also cover conservation of medicinal plants and other natural resources many of which are threatened with extinctions. Health education should be launched in towns and cities to encourage people grow plants in their backyards.

Information Technology

There has been tremendous growth in information technology in the recent past. The growth will be continuous in the future. Information technology should be channelled for the benefit of villages. Availability of internet facilities in villages can be used for the spread of knowledge. Telemedicine can be used to support the works of medical officers at primary health centres. Telephone facilities will facilitate the control of communicable diseases easier. Video cassettes can be used to promote health education is groups. The work of community group of the grass roots level should be facilitated and strengthened through modern information technology.

Strengthened Health Education Programme

The concept of health education has undergone tremendous changes over the decades. From the initial concept of providing knowledge, changing attitudes and bringing about behaviour changes among individuals, the term health education is currently defined as a combination of planned social action and learning experiences designed to enable people to gain control over the determinants of health and health behaviour and to conditions that affect their health status and the health status of others. In order to operationalise this definition, three principal strategies are to be adopted for health education. These are advocacy, empowerment and systems support. As already stated, advocacy is to be directed at policy and decision-makers, professionals, political and religious leaders, power brokers and interest groups to support health and place health issues high on the public agenda. Empowerment is aimed at equipping people, individuals, families and communities, with the knowledge and skills that will enable them take positive action for health and make appropriate health choices. Information, communication, and health education should aim at promoting learning, which is at the heart of the empowerment process. Strategies to strengthen social support are directed both at community organizations and institutions that provide legitimacy and support to new behaviours as social norm and provide community action in support of these. It also aims at and generating support from systems that provide infrastructure for health care services and from health related systems like education, agriculture and many others that can influence health.

Conclusion

India as of now, is passing through a number of

transitions simultaneously. These are demographic transition, epidemiological transition, transition from an agricultural to an industrial society; transitions in life-styles, transitions from a controlled to a market economy and others. All these transitions have a deep bearing on health. We are also not so fortunately placed in regard to the major determinants of health as the nation and present encounters large scale poverty, backwardness in education and literacy, unemployment, inadequate housing, increasing population, environmental degradation, etc. The scenario where we have to tackle simultaneously communicable diseases, non-communicable diseases, and health problems of the elderly is also alarming. In spite of these, the progress achieved today is not insignificant. Added to that, a number of demonstration projects carried out in different parts of the country have also shown that we need no despair and can meet the challenges thrown successfully. We know how to do it. But do we have the determination and commitment to get it done? Much depends upon an answer to this question.

4

Nutrition Intervention and Education for Promotion of Health

Dr. S. Premakumari*

Good nutrition is an important determinant in the allround socio-economic upliftment of any community. Good nutrition fosters sound health, improves working capacity and facilitates national development while health stress the importance of mental, physical and social well-being as opposed to the absence of diseases.

The largest public health problem faced by the developing world today is malnutrition which is extensively prevalent among the majority of the population. It is a problem of considerable magnitude especially among the vulnerable sections of society, namely pre-school children, expectant women, nursing mothers and the aged. The causative factors for the widespread malnutrition include primarily lack of food, poor purchasing power, inadequate knowledge of nutrition and recurrent infections.

According to the global situation analysed by the United Nation's Children's Fund (UNICEF, 1998), 30 per cent of children under five years of age are underweight, 199 million children suffer from vitamin A deficiency disorders, and two billion people are affected by or at risk from iron deficiency anaemia.

---

* Professor and Head, Department of Food Science and Nutrition, Avinashilingam Deemed University, Coimbatore-641043, India.

Around 790 million people in the developing world are chronically undernourished. Nearly 13 million children under five years of age die every year from preventable diseases and infections such as measles, diarrhoea, malaria, pneumonia or from a combination of these ailments.

According to the reports of the National Nutrition Monitoring Bureau, in India there has been a marginal decrease in the intake of protein over the years. But this is not significant since the intake is above the RDA (Table 1). However, the decrease in energy consumption, though marginal, is somewhat significant in the sense the lower availability/consumption of food grains.

Table 1: Average Consumption of Nutrients (Per Consumer Unit Per Day)

Nutrient	Year	Pooled average consumption	Recommended dietary intake ICMR
Protein (g)	1975-79	62.9	55
	1988-90	61.8	
Energy (kcal)	1975-79	2340	
	1988-90	2283	2350

Apart from the widespread prevalence of Protein Energy Malnutrition particularly among pre-schoolers, anaemia is reported to be prevalent between 47 to 87% in pregnant and lactating mothers, 38 to 69% in adolescent girls, and 14% to 90% in school children in the country. Around 167 million people in India are at risk from iodine deficiency disorders and about 66 million have mild neurological disorders.

Malnutrition and under-nutrition which manifest themselves among major sections of the poor, particularly women and children are the result of poverty, chronic diseases and persistent hunger. High levels of illiteracy, low purchasing power, inadequate household food security, poor environmental sanitation, lack of safe drinking water, poor housing, lack of regular employment are all the basic risk factors that result in adverse synergistic effect.

Devadas and others (1991) evaluated the influence of mother's education on birth rate and Infant Mortality Rate

(IMR) in five Southern States of India. In every State one district with high literacy level and another with low in all literacy level, ten districts were selected for investigation. In every district 100 women in three different levels of education namely illiterate, moderately educated (upto 10th standard) and highly educated (beyond 10th standard) were selected by the random sampling method and interviewed. Table 2 presents the correlation between birth rate, IMR and female literacy levels observed in this study.

Table 2: Birth Rate and IMR in Low Literacy Districts and High Literacy Districts (Number Studied—500 in Each Group)

Area	Educational Level	Birth Rate (a)	IMR (b)	Chi Square Value	
				Birth Rate	IMR
Districts with low literacy level	Illiterate	36	118		
	Medium	29	82		
	High	25	63	4.35 NS	20.26**
Districts with high literacy level	Illiterate	32	101		
	Medium	24	62		
	High	18	50	2.04 NS	18.35**

(a) Number/1000 population/year. NS—Not Significant.
(b) Number/1000 live births/year. ** Significant at one per cent level.

As the level of education among mothers increased, the birth rate decreased and the IMR got reduced in all the selected districts. This association was found to be significant at one per cent level. Hence the need for concerted efforts on a massive scale to eradicate illiteracy among mothers and educate them on better living is imperative.

The various factors influencing malnutrition exist in the community form a vicious circle as shown in figure 1 (Devadas *et al.*, 1993).

The vicious circle once initiated with poverty or any other factor has a devastating spiral effect on society causing a low level of adaptive functioning, non-application of knowledge of science and technology to daily living, undesirable social customs, infections and insufficiency of food.

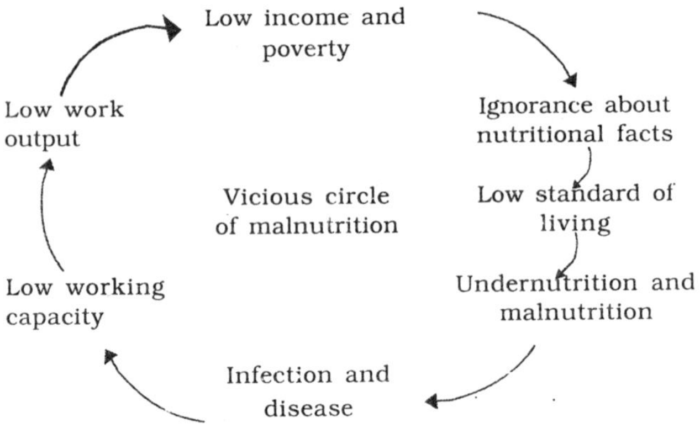

The National Nutrition Policy takes measures for the control and elimination of nutritional diseases and promotion of health. Towards reaching this target a multipronged approach including increased food production, distribution and consumption, nutrition intervention and nutrition education should be considered as the most important focal points.

Among the above strategies, nutrition intervention programmes serve as one of the important short-term strategies to improve the nutritional status of the vulnerable groups. The major ongoing nutrition intervention programmes are the Integrated Child Development Services (ICDS), school meal programme, anaemia and vitamin A prophylaxis programme and goitre control programme.

Each programme has specific objective and provides supplementary nutrition and other services. It has been proven beyond doubt that organized feeding programmes can provide only a temporary solution unless accompanied concomitantly by nutrition education.

Imparting nutrition and health knowledge to the population appears to be practical and promising in the long run because ignorance is one of the most predominant simple factors underlying poverty and malnutrition. The findings of the research accumulated over the past four decades by Devadas and coworkers at Avinashilingam Deemed University, Coimbatore have established the benefits of nutrition education in nutrition intervention programmes.

This article highlights a few of these findings. School lunch programme in Tamil Nadu had been growing steadily in quality as well as coverage since 1925 and it has reached a massive dimension today. The beneficial outcomes of school lunch have been reported through a number of studies by Devadas and coworkers. An effort was made by Devadas and Premakumari (1978) to explore the longitudinal impact of participating in school lunch programme in terms of nutritional status and nutritional knowledge of the children and parents.

Sri Avinashilingam Trust's Basic Elementary School, Coimbatore where nutrition education is built into the school lunch programme was selected for the study. Using the school records, all the children (5 to 11 years old) who had been continuously participating in the school lunch programme starting from the first standard for a period of five years, four years, three years, two years and one year respectively were identified. For each group, a comparable group of children who never participated in the programme were selected as controls. The experimental and the control children were administered special tests and their nutritional knowledge was assessed. Similarly questionnaires were administered to randomly selected 25 parents of children in the control and experimental groups and their nutrition knowledge was determined.

The mean scores obtained by the children in the experimental and the control groups for their nutrition knowledge are presented in Table 3.

Table 3: Mean Scores Obtained by the Children for Nutritional Knowledge (Number: 25 in Each Group) (Maximum Scores: 25)

Details	Years of participation or non-participation in the School Lunch					Groups compared	't' value
	5	4	3	2	1		
School lunch groups	23.3	20.0	18.6	15.4	10.2	School lunch vs non-school lunch	13.97*
Non-school lunch groups	12.2	12.1	8.9	7.7	5.4		

* Significant at one per cent level.

The scores obtained by the school lunch children put together were significantly greater that those of the non-school lunch children (P<0.01). Participation of children in school lunch programme improves their nutrition knowledge and this in turn will improve their food habits and ultimately their nutritional status.

The nutritional knowledge of the 25 per cent of the experimental children and 25 parents of the entire control groups is presented in Table 4. The results revealed that the parents of children in the school lunch groups were better informed about the nutritional facts. It was noted that as the number of years of participation of the children in school lunch where nutrition education was operating as a component increased the nutritional knowledge of the parents also. This is due to the carry home effect of nutrition information by the children from school as well as the orientation given to the parents through parent-teacher meetings.

Table 4: Nutritional Knowledge of Parents of School Lunch and Non-School Lunch Children (Number 25 in Each Group)

Questions	Answers	Years of participation					Control
		5	4	3	2	1	
Why should we consume green leafy vegetables?	For good health	20	12	18	10	10	3
	Supplies iron	11	12	–	2	–	–
	Purifies blood	7	6	8	10	7	4
	Avoids constipation	3	–	–	–	2	–
What are the foods you like the most?	Cereal preparations	12	14	8	5	6	6
	Fruits and vegetables	15	10	10	6	6	6
	Milk and milk products	11	11	8	7	5	6
	Non-vegetarian foods	2	4	2	1	–	–
How do you cook rice?	Absorption method	22	20	20	15	14	10
	Draining the water	3	5	5	10	9	15

In the year 1982, the school lunch programme in Tamil Nadu was converted into a massive nutrition programme covering children of age ranging from 2 plus to 14 years in pre-schools, primary school and high schools, numbering 8.5 millions in all. Devadas and coworkers (1986) evaluated the nutritional outcomes of this programme in terms of nutritional and health status of children, food habits and nutrition knowledge of children and mothers, school attendance, school enrolement and cognitive development of children. The outcomes were extremely encouraging and the programme today is benefiting the participants in a large way.

Nutrition education could be used as an effective tool to promote the nutritional status of pre-school children also. The largest intervention programme operating for pre-school children in the country is the Integrated Child Development Services programme. An effort was made by Devadas *et al.* (2002) to wipe out vitamin A malnutrition among pre-school children of the ICDS programme through strengthening it with components of nutrition education, food production and supplementation.

Two groups of 25 Anganwadis (pre-schools) operating the ICDS programme in Coimbatore urban area were selected for the study and all the children belonging to the 50 centres formed the subjects for the study. The two groups of children received the following treatment for a period of two years.

Group A: Supplemented with 30g amaranthus per child per day in the regular meal which consisted of rice, pulse, oil and vegetables providing 400 calories and 10g protein per meal (No.987).

Group B: In addition to the above food supplements, the children (No.1082) received nutrition education. Vitamin A school gardens and home gardens were promoted.

Table 5 presents the changes in the prevalence of vitamin A deficiency among the children.

As the duration of participation increased, the clinical signs disappeared and by 18 months all the children were completely free from clinical signs of vitamin A deficiency irrespective of the treatment given. However, the rate of disappearance of clinical signs was faster when nutrition education was imparted along with supplementation than when mere supplementation was given. Table 6 presents the knowledge, attitude and practices of mothers quantified in terms of scores (total 40) before and after imparting nutrition education.

Table 5: Clinical Signs of Vitamin A Deficiency in Pre-school Children at Different Intervals

Group	Initial				Six months				12 months				18 months			
	CX		BS		CX		BS		CX		BS		CX		BS	
	N	%	N	%	N	%	N	%	N	%	N	%	N	%	N	%
A	71 (2295)	3.09	40	1.74 (2295)	28	1.22	14 (875)	0.61	5	0.57	-	- (596)	-	-	-	-
B	78 (2340)	3.33	49	2.09 (2340)	25	1.07	10 (886)	0.43	2	0.23	- (663)	-	-	-		

N—Number of clinically affected children.
CX—Conjunctival Xerosis, BS—Bitot spot.
Numbers in parentheses indicate the total number of children who participated in the study.

Table 6: Knowledge, Attitude and Practices of the Mothers Before and After Nutrition Education

Aspects	Groups	Initial score	Final score	Increase	Critical difference A vs B
Knowledge	A (N-948)	5.41 ± 0.86	12.68 ± 0.93	7.27 ± 0.69	247.72**
Max. score-20	B (N-417)	5.78 ± 1.25	17.40 ± 0.98	11.62 ± 0.96	
Attitude	A	3.25 ± 0.80	7.60 ± 0.90	4.35 ± 0.86	57.16**
Max. score-12	B	3.47 ± 0.62	10.44 ± 0.53	6.97 ± 0.57	
Practice	A	2.17 ± 0.67	4.65 ± 0.53	2.48 ± 0.61	48.33**
Max. score-8	B	2.31 ± 0.83	6.96 ± 0.71	4.65 ± 0.75	
(KA)	A	10.83 ± 0.35	25.36 ± 0.93	14.53 ± 0.52	289.59**
Max. score-40	B	11.56 ± 0.39	34.81 ± 0.73	23.25 ± 0.44	

** Significant at one per cent level.

At the end of two years, mothers in both the groups registered greater knowledge scores. However group B mothers registered significantly greater scores than those in group A. This difference was mainly due to the special effort of nutrition education imparted to the children and mothers. The mothers in group B centres had an additional opportunity of observing the Anganwadi gardens being raised and the produce being utilized for feeding the children.

Studies of the impact of nutrition education to the beneficiaries of Lab-to-Land programmes, Special Nutrition Programme, Applied Nutrition Programme and the like have shown similar encouraging results. During the process of imparting education several socio-economic and cultural factors crop up. Problems in convincing the people to change their dietary habits, their lack of awareness, ignorance, food beliefs and fads and fallacies are some of the practical difficulties one encounters in the field of nutrition education. However, past experience has revealed that when intervention programmes are used as channels to improve the food habits of the population, if the beneficiaries are given opportunities to practise what they learn and discuss the problems during their subsequent visit to the centre many of the difficulties mentioned above can be overcome. Hence immediate efforts are needed to strengthen the component of nutrition education in all the existing intervention programmes. Specific allocation of funds must be there to produce relevant audio visual aids and distribute them. Proper use of these aids must be ensured and the outcomes evaluated through an inbuilt component.

References

1. Devadas, R.P. 1984. Report of the project determining the scope for adding a Nutrition/Home Science dimension to the Lab-to-Land and Food for Work Programmes. Sri Avinashilingam Home Science College for Women, Coimbatore.
2. Devadas, R.P. and Premakumari, S. 1978. Nutritional impact of a school lunch programme on children over a period of five years, Indian Journal of Nutrition and Dietetics, Vol. 15, pp. 257-263.
3. Devadas, R.P. 1986. Nutritional outcome of a massive feeding programme in Tamil Nadu, Report of the Nutrition Society of India, No. 32, pp. 1-13.
4. Devadas, R.P., Chandrasekhar, U., Premakumari, S. and Geetha, G. 1991. Correlation between female literacy, birth rate and infant mortality rate. Paper presented at the VI Asian Congress of Nutrition held at Kualalumpur, Malaysia, 16 - 19, September.
5. Devadas, R.P., Chandrasekhar, U. and Premakumari, S. 1993. Nutritional challenges India faces today, Indian Journal of Nutrition and Dietetics, Vol. 30, pp. 271-278.

6. Devadas, R.P., Chandrasekhar, U. and Pramakumari, S. 2002. Nutrition education: Effective tool to wipe out vitamin A malnutrition. Health promotion and education in South East Asia, Quarterly official publication of IUHPE-SEARB, Vol. 17, No. 2, pp. 41-48.

7. UNICEF. 1998. The state of the World's Children Report, Vol. 20, p. 25.

5

Health Education at Primary Health Centre and Beyond: Search for New Alternatives

K. Mahadevan, Iqbal Shah, Lorry Laing and V.M. Sandeep

Introduction

Health education, so far, has not received the priority and importance that it deserves at the peripheral level both in rural and urban areas in India and the other developing countries. Similarly it has not been given due recognition, like the other subjects of health in the teaching programmes in medical colleges at the under-graduate level. It is partly due to the ignorance of people about the importance of preventive consciousness in health care and partly due to the poor focus and coverage given to this subject by the practitioners themselves. If consumers/clients themselves develop essential ideas about healthy living and prevention of diseases, automatically the demand for health education will increase by leaps and bounds, as in the developed countries. In the absence of such health consciousness in the developing countries, people generally give importance and serious thought mostly to curing diseases reducing pain and suffering; the general tendency is to ignore or neglect non-painful or trouble free morbidity conditions by quite a few till the condition becomes problematic and painful. For instance, due to delicacy or ignorance or both several reproductive health problems of women are neglected in the infant stages and not reported to doctors till they create serious difficulties and suffering. Such a situation exists, largely due to poor education, social stigma, backwardness, fatalism and lack of scientific temper in our society coupled with wrong ideas perpetuated by certain traditional medicine men/magicians over the centuries. In other words, people in general have yet to realize the great value and significance of the wise saying *"Prevention of disease is better than curing disease"*.

Therefore, an attempt has been made in this chapter to highlight the problems faced in implementing health education programmes and the salient changes and improvements to be made to promote them. They relate to human resource development on health education, culture and behaviour, coverage of new and salient subject-matter of health education like Ayurveda, Yoga-cum-exercise, appropriate dietary habits and life style and educating people from childhood onwards to understand and assimilate health education concepts. In addition, necessary importance must be given to communication and the media employed such as films, TV and the other mass media in the dissemination of ideas on health even in far off places. Further, successful experiences in health education have to be adopted as models to bring about overall behavioural changes especially among the backward so that they can absorb these technical programmes quickly and effectively. Hence the discussion here commences with Human Resource Development in Medical Education at the under-graduate level.

Human Resource Development for Education and Service

At present the clinically oriented general physicians serving in most Health Centres (HCs) in India have not been able to deliver health education to the population at the PHC level. Because the doctors themselves were inadequately exposed to the subject of health education during their graduate programme. At present only nominally community medicine is taught at the graduate level and is not given any importance in the medical curriculum; often most medical students neglect the study of this subject, and are indifferent to the classes: Therefore there is an urgent need to rethink now regarding the course content, teaching the methodology, providing field training for under graduates to gain experience. The subject itself has to be given high priority in the overall curriculum of medical education besides making compulsory for all medical graduates. In addition, certain concepts of Health Education must be incorporated into the other papers at the under-graduate level such as preventive cardiology and so on.

Parallely periodic training in human resource development may be imparted to the PHC doctors by making them participate compulsorily in biannual in-service workshops and seminars. They also may be made accountable for promoting health education in different ways at the PHC. For example, in their annual progress report on activities carried out, health education must be given priority. At regular intervals the administrators at the district level may inspect and assess how far health education has been adopted by the PHC doctors, and the results they have achieved.

The PHC doctor alone cannot promote health education at the peripheral level without the complementary efforts of his/her team. For instance, all the ANMs, health visitors, multipurpose male and female-health workers must be given condensed training to promote health education at the peripheral level. Correspondingly necessary administrative changes may be made to reduce the size of worker population ratio to reasonable level so that each worker can deliver the goods satisfactory. *Why is the PHC not utilised by a very large section of population?* Today the utilization of the PHC ranges from 10 per cent to 90 per cent in UP and Kerala respectively. This colossal waste of investment made on the PHC remains in corrected even after 53 years of our independence. *Revamping the PHC services is the most urgent task before us.*

If doctors and paramedical staff reverse their present pattern of services and visit patients in their homes in villages at least fortnightly large scale increase and utilisation of the PHC service will be possible. In order to make such changes effective *inter-sectoral co-ordination between* the *transport department* and *the PHC timing* for service must be co-ordinated and improved to prevent wastage of investment on the PHC services. Unfortunately no systematic study has been carried out on this aspect so far. Under the existing constraints of poor transport and communication and absence of suitable conveyances at the peripheral level even the well-meaning workers have not been able to do their service. *Therefore this problem* has to be *viewed holistically* and *in-depth* to make *suitable changes expeditiously.*

Changes in Strategy Needed

The present day curriculum for health education is not comprehensive, appropriate and need-based, considering the skill development and competence needed to be developed among doctors and paramedical staff who have to tackle mostly illiterate/backward population. For instance, skill in inter-personal communication is very poor among the newly graduated doctors. When they are poor in communication how can they impart health education? Similarly doctors are not adequately equipped with appropriate knowledge of the psychology of human relations. Without such psychological orientation, doctors cannot make the advice credible and acceptable to the patients. In addition, under the existing overcrowing of the PHCs doctors hardly get enough time to impart properly any useful concept of health education. Therefore, all these aspects are to be tackled either at the under-graduate level or subsequently through condensed courses to the doctors before they are posted, to the PHCs for rendering effective curative and preventive services.

Sex Education for AIDS Prevention

In the context of the HIV/AIDS infection spreading like wildfire, very high priority has to be given now for sex education under health education. Therefore, there is urgent need to integrate sex education, family planning education, and nutrition education under one package. Such education cannot be made successful without repeated efforts made among the clients at the PHC, at home and also in small group meeting not only by the doctors but also by the entire peripheral staff of the PHCs. In order to make this programme successful the conventional face to face counselling alone may not be sufficient. It has to be supplemented with effective exposure to films or film strips, which convey the message powerfully with suitable live photographs depicting the miserable life of AIDS/STD patients. *Therefore* a *suitable* mix of *audio-visual aids must* be *standardised* at the *earliest* to make *health education successful.*

For prevention of AIDS and STD, the single most precaution is to promote safe sex. According to Indian experience nearly 80 per cent of the AIDS patients get infection through unsafe sex. Added to it nowadays AIDS has emerged as the single most killer of human being in Africa and Asia. Unfortunately, due to tobacco on discussion related to sexuality, it has not been covered adequately under Health Education literature. In fact, sexuality must get the highest priority now onwards, not only under Health Education but also with every subject of human concerns. Therefore, it is all the more important and timely now to give the highest priority for sexuality, under Health Education in view of laxity noticed in pre-marital and extra-marital sex and weakening of more value system on chastity and virginity. For details on sexuality, readers are directed to refer to our comprehensive paper elsewhere in a book (Mahadevan, *et al.*, 2001).

Parallely, certain decentralised approach to doctors visiting patients at different places has to be adopted instead of expecting the patients to go to the overcrowd centres like the PHCs; is it not appropriate for the doctors to spend the mornings at the PHC and the afternoons at the subcentres in turn? When private doctors practice during mornings and evenings, should the government doctors practice only in the morning time alone? Therefore, urgent changes are needed at the PHC level to improve the utilisation of the existing facilities which have been created at exorbitant cost in the PHCs, Health sub-centres. *Therefore, in terms of cost-benefit the PHCs have been terrible waste now as people are deprived of* essential health service facilities to them. When are we going to put an end to this colossal waste, which as a poor developing country we can ill afford?

Culture Behaviour and Health

Like food and nutrition, which mould the body and physiological growth, the mind is shaped and conditioned largely by one's culture and environment, social and psychological situation. Formal education too contributes to it. Since most people in developing countries like ours are socially backward and largely illiterate or semi-literate the culture they inherit influences the moulding of their etiological concepts of diseases and reproductive processes. Traditional culture has both beneficial and harmful effects on the life style of people and their health. In fact the nature and consequences of cultural influence on human behaviour related to health, vary depending upon the sub-cultural values, beliefs, customs and habits of different communities. Now let us examine first the benevolent aspects of culture, followed by its deleterious effect on health related behaviour of certain communities.

Brahmins and the Kurichia Tribe in India are proverbial for their hygienic and sanitary practices. The concepts of pollution and purification through bath that they follow have beneficial effect to prevent skin diseases and communicable diseases. In fact, the concept of pollution helps them to avoid extra or premarital sex and enable them to prevent STD and HIV infections. For Brahmins traditionally sex is sacred and therefore the commencement of sexuality after marriage is auspiciously determined, which is popularly called "Shantimuhurtham". Similarly strict observation of monogamy and practice of pollution and virginity help the Kurichia tribe to protect themselves against getting infected by such dangerous communicable diseases like TB, STD and HIV infections. Yet another example of the culture of traditional Brahmins is that they wash their mouth after taking food, at least 7 times, which invariably helps their dental health and promotes their longevity. These are positive aspects of culture that need to be reinforced and can be suitably popularised among other communities without prejudice for healthy living.

The word "etiology" itself means the scientific study of the causes of diseases. However, most traditional cultures explain the causes of many diseases fatalistically. In the absence of proper etiology of diseases, due to ignorance and poor knowledge of physiology, people generally attribute the causes of diseases to fate and divine displease. Even educated people often attribute the sex determination of children and the number of children borne to a parent to divine blessings exclusively. When procreation is believed by people to be purely as a phenomenon of sacred creation, such people cannot be easily convinced of the role of contraception in family formation. Therefore, popular *notion of procreation need, to be changed through syncretic approach and a scientific knowledge of the physiology of reproduction must replace the one-sided notion of making the divine responsible of all procreation.* A similar strategy of syncretism, needs to be adopted to change harmful effects of traditional culture to promote good health, procreation and progress.

Emancipation of Women for Sustainable Health

Women have a very great and varied role to play in the family to promote health or obstruct a healthy way of life. If they are backward, both educationally and culturally, they can do more damage to the entire family, because such function as socializing children, processing food and maintaining sanitation and hygiene in the family are in their hands. Therefore, through formal or non-formal means, education and health education must be imparted to women without failure to make the entire family healthy and happy. Otherwise their backwardness can perpetuate unscientific socialization of children and child development, ruin the nutrition value of food by wrong selection of food items and destruction of the nutrition value of food by over cooking. They may fail to promote a scientific environment in the family. *Therefore, emancipation of women is very essential to promote and sustain healthy family and society in a big way.*

Integration of Other Systems of Knowledge

It is a well-known fact that not only allopathy but the other systems of medicines also like Ayurveda, Homoeopathy and Unani, can cure several diseases effectively *without side effects.* For instance, Ayurveda has the best remedy for jaundice and similarly for degenerative diseases like arthritis, diabetes, spondylitis, control of cholesterol, etc. It is needless to say that allopathy cannot render much help to those suffering from arthritis, whereas Ayurveda can fully rehabilitate even chronic patients of arthritis. Therefore, without prejudice allopathic doctors must be oriented through in service training towards selected effective Ayurvedic, Homoeopathic and Unani therapies for appropriate problems.

Yoga and Health

In addition to the integration of the above-mentioned systems of Medicine, Yoga too must be integrated with health education. In fact, there are several Yoga therapies, which can reduce/cure many morbidity conditions. For instance, to control hypertension, pranayama, savasana and meditation can be successfully adopted. Similarly suryanamaskar is believed to rejuvenate the entire physical system. To prevent/control vertigo, Sarvangasana and Dhanurasana, which give exercise to the neck can be successfully adopted. Even to reduce the adverse effects of diabetes mellitus, two to three *asanas* can be practised daily to revitalize the pancreas, viz., Dhanurasana, Pastchimottasana and Arthamatschendrasana, which can certainly rectify/rejuvenate such degenerative organs and can also be adopted at young ages to prevent this disease. Therefore, Allopathic doctors must be reoriented to integrate certain yoga aspects in their practice without prejudice and reservation.

Ayurveda and Rejuvenation

There are several minor and major retinal problems occurring now-a-days and the present knowledge of allopathy has negligible explanation for their prevention. For example, retinal pigmentation leading to partial or full blindness later on and other types of retinal damages, allopathy has no preventive care. On the other hand, Ayurveda has well developed rejuvenative therapies, which not only cure the damage already happened but also can prevent future degeneration of the retina. Ayurveda preaches to control the problem first with diet, followed by Krias and then medicines.

Prevention of Retinal Detachment by Ayurveda

Mr. X developed a hole on the right retina and an ophthalmologist did cryo-operation and sealed it. Again, after an year, another hole developed on the left retina and a second cryo-operation was carried out. The unhappy patient sought the help of a super speciality ophthalmologist to give preventive ideas and medicines to avoid recurrence of such degeneration of the retina in future. The expert said that there was no medicine in allopathy to prevent the recurrence of such problem. The patient being an eminent and able researcher turned to an Ayurvedic expert of ophthalmology for his retinal problem.

Dr. Ravindranath is an Allopathic surgeon and also an Ayurvedic physician specialised in ophthalmology, and practising in Trivandrum. This doctor has prevented/cured hundreds of cases of retinal/eye problems using Ayurvedic therapy. He prescribes three types of oral and external therapies. He first arranges 'Tharpanam' treatment for the eye. Tharpanam is medicated ghee poured in to eye for a few minutes on seven days during the evenings using the Ayurvedic procedures. After completing Tharpanam he prescribes 'Shirovasti' another treatment, for strengthening the central nervous system through the head by keeping one litre of medicated oil for a few minutes on the head and repeating the practice for another 7 days. Parallely, oral medicine is also given for three months to strengthen nerves. These treatments are repeated for three years as a requirement. However, the patient has continued Tharpanam alone for 12 years, so far. Ever since the patient took Ayurvedic treatment, there has never been a recurrence of any retinal problem, and not even irritation in both eyes. If the patient had not resorted to Ayurveda treatment, he fears he would have been forced to undergo cryo-operation several times more leading at least to partial handicaps to use the eye normally. Similarly, another patient, who returned from the USA, after failing to get cure for his retinitis, was successfully cured by the same doctor, and the patient has not faced any recurrence of this trouble since then. Think for a moment, why should we not integrate the valuable experiences of Ayurveda in our health education and also curative system of medical care.

No Side Effect

Integration of Ayurveda with health education must be made forthwith in order to prevent degeneration of organs like the retina, knee, neck, and for the curing of diseases like amoebiasis, jaundice and for strengthening the reproductive system and several other organs and for curing many common diseases. It should be particularly stated that for the selected troubles mentioned above, Ayurveda is not only more effective than allopathy but it is without any side effects. In the present century people will become more conscious of the side effects of allopathic drugs and therefore Ayurveda will certainly replace allopathy on a selective basis at least for a number of preventive and curative therapies, for the reason already mentioned. But it is necessary to dispel many of the prejudices perpetuated against Ayurveda and other system of medicine by vested interests.

Life Style, Health and Longevity

The concept of life style forms a central theme to health education. In fact several aspects of life style, viz., smoking, alcoholism, drug addiction, chewing tobacco, food habits, exercise regimen, work culture, meditation entertainment etc., differ among people and these attributes of life style have differential influence on the health and longevity of people. Normally longevity depends on health and on Indian's average longevity is around 65 years. Developed countries like Japan and the Scandinavian countries have longevity between 70 to 80 years. However, there are not many centenarians in the developed countries but interestingly several centenarians live among the Kurichia Tribe who live in Wayanad district of Kerala in India (Aiyappan and Mahadevan, 1990).

In a study of more than 3000 adults with or without bladder cancer, researchers found that when smoking habits were compared, women had a higher risk for the disease than men did. The finding is surprising, investigators say, because bladder cancer, which has long been linked to smoking, is more common among men (Donald Ross, 2001). Ross and his colleagues report the findings in the Dumal of the National Cancer Institute. Men get bladder cancer about three times as often as women do according to the National Cancer Institute. While smoking is a major risk for the disease, it has seemed to have a stronger effect on white males susceptibility. For example, Ross noted, black men in Los Angeles have higher rates of smoking but lower rates of bladder cancer compared with white men in the area. In this study, he and his colleagues were tying to figure out why smoking affects groups differently.

They unexpectedly found that women seem more vulnerable than men to smoking effects on bladder cancer risk. For example, among smokers who lit up 40 times a day for 40 or more years, women were more than twice as likely as men develop bladder cancer. According to Ross, women and men may differ in how they process certain cancer causing compounds in tobacco smoke. Research in lung cancer, he noted, has also suggested that women are more vulnerable to ill effects of smoking.

Kurichia Tribes' Longevity: A Model for Education

A classical study completed on the determinants of prolonged longevity beyond 80 years among the Kurichias by Mahadevan and Subramanyam* (1992) have revealed fascinating findings for the civilised population regarding the healthy life style of the Kurichias as a major determinant of their centenarian life. The Kurichias are mostly illiterate and do not take any allopathic medicine. In fact, they do not suffer from most of the communicable diseases like TB, STD, HIV, skin trouble etc. There is so far no reported case of HIV and the other reproductive health problems among them. How could they succeed in living for hundred years, that too, without any of the common ailments? According to our study of the Kurichias the following life-style factors have mostly contributed to their health and longevity. They are very clean and highly hygienic, they never touch other people and if it happens they take several baths daily, when they go out of their houses. They live in massive joint families, owning property jointly and not individually. They have least

---

* This study was presented at an International Gerontological Conference in 1992, held in Sweden and received extensive appreciation from all the delegates.

worry about the security and the future of their children, since the family head and the members collectively take care of everything. No dowry allowed and marriage is simple. All marriages are arranged and no love marriage is reported and no extra and premarital sex reported so far. They live in the salubrious hilly forests and hinterland of Wayanad, close to the Ooty and Coorg hill ranges. They own fertile land and collectively grow paddy, coffee and other cash crops themselves and never employ outsiders. Hence they have very good physical exercise through ploughing/digging etc. They eat a balanced diet without adulteration and pollution. Finger millet (Ragi), leafy vegetables and meat of wild animals are their staple food. Except drinking palm toddy occasionally they do not have any other bad life style. Late in the evening they all sit together around the fire and sing songs for an hour before going to bed. All these life style factors together made them healthy and live upto 100 years and even beyond. Thus, health education must concentrate on dissemination of successful case studies of life style of Kurichias and the others with suitable modification.

Dietary Habits and Fast Food

Mechanisation, hectic life, constrains of time, and cost of living have drastically changed our dietary habits. Added to these, changes in taste and the need for easy and fast cooking and eating have changed the selection and preparation of food items and the menu, as a result fast foods have emerged as an attractive menu for urbanites and migrating population. These changes are likely to create the following hazards for health in future.

Most of the fast food items contain least fibre, resulting in fast absorption of excess sugar, carbohydrates and fat by the body. Fibreless food may cause miseries of constipation also. For the sake of taste and appearance, rice and wheat are polished excessively causing loss of certain nutrients like B-complex and fibre. For further attraction, in fast food shops people add permitted and non-permitted colour also which may in the long run cause cancer. In addition, essential leafy vegetables are avoided in fast food, which in fact formed a part of the traditional diet. Think for a moment?

The cow that gives us complete balanced diet of milk consumes different leafy vegetables and grass. Nowadays how much leafy vegetables do we really consume daily to get a balanced diet. Therefore, health education must lay emphasis on dietary habits during the course of discussion between doctor and patients and also by peripheral workers and through periodic attractive dialogue in the TV and the other mass media.

Food for Health and Happiness

According to age old wisdom to traditional life in India, a number of natural Medicinal Plants, Fruits and grains grown in our country can protect health, prevent diseases and enable trouble free life, however, they are not effectively and regularly used nowadays *out* of fads and fallacies of modern life. The following items of leafy vegetables, fruits, cereals and milks products are good for health, in this regard. For Kurichia tribe Finger millet (Ragi) is a staple diet, which provides 7.5 per cent of protein as against only 2.5% in rice, B-complex, calcium, and necessary fiber for balanced diet for their centenarian life. Similarly Ayurveda proved that sweet neem leaf decoction or pulp (Chatni) regulates cholesterol at 160 to 180 range, eradicates/prevents Amoebiasis, Gastritis and its Magnesium protects heart and it acts as a fiber to prevent constipation. Unfortunately we use it only for flavour and throw it away after cooking and while eating. In addition, taking defatted curd/butter milk with 3-4 garlic pearl daily regulates Cholesterol and prevent Gastritis. Moreover using spinach alone or with all as a daily curry can provide enough protein, minerals, vitamins and fiber for a healthy life. There are many such raw materials of food available in India that can prevent diseases, cure them and promote health. Unfortunately Health Education literature does not bother about them. Therefore, we must popularise them forthwith for the good health of posterity.

Pesticide and Cancer

Several pesticides are used in paddy fields, cashew plantations, vegetables, gardens and horticultural fields, which are supposed to be safe according to the knowledge existed till recently. However, it is not true according to the latest science evidences. In fact, most of these pesticides in the long run causes cancer of intestine. How pesticides reach our body from the plants has not been published through education. For instance, when excessive chemical pesticides are sprayed on the paddy/wheat, its residues sticks on to the leaves and stack, which will be consumed by the cows and in turn through their milk or meat, the pesticides infected animal products get consumed by human beings. Thus, it reaches our body through plants and animal products. Similarly when apple and grape fruits are consumed without sufficient washing, pesticide residues again enter our body, when we consume them. Why health education did not give any coverage on this dangerous process so far?

However, very recently in Europe chemical pesticides are being replaced with organic/neem based pesticides, which will certainly minimize the risk of cancer out of chemical pesticides. However, it will take years for developing countries to relearn about the production and use of organic pesticides and use them in a large scale in our agriculture. In fact, we produce the maximum neem in the world and efforts so far made are drops in the ocean in our agriculture. Therefore, it is a very high priority area of health education for the future generation.

Exercise and Health

Nowadays those with white collar jobs, executives, teachers, researchers, business people and many other employees are busy due to pressure of work and hectic travel in over crowded vehicles, which make them miserable. Therefore, they get little time to do exercise. In our work culture there is no built in mechanism, for half an hour exercise at least on the office premises after working hours. Lack of exercise and laziness make people sleep longer than required. All these changes in society have led to a sedentary living, which has dangerous consequences.

Exercise has multiple benefits, which is not included in most health education literature. First of all, exercise improves the body's resistance against diseases. It improves mental alertness and paves the way for better productivity.

It reduces fatigue for prolonged productivity. It improves digestion, reduces acidity and prevents gastritis, which are common problems of sedentary people, exercise—burns the excess calories and fat in particular, leading to prevention of fat accumulation (pot belly) and the risk of cardiac and diabetic diseases.

Obesity and Cancer

Obesity is largely due to wrong life style, sedentary life and genetic factors. However upto one third of cancers of the colon, breast, kidney, and digestive tract are attributable to too much weight gain and too little exercise, the World Health Organisation cancer agency said. Half the adults in Europe and 61 per cent of American adults are overweight, and the epidermic is spreading round the globe as Western Lifestyles infiltrate new areas, experts say. Putting on weight, even if you are in the normal range increases your risk, said Dr. Harri Vainio, chief of the chemoprevention unit at the International Agency for Research on Cancer, which convened an expert panel for the first analysis of the contribution of obesity and sedentary lifestyle to worldwide cancer. The most important thing is not to gain weight, however much you already weigh. The evidence is not as strong for intentional weight loss "There is no evidence that weight loss reduces the risk of cancer, but that doesn't mean it doesn't." Vainio said, "Nobody has been able to track it because people haven't maintained their weight loss long enough to see if it makes a difference in cancer risk" (WHO, 2001).

Exercise and Control of Degenerative Diseases

Normally, sedentary people with obesity are at risk to get hypertension and diabetes mellitus. Such risk increases when people are short-tempered and irritable. Normally, when BP patient approaches a cardiologist, he advises him/her to go for an evening or morning walk and not to play any strenuous games. Generally slow walk gives only negligible exercise and hardly burns 150 to 200 calories of energy. It is not at all sufficient.

An experiment was carried out by one of this authors by playing indoor shuttle cock to reduce hypertension against the advice of the cardiologist. When his BP count was taken before the exercise it was 140/90 and after playing two games of shuttlecock, and half an hour rest, the BP came down to 120/85. How can it happen? Sweating profusely, flexibility of every organ and the consequent free flow of blood and the other concomitant several physiological and metabolic changes together regulated hypertension. Of course such experiment is desirable only when the person concerned has not developed any cardiac problem. In addition, the overall alertness, endurance, ability, good sleep absence of fear to eat a little more food and no fatigue make life more healthy, pleasant and rewarding through two to three games of shuttle cock daily. Therefore, suitable exercise must be standardised for different people with diabetes, hypertension, cervical spondylosis, and so on. In fact exercise can reduce the need for medication also. It is a wonder that no serious effort is made, so far, to give high priority for exercise in health education programme.

Literacy and Ignorance

The present day general education in schools and colleges, which in the absence does not include health education produces only, literates ignorant of the essential aspects of health. It is a pity that even a doctorate in an arts subject is found to behave like a rustic in rural areas, while selecting water for drinking. He/she does not know that poor quality of water taken from hotels causes diseases like jaundice, diarrhoea, dysentery and several other water-borne diseases. Similarly ignorance of simple causes of other diseases are equally noticed among most of the educated people. What can be done to bridge this knowledge gap must be a priority of health education. Therefore, communication through all the available and effective mass media must be explored for extensive health education to one and all.

Mass Media for Health Education

The vehicle of health education must not be merely the text books, but it as to be carried by all the available mass media. Unfortunately powerful and effective mass media like the television have been mostly monopolised by entertainment, political news and advertisements, which contribute little to healthy life. In fact, getting glued to the TV over a long period of time after sedentary life in the office affects one's health badly. Nearly 80% of newspapers coverage is political and the rest is taken up by advertisements. Hardly many space is given to spreading the ideas of health and health education. Neither the government nor the NGOs make any effort to spread message of health education through mass media.

An urgent rethinking is needed now on what is going on in the mass media to save the health of our millions. At least weekly once certain feature articles on health must appear in all the newspaper. *The Hindu* for example publish very useful articles on health on every Sunday. Such policy must be made compulsory by the government. Similarly, during evenings all the TV channels must be made to carry some message on health education on a regular and compulsory basis. In fact some of the on going serials must be built on themes related to health and happiness instead of showing only romantic serials. The reality is that even romance cannot prolong without health.

High Priority Perspective Needed Now

1. Review critically the opportunities available at the PHC now for health education.
2. On going poor health education at the PHC must be modified.
3. Explore how additional opportunities for health education can be created at the PHC and peripheral areas.
4. Need for retraining the staff for better delivery of health education is a must.
5. Impart health education to idle and waiting patients. In fact valuable 1-2 hours are lost to most patients at the PHCs and other hospitals while waiting for getting service from the doctor? At that time, the waiting patients may be exposed to suitable film on health education, which should educate them regarding preventing diseases. Through films show systematic interventions to prevent anxiety and fear and ignorance on nutrition, safe sex, communicable diseases can be

got rid off. Population regulation can also be achieved. It is a golden opportunity for health education.

6. Adopting new strategies from all available sources for revamping health education not only at the PHC level, but also on a universal basis in schools and public places in a big way are immediately needed.
7. Behaviour of doctors with patients must change. It is well known that most patients suffer from anxiety and fear, when they are sick. If their anxiety and fear are removed by proper counselling at the PHCs, more than fifty per cent of the problem of disease can be cured. A busy PHC doctor, who is not trained in counselling-cum-human behaviour dynamics, cannot look into this basic requirement. As a result, patients returns home very often with half satisfaction and their anxiety and fear may not allow them to get full relief from the sickness. If proper counselling is done by the doctor or the nurse during or after the screening of patients, many patients with minor ailments may not need to visit the PHC and such change can reduce the over-crowding at the PHCs in future. Therefore, appoint a well-versed nurse on health education to counsel patients after the diagnosis of illness by the doctor to alleviate their fear and anxiety and to educate them in care, precaution and follow up.

Adopt Successful Health Education Strategy of China in Indian Schools

China has given the highest priority through all the developmental programmes to

1. clearing the environment,
2. disposal of the waste regularly,
3. prevention of stagnation of waste water,
4. and control of mosquitoes and flies. For instance, in the Beijing City there is no slum settlement. Although Chinese extensively eat watermelon, no fly is seen anywhere around it in the whole of Beijing. In fact no one spits and throw rubbish/waste in public places in China. This civilized behaviour is politically enforced

not only in China but throughout Singapore. No one defecates in and around public places in China and Singapore. But in Tamil Nadu and elsewhere in India the roadside is used as an open and attractive public latrine causing dangerous public health hazards. Should we continue this uncivilized behaviour even after 53 years of independence?

In China and Singapore high priority is given to sanitation, cleanliness of environment, personal hygiene and prevention of flies and mosquitoes. These are taught to children right from school days. Therefore, health education is universal in China and not confined to medical and paramedical staff. Let us adopt these priority subjects in our school curriculum. The need of the hour is health education at all levels of the school to make it universal in the society. The present focus of health education at the PHC level by the busy doctor, who is untrained in this subject, alone cannot solve this problem.

References

1. Aiyappan, A. and Mahadevan, K. 1990. Ecology, Economy, Matriling and Fertility of Kurichias, BRPC, 1990.
2. Mahadevan, K. 1992. Health Education for better quality of Life, BRPC, New Delhi.
3. Mahadevan, K. and Subramanyam, G. 1992. Life style, health and longevity of Kurichias, paper presented at International Gerontological Conference, in Sweden.
4. Ronald, K. Ross. 2001. "Women smoker more valuable to bladder cancer", Journal of the National Cancer Institute, Republished in the *Times of India*, April 4, 2001.
5. Obesity can lead to Cancer: WHO. *Times of India*, April, 2001.
6. Mahadevan, K., Sivaraju, S., Jayasree R. and Sandhyarani, P.M. Human Sexuality and Reproductive Health: A Conceptual Model and Policy Implications. A chapter in a forthcoming book by TISS, Mumbai.

6

Strategies Followed for Education, Health and Population Regulation in Gandhigram, India

R. Kausalya Devi, K. Mahadevan, K.A. Pisharoti, K.V. Renganathan and R. Subramanian

Introduction

The focus of this paper is on the successful rural based, development and welfare activities promoted by the main Institutions of Gandhigram with emphasis on Health promotion, rural welfare activities, and population education with community involvement. Gandhigram has been named after Gandhiji the Father of our nation, who attached the greater importance to rural reconstruction. His philosophy of service is associated with rural development focusing on rural health services, sanitation-cum-health education, small family norm, agricultural development and so on. Therefore, in order to translate the Gandhian Philosophy of rural reconstruction into action, the founders of Gandhigram, Dr. G. Ramachandran and his spouse Dr. (Mr.) Soundaram Ramachandran, selected an extensive rural area covering over 1000 acres at the foot of Sirumalai (Hill) close to the National Highway 7, in Dindigul District and about 55 Kms. north of Madurai city in Tamil Nadu. They established it in the year 1947, coinciding with the independence of India. This distinguished couple earlier had worked under the leadership of Gandhiji in Sevagram, Wardha for several years and it was their ambition to expand rural development programmes in the southern parts of India. Gandhi blessed their efforts to establish a complex of institutions at a site which they named as "Gandhigram" (Gandhian village).

When the Gandhigram was established, the main centre and its activities was the rural institute, and later on, it expanded its activities one after another. Kasturba Hospital was added to render health care services to rural population. Next for the promotion of education-cum-service on environmental sanitation, a sanitation faculty was added on to the institutions. For rendering composite health education-cum-population education, a premier institution for such purposes was set up. When the Gandhigram Rural Institute got expanded with the addition of activities of training and extension programmes, it was upgraded to the status of a Deemed Rural University. At that time, the rural service aspects were de-linked from the University and organised into a separate NGO to continue and expand the service components of Gandhigram. Thus, the original Gandhigram has been expanded and decentralised into several institutions, for rendering education, health services, training in health-cum-population education, welfare activities like institutionalised care for destitute women, orphan children, and to promote the indigenous system of medicine namely Ayurveda. However, in the present chapter, relevant rural education-cum-services of Gandhigram related to health, population and rural welfare in general are presented.

Pilot Project for Health Planning, Education and Service

The pioneering founders of Gandhigram, very rightly promoted a pilot project covering the present Dindigul District, consisting of such major panchayat unions as Chinnalapatti, Batlagundu, Kodaikanal and Dindigul regions. Of them 24 major villages covering a total of 6,036 households were included in this pilot project. The major aims of this project were to study the socio-economic and cultural background of the local population, since no data was available at that time, through primary and secondary sources, identify the major local problems and needs of the people, their dietary habits and level of nutrition, environmental problems and needs, health facilities, hospital utilisation for the prevailing morbidity conditions and population characteristics and so on. In fact, such a database was needed for any pioneering efforts to promote need-based multiple welfare programmes.

The findings of the pilot project revealed the heartbreaking, miserable and all round backward conditions that prevailed half a century ago in this part of India. Regarding the population characteristics, 84.4 per cent, 9.9 per cent and 3.7 per cent were Hindus, Christians and Muslims respectively. Among them the majority (63.6%) were engaged in agricultural pursuit but only 42.2 per cent among them owned land. The density of population was moderate (1104 per square mile) and most of the girls were married off before the age of 18 years. The average size of a household was 4.76 at that time, but it steadily increased in the 1960s. Economically most of them were poor and the bulk of them lived in "kutcha" houses (poor). Most of them depended on tube wells and open wells for their water requirements, but only 7.2 per cent of the households had a safe water source. The condition of sanitation was pathetic, since only 3.43 per cent of the houses had their own latrines and 7.2 per cent of the population used latrines. The remaining 92.8 per cent resorted to open-air defecation. Such miserable and risky environmental hazards, exist even today in Tamil Nadu. Poverty and malnutrition were also widespread at that time in the state as a whole.

Communicable diseases occurred sporadically in most villages. Most common among them at that time were: Small Pox, Tuberculosis, Cholera, Typhoid and skin diseases. There was widespread ignorance among the people about their cause, and prevention. Only a minority of respondents knew treatment procedures partially. Communicable diseases were attributed generally to fate, to forces beyond they control. Such findings necessitated the establishment of a hospital and a health education institute by Gandhigram.

Kasturba Hospital

Kasturba Hospital was established in 1947, when hospital facilities under the state government were just beginning to come up in certain places only. Rural-based primary health centres were established all over the country only after the early 1950s. Even private hospitals were not available in most places near the field area of Gandhigram. Therefore, the establishment of Kasturba Hospital with 100 beds for in-patients was a great boon and met a long felt need. The founder of Kasturba Hospital, Dr. Soundaram used to advise the first author, and her predecessor "*You work in the hospital for eleven months and go to the field and meet the community for one month to give follow up care and also to learn from them their needs.*" Since then field visit, which is a rare feature of government hospitals, became an integral and essential feature of Kasturba Hospital.

Kasturba Hospital provided suitable facilities for the relatives of patients to stay on the hospital premises. Food was also provided to them through the attached canteen at a reasonable cost. Doctors and nurses treated the patients with a human touch. Formality and rigid restrictions were absent. However, all medical procedures were religiously followed. More than all these, the love and concern shown by the doctors and the paramedical staff to all the patients and their humane treatment, irrespective of the patient's economic background become proverbial. This altruistic and humanitarian attitude of the staff brought the Hospital name and fame which no other private or government hospital could ever dream of. For the patients the chief doctor of the hospital is "Amma" (mother) and addressed her as such instead of doctor. Such favourable doctor-patient relationship has strengthened confidence and loss of fear to most of the operations; sterilisations conducted there to the full confidence of patient care in general and were successful and satisfying to the patients. Thus, today Kasturba Hospital has become a model of excellent medical care in this part of India deserving to be emulated by all other hospitals in the state and elsewhere.

Service Strategies

A team of dedicated workers joined the founders of the institution for health and population education services. Accordingly, a maternity centre was started at Chinnalapatty with a number of peripheral centres located in the villages around. *Arogya Sevikas* as the peripheral workers are called who had intensive training under *Kasturba Gandhi National Memorial Trust* were placed in-charge of these peripheral centres to play several role. They functioned as doctors where there was no doctor, as teachers where there was no school and as close friends of the community where there were communal differences.

Dr. Soundaram herself being a doctor, started with health activities in the villages. She gained the confidence of the village leaders and made them feel that they too could think on their own about their needs and problems, talk among themselves and decide upon their needs. Mahila mandals were formed where decisions were made by women and they would express their needs. Dr. Soundaram felt that it is our duty to give the rural people knowledge of health care and create awareness among them; it was their duty to demand and the duty of Gandhigram was to provide the services required within their easy reach.

A team of dedicated workers from Gandhigram would visit the villages regularly, talk to the people there either through the Mahila mandals, or to individuals about nutrition, health, diseases, treatment facilities, care of pregnant mothers, immunisation for children, family welfare programmes and so on which are all of great importance to them. In course of time, Rural-based Health Education became a part of the extension services of Gandhigram. Programmes were organised in villages where women participants could raise incessantly their doubts and get them cleared, or discuss all issues touching upon their well being.

During the discussions on family welfare programme, the participants from the community expressed the view that if some one could give them assurance about the welfare and survival of their children, they would like to limit the number of children. As things stood, they felt, if a mother gave birth to 6 children, at least two were likely to survive to care for them when they became old. So it became necessary not only to educate the rural people but also provide immunisation services in all the villages. The need for immunisation of children against killer diseases was explained to the rural community quoting examples of preventable deaths due to Tetanus, Diphtheria and whooping cough (DPT). The Arogya Sevikas posted in the villages took it up as their responsibility to create such awareness in the rural people. Once they consented to immunise their children, services and follow up care were provided by the team from the Gandhigram Institute of Rural Health and Family Welfare Trust and Kasturba Hospital thus immunisation of children became an accepted practice.

Government of India planned to introduce Intra-Uterine Contraceptive device as a method of temporary contraception. Dr. Soundaram Ramachandran was then Deputy Minister of Education and her friend a devout Gandhiite Dr. Sushila Nayyar was the Health Minister. Health education teams went to villages explaining the importance of temporary contraception and the use of Lippie's loop, an Intra-Uterine contraceptive device, then in vogue. After group talks, and house to house visits explaining the use of the loop, several rural mothers accepted the idea and promised services. Here again the Health Education given by the Gandhigram Institute of Rural Health and Family Welfare Trust team made a significant impact. The Kasturba Hospital Doctors and Nurses participated in providing the required services at not only the Kasturba Hospital but also in the nearby villages arranging camps for this programme. The inventor of Lippies loop; Lippie himself was present at one of the camps and appreciated the Rural Family Welfare Programme undertaken by the Institute.

When Government of India and Tamil Nadu Government thought of conducting Family Welfare camps to popularise the Family Welfare programme, the first few camps were conducted at Kasturba Hospital, Gandhigram, which made the acceptance of the family welfare programme by the villagers easy. Many mothers started coming to Kasturba Hospital for Family Welfare surgery. The Hospital continued the health education programme at the hospital during the family welfare acceptors' stay at the hospital and this encouraged the satisfied mothers to spread the message of family welfare among other mothers who felt encouraged to accept the programme.

Kasturba Hospital had started doing puerperal sterilisation even before the Tamil Nadu Government started it as a programme. Initially camps were arranged for family planning surgery (Tubectomy Operation) at Kasturba Hospital and Government doctors like Dr. Bhasker Rao participated and expressed their satisfaction about the work. During their stay in the hospital, the acceptors were encouraged to bring all their children who were looked after by the hospital providing food, medical check up to the children, immunisation, nutrition education and so on. This service again popularised the programme, much to the satisfaction of the acceptors and the Government. During the camps conducted at Government Hospitals, such services were extended to the children of mothers, who accepted family planning.

It was then that the Government thought of popularising Trans Vaginal Tubectomy (TVT), which a number of mothers felt was a minor surgery as no scar was seen on the abdomen. But Kasturba Hospital, Gandhigram was not very happy about it though 8,000–10,000 and odd mothers every year underwent the TVT at this Hospital. Therefore, the likelihood of pelvic infection was explained to them by the Hospital team as part of its Health Education about TVT. Some mothers developed complications like pelvic infection especially pelvic abscess, which had to be incised and drained. As a result, their hospital stay increased.

Health education in their respective homes was continued and the reason for pelvic infection was explained to them. They were told that pelvis cannot be kept as clean as the abdomen since a number of women could not get the cooperation of their husbands. The acceptors of TVT were advised to avoid sexual relationship for six weeks following surgery but they were forced by their husbands into sexual relationship after a week or two.

Health education and response from the acceptors and other women made women realise that any day abdominal surgery was far superior to vaginal sterilisation. By then the acceptance of the programme was satisfactory, and Tubectomy had become an accepted norm. During the first year of follow-up visits, the community suggested that

Medical Termination of Pregnancy (MTP) could be resorted to for mothers who wanted to induce abortion after they conceived. The first author who belongs to an older generation, had taken a vow at the time of Graduation, not to do abortion! That was deep in her mind and she refused to do MTP. It was Dr. Soundaram who explained to her to try it on a selected few. Vasectomy was very popular then. But there used to be cases of failure and the wife conceived after the husband had vasectomy! Medical personnel, could understand why vasectomy failed and husband also would accept it when his seminal fluid examination showed millions of active male sperms. But the community would take the conception in a different way, even suspecting the wife's character. To save the honour of such mothers the medical team felt that it was its moral responsibility to do MTP. At that time Professor Dr. Bhaskar Rao, asked the first author to attend a seminar on MTP. She participated in the seminar half-heartedly but later on she realised that the MTP was not a sin. By not doing it and by letting a pregnant mother undergo a septic abortion *and* ultimately lead for her death that would be far more sinful than doing MTP. After this experience it was accepted by Kasturba Hospital, the MTP programme was undertaken. Since then maternal death due to septic abortion at the hospital has become practically nil. Till then, cases of septic abortion were frequent and every month one or two mothers lost their lives due to the complications of it. This experience was an education for all the medical staff. Thus the Hospital accepted the MTP and made many rural mothers happy.

Then came Laparoscopic sterilisation. It was at the request of rural mothers the hospital introduced this programme, especially for those mothers who for some reason or other wanted to reduce the hospital stay from 7 days to 2 days. The demand for Laparoscopic sterilisation has been increasing.

During one of the annual, one-month follow-up programme, the village leaders asked the visiting team: "what is the solution to the couple who lost their child/ children after Tubectomy operation?" That made the team realise the need to take up Recanalisation Surgery as an answer to their just fear. This surgery is not being done except rarely even in teaching/medical college hospitals. The results so far have been fairly satisfactory and the happiness that the family gets adds to our happiness.

The next question from the village community as part of its response to Health Education was: "What is your answer to couples, who do not have children even after a few years of married life?" That encouraged the team to take up investigation of infertility. The traditional rural belief was that if a couple was not blessed with a child, it was due to some defect in the wife and it has little to do with the husband. The villagers had to be therefore educated and changed their mistaken notions. This is now an accepted fact that the husband is also responsible for infertility and therefore in cases of infertility it is necessary for the couple to go together to consult a doctor regarding infertility. At Kasturba Hospital, first the couples are counselled individually and together. As there is no facility for high level treatment for infertility, simple investigations are carried out and based on the need follow Allopathy and Siddha/ Ayurveda systems of medicine, and there have been fairly satisfactory results. But it does require a lot of patience and perseverance to make the rural community interested in Health Education. But from experience, it is realised that it is our responsibility to give health education to all concerned and that the satisfaction it gives the giver and the benefits that the rural community gets from it are encouraging rewards in themselves.

Achievements of Kasturba Hospital

When this hospital was started it had only 100 beds. Now there are 260 beds for various categories of in-patients. Such progress in bed strength is no mean achievement since very moderate fees are charged from all the patients. Even Sri Chitra Tirumal Super speciality hospital of Government of India in Trivandrum, has only 236 beds and the Sri Venkateswara Institute of Medical Sciences (SVIMS) of Venkateswara Devasthanam at Tirupati has only 265 beds. *What is more the mortality rate of Kasturba hospital is extremely negligible (0.7%) compared with the rates of Sri Chitra Thirumal*

Hospital (2%), All India Institute of Medical Sciences (4%), JIPMER (15%) and SVIMS (8%). Of course, patients attending these other hospitals mostly have cardiovascular complications, and most cases treated at Kasturba Hospital are delivery cases of women and of morbidity of children. Even then, it is no mean achievement to have the lower mortality rate as annually reported at the Gandhigram Hospital (Mahadevan, 2003). Another notable success is the phenomenal increase in the number of in-patients (1,16,555), and out-patients (76,124). Among the patients women outnumber men by almost two times during 2003. On a daily basis more than 300 patients get treatment here either as in-patients or outpatients. In fact, Kasturba Hospital has been carrying out a record number of sterilisations and the other family planning services more than any other hospital. In recognition of such distinguished services rendered here, the architect of such services, Dr. Kausalya Devi, was honoured by the Central Government. Thus, Kasturba Hospital can be justly proud of its achievements.

Research for Strengthening the Programmes

The two sister-institutions of Kasturba Hospital and Institute of Health and Population jointly carried out a very valuable action research led by Mahadevan and others for the successful promotion of both hospital service utilisation and acceptance of family planning. The research theme was "Utilization of successful adopters of female sterilization for diffusion of the same message to non-adopters of family planning". Therefore, all eligible women, who underwent sterilisation at Kasturba Hospital during one year period early in the 1970 were given each a set of 5 identity cards of this hospital, to pass them on to a similar number of non-adopters and explain to every one of them the success and satisfaction of their sterilisation experiences. Such planned communication strategy between the satisfied sterilised women and non-adopters was not only successful but increased the sterilisation rate during the one year-study period by leaps and bounds. After establishing the worthwhileness of the action research at the hospital level, it was later on extended as an experimental study to two

Community Development (CD) blocks also by Mahadevan and his team. That field level study further confirmed the tremendous credibility of satisfied adopters in promoting family planning. It was a successful and exemplary and a real advancement in strategies for promoting expeditiously family planning in the world. When it was published in studies in family planning, *Journal of Population Council*, New York, Dr. M.H. Heidegger, a German professor complimented it on the following lines.

"We think that your (Mahadevan) project described there is one of those "Model projects", we are looking for. Of course we are even interested in your later publications mentioned. Obtaining this paper of yours would be great value for our work (University of Heidelberg, West Germany, January 11, 1978)". This strategy of Gandhigram has been adopted all over the world for successfully promoting family planning and also it was adopted as a job function for all peripheral workers by the Government of India. This study was liberally funded by the Ford Foundation.

Institute of Health and Family Planning

This Institute came into being, as an offshoot of the Pilot project mentioned above to institutionalise proper human resource development of health and family planning workers, carry out research to develop these programmes, and also to experiment with different strategies at the field level for strengthening the implementation of the programmes at primary health centre (CD Block) level. The pioneering training research and field experiment carried out by this Institute were totally successful and the findings of this Institute were adopted in several countries in the world and states within India for the successful promotion of health education and family planning. Such experiences have been lucidly documented and jointly published by the North Carolina population centre in the USA and the Gandhigram Institue (K.A. Pisharoti *et al.*, 1972) and interested readers may refer to it for further details.

Training on Health Education and Family Planning

This Gandhigram Institute is a pioneer in the world for

successfully imparting job-oriented training for Health Educators and family planning personnel working at different levels, peripheral, block, district and national. Integrated health and population education sandwiched between classroom teaching and concurrent field training really provides self-reliance and full confidence to all the trainees. The strategy of training was based on the job functions of each category of staff operationalised and synthesized with relevant interdisciplinary subjects to develop professional capacity, gain suitable experiences and to achieve self-reliance to carry out the expected work efficiently.

This Institute offered short-and long-term training programmes on Health and Population Education. The trainees came from all over India and abroad. In addition, the entire staff from Indonesia working on Health and Population projects there were trained in this Institute. Several other Asian and African countries deputed their candidates to Gandhigram for similar training. In fact International agencies like World Bank and WHO deputed trainees from several developing countries to this Institute for similar human resource development of different categories of staff. Thus the Institute of Gandhigram has pre-eminently helped the developing countries in their Health Education and Family Planning Programmes.

Research and Evaluation

In the field of research as stated above, this Institute has contributed several valuable ideas to (a) strengthen strategies to promote the programmes successfully, (b) evolve policies, (c) evaluate the impact of the programmes and (d) explain the unresolved problems faced during the implementation of Health and Family Planning Programmes. The research compendium (1964-1987) published by this Institute gives glimpses of its manifold research and evaluation programmes carried out in the past. International collaboration in the field of research with funding from WHO, Ford Foundation, Rock Feller Foundation also eminently helped in executing various research projects and programmes. A joint research project undertaken by North Carolina University and Gandhigram, funded by WHO, led to the development of the valuable book "FAMILY FORMATION PATTERNS AND HEALTH", which form a major contribution to the subject. (Abdul Omran, *et al.*, 1976, WHO). There are many such research projects carried out in this Institute.

Field Training

Practical field training given to the trainees at Gandhigram forms a unique feature. Trainees without exception have found it valuable. During the training the theory taught in class is translated into practical field situations. Such field experiences are provided concurrently with learning in classroom on a regular basis, and after formal classroom training exclusively for a longer period, supervised field training is provided. After the completion of classroom assignments includes the development of a dissertation based on empirical data and observation, which strengthens the practical capacity of the trainees. Such training enables trainees to develop self-confidence, practical wisdom and realistic approach to the problems faced in the respective countries of the trainees. Thus field training imparted during Health and Population training programmes has significantly promoted Human Resource Development.

Achievements of the Institute

In Asia, this institute is a pioneer in carrying out valuable job-oriented health education-cum-family planning training, research and consultancy services. In recognition of such commendable services rendered in the past, World Bank deputed family planning staff of several countries to the institute for human resource development to strengthen family planning in their countries. As noted earlier the Indonesian family planning programme succeeded with the training offered at Gandhigram for its entire staff. World Bank appointed two of its former directors, Dr. K.V. Ranganathan to the head office of World Bank to help the successful implementation of family planning in several other countries, and Dr. K.A. Pisharoti as adviser to Bangladesh Government to strengthen family planning in that country. In fact Bangladesh had the highest birth rate at that time in South Asia. However, today its birth rate has come down considerably and is only 30 at present as against 36.5 in Pakistan, and 24 in India (UN: 2003). Many erstwhile staff members of Gandhigram have occupied very important positions in several other institutions in India and abroad and shared with them the Gandhigram experience. Dr. Mahadevan carried out a number of research projects, guided several doctoral students (40) and produced 33 valuable books. And according to Dr. D.J. Reddy, former Vice Chancellor, of Sri Venkateswara University, he brought the population centre of S.V. University international recognition. Similarly Dr. K. Srinivasan served in ESCAP and at I.I.P.S. Institute etc. successfully.

The community participation approach developed by Gandhigram can be adopted by all the developing countries for promoting health and family planning programmes successfully among them. There are approaches for the involvement of community leaders and satisfied adopters for the promotion of health and family planning programmes. In this approach, all the community leaders from the villages were first identified using a scientific methodology developed by this Institute and were periodically trained, made them coordinator of local health committees along with a dozen or more eligible couples for planning, cooperating and implementing health and family planning at the grass roots level. This method of community participation gave the paramedical workers, easy access to the people, reduced people's resistance, and encouraged them to volunteer to strengthen the efforts of the workers to promote family planning. Such efforts were further augmented when satisfied adopters facilitated interaction with one another in the periodic group meetings, as cited earlier. This twin methodology of successful community participation was adopted widely in India and abroad through the former trainees of Gandhigram.

This Institute established a world record during the early 1970s in the Athoor block, which was their experimental field demonstration area for several years. Using the community participation strategy and the well-trained health-cum-population education peripheral staff, the birth rate in this block was drastically reduced to 28, when the national birth rate was 35 plus. At that time this block alone had such low birth rate in the entire country. It was referred to several times in Indian Parliament and in several other forums by the Ford Foundation, who liberally financed this programme. In addition, the natural low fertility (CBR 24.5) was exceptionally low among the Kongu Vellala (Gounders) community living in Coimbatore, Salem, Dharmapuri, Ooty, and Palani regions, according to a major study on fertility carried out and reported for the first time in the developing countries (Mahadevan, 1979). It was the first of its kind in Asia at that time, which was reviewed extensively at a seminar in Delhi by Ford Foundation for the benefit of others. Dr. Mahadevan has produced the largest number of 33 diverse developmental books on all aspects of population sciences, methodology, health, women development, communication etc., which is a world record. Similarly he produced the largest number of Ph.Ds. (40) in Asian Universities.

Another landmark achievement of this Institute was in revolutionising the eradication of universal open-air defecation in this region by promoting widespread use of community and family latrines. This dramatic development was possible through the strategies of health education pioneered by Dr. Pisharoti and his dedicated team of workers. Even to day, open-air defecation is the general practice in the rural areas of Tamil Nadu. Therefore, total eradication of open-air defecation, particularly at Chinnalapatti and several other villages deserves special recognition by all health educators. In fact according to the pilot health project findings of 1947 referred to above 93 per cent of the population were accustomed to open-air defecation in this area. It was possible to eradicate this unhygienic practice with the liberal funding by the International Development Research Centre, Canada and Ford Foundation. There are many more such landmark achievements of this institute, which can be seen in the book "*The Athour Experience*" and the other publications of the GIRH and FWT.

Gandhigram Rural Institute

1. The founding of Gandhigram Rural Institure (GRI) was wholly the overriding conceptual notion (its vision) for

the founders of Gandhigram, inspired by the long-felt need for taking "higher education" to the doorstep of villages to free them from centuries of economic and social backwardness. The Government of India seized of the imperative need for rural upliftment, around 1955 and took a decision to introduce in its educational system with the support of the Ford Foundation, New Delhi, a new type of institutions—Rural Higher Institutes—specially designed to better life in the villages and make them join the mainstream of national development. It looked for already existing institutions which were providing such service in villages in the country. Fourteen such places were identified. And Gandhigram was one of its primary choices to establish one such rural institute, on account of Gandhigram's rural setting and proven ability to deal with the problems and issues of village development within GANDHIAN AMBIENCE. In consequence the GRI inherited the mission already started by the Founders of Gandhigram. The year 1956 saw, then, the establishment of GRI, mandated by the Government of India as welcome addition to the Gandhigram complex of educational and service institutions. The new institution, GRI, attracted a band of dedicated persons, (V. Rengarajan, M. K. Selvaraj, M.G. Gopalakrishnan R. Subramanian and S. Sivasubramanian) who were recruited to form the faculty headed by Mr.V. Krishnamurti, who acted as its Executive Secretary.

2. GRI has as its goal the application of an educational and information package to virtually every area that challenges the nation in village development—from the wiping out of illiteracy to improving rural health and village environmental sanitation; from the development of sustainable agriculture to efficient management of homes and better farms; from providing the background for emerging leadership in local self-government: from alleviating poverty to finding means to live a well-informed life.

3. Therefore, the GRI has had the opportunity to experiment with innovative approaches in order to

achieve excellence in higher education, through teaching, research and extension education/service (for rural development) in its rural hinterland—100 villages—within the framework of Gandhian educational philosophy and ethics. The Institute's background, years and growth provide rich field experience to mould its academic programmes to efficiently operate in the field and simultaneously strengthen teaching in the classroom. Consequently its curriculum for the various multi-disciplinary academic courses, initially at the graduate level and later at the post-graduate level, along with a built-in rural extension/service component, has a major bearing on the varying emphasis on approaches to rural development. Today the Institute's academic offerings are tailored to meet the cutting edge of the sciences, intermediate technology, IT, social sciences, ethics and politics so that these approaches become invariably multi-disciplinary in finding possible solutions for village problems and issues.

GRI in the Beginning

4. The Institute's formative years (1956-1976) were marked by experiments in inter-linking graduate programmes with extension activities plus village camps and action research. Various disciplines were used to identify the rural problems for lab-treatment (research) before taking the result into the field. The major highlights were improving agriculture by scientific farming technologies. The strategy was that the GRI, after picking up the need in priority would let the clients (parents) and the agency (Block or Bank) sort out the problems and figure out possible areas of assistance. Another area for development was the organisation of cooperative societies for various purposes such as lime-kiln and lift irrigation. Rural services development then, comprised creation of self-employment opportunities among landless agricultural labourers, better housing and drinking water supply, adult literacy programmes, founding of pre-school

education centres for children, formation of rural Women's Clubs, which proved to be viable, relevant and functional for rural women-folk development and rural health and sanitation. Applied research activities involved, besides teaching research methods and statistics, guidance in the preparation of students project reports, coordination of extension and action research programmes, direction of nationally-funded research projects, surveys, attitudinal and opinionated studies etc. In all such activities, rural community participation, agency (Block and District level) involvement and the Institute's catalyst role were emphasised.

Over the years the GRI, in the lights of its successes and failures, has developed its own a strategy of action for rural development. Its various steps are the following:

i. Determining the status quo of the people, their numbers and resource availability;

ii. Leadership survey in the villages with a view to identifying dynamic leadership;

iii. Meeting the village assembly and discussing on the conditions (position status) of the village and its needs. (The officials/non-officials/specialists of the Panchayat Union/Panchayats were invited to participate in the meet);

iv. Meeting of the village community for discussion of economic/social needs and fixing priorities;

v. Execution of the projects after planning in the light of local resources—men and material for the project—with the assistance of voluntary organisations, local bodies and the village committees.

Recognition—Expansion and Consolidation 1976 to Present

5. Recognition of GRI's achievements in the innovative stream of education came in 1976 from the University Grants Commission (UGC). Based on an evaluative study, the GRI was rated high for its academic

achievements, research and extension. As a result, the status of a Deemed University was conferred statutorily upon it in 1976. This was a great leap forward for the GRI. Propelled by this new status, and further expansion and development were undertaken in several directions diversifying, innovating and strengthening academic programmes, undertaking nationally and internationally funded research projects, and extensive village and home improvement programme using development education as the tool. An impressive range of teaching programmes, including Ph.D. in several related disciplines and participatory development were introduced. Very recently the U.G.C. initiated an assessment of the current state in the Institute's work and activities-academic, research and rural community development. In consequence, GRI earned the *Five Star* status—a national symbol of its recognition as an important university in the country.

6. One of the thrust areas in the GRI, over the years, has been the spectrum of studies, funded nationally and internationally, including descriptive, statistical, analytical, action-oriented evaluative studies for the state of Tamil Nadu, policy-oriented advisory projects for the Tamil Nadu Planning Commission, research in development indicators and impact studies—studies in health and nutrition, and environmental sanitation; in the economics of home and the farm and child development; in adult literacy; in rural industries and small/micro-entrepreneurship; and in local self-government. In this effort the Faculty of Rural Development has drawn upon the researches from the Faculty of Rural Oriented Sciences and Technology. Faculty of Rural Social Sciences, Department of Applied Technology for Rural Development, Faculty of Agriculture and Animal Husbandry and Faculty of Rural Health and Sanitation.

Development of Strategies

7 a. Extension is central to teaching and research in the GRI, its prime objective being development of self-

reliant, well-informed and autonomous rural communities. With this as the centrepiece, GRI has employed several strategies in its extension programmes. The key players in all these have always been the people. The GRI applies the concept of participatory development—an innovative approach—with a specific focus on "Putting the People First" as the nucleus of development intervention. The starting point is enabling and empowering the people to analyse their own situation and contexts and finding ways and means to better their situation through a set of participatory appraisal tools and techniques. The GRI with a core team led by N. Narayanasamy, has used the concept extensively in outreach activities. The areas wherein the PRA technique (Participatory Rural Appraisal) was applied included: the understanding of the broad patterns and trends in rural societies; exploration of different dimensions of a given theme; deductive PRA's for dealing with sensitive issues—for e.g. resettlement and rehabilitation of farmers affected by the reservoir project; researching on the forms of participation, process and methods as well as analysing the efficacy of participatory methodology; planning and implementation with a designing project for implementation; monitoring and evaluation of projects/programmes. Recently the PRA was successfully applied in the project, "Hunger-Free Area Programme", conceived and implemented by the GRI in collaboration with the MSSRF (Swaminathan Research Foundation, Chennai). A quick participatory evaluation of the project, "Hunger Free Area Programme", revealed better awareness of various schemes of the government, especially among the poor and villagers who demanded services from the government.

7 b. The GRI has been experimenting with the idea of linking extension in higher education and its quality up-gradation with students' research and funded research. The Department of Home Science has done appreciable in this regard. One of the primary strategies developed by the faculty under the leadership of

Kamalamma and Vasantha Devi is integrated educational intervention on do-hows for a target group of women and children with anaemia. They created a replicable package, which is used as an educational module. Another approach used has been taking programmes to the target group—by means of student involvement in schemes like Dr. Jayalalitha's Girl Baby Scheme, Dr. Muthulakshmi Reddy Scheme, Old age Pension Scheme, etc.; and hand-outs for dissemination of information have been prepared for five schemes based on field experiences. The impact on the target group was positive since the strategy brought an awareness of schemes and benefits to them. Yet another approach has been needed identification and assessment through participatory rural appraisal in six villages for programme planning for students' extension: This model has been found very effective in classroom and field situations. Another valuable area of action has been the development of suitable technologies for improving water management and sanitation practices with the support from the DST under the project "Water, Health and Sanitation". The technologies used for sullage disposal, spill water disposal/recycling at community water sources, roof water harvesting models, improved design for community toilet are being replicated by several agencies, NGOs, research organisations, Centre for Science for Villages, (Wardha), to name a few. The department in collaboration with the TTK, Chennai, also facilitates de-addiction of alcoholics in the villages around the GRI .

7 c. Another major achievement of the GRI is the promotion of Self Help Groups (SHGs) in and around Gandhigram—a kind of sustaining "SHG revolution". The main object is to build up the capacity of men/women for the purpose of eliminating poverty by helping them to form themselves into small, informal affinity groups of not more than 20 members. The Departments of Adult and Continuing Education, of Extension Education, of Rural Development, of Agriculture and Animal Husbandry and the Krishi Vigyan Kendra (KVK) have undertaken this

task. The Department of Extension Education has designed a curriculum for SHG management and organised 2-3 months training programmes for strengthening the capacity of field level functionaries of the SHGs (Easwaran and L. Raja). Action Research Programmes on SHGs, and SHG promoting institutions in Dindigul district have their focus on mainly skill training, capacity building and on various issues in running and sustaining the SHGs (N. Lalitha).

The major impact of the SHGs has been on the marginalisation of moneylenders, the inculcation of savings habit among group members, improvement in livelihood opportunities, development of capacity to manage groups, creation of "Community" sense among the members and improvement in knowledge and skills.

7 d. The introduction and installation of 7200 SUKHAD model of smokeless Improved Chulha in 112 villages spread out in 7 blocks with financial back-up from the KVIC and DRDA by the Physics Department is another aspect of GRI's extension service. Involvement of students and Faculty team under the guidance of Balasubramanian and extending the project beyond the target area by the adopters themselves are the strategies that really helped in its dissemination. The impact is seen on the fact that women have a healthy, unpolluted kitchen environment.

7 e. The Rural Technology Centre of the GRI has its own innovation in planning, guiding and assisting rural house-building activities using the technology the Centre created namely, cost-effective building technology with hollow block brick panel and pre-fabricated structures. It has covered Gandhigram and extended to villages in the neighbourhood.

7 f. Started in 1989, the Krishi Vigyan Kendra (KVK) of GRI can boast of some laurels. It was created specially to meet the needs of the farmers of Dindigul District; and the funds came from the Indian Council of Agricultural Research, New Delhi. Its strategies of extension activities, are primarily in agriculture (Dry-farming), Animal Husbandry, Horticulture, Forestry and Home

Science. Particular mention must be made of the strategy—organisation of Farm Science Clubs (FSCs)—evolved by the Kendras which has proved effective in the diffusion of new technology from farmer to farmer. The KVK imparts training to extension workers, NGOs, students, teachers and housewives. It has a well spread out network with state and national agencies, private organisations, NGOs, financial and research institutions. Its impact has been on improved nursery practices, improved practices of fertilizer application, wide-spread adoption of improved HY varieties of paddy, groundnut, sun flowers, etc.

7 g. The GRI's Centre for RE IRD implemented the Social Forestry Project, which had for its components training rural men/women, raising nurseries in villages and generating employment opportunities for more rural women in the villages at the foothills of Sirumalai. Fresh nurseries were raised in the identified villages around Gandhigram for future development into tree-plantations as well as afforestation along the Western Slope of Sirumalai Hills. The GRI-service village sector was one of the locations for it. The project helped women/men to get economic benefits. The strategy adopted was participatory development, training and skill orientation for men and women. The social forestry project was funded by the SIDA for about ten years. A faculty team and field staff under the leadership of R. Subramanian with the assistance from the Social Forestry Training School at Vaigai Dam, the Department of Agriculture and Animal Husbandry, the KVK, village leaders and rural women trainees was in-charge of it. Manpower to plant the nursings came mostly from the village leaders, people beneficiaries and students.

7 h. From the dizzy heights of abstraction, mathematics has its own attraction to the rural 'concrete'. The journey is bumpy when it moves from math-broadways to the lanes of rural reality. Yet maths moved, when set in motion research mode in its application and resulted in the creation of optimisation (mathematical) models for use in dealing with energy crisis in the villages, in

increasing the income of small-scale industries in the villages; in augmenting farm income by rotation of crops in an efficient, result-oriented manner and in optimisation of rural credit utilisation for the beneficiaries—(and team).

7h(a) Recognition of the work of the Centre for Research, Extension and IRD (Later Faculty of Rural Development) came when the UNESCAP, Bangkok, Thailand, invited the Director of the Centre as Resource Person (1977) to organise a Regional Workshop on methods and techniques of promoting people's participation in Local Development. The above mentioned team devised the strategies through village extension and action-research, and the invited specialists formed the core of the workshop personnel, the workshop had as part of its activity, field visits, conference with panchayat, block and district level officials, village leaders—men and women and specialists. The first phase of the workshop for the participants from Australia and South Pacific region, was held in the GRI followed up by its second phase in Bangkok, Thailand. The UNESCAP applauded the conduct of the workshop Phases I and II.

7h(b) The Good Samaritan Foundation, Seattle, USA invited the Centre for RE, IRD, GRI to participate in an international study of the impact of social experiment in Family Planning Services. One location was Thanjavur where a survey was undertaken. This social experiment was well monitored and analysed. The survey was well designed and executed, yielding clear, and useful data; the theme and the design were presented at the World Bank's Annual Conference on Development Economics, 1990. That became a model later on. This brought the World Bank acclaim to GRI.

7h(c) The chemistry department (Karthikeyan and team) successfully tackled the FLUOROSIS problem in the drinking water, which badly affected the health of rural people, who depended on mostly on bore wells for water consumption. This department on a cost effective manner using local technology made the hand pumps shaft with alumina and neutralised the bad effect of fluorosis. For want of space for the time being we stop here for the present.

7h(d) The economic department of GRI is a pioneer in India, in promoting applied economics integrating financial and other management concepts. In addition, its this department published a pioneering and comprehensive book on WOMEN IN DEVELOPMENT IN INDIA, (Philomena and Sumangala, 2001) which is a text book all over India. Thus, the Gandhigram institutions as a whole pioneered and promoted innovative, valuable and replicable several strategies for the better quality of life of rural people in southern part of India.

Note

Personal experiences of K. Mahadevan, and R. Subramanian have been extensively adopted into this chapter. Similarly certain ideas provided by R. Kausalya Devi and K.A. Pisharoti have also been incorporated in this chapter. Information available was also collected from Departmental (GRI's) sources about strategies adopted in extension and their impact.

References

1. Pisharoti, K.A., Ranganathan, K.V., Sethu, S. and Dutt, P.R. 1972. *The Athoor Experience: Implications for a Statewide Family Planning Programme*, GIRH and FWT, Gandhigram and Carolina Population Centre, at Chapel Hill, the U.S.A.
2. Ramakrishnan, N.R. 1963. *Report on the Baseline Survey*: Pilot Health Project, Gandhigram.
3. Kausalya Devi, R. 2002. *Kasturba Hospital-Gandhigram, Hospital Statistics for 2002*, (Mimeo).
4. Subramanyam, G. 2003. *Sri Venkateswara Institute of Medical Sciences: A Deemed University in Expeditions Empowerment of Women, through Innovative Strategies in A.P.*, Edited by K. Mahadevan, BRPC, New Delhi.
5. Mahadevan, K. 1996. *Demographic Transition and Development Strategies in India*, BRPC, New Delhi.
6. Mahadevan, K., Rajaram, P. and Sandeep, V.M. 2003. K.V. Ranganathan: *A Dynamic Administrator and Educator, in Mahadevan Edition*, 2003.
7. Omran Abdul, Standley, C.C., Azar, J.E., Bertan, M., Guzman, V., Nahapetian, V. and Pisharoti, K.A. 1976. *Family Formation Patterns and Health*. World Health Organisation.

8. Reddy, D.J. 1990. *Personal Communication with K. Mahadevan* (Mimeo).

9. Kapali, V. and Hassan, H. 1990. Profile of K.A. Pisharoti, Chapter in "Policies and Strategies for Child Survival: Experiences from Asia", Edited by K. Mahadevan, BRPC, New Delhi.

10. Subramanian, R. 1977. *Scope and Nature of the Gandhigram Rural Institute (Deemed University) and Their Relationship to National Rural Development* (Mimeo); paper prepared for the Regional Workshop on Methods and Techniques of Promoting People's participation in Local Development for United Nations' Economic and Social Commission for Asia and the Pacific (UNESCAP), Bangkok, December 1977. (The first phase of the workshop was held in GRI, Gandhigram and the second phase in Bangkok, December 1977.)

Part - II

REPRODUCTIVE HEALTH

7

American Experience in the Prevention of HIV/AIDS: Risk Behaviours among Bisexuals, Hispanic Males and Black Males

Guang-zhen Wang and Vijayan K. Pillai

Introduction

The prevention of HIV/AIDS has become the most efficacious way to cope with the risk of transmission as there are no substantial measures for curative treatment of AIDS. The AIDS epidemic continues to expand and it affects all kinds of people. As of December 2001, the number of people living with HIV/AIDS totalled 40 million, of whom 28.1 million in sub-Saharan Africa and 940,000 in North America (UNAIDS, 2001). The National Institute of Allergy and Infectious Diseases (2002) and the National Institutes of Health (2002) identified three types of risk behaviour: (1) sharing drug needles or syringes; (2) having sexual contact with an infected person without using a condom; and (3) having sexual contact with someone whose HIV status is unknown. HIV virus is spread most commonly by having unprotected sex with an infected partner. The Centers for Disease Control and Prevention (CDCP) (1999) estimated that between 920 million and 1.7 billion injections by injecting drug users (IDUs) take place every year in the United States. IDUs make the second largest exposure to HIV/AIDS infection representing 15 and 26 per cent of HIV/AIDS cases respectively (CDCP, 1999). Given the number of unprotected sex and IDUs, this population has become a primary focus in preventing the spread of the disease (Zagumny and Holt, 1999).

Using data from Cooperative Agreement for AIDS Community Based Outreach/Intervention Research Program1992-1998 (CA), the study attempts to evaluate the effectiveness of the experimental interventions taken to prevent the transmission of HIV/AIDS and to assess the socio-economic and demographic factors in predicting risk behaviours for the Americans.

Data

The data used for the study consist of 31,088 adult respondent records collected from 21 CA facilities in the United States and one facility each in Puerto Rico and Brazil. The data were prepared by the United States Department of Health and Human Services; National Institute of Health; and National Institute on Drug Abuse. The respondent data include risk behaviour assessments of both a baseline risk behaviour survey and the post-intervention survey conducted either three or six months after the baseline risk behaviour survey. The standard interventions consist of street-based outreach and HIV prevention counselling that include support group activities, educational videos, and social gatherings. Interviews were used to collect data from multi-racial/ethnic male and female drug injectors and cracker users at risk for HIV.

The data were collected using a randomized and quasi-experimental design. A targeted sampling strategy was used to map geographic areas of local drug use activity and HIV infection. Each site chosen had a monthly recruitment of 35 multi-racial/ethnic drug injectors and crack users who were at risk for HIV. The sample consists of 69 per cent of males and 57 per cent of Blacks.[1] Most of the respondents were heterosexuals, with 4 per cent being bisexuals. Forty five per cent of the respondents had less than high school education. Only 18 per cent of the respondents were either married or common law couples. Of all the participants, over 67 per cent had some chance of getting AIDS (from 25 per cent of the chance to 100 per cent of the chance). Table 1 shows the demographic characteristics of the participants in the sample.

Table 1: Demographic Characteristics of Respondents

Variable		Frequency	Valid %
Sex			
	Male	21,494	69.1
	Female	9,594	30.9
Race/ethnicity			
	Black (not Hispanic)	17,719	57.0
	White (not Hispanic)	5,185	16.7
	Hispanic	6,542	21
	Asian/Pacific	72	0.2
	Native American	786	2.5
	Other	784	2.5
Education			
	Less than high school	13,880	45.0
	High school graduate	11,294	36.0
	Some college or above	5,889	19.0
Considered homeless			
	Yes	8,748	28.3
Marital status			
	Single/separated/divorced/widowed	23,663	76.0
	Married and common law	5,567	18.0
	Same sex partner	173	0.6
	Opposite sex partner	1,649	5.3
	Other	16	0.1
Sexual preference			
	Heterosexual	29,009	93.6
	Gay	368	1.2
	Lesbian	323	1.0
	Bisexual	1,220	4.0
	Other	60	0.2

Variables and Analysis

There are few publications on HIV/AIDS prevention research and evaluation of prevention programs in general (Mallory and Fife, 1999). Eight variables were used to assess the risk factors and the efficacy of the experimental interventions to prevent or reduce HIV risk behaviours.

The first variable is the survey question "In the last 48 hours/two days when you used drugs, did you inject them?" "Yes" is coded as 1 and "No" is coded as 0. Figure 1 presents the results for various groups before and after the experimental interventions.

Hispanic males were most likely to inject drugs compared with other groups before the intervention: 73 per cent of Hispanic males answered "yes" to the survey question. Black females were least likely to inject drugs before the intervention (mean=0.28) compared with other groups. Interventions were most effective in reducing the risk behaviour among the gay and bisexual people (mean differences are 0.16; 0.13 respectively).

For the second variable "Have you ever given someone sex (tricked) to get drugs?" 51 per cent of the bisexuals answered "yes" before the interventions. Experimental interventions seemed to reduce the risk behaviour for most of the groups except for bisexuals and white females (Figure 2).

The third variable is "Have you ever given someone drugs to have sex?" Black males seemed to be more at risk. Fifty two per cent of the Black males who answered the question admitted they had. Intervention programs did not seem to reduce the risk behaviour significantly; 46 per cent of Black males still gave drugs to have sex after the interventions (Figure 3).

The fourth variable is "Have you ever given someone sex to get money?" Bisexuals were most likely to engage in the activity compared with other groups, 69 per cent of the bisexuals answered "yes" to the survey question. Interventions did not seem to alter the risk behaviour in substantial way for bisexuals. Intervention programs helped reduced the risk behaviour for gays and Hispanic females (Figure 4).

The fifth variable is "Have you ever given someone money to have sex with you?" Black males were most likely to engage in the risk behaviour. Interventions did not seem to reduce the risk behaviour among Black males. Interventions helped reduced the risk behaviour for most of the groups (Figure 5) .

Figure 6 displays the variations in the number of times that respondents cleaned the works (needles/syringes) previously used by someone else only with tap water before shot up.

Hispanic females were most likely to engage in the risk behaviour before the interventions compared with other groups. The intervention programs appeared to be effective in reducing the number of times among Hispanic females. The interventions did not seem to work among Native American males.

In terms of the number of times that respondents cleaned works (needles/syringes) used by someone else only with alcohol and water and peroxide and water before shot up, the data showed that Hispanic males were most likely to do so. The intervention programs seemed to be effective to reduce the number of times except for the lesbian group (Figure 7).

Figure 8 presents the results for the variable "number of sex partners who used drug." Bisexuals had most sex partners who used drug compared with other groups. Interventions seemed to be effective in reducing the number of sex partners for all groups.

The findings indicate that the three groups of people who were most likely to engage in risk behaviours are bisexuals, Hispanic males, and Black males although the overall intervention programs seemed to be effective in reducing the likelihood of risk behaviours.

Table 2 presents the demographic characteristics of bisexuals, Hispanic males, and Black males. Most of them were single and had less than high school education.

Although the data suggest some success in reducing risk behaviours, a number of factors have been identified to predict risk behaviours in relation to HIV/AIDS infection including knowledge about testing and the nature of HIV (Jemmott and Jemmott, 1991, 1992; Kline, Kline, and Oken, 1992; Nyamathi *et al.*, 1993; Ford, Wirawan, and Fajans, 1995; Sikkema *et al.*, 1995; Zagumny and Holt, 1999), poverty and homeless status (Wingood, Hunter-Gamble, and DiClemente, 1993; Nyamathi, Stein, and Brecht, 1995; Peragallo, 1996; Mallory and Fife, 1999; Malow *et al.*, 2000), and characteristics of intervention participants (Knodel *et al.*, 2001; Strauss and Falkin, 2001; Warner and Leukefeld, 2001, Ziek *et al.*, 2001).

Table 2: Demographic Characteristics of Bisexual, Hispanic Male, and Black Male

Characteristics	Frequency (valid %)		
	Bisexual	Hispanic male	Black male
Highest grade of school completed			
Less than high school	495 (40.6)	3,010 (61.3)	4,361 (36.8)
High school/trade/technical graduate	404 (33.1)	1,353 (27.5)	4,910 (41.5)
Some college	240 (19.7)	440 (9)	1,968 (16.6)
College graduate	81 (6.6)	110 (2.2)	605 (5.1)
Marital status			
Single/separated/divorced/widowed	960 (79)	3,704 (75.5)	9,610 (81.1)
Married/common law	156 (12.8)	1,022 (20.8)	1,717 (14.5)
Same sex partner	35 (2.9)	14 (0.3)	35 (0.3)
Opposite sex partner	64 (5.3)	168 (3.4)	488 (4.1)
Considered homeless			
Yes	411 (33.9)	1324 (27.1)	3,678 (31.2)
Sex			
Female	791 (64.8)	0	0
Male	429 (35.2)	4,916	11,857
Race			
Black	712 (58.4)	0	11,857
White	252 (20.7)	0	0
Hispanic	174 (14.3)	4,916	0
Native American	38 (3.1)	0	0
Asian/Pacific	5 (0.4)	0	0
Other	39 (3.2)	0	0
Sexual preference			
Heterosexual		2,315 (97.4)	6,753 (96.3)
Gay		35 (1.5)	138 (2)
Bisexual		26 (1.1)	123 (1.75)
Lesbian		0	3 (0.04)

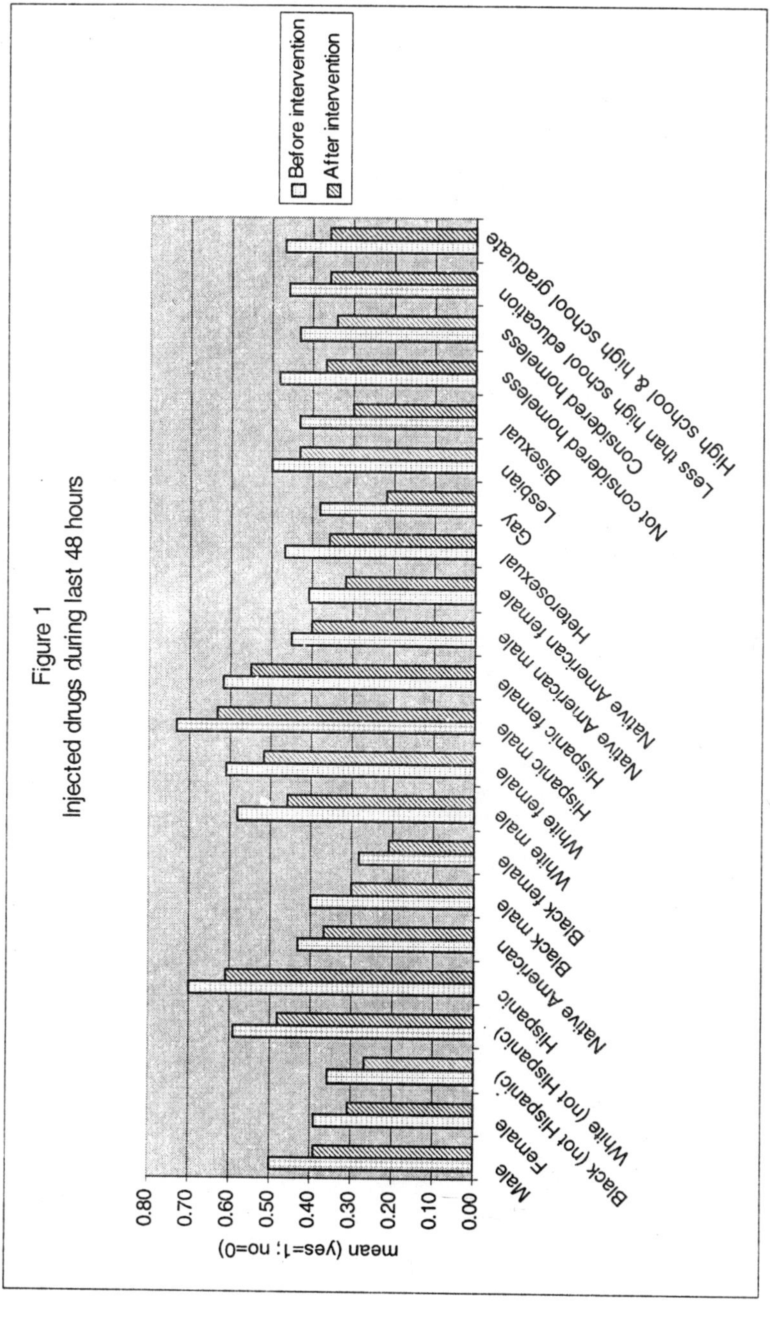

Figure 1
Injected drugs during last 48 hours

Figure 2
Ever given sex to get drugs

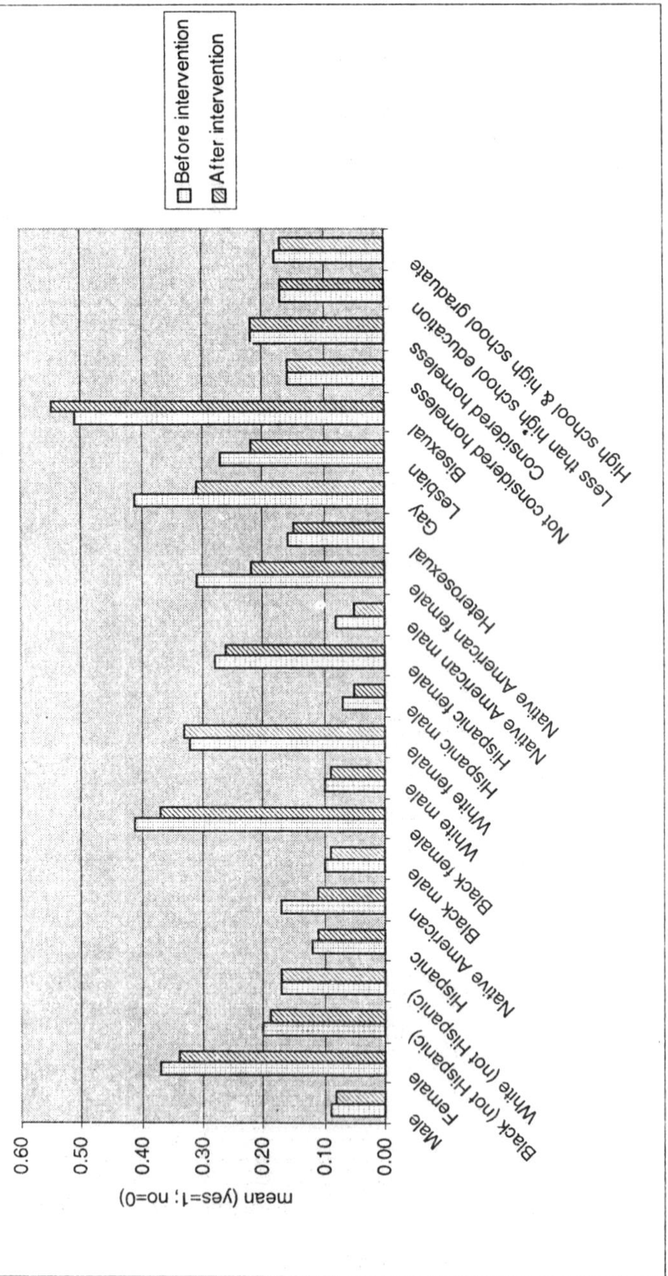

Figure 3
Ever given drugs to have sex

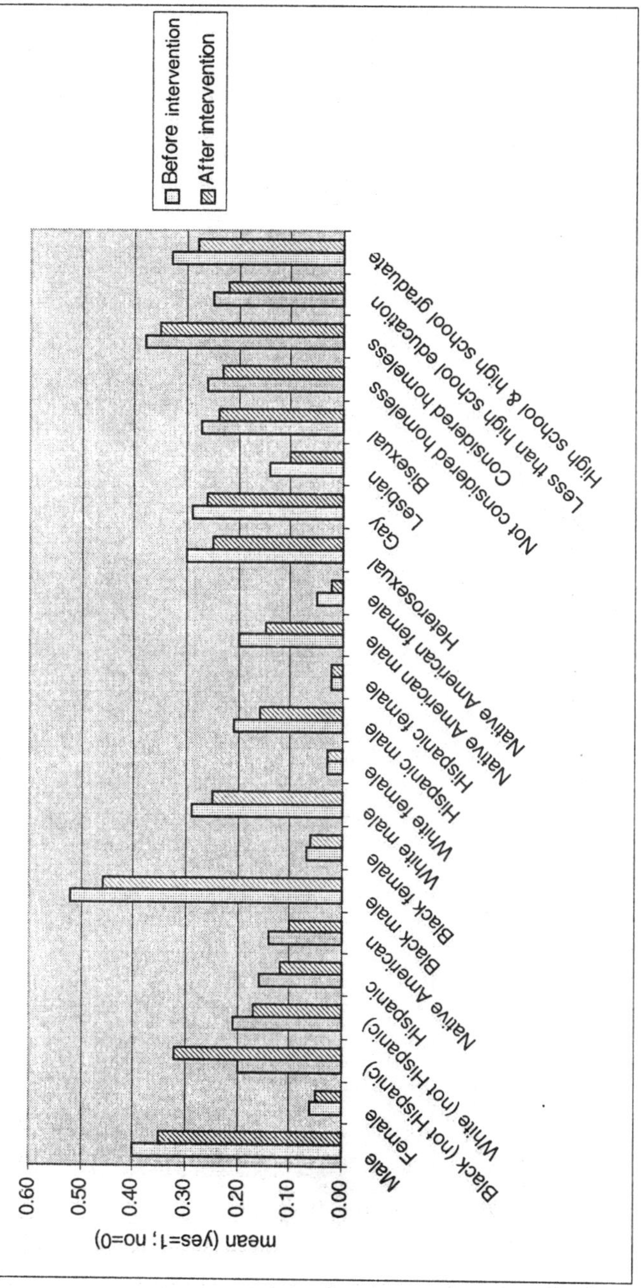

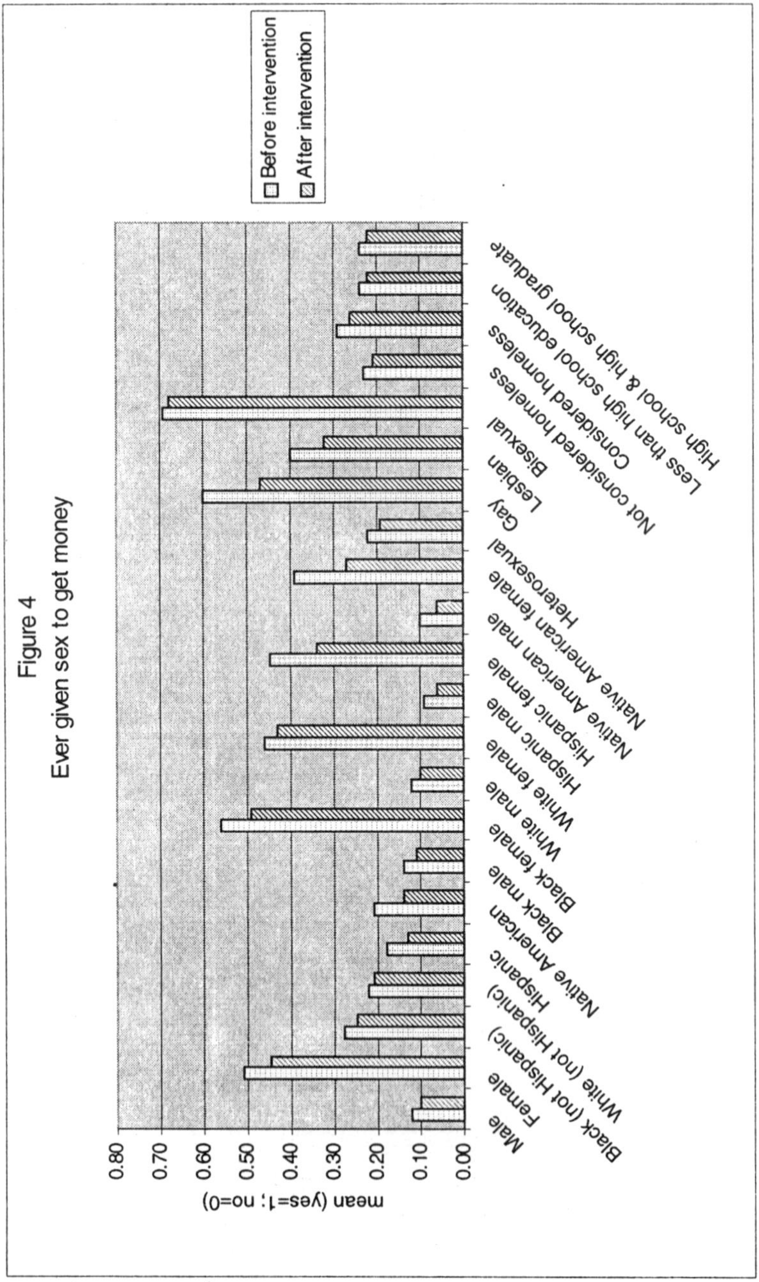

Figure 4
Ever given sex to get money

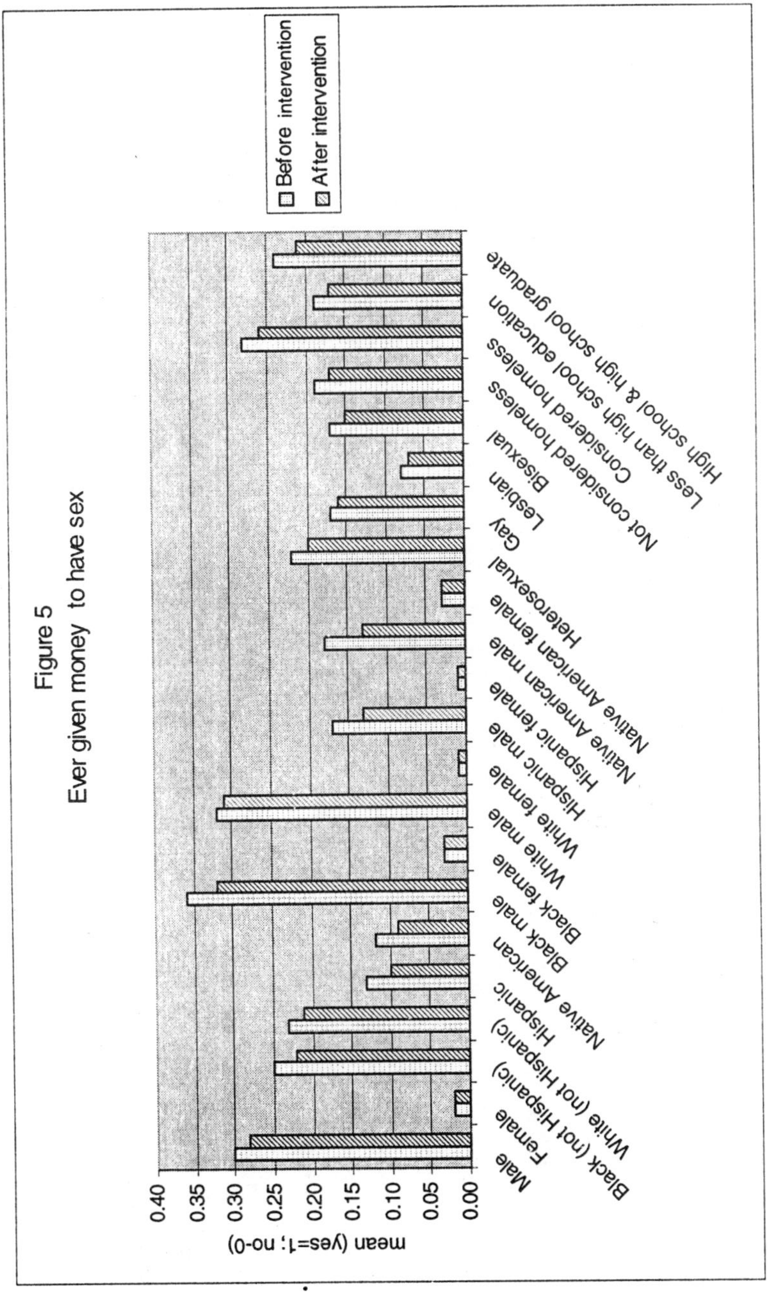

Figure 5
Ever given money to have sex

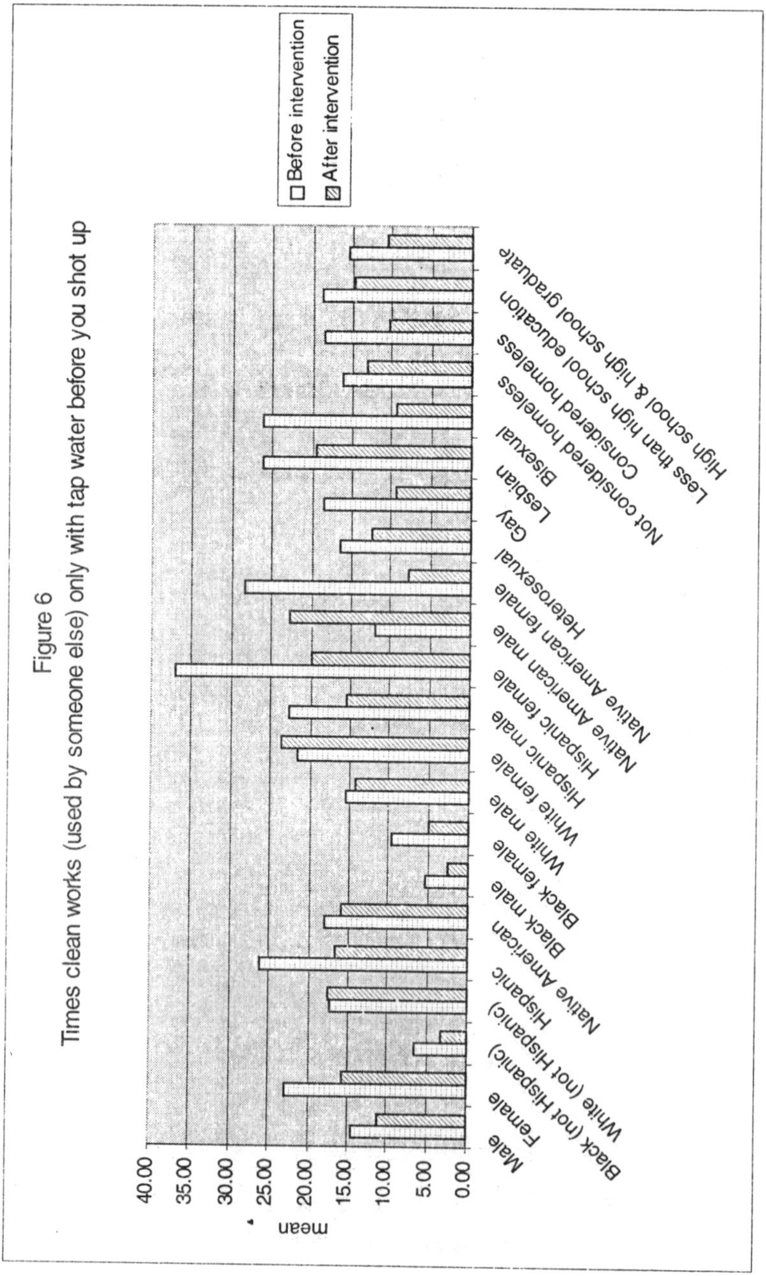

Figure 6
Times clean works (used by someone else) only with tap water before you shot up

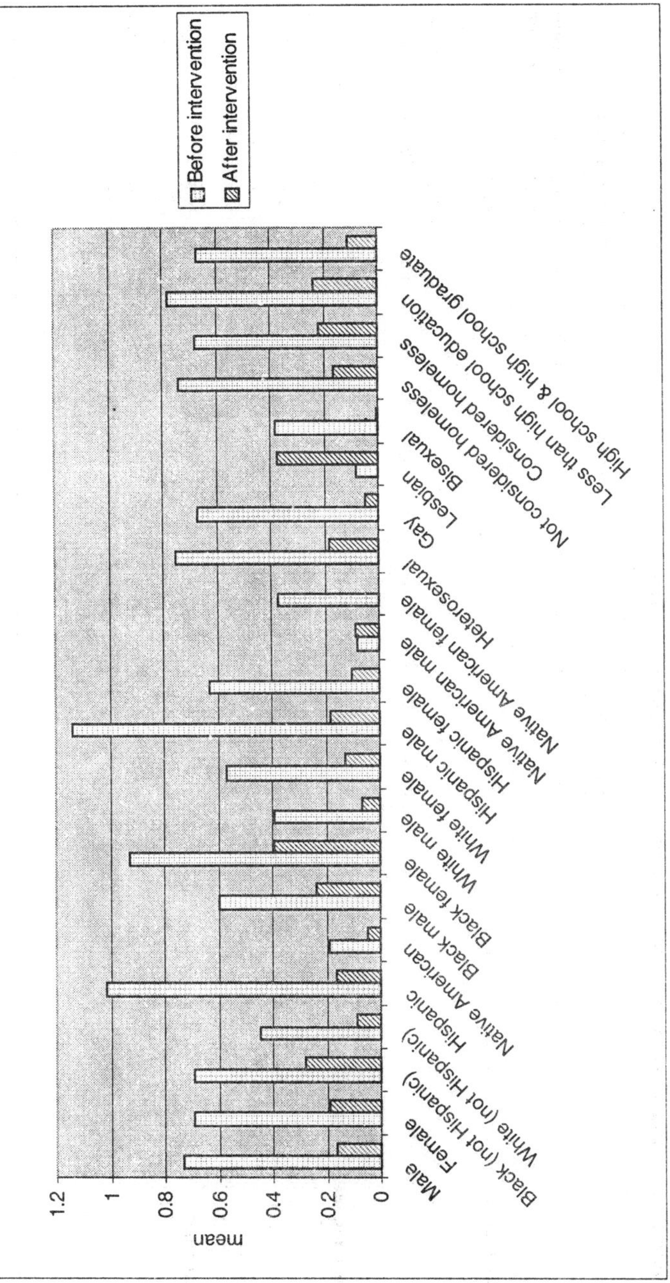

Figure 7

Times clean works (used by others) only with alcohol/water and peroxide/water before you shot up

Table 3: Crosstabulation of Risk Behaviours with Selected Variables

Variables			Considered homeless		HIV testing		Marital status	
			Yes (%) (1)	No (%) (0)	Yes (%) (1)	No (%) (0)	Married/common law (1)	Single/div/sep/ wid (0)
Black Male	Risk behaviours	Low (1)	77.4	82.7	81.1	82.7	84.2	80.5
		High (2)	22.6	17.3	18.9	17.3	15.8	19.5
		(N)	3,509	7,789	9,890	1,138	1,652	9,193
			Chi-square (df=1): 45.510		Chi-square (df=1): 1.688		Chi-square (df=1): 12.589	
			Phi: 0.063*		Phi: 0.012		Phi: -0.034*	
Hispanic Male	Risk behaviours	Low (1)	83.4	90.9	89.5	83.9	91.6	88.2
		High (2)	16.6	9.1	10.5	16.1	8.4	11.8
		(N)	1,286	3,482	4,183	528	994	3,609
			Chi-square (df=1): 53.381		Chi-square (df=1): 14.740		Chi-square (df=1): 9.588	
			Phi: 0.106*		Phi: -0.056*		Phi: -0.046*	
Bisexual	Risk behaviours	Low (1)	61.4	66.9	64.9	67.8	62.0	65.1
		High (2)	38.6	33.1	35.1	32.2	38.0	34.9
		(N)	386	764	1,042	90	150	911
			Chi-square (df=1): 3.394		Chi-square (df=1): 0.307		Chi-square (df=1): 0.539	
			Phi: 0.054		Phi: 0.016		Phi: 0.023	

*p<.01

Warner and Leukefeld (2001) suggest that intervention programs do not reduce HIV/AIDS risk behaviours randomly. Identifying participant characteristics related to both intervention programs and reduction in risk behaviours is useful for developing explanatory models of health behaviour and for targeting and customizing intervention populations (Warner and Leukefeld, 2001). An examination of some social-economic and demographic variables suggest that homeless status and marital status are important predictors of risk behaviours for both African-American and Hispanic males.[2] (Table 3).

Homeless people are more likely to engage in risk behaviours than non-homeless people. Single, divorced, separated, and widowed persons are more likely to engage in risk behaviours than married and common law persons. Among Hispanic males, those who had HIV testing show less risk behaviours than those who did not have HIV testing. None of the three independent variables can explain the risk behaviours for bisexuals.[3]

Conclusion

The U.S. HIV/AIDS epidemic has expanded from one that primarily impacted white gay men in the late 1980s to an epidemic that represents an increased risk for racial/ethnic minorities (CDCP, 2000). CDCP has directed the largest portion of HIV/AIDS prevention to the African American community. AIDS is the leading cause of death among Blacks aged 25 to 44 (CDCP, 2001). African Americans represent close to 13 per cent of the U. S. population, yet they represent 55 per cent of the new HIV infections while HIV prevalence among white men declined by 50 per cent between 1988 and 1993.

The findings indicate Black males are more likely than other groups to give someone drugs to have sex, to give someone sex to get money, and to give someone money to have sex both before and after the interventions. The risk behaviours among Black males can be significantly explained by their homeless status and marital status.

CDC's funding of HIV/AIDS prevention programs specially targeted to the African American community has increased substantially over the last decade. Yet, the study has found that Hispanic males and bisexuals are among the three groups of people who have demonstrated high levels of risk behaviours. Latinos overall represent an estimated 20 per cent of new HIV infections. Hispanic males are more likely than other groups to inject drugs and use uncleaned needles and syringes that have been used by someone else. All three independent variables, homeless status, HIV testing, and marital status can significantly explain the risk behaviours among Hispanic males.

The bisexuals in the data are found to have the most number of sex partners who used drugs, to give someone sex to get money, and to give someone sex to get drugs. For bisexuals, close to 60 per cent of the participants are women. Zagumny and Holt (1999) found that females who are more likely to engage in risk behaviours report fewer perceived benefits to safer sexual practices than males. AIDS cases are increasing faster among women than among men in the United States (Sobo, 1995; Lauby *et al.*, 2000). CDCP (1997) reported that women make up 20 per cent of the population diagnosed with AIDS and that AIDS cases contracted via injection drug use among women aged 15 to 24 years exceeds men by more than two to one. AIDS has become the third leading cause of deaths among women 25 to 44 years of age and the leading cause of deaths for Black women in same age range (CDCP, 1999). Although deaths resulting from AIDS among men have recently declined nationwide, deaths among women have increased by 3 per cent (CDCP, 1997).

Mallory and Fife (1999) pointed out that research in the area of prevention and evaluation of interventions of HIV/AIDS infection among bisexuals and women remains scant despite the growing public awareness of women's vulnerability to the virus. The lack of theoretical concepts and preventive intervention research specific to bisexuals and women has resulted in serious limitations in research on women's health behaviour and prevention of HIV/AIDS (Zagumny and Holt, 1999; Lauby *et al.*, 2000; Malow *et al.*, 2000). There is a need for gender-sensitive and continued research that specifically addresses women's needs in the prevention of HIV/AIDS (Wortley and Fleming, 1997; Mallory and Fife, 1999; Elwy *et al.*, 2002; Malow *et al.*, 2000).

AIDS is a stigmatized disease both in the United States and throughout the world (Price and Hsu, 1992; Herek and Capitanio, 1997, 1999; Pryor, Reeder, and Landau, 1999). The findings from this study have indicated the necessity for an integrated approach to the prevention of HIV/AIDS among some vulnerable groups. It will be important for future intervention programs to target more toward Black and Hispanic males, bisexuals and women, and homeless people.

Notes

1. Asian/Pacific Islanders were excluded from the analysis due to very small sample size.
2. HIV/AIDS risk behaviour is indicated by an additive measure of five variables: injected drugs during last 48 hours, ever given sex to get drugs, ever given drugs to have sex, ever given sex to get money, and ever given money to have sex. The additive measure is then recoded into two categories, low risk behaviour (0-2) and high risk behaviour (3-5).
3. Chi square was used to test the relationship between risk behaviours and the socio-economic and demographic variables. It is a test of statistical significance based on a comparison of the observed cell frequencies of a joint contingency table with frequencies that would be under the null hypothesis of no relationship. The sensitivity of chi square to the sample size points to an important distinction between statistical significance and substantive importance in relationships between the variables.

References

1. Centers for Disease Control and Prevention, 1997. "Update: Trends in AIDS Incidence, Deaths, and Prevention—United States 1996." *Morbidity and Mortality Weekly Report* 46 (8): 165-172.
2. Centers for Disease Control and Prevention, 2000. *Protecting the Health of Latino Communities Combating HIV/AIDS.* www.cdc.gov/nchstp/od/nchstp.html.
3. Centers for Disease Control and Prevention, Divisions of HIV/AIDS Prevention, 2001. www.cdc.gov/hiv/pubs.
4. Elwy, Rani, A., Hart, Graham, J., Hawkes, Sarah and Petticrew Mark, 2002. "Effectiveness if Interventions to Prevent Sexually Transmitted Infections and Human Immunodeficiency Virus in Heterosexual Men: A Systematic Review." *Archives of Internal Medicine* 162 (16): 1818-1833.
5. Ford, K., Wirawan, D.N. and Fajans, P. 1995. "AIDS Knowledge, Risk Behaviours and Condom Use among Four Groups of Female Sex Workers in Ball, Indonesia." *Journal of Acquired Immune Deficiency Syndromes and Human Retrovirology* 10 (15): 569-576.

6. Herek, Gregory, M. and Capitanio, John, P. 1997. "AIDS Stigma and Contact with Persons with AIDS: The Effects of Personal and Vicarious Contact." *Journal of Applied Social Psychology* 27: 1-36.
7. Herek, Gregory, M. and Capitanio, John, P. 1999. "AIDS-related Stigma and Attitudes toward Injecting Drug Users among Black and White American." *The American Behavioural Scientist* 42 (7): 1148-1161.
8. Jemmott, L.S. and Jemmott, J.B. 1991. "Applying the Theory of Reasoned Action to AIDS Risk Behaviour: Condom Use among Black Women." *Nursing Research* 40 (4): 228-234.
9. Jemmott, L.S. and Jemmott, J.B. 1992. "Increasing Condom-use Interventions among Sexually Active Black Adolescent Women." *Nursing Research* 41 (5): 273-279.
10. Joint United Nations Programme on HIV/AIDS (UNAIDS), 2001. *Global Summary of HIV/AIDS Epidemic.* www.unaids.org/worldaidsday/2001.
11. Kline, A., Kline, E. and Oken, E. 1992. "Minority Women and Sexual Choice in the Age of AIDS." *Social Science and Medicine* 34: 447-457.
12. Knodel, John, Saengtienchai, Chanpen, Im-Em, Wassana and Landingham, Mark Van, 2001. "The Impact of AIDS on Parents and Families in Thailand: A Key Informant Approach." *Research on Aging* 23 (6): 633-670.
13. Lauby, Jennifer, L., Smith, Philip, J., Stark, Michael, Person, Bobbie and Adams, Janet, 2000. "A Community-Level HIV Prevention Intervention for Inner-City Women: Results of the Women and Infants Demonstration Projects." *American Journal of Public Health* 90 (2): 216-222.
14. Mallory, Caroline and Fife, Betsy, 1999. "Women and the Prevention of HIV Infection: An Integrative Review of the Literature." *The Journal of the Association of Nurses in AIDS Care* 10 (1): 51-63.
15. Marlow, Robert, M., Cassagnol, Theresa, McMahon, Robert, Jennings, Terri, E. and Roatta, Victoria, G. 2000. "Relationship of Psychological Factors to HIV Risk among Haitian Women." *AIDS Education and Prevention* 12 (1): 79-90.
16. National Institute of Allergy and Infectious Diseases, 2002. *HIV Infection and AIDS: An Overview.* www.niaid.nih.gov/factsheets/hivinf.htm.
17. National Institutes of Health, 2002. *HIV Infection and AIDS. An* Nyamathi, A.M., Bennett, B., Leake, C., Lewis, C, and Flaskerud, J., 1993. "AIDS-Related Knowledge, Perceptions and Behaviours among Impoverished Minority Women." *American Journal of Public Health* 83: 65-71.
18. Nyamathi, A.M., Stein, J.A. and Brecht, M.L. 1995. "Psychological Predictors of AIDS Risk Behaviour and Drug Use Behaviour in

Homeless and Drug Addicted Women of Colour." *Health Psychology* 14: 265-273.

19. Peragallo, N. 1996. "Latino Women and AIDS Risk." *Public Health Nursing* 13 (3): 217-222.

20. Price, V. and Hsu, M. 1992. "Public Opinion about AIDS Policies: The Role of Misinformation and Attitudes toward Homosexuals." *Public Opinion Quarterly* 56: 29-52.

21. Pryor, J.B., Reeder, G.D. and Landau, S. 1999. "A Social-psychological Analysis of HIV-related Stigma: A Two-factor Theory." *American Behavioural Scientist* 42 (7): 1193-1211.

22. Sikkema, K.J., Koob, J.J., Cargill, V.C., Kelly, J.A., Desiderato, L.L., Roffman, R.A., Norman, A.D., Shabazz, M., Copeland, C., Winett, R.A., Steiner, S. and Lemke, A.L. 1995. "Levels and Predictors of HIV Risk Behaviour among Women in Low Income Public Housing Developments." *Public Health Reports* 110 : 707-713.

23. Sobo, E.J. 1995. *Choosing Unsafe Sex: AIDS-Risk Denial among Disadvantaged Women.* Philadelphia: University of Pennsylvania Press.

24. Strauss, Shiela M. and Falkin, Gregory, 2001. "HIV Negative Women's Communication of their HIV Status to their Intimate Partners." *AIDS Education and Prevention* 13 (5): 403-412.

25. Warner, Barbara, D. and Leukefeld, Carl, G. 2001. "Assessing the Differential Impact of an HIV Prevention Intervention: Who Putting the Message into Practice?" *AIDS Education and Prevention* 13 (6): 479-494.

26. Wingood, G.M., Hunter-Gamble, D. and DiClemente, R.J. 1993. "A Pilot Study of Sexual Communication and Negotiation among Young African American Women: Implications for HIV Prevention." *Journal of Black Psychology* 19: 190-203.

27. Wortley, P.M. and Fleming, P.L. 1997. "AIDS in Women in the United States." *Journal of the American Medical Association* 278 (11): 911-916.

28. Zagumny, Matthew J. and Holt, Tamala Ray, 1999. "Gender Differences in Sexual Practices and Beliefs among Rural Injecting Drug Users in Treatment." *Journal of Alcohol and Drug Education* 44 (2): 1-6.

29. Ziek, Kristine, Goldstein, Marjorie F., Beardsley, Mark, Deren, Sherry and Tortu, Stephanie, 2001. "Factors Associated with HIV Testing and Returning for test Results in a Sample of Out-of-treatment Drug Users." *Journal of Drug Issues* 30 (3): 675-685.

8

Chinese Experience in Reproductive Health and Prevention of AIDS

Gao Ersheng, Dou Lixia*

Current Situation and Achievement of Reproductive Health in China

China is a developing country with the largest population in the world and family planning is a basic state policy. Since the mid of 1990's, Chinese family planning program has achieved a great success. In 1990s, contraception-use rate of married reproductive-age women stabilized at about 80%. After implementation of informed choice on contraception, contraceptive method construction of married reproductive-age women modified a little. But long-term contraceptives are still the main contraceptive methods and its proportion remained more than 90%.[1]

Family planning service stations in different levels were set up from the early 1980s to increase the availability and accessibility of contraceptive services. The Family Planning Service Network covers all cities, townships, and villages in China. The network distributes contraceptive devices and agents and disseminates information on population and reproductive health to people. There are totally more than 400,000 service workers for family planning service. They implement state family planning policies and provide relative services to people. At the grassroot levels, full and

* Shanghai Institute of Planned of Parenthood Research.

part-time family planning workers are staying in close touch with the women and maintaining variety of contraceptive and reproductive service. Accordingly, a national training system on reproductive health has been building.

Contraceptive method construction of married reproductive-age women (%)

Contraceptive method	1992	1997	2000
Male sterilization rate	12.1	9.8	8.9
Female sterilization rate	39.6	39.1	37.6
IUD prevalence	39.1	43.7	46.3
Subcutaneous contraceptive implants	–	0.4	0.4
Oral or injectable contraception prevalence	4.1	2.5	2.1
Condom prevalence	3.9	3.8	4.2
External application prevalence	0.7	0.4	0.3
Others	0.5	0.3	0.2

In addition, remarkable social effectiveness has been achieved. Reproductive programs directly benefit reproductive population. They are provided with education, consultation and technical services about birth, contraception, STD prevention and infertility. So their knowledge about family planning and reproductive health are raised.

Development of Quality Care for FP/RH in China

The definition of reproductive health has been accepted and adopted widely since the International Conference on Population and Development in 1994. In responding to the recommendations of ICPD Plan of Action, the Chinese Government has earnestly implemented the ICPD "Program of Action" and the State Family Planning Commission sponsored a national project "Quality of Care on Contraception" (QOC). This project poses a major innovation for family planning and reproductive programs and it is a concert action in achieving the goal to serve the people.

In 1995, the SFPC decided to carry out a pilot project for the quality of care in China. In 1996, the pilot project for the quality of care began to be initiated in the country. In 1997, with the continuation of the pilot project, international institutes participated in QOC of China, for example, experts from Population Council attended the workshop on the quality of care in Yancheng, Jiangsu province. In 1998, the SFPC started international cooperation with Ford Foundation, the Population Council, and University of Michigan. In 2001, the State Family Planning Commission carried out three major programs—reproductive tract infection control, birth defect control and quality care for contraception service—to improve the reproductive health of adults and prevent birth defects. The Quality of Care program has served 827 counties in China. China is bringing about or has brought about some changes in the strategy for population and family planning.

The six-element framework of quality of care that has been accepted in China include choice of methods, information given to clients, technical competence, interpersonal relations, follow-up and continuity mechanisms, and the appropriate constellation of services. In order to provide better reproductive health service, the Chinese government switched the work focus from only family planning to reproductive health; from population control to client-centered services; from mere contraceptive methods to informed choice; from administrative order to providing quality of care services. Quality of Care in family planning has been developed all over the country.

Strengthening of Scientific and Technological Research

Systematic research network of reproductive health and family planning has been formed. China has 27 special family planning institutes including 6 WHO collaborating centres. They conduct research projects covering all Family Planning/ Reproductive Health area, including sociology, demography, economics and biomedicine. Scientific and technological research are being conducted to find new method to meet people's reproductive health need. Contraceptive development research are promoted, efforts are being made to produce new contraceptive methods and techniques which are safer, more effective and more convenient. The researchers have developed some new type of IUD, subcutaneous contraceptive implants, emergency contraceptives, medical abortions service with mifepristone and so on.

Providing and Distributing Good-Quality Contraceptive Devices and Agents

Diversity of contraceptive devices and agents such as IUDs, condoms, vaginal spermicides and suppositories, oral contraceptive tablets are widely available in Chinese social market. They are mostly distributed free of charge through the nation-wide contraceptive distribution and management network.

Promoting Informed Choice of Contraceptive Methods

Informed choice refers to the process by which an individual arrives at a decision about contraceptive use. It must be based upon access to, and full understanding of, all necessary information on the client's perspective. The process should result in a free and informed decision by the individual about whether or not the client desires to obtain health services and, if so, what method or procedure the client will choose and consent to receive. The family planning service providers should respect the clients and their right and shift their working way from traditional "pure administration" to "services-oriented". Training has been conducted for grassroot family planning workers and the relevant service has been improved. People at childbearing age can choose satisfactory contraceptive methods on the basis of the acquisition of adequate information and advice. Quality care on family planning programms can improve the degree of satisfaction for reproductive women with reproductive health or family planning services. Among all factors, informed choice on contraception is most important to improve the women's satisfaction degree to services.[2]

Stressing and Participating in the Prevention of AIDS and Other Sexually Transmitted Diseases (STDs)

The HIV/AIDS and STDs epidemic has spread fast recent years and proves to be a crucial social problem. China family planning network covers widely and can carry out large scale IEC (Information, Education and Communication) campaign on HIV/AIDS and STDs prevention.

The Quality Care helps maintain stability of low fertility rate. Method use of family planning is a main factor affecting fertility rate. Implementation of Quality Care on Family Planning improved the reproductive people's self-consciousness of contraception use. In fact, quality of care can stabilize fertility rate instead of increase.[3] Since 1998, the Reproductive Health/Family Planning project of UNFPA fourth cycle program has been launched in 32 counties of 22 provinces in China. According to the project Mid-term Review, the women of childbearing age can name more than 3 contraceptive methods, and the knowledge about STIs and HIV/AIDS increased a lot, compared with the result from the baseline survey. Women's awareness on self-health care was also enhanced.[4]

Changes in Some Indicators Since UNFPA Program Implementation

Indicators	1998	2000
Birth Rate (1/1000)	11.44	10.62
Abortion ratio	0.18	0.11
Infant mortality (1/1000)	22.7	21.0
Maternal mortality (1/100,000)	62.9	52.2
Female sterilization rate (%)	35.8	25.5
IUD prevalence (%)	50.8	60.9

Issues Concerned

Sex and Reproductive Health Education Among Adolescents

Each year in China, there are 11 million students newly enrolled in secondary schools. Noticing the experience of population and family planning practices abroad, China has emphasized sex and reproductive health education in recent years. Some relevant courses have been offered in secondary schools to help adolescents form a comprehensive understanding on population and reproductive, develop a strong sense of social responsibility and good behaviour norm, and learn communication and life skill. In addition that courses on sex physiology, sex psychology and sex moral ethic are provided in the school, puberty hotline, anonymous call-in radio talk, lectures, workshops and exhibitions are held to help people better understand the issue.

Provide Special Service to Vulnerable Population

The number of people who migrated increased from 70 million in 1993 to 140 million in 2000, doubled in a decade. The main migration flow was from the rural to the urban and the principal reason of migration was employment. Most of migrants are at reproductive age while reproductive health services are not conveniently available for them. Currently, family planning system tries to reach this population and support them. For example, to tackle this problem, some local family planning stations provide specific service for migrants' hometown.

Reproductive Health Service Applicable to Local Conditions

At present, the fertility is low and maternal mortality and infant mortality are decreasing in China. But induced abortion rate and cesarean section rate are still high and STIs prevalence among women is increasing. All of these do harm to women's reproductive health.[5] In poverty-stricken area, the poor awareness of self-care and inadequate knowledge about health care, as well as poor quality of care are main factors that influence women reproductive health. Different areas have different economic and natural conditions. Service agencies should provide better, convenient and effective service according to people's need and the local conditions by taking advantage of existing resources.[6]

Epidemic Situation of HIV/AIDS in China

The rapid spread and high cost of treating AIDS endangers the lives of people, mainly young and middle-aged people. Since the first AIDS case in China was discovered in 1985, the incidence of the disease has increased rapidly. By September 2001, all China's 31 provinces, autonomous regions and municipalities had reported HIV cases. AIDS is not only a health problem, but also an issue that seriously affects economic, social and cultural development, and therefore demands paying high attention from all sectors in society.

China has a rapid increase of HIV/AIDS epidemic since 1985 when the first case of AIDS in China was reported.

Up to September 30, 2001 the Chinese Ministry of Health reported a total of 28,133 people infected with HIV, of whom 1,208 had developed AIDS and 641 died. Experts estimated that the number of infection cases in the country might surpass 600,000-1,000,000.

China's HIV/AIDS epidemic can be divided into three phases.

- Imported and sporadic phase (1985-1988). This phase involved a small number of imported cases in coastal cities—mostly foreigners and overseas Chinese. By the end of 1988, there were totally 19 case of HIV infection in Mainland China, 3 of whom were AIDS cases.
- Geographically limited epidemic phase (1989-1995). In October 1989, 146 cases of HIV infection were found among drug users in Yunnan Province in Southwest China, adjacent to the "Golden Triangle" bordering Myanmar, Laos, and Vietnam. Since then, numbers of new cases were found every year, mostly from drug users. The epidemic situation was rapidly extended to 21 provinces of China.
- Spread epidemic phase (1995-present). Since 1995, HIV/AIDS epidemic situation in China has increased and spread rapidly. By 1998, HIV infection had been reported from all 31 provinces, autonomous regions, and municipalities in Mainland China.

Annual Reported Cases of HIV/AIDS in China (1985-2000)

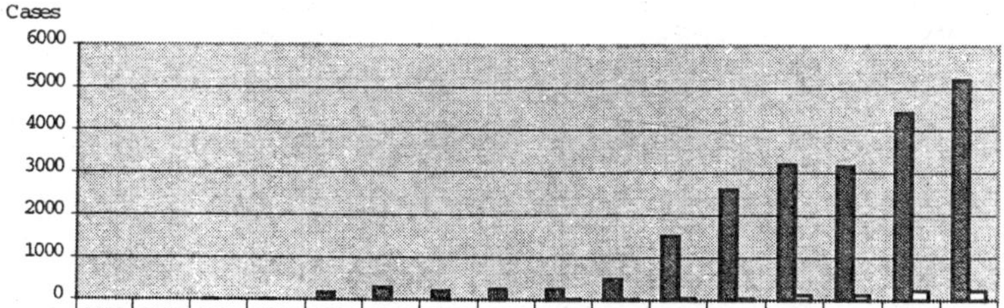

	1985	1986	1987	1988	1989	1990	1991	1992	1993	1994	1995	1996	1997	1998	1999	2000
■HIV	4	1	7	7	171	297	213	256	251	502	1515	2611	3217	3170	4447	5201
□AIDS	1	0	2	0	0	2	3	5	23	29	52	58	126	136	230	233

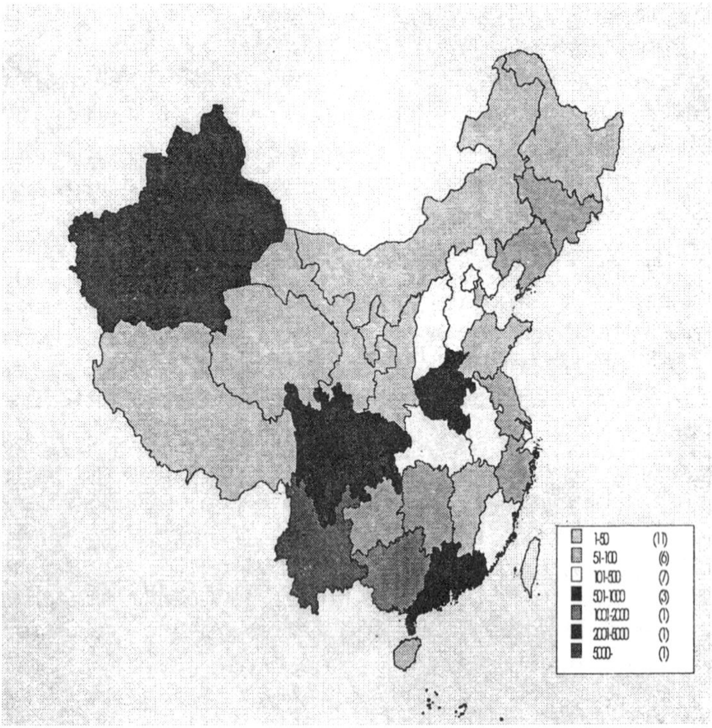

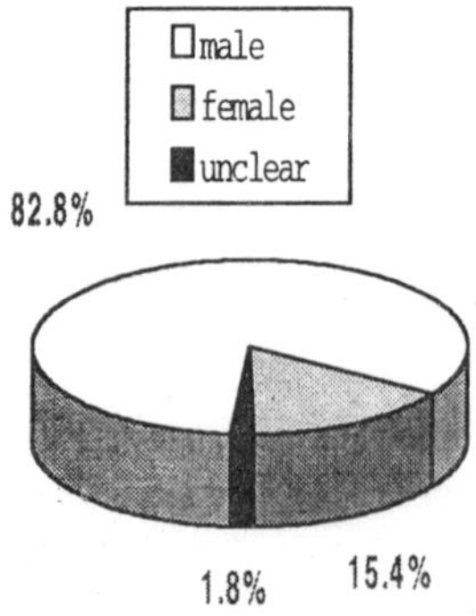

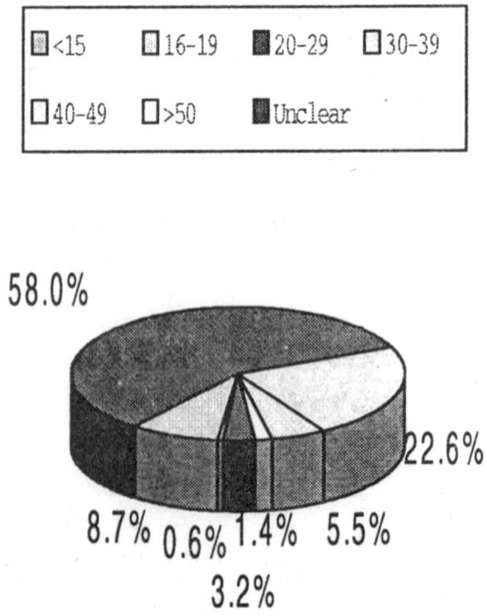

HIV/AIDS Gender and Age Distribution in China (1985-1999)

Epidemic characters of HIV/AIDS in China can be summarized as following: At present HIV/AIDS incidence is low in China, the carriers and cases are distributed in cluster. Most of them lived in countryside. This disease is mainly among youth and middle aged people and it is transmitted through diversified routes. It is possible to outbreak if no effective methods were adopted.

High Risk Activities

High risk activities relating to HIV transmission in China mainly include injecting drug use, the use of infected syringes, blood transfusion relating to blood products use, and unsafe sexual practices. Mother-to-child HIV transmission was also found in China.

Injecting Drug Use

Injecting drug use is absolutely the most important way of HIV transmission in China. It is estimated that nearly two thirds of all HIV cases got infected through drug use.[7] The main heroin-producing region of China is in the southwest of the country, near the borders of Laos, Myanmar, and Thailand. The region, better known as the Golden Triangle, now has a very high level of HIV infection due to injecting drug use (IDU) and needle sharing. The term 'drug abuse' has been used in China for more than a hundred years and originally it referred only to the smoking of opium. But a progression from non-injecting to injecting drug-use (IDUs) is increasingly common, largely because injecting is seen as a more cost-effective way of experiencing the effects of the drug. The geographic environment and the large market for drugs makes it very difficult to eliminate and control drugs use effectively. And with respect to the rapid spread of HIV among drug users, the really risky behaviour is needle sharing. HIV prevalence is about 1% among IDUs, but it is much higher in Xinjiang autonomous regions.[8]

Blood Products and Blood Transfusions

In 1988 the Chinese government prohibited the importation of blood and blood products in order to prevent the transmission of HIV by blood products. There are two main sources of donated blood in China. One is unpaid donations (either requested or voluntary donations) and the other is paid donations, the latter is mainly illegal. At some local illegal blood banks, blood was often collected from several people at the same time and mixed together in a container, where the plasma was removed. The remaining blood was often given back to the donors, mixed with the blood of others, and all were easily contaminated with HIV. Such procedures, plus the reuse of needles and unsterilised equipment gave the disease an easy route to spread rapidly through the local population. Up to June 2001, Chinese government reported that totally 966 cases got HIV infection through illegal blood donation. Experts estimated the real number was much higher.[9]

Commercial Sex Workers

Since the 1980s there has been a resurgence of prostitution in China, starting in coastal cities and large metropolitan areas and gradually extending inland to smaller townships. The main reason for this resurgence is economic. City dwellers have higher working and living standards than residents in rural areas. This attracts young women to the cities, where some become prostitutes in an effort to quickly make enough money to return home or start up their own businesses.

Homosexuality

In China, homosexual activities are not socially acceptable in society. Most homosexual people are still under social pressure to hide their sexual orientation and to be married. There are complicated social-psychological factors for playing homosexual relationships: since activities are not widely accepted, there is some secrecy about interactions. This often makes education about safe-sex practices extremely difficult. It also means that the HIV prevalence rate among this high-risk group is hard to predict. In addition the bridge populations' sexual mixing behaviour could get their opposite sex partner at the risk of infecting HIV.

HIV transmission routes in selected sentinel sites in 2000 in China

Transmission routes	Per cent (%)
Injecting drug use	71.1%
Sexual contact	7.0%
Transfusion	0.8%
Mother-to-child	0.1%
Unknown (including paid blood donation)	21.0%

Migration-Fueling the Development of the Epidemic

The current large-scale migration of the rural labour force is both a spontaneous response to, as well as a consequence of the economic reform process. But the large-scale migration carries a risk of contributing to the development of an HIV epidemic throughout China. Large numbers of people in constant movement between cities and between regions could promote rapidly transforming a local HIV epidemic to a country-wide one.

A number of factors make migrant labour forces particularly vulnerable to HIV infection. Migrants are often young, and living for extended periods of time away from the social pressure of their families and communities. They are often unmarried or live apart from their spouses and children. They tend to have more available cash money than they were used to having in rural areas. All these factors make them likely to have sexual interaction with casual partners, in some cases with prostitutes.

As the migrants are mobile, it means they are not easily accessible, and migrants can easily escape efforts at education and health promotion. Since the migrants are often poorly educated and sometimes not fluent in the languages or dialects of the regions they have migrated to, raising their awareness of HIV/AIDS becomes even more challenging.

HIV/AIDS Prevention

The spread of HIV/AIDS in China will create a national disaster if the number of virus carriers continues to swell while intervention measures remain weak. Fortunately the

Chinese government has realized the problem and is trying to tackle the spread of HIV. Relative polices and measures are made to prevent and control HIV/AIDS. The government aims to keep the annual growth rate of new cases to less than 10 per cent, compared with the reported growth rate of above 30% in recent years.

China's current HIV/AIDS Surveillance Program has two major components: HIV/AIDS case reporting, started in 1985, and HIV sentinel surveillance, begun in 1995. These systems exist both at the national level within the National Centre for AIDS Prevention and Control (NCAPC), and at the provincial level within the respective Provincial Centres for AIDS Prevention and Control located within the Provincial Centre for Disease Control. There are 101 HIV/AIDS sentinel surveillance sites, 24 STD sites, doing surveillance of 5 population groups (STD clinic patients, prostitutes, drug users, long-distance drivers and pregnant women). The surveillance sites find the trend of HIV/AIDS incidence among the target population and discover the risk factors, providing information for policy makers. Additionally, over 1,500 screening and 41 confirmation laboratories have been established.[10]

In order to control HIV/AIDS, interventions were carried out throughout the country, including policy intervention, behaviour intervention and medical intervention. China's experience of HIV/AIDS prevention focuses on the following aspect:

(1) *Government Support*

The key to stopping the spread of AIDS in China is that every level of government and all government departments consider AIDS as a crucial issue and take effective measures to prevent its spread. China gave both policy and financial support for HIV prevention. Both central government and local government investment increased from various sources. The government has made The Mid-Long Term Plan of HIV/AIDS Prevention and Control in China (1998-2010) and China Action Plan to Contain, Prevent and Control HIV/AIDS to stop the rapid increasing trends of the HIV/STD epidemic and decrease the HIV/STD prevalence.

(2) *Health Education to Increase HIV/AIDS Awareness*

Health education is now considered as the most effective 'vaccine' to prevent and control HIV/AIDS.[11] Unfortunately, there is now no enough basic information about HIV and AIDS available for the general public in China. HIV/AIDS patients often face social exclusion, prejudice and stigma from other people who tend to think of HIV as a death sentence. More awareness of HIV/AIDS in the society through health education will help a lot in the fight against the epidemic. The Ministry of Health and the Ministry of Publicity jointly formulated the Principles for Publicity and Education on HIV/AIDS Prevention. Alternative ways are developed to carried out health education program, including mobilization of the mass media to conduct an array publicity and education activities at a given point in time to create needed momentum, HIV/AIDS education via public service advertisements, and incorporation of HIV/AIDS education into the health education curricula for high school students. Health education can mobilize the whole society to show concern and support for HIV/AIDS prevention and control.

(3) *Behavioural Intervention among High Risk Populations*

Most of people with HIV infection in China have contacted it through intravenous drug use or unsafe blood transfusions. Pilot studies are being conducted to promote health education and open needle and syringe social marketing for IDUs. A methadone preparation for replacement therapy among IDUs is also tried. We hope all these efforts can help prevent and control HIV in IDUs. The illegal status of prostitution in China is often cited as a barrier to studying and otherwise working with this population. However, there have been studies and interventions with commercial sex workers (CSWs) and sex establishment owners conducted in several provinces (e.g., Yunnan, Guizhou), which suggests that this barrier can be surmounted. Health education and condom use can be promoted among this population. In addition, since sexually transmitted diseases may facilitate HIV transmission, health providers should counsel and educate STD patients and provide educational packages and condoms for them.[12]

(4) *Safe Blood Transfusion*

Considerable legislative efforts have been made to ensure safe blood supply. Chinese government strictly prohibits illegal blood donation and collection, to protect the human right of population and patients. Illegal blood collectors and doctors who collude with them must be punished.[13]

(5) *Strengthen International Cooperation*

Statistics show that China has been engaged in cooperative efforts with more than 30 international organizations, countries and regions. International cooperation has provided not only funds, but also new ideas, advanced techniques, and valuable experiences.

(6) *Capacity Building in AIDS Control for NGOs*

Central and local STD/AIDS Prevention and Control Associations are established to Support STD/AIDS Prevention and Control. The Youth League, the Women's Federation, the Labour Union and the Red Cross Associations are mobilized to conduct AIDS control. All these Chinese NGO's will also participate and collaborate with international NGO's in project activities.

(7) *AIDS Treatment and Care*

Highly Active Anti-retrovirus Theropy (HAART) is used to cure HIV carrier. But this kind of drug are very expensive and most patients can not afford it. Many measures should be taken to decrease the price of the drug. In addition, public awareness about respecting and understanding HIV/AIDS patients will be stressed and the rights of HIV/AIDS patients and their widows and children will be better protected. The Treatment and Care Department of the National Centre for AIDS/STD Prevention and Control under the Chinese Centre for Disease Prevention and Control is preparing a national comprehensive care strategy to create a better living environment for HIV/AIDS patients. Patients are encouraged to seek health care in normal hospitals instead of quack. These health sectors keep it secret for them. Comprehensive care centres will soon be established in some provinces with comparatively more HIV/AIDS cases, such as Yunnan

Province, and if the centres thrive, a national network of such sites will be set up in the future. Some treatment therapy for HIV/AIDS has been developed in China. It is expected that the medicine will be on marketing soon.

References

1. State Family Planning Commission of China, http://www.sfpc.gov.cn/cn/news20010720-2.htm.
2. Fang Liwen, Hu Hongtao, Zhao Baige. Study on the Satisfaction Degree of Reproductive Women with Reproductive Health/Family Planning Services and its Influencing Factors. *Reproduction and Contraception* 22(1): 2002, 40-6.
3. Wu Xuehong, Li Fuxiang. Provide high quality family-control service, control people increasing speed. *China Maternity and Child Care* 15(1): 2000, 25-7.
4. State Family Planning Commission of China, http://www.sfpc.gov.cn/en/enews20010911-1.htm.
5. Hua Jiazeng. Reproduction health new needs in 21 century *China Maternity and Child Care* 15(5): 2000, 316-8.
6. Wang Fengqing, Jin Hui, Li Yanqin, *et al.* Qualitative Study on the Needs for Reproductive Health/Family Planning Service. *China Maternity and Child Care* 17(4): 2002, 223-5.
7. Zhang Konglai. Review: Epidemic situation and trends of AIDS in Asia and China. *Chinese version of BMJ.* 2002, 5(1): 38.
8. Liu Dechun. HIV/AIDS Epidemic in Our Country. *Journal of Bengbu Medical College.* 2001, 26(1), 86-7.
9. Cai Jianzhang. Characteristic, reason and counter-measure of AIDS epidemic in China. *Medicine and Philosophy.* 2002, 23(7): 24.
10. Zheng Xiwen. Epidemic situation, prevention and control of AIDS in China. *Liaoning Medical Journal.* 2000,14(1): 3.
11. Yi lijun, *et al.* Health education is the most effective 'vaccine' to prevent HIV/AIDS. *Chinese Journal of Health Education.* 2000, 16(1): 47.
12. Li Dongli. AIDS/HIV prevention in the changing times. *Market and Demographic Analysis.* 2002, 8(3):48.
13. Zeng Yi. Epidemic trends, study progress and preventive strategy of AIDS. *China Public Health.* 2001, 17(12):1061-2.

9

Global Problems of HIV/AIDS and Role of Health Education

T.S. Sunil

Introduction

Several notable demographic events took place during the second half of the twentieth century at the global level. The two most important events that have caught the attention of demographers are the steady decline in fertility, particularly in developing countries, and the emergence and widespread of global HIV/AIDS pandemic. Although the decline in fertility levels in developing countries was expected, the impact of HIV/AIDS on demographic structure is unprecedented.

Recent estimates on the prevalence of HIV/AIDS show that at the end of December 2001, over 40 million people were living with HIV/AIDS, which include 2.7 million children under fifteen years of age and 17.6 million women (UNAIDS, 2001). That is, about 50 per cent of people infected with HIV/AIDS is men aged 15 or above. This figure is 50 per cent more than that projected in 1991 by the World Health Organization (WHO). Since the first clinical evidence of AIDS was reported in 1981, nearly 25 million people had died of this disease. About 5 million people became newly infected with this disease in 2001 around the world, out of these 800,000 of them are children under fifteen years of age. With little intervention and withering access to treatment and care to control the situation, these men, women and children will join death toll in the next five years. Although the numbers at the global level is quite alarming, the levels at the regional level are shocking. Following sections present the regional differences in the prevalence of HIV/AIDS.

Sub-Saharan Africa

It is geographically, demographically, socially, and culturally heterogeneous. This makes the generalization of AIDS situation within the region a bit complicated. This region is considered as the worst affected region in the world in terms of the prevalence of HIV/AIDS. Over 40 million people living with HIV/AIDS in the world, nearly 70 per cent of the infected people are from this region, which carries only 10 per cent of the world's population. Approximately, 3.5 million new infections occurred in 2001, adding to a total of 28.5 million people infected with HIV/AIDS in sub-Saharan Africa. While HIV/AIDS epidemic was first discovered in Central and East Africa, recent studies have recognized that the epidemic is spreading more rapidly into West and Southern Africa (Dada *et al.*, 1993; Olaleye *et al.*, 1993). For example, in Abidjan, Cote d'Ivoire, in West Africa, HIV-1 prevalence among adults increased from 1 per cent in 1986 to more than 15 per cent in 1992. Similarly, studies have also suggested that in Nigeria, the prevalence of HIV-1 and HIV-2 among prostitutes is rapidly increasing and it is highest in the region (Dada *et al.*, 1993). However, to date the epidemic has disproportionately affected Eastern and Southern Africa. Recent statistics on HIV prevalence show that certain urban populations in Kigali, Rwanda, and Kampala, Uganda, about 1 in every three adults is infected with HIV. It is also shown that HIV seroprevalence is comparatively lower in rural areas than in urban settings. In addition, some population groups are disproportionately affected by the epidemic. It is generally observed that the infection rates are higher among men-women between 20 and 40 years of age, people with tuberculosis and certain occupational groups. These occupational groups include long-distance truck drivers, military personnel, and women employed in commercial sex and entertainment industries (Piot *et al.*, 1988). Pregnant women are also considered to be higher risk than the general population because they are sexually active. Seroprevalence data from a number of studies of pregnant women conducted since mid-1980s demonstrate heterogeneity in prevalence rates (U.S. Census Bureau of the Census, 1994). However, there has been a consistent and rapid increase in HIV infection among pregnant women in different countries in sub-Saharan Africa. These include, pregnant women in Francistown, Botswana; Blantyre, Malawi; and Kampala, Uganda. By 1992, between 25 and 35 per cent of pregnant women were infected with HIV. Current estimates show rapid increase in these figures in these cities and other major cities in this region. Although HIV/AIDS epidemic marks a social, economic and political crisis in this region, several countries in this region are progressively taking the lead in responding to the epidemic in the past decade.

Asia and the Pacific

According to UNAIDS (2001) report, Asia and the Pacific is the second largest region with a large number of people living with HIV/AIDS. In the South and South-East region, an estimated 6.1 million people were living with HIV/AIDS in December 2001. The most affected countries in this region include India, Thailand, Myanmar and Cambodia. On eastern region, in East Asia and Pacific region, an estimated one million people were living with HIV/AIDS by the end of December 2001. Major countries from this region affected by this epidemic include China, Japan and Papua New Guinea. Comparing these numbers with African region, the rates of HIV infection in the general population in Asia remain low. However, these numbers should be interpreted taking into account the population size of the respective countries. Many Asian countries with huge populations have a large number of infected people, even if the prevalence rates among the general population remain very low. It is possible that many of these Asian countries have more number of people living with HIV/AIDS than many countries in Africa. There are several reasons mentioned in the literature to explain the spread of HIV/AIDS in this part of the region. Sub-populations that have been consistently identified as having higher risk of HIV infection than the rest include IV drug users, heterosexuals and blood and plasma donors (UNAIDS, 2001). In India, several groups of people are identified as high-risk groups. In parts of North-East India, use of unsterilized needle exchange among drug users is the major reason for the high prevalence of HIV/AIDS. Majority of the affected people are men who then eventually pass HIV to their wives, girlfriends or other sexual partners through unprotected sex. But in southern and western states of India, the prevalence of HIV among sex workers is very high and is considered as the predominant mode of HIV transmission. By 1997 the prevalence of HIV among sex workers in Mumbai reached 71 per cent (UNAIDS, 2001). Heterosexual activities are considered as the main route of transmission in Thailand. Differently from India and Thailand, in sharp contrast with the HIV infected sub-populations in India and Thailand, one of the major high-risk groups found in China is among blood and plasma donors. These donors are mostly from Henan province in China who became victims of negligence and malpractices of medical professionals at the medical facilities. Studies have documented that a range of blood-born infections including HIV are transmitted to people during the process of pooling of red blood cells separated from plasma donors, before those red blood cells were returned to the donors. In addition, spread of HIV/AIDS through heterosexual contact is also common in other parts of China.

Cambodia is considered as the most severely HIV affected area in Asia. It is estimated that about 4.04 per cent of the adult population is affected with HIV/AIDS by the end of 2001. The epidemic has spread mainly through unprotected sex. But in Myanmar it is spread mainly through three groups—injecting drug users, men who have sex with men and heterosexuals. Recent statistics reveals that about 2.0 per cent of the adults are infected with HIV/AIDS in Myanmar by the end of 2001. In Japan, although the number of people infected with HIV/AIDS is low as compared to other countries in the region (0.02 per cent of adult population), the major route of transmission is through homosexual contacts. The proportion of people infected through homosexuality increased more than double the proportion of people infected through heterosexual activities.

Eastern Europe and Central Asia

According to current estimates, there are about 1 million people living with HIV/AIDS in Eastern Europe and Central Asia, by the end of December 2001 (see Table 1) (UNAIDS, 2001). The major route of transmission in this region is considered to be through IV drug use. The estimates show that even though there is a proportionate increase in the number of persons infected through heterosexual contact has increased, this increase is largely due to sexual contact with IV drug users. Infection among gay and bisexual men in this region remained low. Differently from other regions, in Eastern Europe majority of the newly infected cases are likely to be less than 30 years old. The most affected countries in this region include Ukraine, Russia and Belarus. It is estimated that these countries have high proportion of IV drug users. Policy makers and government officials are concerned about the diffusion of HIV into sexually active population. For example, current estimates show that there were 130,000 people infected with HIV/AIDS in Russia by the end of 2001. On the other hand, reports indicate that, in Russia, there are about 2.5 million drug users. If the current rate of infection among IV drug users continues, this may begin to infiltrate other parts of the population, particularly heterosexual people. This would make a larger potential group of people in the high-risk category. UNAIDS (2001) reported that, in Russia, although the rate of transmission is very low but the speed of transmission is very high. Estimates show that the new infections in Russia during the first half of 2000 have increased by 305 per cent compared to 1999, with a total of 22,068 cases being reported during the first six months of the year.

Australia and New Zealand

The prevalence of HIV/AIDS in these populations is not considered as a major national threat. In Australia an estimated 14,000 people and in New Zealand an estimated 1,200 people are living with HIV/AIDS by the end of 2001 (see Table 1). These numbers were 15,000 and 1,200 in Australia and New Zealand respectively at the end of 1999 (see Table 2). Studies have shown that in Australia, the major mode of transmission is through homosexual activities.

Table 1: Estimated Number of People Living with HIV/AIDS, End 2001, in Major Regions and Countries. (Percentage of the Total Population in Parantheses)

Country/Region	Adults and children	Adults (15-49)	Women (15-49)	Children (0-14)
Sub-Saharan Africa	28,500,000 (4.5)	26,000,000 (4.1)	15,000,000 (2.4)	2,600,000 (0.41)
Kenya	2,500,000 (8.0)	2,300,000 (7.4)	1,400,000 (4.5)	220,000 (0.7)
Nigeria	3,500,000 (3.0)	3,200,000 (2.7)	1,700,000 (1.5)	270,000 (0.2)
South Africa	5,000,000 (11.4)	4,700,000 (10.7)	2,700,000 (6.2)	250,000 (0.6)
Zambia	1,200,000 (11.3)	1,000,000 (9.4)	590,000 (5.5)	150,000 (1.4)
Zimbabwe	2,300,000 (17.9)	2,000,000 (15.6)	1,200,000 (9.3)	240,000 (1.9)
East Asia and Pacific	1,000,000 (0.1)	970,000 (0.1)	230,000 (0.02)	3,000*
China	850,000 (0.1)	850,000 (0.1)	220,000 (0.02)	2,000*
Japan	12,000 (0.009)	12,000 (0.009)	6,600 (0.005)	110*
Papua New Guinea	17,000 (0.4)	16,000 (0.3)	4,100 (0.08)	500*
Australia & New Zealand	15,000 (0.07)	14,000 (0.06)	1,000*	<200*
Australia	12,000 (0.06)	12,000 (0.06)	800*	140*
New Zealand	1,200 (0.03)	1,200 (0.03)	180*	<100*
South & South-East Asia	5,600,000 (0.3)	5,400,000 (0.3)	2,000,000 (0.1)	220,000 (0.01)
India	3,970,000 (0.4)	3,800,000 (0.4)	1,500,000 (0.2)	170,000 (0.02)
Thailand	670,000 (1.01)	650,000 (1.0)	220,000 (0.4)	21,000 (0.03)

Country/Region	Adults and children	Adults (15-49)	Women (15-49)	Children (0-14)
Vietnam	130,000 (0.2)	130,000 (0.2)	35,000 (0.04)	2,500*
Eastern Europe & Central Asia	1,000,000 (0.3)	1,000,000 (0.3)	260,000 (0.07)	15,000*
Belarus	15,000 (0.15)	15,000 (0.15)	3,700*	—
Russian Federation	700,000 (0.5)	700,000 (0.5)	180,000 (0.1)	—
Ukraine	250,000 (0.5)	250,000 (0.5)	76,000 (0.2)	—
Western Europe	550,000 (0.14)	540,000 (0.13)	140,000 (0.03)	5,000*
France	100,000 (0.17)	100,000 (0.17)	27,000 (0.05)	1,000*
Germany	41,000 (0.05)	41,000 (0.05)	8,100*	550*
Italy	100,000 (0.17)	100,000 (0.17)	33,000 (0.06)	770*
North Africa and Middle East	500,000 (0.14)	460,000 (0.13)	250,000 (0.07)	35,000*
Sudan	450,000 (1.4)	410,000 (1.3)	230,000 (0.7)	30,000 (0.1)
Yemen	9,900 (0.05)	9,900 (0.05)	1,500*	—
North America	950,000 (0.3)	940,000 (0.3)	190,000 (0.1)	10,000*
Canada	55,000 (0.2)	55,000 (0.2)	14,000 (0.01)	<500*
United States of America	900,000 (0.3)	890,000 (0.3)	180,000 (0.06)	10,000*
Latin America	1,500,000 (0.3)	1,400,000 (0.3)	430,000 (0.09)	40,000*
Argentina	130,000 (0.4)	130,000 (0.4)	30,000 (0.08)	30,000 (0.08)
Brazil	610,000 (0.4)	600,000 (0.4)	220,000 (0.13)	13,000*
Colombia	140,000 (0.3)	140,000 (0.3)	20,000 (0.05)	4,000*
Mexico	150,000 (0.15)	150,000 (0.15)	32,000 (0.03)	3,600*

* percentage not included due to small values. *Source*: UNAIDS, 2001.

Table 2: Estimated Number of People Living with HIV/AIDS, End 1999, in Major Regions and Countries. (Percentage of the Total Population in Parantheses)

Country/Region	Adults and children	Adults (15-49)	Women (15-49)	Children (0-14)
Sub-Saharan Africa	24,500,000 (4.1)	23,400,000 (3.9)	12,900,000 (2.2)	1,000,000 (0.2)
Kenya	2,100,000 (7.1)	2,000,000 (6.8)	1,100,000 (3.7)	78,000 (0.3)
Nigeria	2,700,000 (2.0)	2,600,000 (1.9)	1,400,000 (1.0)	120,000 (0.09)
South Africa	4,200,000 (10.6)	4,100,000 (10.3)	2,300,000 (5.8)	95,000 (0.2)
Zambia	870,000 (9.7)	830,000 (9.2)	450,000 (5.0)	40,000 (0.5)
Zimbabwe	1,500,000 (13.0)	1,400,000 (12.2)	800,000 (7.0)	56,000 (0.5)
East Asia and Pacific	530,000 (0.04)	530,000 (0.04)	66,000*	5,200*
China	500,000 (0.04)	500,000 (0.04)	61,000*	4,800*
Japan	10,000 (0.008)	10,000 (0.008)	1,300*	<100*
Papua New Guinea	5,400 (0.1)	5,200 (0.0)	2,600*	220*
Australia & New Zealand	15,000 (0.07)	15,000 (0.07)	1,100*	190*
Australia	14,000 (0.08)	14,000 (0.08)	900*	140*
New Zealand	1,200 (0.03)	1,200 (0.03)	180*	<100*
South & South-East Asia	5,600,000 (0.3)	5,400,000 (0.3)	1,900,000 (0.1)	200,000 (0.01)
India	3,700,000 (0.4)	3,500,000 (0.4)	1,300,000 (0.1)	160,000 (0.02)
Thailand	755,000 (1.2)	740,000 (1.2)	305,000 (0.5)	13,900 (0.02)
Vietnam	100,000 (0.1)	99,000 (0.1)	20,000 (0.03)	2,500*
Eastern Europe & Central Asia	420,000 (0.1)	410,000 (0.1)	110,000 (0.03)	15,000*

Country/Region	Adults and children	Adults (15-49)	Women (15-49)	Children (0-14)
Belarus	14,000 (0.1)	14,000 (0.1)	3,500*	<100*
Russian Federation	130,000 (0.09)	130,000 (0.09)	32,500*	1,800*
Ukraine	240,000 (0.5)	230,000 (0.5)	70,000 (0.1)	7,500*
Western Europe	520,000 (0.1)	520,000 (0.1)	130,000 (0.03)	4,100*
France	130,000 (0.2)	130,000 (0.2)	35,000 (0.06)	1,000*
Germany	37,000 (0.05)	37,000 (0.05)	7,400*	500*
Italy	95,000 (0.2)	95,000 (0.2)	30,000 (0.05)	700*
North Africa and Middle East	220,000 (0.07)	210,00 (0.07)	42,000 (0.01)	8,000*
Sudan	—	140,000 (0.5)	—	—
Yemen	—	900*	—	—
North America	900,000 (0.02)	890,000 (0.02)	180,000 (0.06)	11,000*
Canada	49,000 (0.2)	49,000 (0.2)	5,600 (0.02)	500*
United States of America	850,000 (0.3)	840,000 (0.3)	170,000 (0.06)	10,000*
Latin America	1,300,000 (0.3)	1,200,000 (0.3)	300,000 (0.06)	28,000*
Argentina	130,000 (0.4)	120,000 (0.4)	27,000 (0.07)	4,400*
Brazil	540,000 (0.3)	530,000 (0.3)	130,000 (0.08)	9,900*
Colombia	71,000 (0.2)	70,000 (0.2)	10,000 (0.02)	900*
Mexico	150,000 (0.2)	150,000 (0.2)	22,000 (0.02)	2,400*

* percentage not included due to small values. *Source*: UNAIDS, 2001.

Latin American and the Caribbean

This region is considered as the third most affected region in the world followed by sub-Saharan Africa and Asia and Pacific. AIDS is considered as a major cause of death in this region. By the end of 2001 an estimated 1.5 million people are living with HIV/AIDS in Latin America and this was 1.3 million at the end of 1999 (see Table 2). The worst affected countries in this region include Brazil, Mexico, Argentina, Guyana, Belize, Honduras, Panama, and Guatemala. The prevalence in these countries varies from 1 per cent to 3 per cent among all adult population. In the Caribbean region, an estimated 420,000 people were living with HIV/AIDS by the end of 2001, about 2 per cent of all adult population. The major affected countries in the Caribbean region include Haiti, Dominican Republic, Bahamas, and Trinidad and Tobago. The percentage of people affected in this region varies between 1 per cent to 4 per cent among all adult population. It is documented that the major route of transmission in Latin America and the Caribbean region is through heterosexual contacts. However, the infection is also found to be concentrated among men who have sex with men, and those who inject drugs in this region. For example, while the majority of transmission in Brazil is through sex between men and women. In Argentina, Mexico and Columbia it is mainly through heterosexuals and injecting drug users. However, infection is concentrated among injecting drug users in Puerto Rico and among men who have sex with men in Jamaica and Haiti.

North Africa and the Middle East

An estimated 500,000 people were living with HIV/AIDS in this region by the end of 2001 (see Table 1). This number was 220,000 at the end of 1999. The worst affected countries include Sudan, United Arab Emirates, and Algeria. Out of these countries, in Sudan an estimated 450,000 people are infected with HIV/AIDS, according to UNAIDS (2001). Unprotected sexual intercourse is considered as the major route of transmission in this region, although injecting drug users are also considered as a significant contributor.

Western Europe

In Western Europe, an estimated 550,000 people were infected with HIV/AIDS by the end of 2000, a dramatic increase from 520,000 at the end of 1999. In countries of the Western European region, heterosexual activity is considered as a major transmission route. Studies show that the recent increase in infection in Western Europe is primarily a reflection of migrant population from Africa and other regions where heterosexual transmission is dominant. However, it is important to note that in three of the countries most affected by HIV—France, Italy and Spain—only AIDS cases (and not HIV infections) are reported at national level. In the remaining countries, numbers of new HIV diagnoses are decreasing among injecting drug users and are stable among homo/bisexual men. Since 1996, the number of cases of HIV infection have been increasing among heterosexually infected persons, in particular those originating from sub-Saharan Africa. In France and Italy, an estimated 100,000 people each are living with HIV/AIDS, and in Spain an estimated 120,000 people are living with HIV/AIDS by the end of 2001.

North America

Recent estimates show that in the United States and Canada, about 950,000 people were living with HIV/AIDS at the end of 2001 an increases from 900,000 at the end of 1999. Since the first AIDS cases were reported in the United States in June 1981, the number of cases and deaths among persons with AIDS increased rapidly during the 1980s followed by substantial declines in new cases and deaths in the late 1990s. The most prominent route of transmission is through men who have sex with men (MSM). A wide discrepancy in prevalence of HIV/AIDS is observed within the United States among racial/ethnic groups, with increases in the number of cases among women and of cases attributed to heterosexual transmission.

According to recent CDC report, "as of December 31, 2000, 774,467 persons had been reported with AIDS in the United States; 448,060 of these had died; 3542 persons had unknown vital status. The number of persons living with

AIDS (322,865) is the highest ever reported. Of these, 79% were men, 61% were black or Hispanic, and 41% were infected through male-to-male sex. Of the AIDS cases, approximately one third were reported during 1981-1992, 1993-1995, and 1996-2000 (CDC, 2000). In the early 1980s, most AIDS cases occurred among whites. However, cases among blacks increased steadily and by 1996, more cases occurred among blacks than any other racial/ethnic population. Cases among Hispanics, Asians/Pacific Islanders, and American Indians/Alaska Natives have increased also" (CDC, 2000, p.17).

Male-to-male sex has been the most common mode of exposure among persons reported with AIDS (46%), followed by injection drug use (25%) and heterosexual contact (11%). The incidence of AIDS increased rapidly in all three of these risk categories through the mid-1990s; however, since 1996, declines in new AIDS cases have been higher among MSM and injection drug users than among persons exposed through heterosexual contact. The HIV infection through transfusion of blood or blood products is also reported in different parts of the country, but this mode of transmission is considered to be lower than MSM.

The spread of HIV/AIDS in Canada is not that different from the neighbouring United States. At the end of 1999, Health Canada's Bureau of HIV/AIDS, STD and TB estimated that 49,800 Canadians were living with HIV/AIDS, a 24 per cent increase from the 1996 estimate of 40,100. Although the number of persons that were newly infected with HIV was about 4,200 per year in both 1996 and 1999, significant changes have occurred in infection rates within population subgroups. The estimated number of new HIV infections among men who have sex with men, increased by 30 per cent between 1996 and 1999. In 2000, for the first time since the mid-1980s, an increased number of newly diagnosed HIV cases among MSM is reported. Shifts in the epidemic are also occurring among other populations. The estimated number of new infections among injection drug users decreased by 27 per cent between 1996 and 1999. The annual number of newly diagnosed HIV cases among this population has also decreased in the national surveillance data. However, targeted studies across Canada have found that HIV infection rates among injection drug users are not declining in all areas of the country (Minister of Public Works and Government Services Canada, 2001).

Several implications can be drawn from the above description of HIV/AIDS situation in different regions around the world. First, there is no region in the world which is immune to HIV/AIDS infection. The condition is particularly alarming in many developing countries namely, countries in sub-Saharan Africa and many countries in Asia and Pacific regions. Although the number of deaths caused by HIV/AIDS is not quite large in developed countries, the conditions are still precarious. Second, one could imagine the consequences of increase in AIDS related mortality. It is not only likely to reduce the population growth but is also likely to bring about severe distortions in the age-sex structure of the population (Baylies, 2000). In addition, the consequences further extend to distortions in social and family institutions. As AIDS death rates increase, yet another epidemic of orphans and vulnerable children is developing. Toward the end of 2000, approximately 1.25 million children (27.4 per cent of children below age 15) were orphaned, and the number of children who did not attend primary school exceeded 700,000. The situation is more vulnerable in many African countries. For example, in Zambia, the number of Zambians orphans was projected to reach about 600,000 by the year 2000 (Baylies and Bujra, 2001). Third and the most important implication from the above description is about the mode of transmission of HIV infection. It is clear from the above description that, irrespective of the region, the major route of HIV transmission is purely a behavioural phenomenon. For example, while several countries in sub-Saharan Africa, the major mode of HIV/AIDS transmission is through heterosexual activities, countries in Asian and Pacific region countries it is mainly through heterosexuals and blood donors, and IV drug users. On the other hand, in developed nations such as the United States, Australia, and New Zealand, the route of HIV/AIDS transmission is through homosexual activities and IV drug use. Thus, controlling individual behaviour is the important task before every country. It is clear from the above description that the prevalence of HIV/AIDS in many societies can be controlled to a great extent through interventional programs specifically controlling individual behaviour. In the absence of effective medical cures, current public health strategies focus on social prevention strategies such as bringing about safe sex practices and behavioural changes among populations exposed to the AIDS risk (Cleland, Cara, Deheneffe, and Ferry, 1992; Janowitz *et al.*, 2000). Available prevention method right now is to control high-risk behaviours associated with its transmission.

Now the question becomes what are the different ways individual behaviour can be controlled. Today there exists a wide range of intervention programs to control individual behaviour on the spread of HIV/AIDS. These include among others, programs such as community-based distribution of contraceptives in Asia, School-based HIV/AIDS Prevention Project in Sichuan Province, China; the School Health and Nutrition Project in Senegal, the Life Skills and HIV and AIDS Education in School Project in Vietnam; the Regei DziveShiri in Zimbawe; Tap and Reposition Youth (TRY) Savings and Credit Scheme Project in Nairobi, Kenya; the Deepak Charitable Trust's Men's Health Project in India; the Young People's Sexual and Reproductive Health Project in Malawi; and the Youth Zone (YZ) project in the Philippines. Even in the midst of all the on-going intervention programs around the world, according to a recent UNICEF report, about 50 per cent of young people age 15-24 in more than a dozen countries, including Bolivia, Botswana, Cote d'Ivoire, the Dominican Republic, Ukraine, Uzbekistan, and Vietnam, have never heard of AIDS or its transmission (UNAIDS, 2001). The major reasons for failure to reach the targeted people are often related to the significance of the program itself. Many programs were often criticized for not linking information and education for young people to the provision of sexual and reproductive health services. Sometimes it is related to having only offering a narrow range of options in the prevention program such as focusing only abstinence. The reasons for failure of many intervention programs in

African region are attributed to not taking into account the traditional and deep-rooted African beliefs and customs in the society (van Dyk, 2001).

In this situation, it is pertinent to have an acceptable and effective program to control the unprecedented spread of HIV/AIDS infection around the world. A large number of fertility studies suggest that improving educational level of people has a tremendous influence on controlling population growth, particularly limiting fertility in a society (Caldwell, 1980; Caldwell, 1982). Analysis of data from 100 countries suggest that an additional year of female education reduces the total fertility rate by 0.23 births (World Bank, 2001). Studies also have documented that the benefits of education, particularly female education, contribute towards reducing infant and maternal mortality, enhancing family health and welfare and increasing economic productivity (Odaga and Heneveld, 1995). Improvements in educational levels are highly correlated with higher age at marriage, delay in childbearing, have fewer children, high self-esteem and avoid commercial sex (UNAIDS, 2001). Substantial evidence shows that increase in educational levels have similar benefits of individual economic growth (Krueger and Mikael, 2000). On the other hand, increase in educational levels at the individual level not only increases economic growth at the individual, but it also affects the national economic growth as well. Thus, improving educational levels brings about benefits to the individuals and positive changes to the nation. Thus, in the past few years, translating this influence of education to control the spread of HIV/AIDS infection is the top priority of many nations around the world. There are several successful educational programs which have received much recognition in controlling the spread of HIV/AIDS in developing countries, particularly among young adults. It is assumed that the impact of education on behaviour is strongest among the young, because it gives them a better direction to practice good health when he/she grows up, as compared to changing the behaviour of a grown-up adult (UNAIDS, 2001). Following section describes two successful educational intervention programs which have made a breakthrough in controlling the spread of HIV/AIDS among youths. Helping Each other Act Responsibly Together

(HEART) in Zambia: Zambia is considered as one of the worst affected countries by HIV/AIDS epidemic. A recent report showed that, in 1999, about 20 per cent of adults in 15-49 years are infected with HIV/AIDS (UNAIDS, 2000). Siamwiza (1998) reported that there exists low enrollment rates and high dropout rates, most children 14 years old or older are not in school. The Central Board of Health in Zambia reported that nearly one out of every five adults is infected with HIV. This represents close to 20 per cent of the adult population in the country. On an average about 300 adults become infected everyday, and that more than 70,000 have the virus that causes AIDS. The program, HEART, is a good example of an intervention program with an impact on behavioural change among youths in Zambia. The program HEART is designed specifically for youth and by youth, for informing young people about HIV/AIDS, discuss ways to protect oneself from HIV/AIDS and promote abstinence and condom use. The campaign was designed to provide a social context in which prevailing social norms are discussed, questioned and reassessed. By creating an atmosphere conducive to changes in social norms as well as in individual sexual behaviour the campaign was intended to contribute to the nation-wide effort to enhance the likelihood that young people would reduce their risk of HIV infection through either abstinence or consistent condom use and, thereby, reduce the incidence of HIV/AIDS and other sexually transmitted infections. Young people ages 13-19 were the intended audience for the campaign. The program has received an overwhelming response from the audience throughout the nation. Several positive behavioural changes were observed among program participants during the study period. Some of the highlights include among women who are sexually experienced, 82 per cent of campaign viewers contrasted with 69 per cent of baseline and 64 per cent of impact survey non-viewers reported they feel confident that they have "the ability to say no to unwanted sex." Approximately 74 per cent of males and 68 per cent of female viewers participating in the program felt skilled enough to talk to others about sex and also decide either to abstain from sex until becoming an adult, or use a condom. Given the success of the program to make behavioural changes among youths, HEART, is now further extended to other countries in the sub-Saharan region.

School Health Education in Uganda

The major mode of HIV transmission in Uganda is through heterosexual activities (more than 84 per cent). About 1.9 million people have been infected with HIV/AIDS since it was first diagnosed and out of these about 1.4 million are living with HIV, 500,000 have died of AIDS, and about 7 per cent of the adult population is estimated to be infected with HIV. This program has been widely accepted and proven to be a very successful program to improve access to information and other resources for healthy sexual behaviour decision-making. By improving peer interaction regarding information and decision-making related to safe sex, the program has contributed to enhancing the quality of performance of existing school health education efforts. This program was targeted to attract youths in their early to mid-teenage years in an educational setting. This school health education program in primary school primarily aimed at AIDS prevention in Soroti district of Uganda. The program focused on improving access to information related to healthy sexual behaviour among adolescents through peer administration. After two years of intervention, the evaluation results show improvements in sexual behaviour. For example, the percentage of sexually active students fell from 42.9 per cent to 11.1 per cent during the study period. The changes remained the same across gender and place of residence categories. It was also observed that students who were participated in the study became more involved and active in their respective schools as peer educators. Over the study period, these students became more likely to give as reasons for abstaining from sex those associated with a rational decision-making model rather than a punishment model. A primary school health education program which emphasizes social interaction methods can be effective in increasing sexual abstinence among school-going adolescents in Uganda.

The above two programs are examples of two successful programs among several interventional programs towards mitigating the spread of HIV/AIDS. Both programs showed a positive correlation between level of education and rates of infection. That is, once the young adults gain knowledge about better sexual practices they are more likely to adopt it into their behaviour. This truly reflects the importance of education not only in terms of numbers but also as a crucial resource of productive human capital for a country.

Conclusion

The purpose of this paper was to emphasize the importance of public health education in the on-going efforts to control the spread of HIV/AIDS around the world. In the absence of curative drugs and prophylactic vaccines, the only way to deal with the current condition is through developing appropriate standards of behaviour. It is widely accepted in demography and many other disciplines, education serves as a social control mechanism and plays a pivotal role in controlling individual behaviour. It is reported that approximately half of all people who acquire HIV become infected before age 25 (UNAIDS, 2000). Hence it is crucial to target the young generation in every country to have the basic knowledge about sexual health and related matters. Several education intervention programs around the world indicated that education has an important preventive impact in the spread of HIV/AIDS. It develops a healthy behaviour among children and adults to make healthy decisions and give people an opportunity for economic independence. Among girls, it delays their marriage, creates economic independence and work outside the home. Also, among all other programs, educational programs are considered to be cost effective as compared to other intervention programs. Educational programs often incorporate not only the students, but also teachers, parents, and the community. Thus educational programs create an opportunity to bring all the groups together thus reduces other major AIDS related costs of health care and additional educational supply. In addition to these benefits, educational programs are considered as an engine for social and economic development. It is widely known that nations' economic prosperity and alleviating poverty cannot be accomplished unless all children have access to, and can complete, a primary education. For example, studies have shown that one year of schooling for women lowers fertility about 10 per cent while one or two years of schooling for mothers reduces child mortality by 15 per cent.

Although improving health education is considered as a pivotal tool in controlling the spread of HIV/AIDS in any nation, it was shown that HIV/AIDS has a direct impact on the education sector (UNAIDS, 2001). Reports from many countries in Africa show that there is sharp increase in mortality among teachers and administrators at all levels of education. In 1999, an estimated 860,000 children lost their teachers to HIV/AIDS in sub-Saharan Africa. In the Central African Republic, AIDS was the cause of 85 per cent of the 300 teacher deaths that occurred in 2000. On the other hand, it was reported that by the late 1990s, in this country about 100 educational establishments are forced to close. The death toll caused by HIV/AIDS among teachers and school administrators is rampant in sub-Saharan Africa no similar situation is reported in any other region. Thus, in many societies, in order to promote education as a viable option to control the epidemic and also to drive to social and economic prosperity, necessary steps need to be taken to protect the education system.

References

1. Agha, Sohail, 2001. An evaluation of the effectiveness of a peer sexual health intervention among secondary school students in Zambia. Population Services International Research Division Working Paper 41, Washington D.C.: Population Services International.
2. Baylies, C. 2000. The impact of HIV on family size preference in Zambia. *Reproductive Health Matters*, 8(15):77-86.
3. Baylies, C. and Bujra, J. 2001. *AIDS, Sexuality and Gender in Africa: Collective Strategies and Struggles in Tanzania and Zambia.* London: Routledge Publishers.
4. Caldwell, John C. 1980. Mass education as a determinant of the timing of fertility decline. *Population and Development Review*, 6(2):225-255.
5. Caldwell, John C. 1982. *Theory of Fertility Decline.* New York: Academic Press.
6. Centre for Diseases Control, 2000. HIV and AIDS: United States, 1981-2000. Surveillance Branch, Div of HIV/AIDS Prevention, National Centre for HIV, STD, and TB Prevention, CDC.

7. Central Statistics Office, 1996. Living Conditions in Namibia. Government of Namibia.

8. Dada, A.J., Oyewole, F., Onofowokan, R., Nasidi, A., Harris, B., Levin, A., Diamondstone, L., Quinn, T.C. and Blattner, W.A. 1993. Demographic characteristics of retroviral infections (HIV-1, HIV-2 and HTLV-I) among female professional sex workers in Lagos, Nigeria. *Journal of Acquired Immune Deficiency Syndromes*, 6(12): 1358-1363.

9. Minister of Public Works and Government Services, Canada, 2001. Current Realities: Strengthening the Response. Canada's Report on HIV/AIDS 2001. Minister of Public Works and Government Services, Canada, 2001. Health Canada Publications, Ontario: Ottawa.

10. Olaleye, I.D., Bernstein, L., Ekweozor, C.C., Sheng, Z., Ormilabu, S.A., Li, X.-Y., Sullivan-Halley, J. and Rasheed, S. 1993. Prevalence of human immuno-deficiency virus types 1 and 2 infections in Nigeria. *Journal of Infectious Diseases*, 167(3): 710-714.

11. Piot, P., Plummer, F.A., Mhalu, F.S., Lamboray, J.-L., Chin, J. and Mann, J.M. 1988. AIDS: an international perspective. *Science*, 239(4840): 573-579.

12. Siamwiza, R. 1998. A Situation Analysis of Policy and Teaching HIV/AIDS Prevention in Educational Institutions in Zambia. UNESCO/UNAIDS Project on Integrating HIV/AIDS Prevention in School Curricula. UNESCO and UNAIDS.

13. UNAIDS, 2001. AIDS epidemic update.

14. U.S. Bureau of the Census, 1994c. Trends and Patterns of HIV/AIDS Infection in Selected Developing Countries: Country Profiles: June 1994. Research Note No. 14. Washington D.C.: Health Studies Branch, Centre for International Research, U.S. Bureau of the Census.

15. van Dyk, Alta C. 2001. Traditional African beliefs and customs: implications for AIDS education and prevention in Africa. *South African Journal of Psychology*, 31(2):60-66.

16. World Bank, 2001. World Development Report 2000/2001. Washington: World Bank.

10

Women's Health and Health Education

Pagadala Rajaram and P. Mangesh

Introduction

World Health Organisation (WHO, 1947) defined health as, "a state of complete physical and mental and social well being and not merely absence of disease or infirmity". 'Social' is defined as relating to human society, the interaction of the individual and the group or the welfare of human beings as a member of the society (*Webster's dictionary*, 1990). Social well being also involves a society that is free from evil effects of poverty, which are the main causes of physical diseases and the consequences of domestic violence, which mainly affects the mental well being of the women in the family.

WHO in order to expand the definition of 'health' justified its appeal suggesting the following definition: 'The extent to which an individual or group is able to, on the one hand, and to change or cope with the environment on the other hand. Health is, therefore, seen as a resource for every day life and not the objective of living; it is a concept in emphasizing social; and personal resources, as well as physical capacities.' (WHO, 1986, p. 73).

Therefore, social refers to a group of people in the community, having common interest in living. Obviously community consists of units of family and each family consists of group of individuals including the servants under one a head. Usually the head consists of the male. However in reality it is the woman of the house who runs the show and in fact is a combination of wife + man (*Webster's Dictionary* pp. 1356). Hence, it is necessary to consider that the woman plays a major role in the family welfare and thus in the society. To consider the women's health is, therefore, of paramount importance in the socio-economic development of a society.

Public Health

The scope of this chapter is to discuss the physical and mental health. However it is important for us to understand the definitions of public health and community health, which have direct effects on the members of the family and society. In order to specify exactly what is meant by 'public health' and 'community health', Hanlon (1960) clarified thus:

Public health is the Science and Art of

1. Preventing disease,
2. Prolonging life,
3. Promoting health and efficiency through organized community effort for:
   a. The sanitation of the environment,
   b. The control of communicable infections,
   c. The education of individual in personal hygiene,
   d The organization of medical and nursing services for the early diagnosis and preventive treatment of diseases, and
   e. The development of social machinery to ensure everyone a standard of living adequate for the maintenance of health, so organizing these benefits as to enable every citizen to realize his/ her birth right of health and longevity.

Having explained that the key members of the community are women in the family, this chapter deals with some of the issues and diseases that a women can get from the childhood to elderly and that could have profound effects on the development of the family, thus they society. Therefore, for a state, it is the personnel involved in the delivery of the health care services are important for organizing the public health system.

Organized Way of Delivery of Health Care Services

The main objectives of curriculum planning for the medical and paramedical students is to emphasize on 'preventive, curative, promotive and rehabilitative', aspects of teaching and training. In dealing so, the thrust is laid on clean environment including ensuring supply of clean water, sewage disposal, immunization, family welfare program, adequate antenatal check up and appropriate place for safe delivery and ensuring proper health to the mother and the child. Therefore providing basic education and health education is important in order to make the members of the society understand the preventive aspects of diseases.

The health care services in India are one of the best organized in the world. However the utilization of infrastructure by the community is very poor mainly due to lack of manpower manning these stations and inadequate supplies of medicines at Level I (Sub-Centres and Primary Health Centres). In addition apathy on the part of health care providers has disappointed the poor and the need approaching Level II (Community Health Centres and Taluq hospitals). This has resulted in overcrowding of the Level III; tertiary care centres (the so-called District, City and teaching hospitals). The staff and the faculty at these centres failed to respond to the needs of the community. The teaching and training program is far from satisfactory, and the physicians and health care providers like nurses coming out of the institutions are ill equipped for the preventive care.

Level I

One should take measures to prevent problems before it occurs by way of immunization, health education, routine check-ups, screening programs for cancer where applicable, promoting health education and timely referral to the next higher centre.

Level II

To be alert and inquisitive and be conscious to expect the disease and plan for it's early detection and take appropriate measures to treat them adequately. And give a feed back to the referring doctor and take active part in future planning for preventive measures.

Level III

Patients having missed the benefits at the primary and secondary levels, usually land in emergency or in advanced state of disease, when the tertiary level care personnel must take a humane attitude and attend to them promptly to treat in order to reduce the morbidity and mortality rates. In order to equip themselves with the latest, they must ensure sharing their experience with others by continuously organizing continuing medical educational and promoting and imparting health education. Tertiary level health care personnel are usually involved in making policy decisions. They must actively take part to sensitize the politicians, policy makers and bureaucrats.

Staying Healthy and Preventing Common Diseases

Until the discovery of bacteria in 1880s and antibiotics in 1940s diseases were not understood properly and the treatment remained empirical. Later the focus was on curing the existing disease. Slowly with the discovery of vaccines the emphasis shifted in preventing the diseases. However the concept of consumption of certain substances in the food, like fibre, has emerged in order to adopt the preventive aspects of diseases.

Nutrition and Obesity

Women think problem of weight is more of social and cosmetic rather than a health problem. Adolescents feel that their weight is not their problem and the parents treat it as a sign of health. While the parents, if they are overweight, they tend to ignore other's comments. The incident of overweight is increasing continuously despite health care conscious created in the community and more and more resorting to some sort of physical exercise. At the same time weight conscious and desire to cut calories is also increasing. Despite the wide spread fashion to go on diet, installing in houses an exercise machine, nothing seem to be working in most individuals. This can be scientifically explained by the fact that the most people have no idea about what to eat and what not to. They also don't have a basic knowledge as to how the body reacts to overeating and how the fat is deposited.

Body has a tremendous capacity to convert the carbohydrates (rice, biscuits, and junk food) into glucose for increasing its levels in the body. The body is producing more insulin to burn the readily interested sugars contained in sweets and the other foods. However the phenomenon of gaining energy momentarily following consumption of these sweets suddenly drops down lowering the activity and the person begins to feel hungry quickly and resorting to overeating. Whereas more complex carbohydrates contained in the ingested whole grains, pulse, fruits vegetables and in proteins and fatty foods is slowly converted into glucose.

The facts about sugar and its role arc a myth. In our diet over 25 to 30% calories (approximately 500 to 750 calories) are in the form of sugar. In addition some consumes ready sugars in the form of candies and sweets. This continuous process that is taking place in the body for years, unchecked, makes 'insulin resistant' when it no longer metabolizes circulating glucose and glucose in the body converts the subject into adult onset of diabetes.

When the insulin becomes ineffective in metabolizing glucose, liver plays its role in converting this excess glucose into fat and the fat is stored in the body. Therefore in order to shed this stored fat one should avoid taking sugar when naturally the fat is burned to produce energy. Thus the person loses weight. It is to be remembered that when the intake of glucose is reduced, automatically the body switches to burning fats in order to produce energy, which then becomes the primary source.

Obesity has become the main menace to the society resulting in the loss of health. Proper intake of balanced diet with regular exercise, one could make a sound foundation for being healthy. In order to maintain oneself healthy, the way of life should be healthy. Regular eating habits, performing exercises and caring for the personal hygiene makes one remain healthy. The nutritional requirements differ in different individuals. While growing children and pregnant women require more calories and specific type of foods, elderly and people with sedentary habits must take care to control their weight. Cutting down on fats, consuming enough of carbohydrates and proteins and making sure that sufficient amount of fibre in their diet will help prevent many diseases like hypertension, diabetes, etc.

In addition, in order to stay healthy at all ages, one should have a regular health care. But in a huge population it is not only difficult but raises many logistic problems. However some women are bound to suffer from certain conditions, which need special health care. Therefore it is necessary to identify the at-risk women who may require further examination and investigations with an objective of preventing impending problems. Therefore, in order to stay healthy, the health care workers must impart health education sensitizing the members of the community to first screen themselves and approach the doctor whenever it is required. Preventive measures are required either to prevent the disease occurring or detect the condition early so that the management and cure becomes much easier.

Breast Self-Exam and Preventing Cancer

It must be emphasized that in order to prevent breast cancer, the initial step is to make women aware of the condition and its consequences that has with high mortality rates and teach them self-examination of the breast. It is best carried out during daytime with good light, standing or sitting in front of a mirror. A look at the size and altered shape will give a first clue of something going wrong. Placing the arms by the side of the body one should look for any changes in the colour of the skin, area of redness, feel for increased warmth, swelling or a dimple and any discharge coming from the nipple.

The next step would be lying flat on the back placing a pillow under one of the arms and putting the arm over the head observe the breast and feel for changes, if any, as observed while standing. With fingers from the opposite hand keeping flat and together, one should gently feel breast without using any undue pressure. Then slowly in a circular fashion the breast is felt for any possible lumps. As one reaches the nipple forming a closer smaller circle around the nipple one should feel for any possible lumps or discharge from the nipple. Then feel in the armpit, which also contains some breast tissue, and other nearby areas for possible swellings. Any abnormality either felt or suspected, however trivial it may be one should immediately approach their doctor.

Health Education and Achieving Safe Motherhood

Childbearing for a woman is an important factor for her to live in the society in a congenial manner. It depends on the woman's ability to conceive her age at which she conceives and bearing a female child are some of the issues that faces women who are from low socio-economic group. Further tremendous social stigma is attached for a woman who is barren and one who bears female child. The health and well being of the women is therefore in jeopardy. The social outcome and the clinical complications have a direct bearing on the adolescent mothers. Therefore let us consider some of the issues that are involved with pregnancy and how imparting health education, given before and during pregnancy can bring down the complications and ensures a safe delivery. Achieving safe motherhood through health education should be the theme of the practice of future obstetrics.

Age and Fertility

Childbearing and social outcomes, especially in those who are young and adolescents is an important consideration for promoting health education in order to achieve good pregnancy outcome. Adolescent pregnancy always attracts negative impact on the socio-economic development of the family. In addition lower educational standards and violence are some of the factors that are responsible for the poor outcome of the pregnancy. Therefore it is important for us to emphasize on the social consequences of adolescent pregnancy and take appropriate measure to prevent motherhood in adolescent period.

As age advances the fertility declines. In the absence of any disease this is a natural phenomenon and mainly due to decreased liberation of eggs in the female and sperm counts in the male and directly related to the decreased frequency of intercourse. However age related diseases especially in women like, tumors in the uterus (fibroids), irregular bleeding due to hormonal imbalance causing non-liberation of eggs or irregularity in it's release, infections, endometriosis etc. may interfere with conception.

Generally it is considered that women who conceive very young (younger than 19 years) and after the age of 35 may have increased incidence of pregnancy complications. In adolescent and young women complications like excessive vomiting (hyperemesis), miscarriages (abortions), blood pressure (toxemia of pregnancy), low-birth weight babies (weighing less than 2kg), anxiety and apprehensions leading to increased incidence of operative deliveries resulting to mortality and morbidity in the mother and the child. While in women who are older than 35, in addition to having other similar complications as in the very young, may also be associated with diabetes, blood pressure, increased chances of having a baby with birth defect, Downs syndrome, stillbirths (deliver a dead foetus), are also high. Therefore it is essential for the women falling in these groups to have a pre-pregnancy counseling and regular antenatal check up should they conceive.

Taking adequate rest, good protein diet including adequate quantity of green vegetables, pulses, fruits are necessary to minimize the pregnancy-associated complications like anemia. Avoiding smoking and alcohol and limiting caffeine intake will prevent many complications. Regular exercise will help for a normal pregnancy outcome. Routine intake of iron, vitamins, and calcium is necessary to cope with the needs of growing foetus in the womb.

Normal Pregnancy : Eating Right and Being Healthy

Healthy food during pregnancy is very important for the baby to grow and develop. One should consume additional calories for the sake of growing baby in the womb. Although, nausea and vomiting during the first few months of pregnancy can make this difficult, eating a well balanced diet and vitamins prevent many associated conditions that are likely to occur during the pregnancy.

Traditionally some of the common conditions that can be best tackled by home remedies are:

1. *Morning Sickness:* Delay from getting out of bed in the mornings; eating small and frequent meals of choice throughout the day and avoiding fatty and fried foods will help reduce nausea and vomiting due to pregnancy.
2. *Bowel Movements:* Constipation can be avoided by consuming more water and liquids, eating more fresh fruits and vegetables.
3. *Heartburn:* Avoiding hot, spicy and oily foods, coffee, tomatoes, citrus fruits etc., can prevent heartburn.
4. *Food Cravings:* A common feature noticed among many pregnant women is to have a craving for certain food items like ice, tamarind, chalk, black soil etc. Although they can have the food for which they crave but should be without depletion in the intake of required calories. One should also avoid foods that are harmful for the pregnancy. However it is observed that these women have iron deficiency anemia with consequences on the pregnancy outcome, if not treated adequately.

Most pregnant women are not well informed and continue to use household alternative therapies that they are habituated when they were not pregnant. As a general rule there are many alternative therapies that are safe and effective even in pregnant women. For example in nausea in early pregnancy ginger root plain carbonated (soda) water may be very effective in addition to vitamin B1 and B6.

Exercise in Pregnancy for Normal Delivery

Maintaining a routine exercise throughout pregnancy can make one feel well and healthy. Regular prescribed exercise during pregnancy can improve the tolerance to the common discomforts of pregnancy like backaches and is also the best way for preparing for the delivery with a goal to reduce the pain. One should continue routine activity through out of pregnancy unless otherwise advised by the attending obstetrician. To start walking is the best way to initiate exercise for those who have never done earlier.

Weight Management and Prevention of Diseases

It is to be emphasized that weight management during pregnancy is an important factor. Both excessive weight gain and loss must be immediately reported to the attending physician. In normal pregnancy up to 10 kg weight gain is permissibly. However in any given month a gain of more than 2 kg is not advisable and may be heading for some complications like pre-eclampsia where in addition to weight gain is associated with rise in blood pressure and deranged kidney function.

Vaccinations and Prevention of Tetanus

Two doses of Tetanus toxoid are given routinely in order to prevent women contracting tetanus during labour and also giving immunity for short period after the baby born. It is wise to avoid unnecessary medications in pregnancy especially during first three months.

Normal Pregnancy and Health Education

Imparting health education and counselling help prevent many unsafe conditions in pregnancy. The pregnant patient and the attending physician, if both are conscious and inquisitive many of the pregnancy complications can be avoided and the outcome of the pregnancy would by delivering a healthy child. Some of the common complications that the pregnant women must know can be prevented and safe motherhood can be achieved are as follows:

Fatigue: Mothers require extra calories during pregnancy to meet the requirements of the growing foetus in the womb. In adequate intake of food and vitamins might lead to anemia and its deleterious effects. Taking adequate additional rest, especially 2-3 hours in the afternoon and lying on the left side will help reduce several complications associated with pregnancy like pre-eclampsia and tiresomeness is reduced. Maintaining regular activity and exercise increase the demand for addition intake of food with the increased levels of energy.

Nausea or Vomiting

Hormonal changes that are taking place during pregnancy and inability to cope with these hormones might result in nausea and vomiting. Normally they disappear by 4th month of pregnancy. This condition described as "morning sickness" may result from a variety of psychosocial conditions. With the co-operation from the husband and the household members and avoiding getting up early in the morning, eating light liquid food might help in lessening the severity. However in certain cases mild medication might help.

Difficulty in Sleeping and Headaches

A comfortable resting position in a comfortable bed and lying on left side make one feel sleepy. Warm milk at bedtime, trying to relax by doing meditation can improve circulation and feel sleepy. Lack of sleep can cause anxiety, tension and congestion that can cause headaches. But headaches could also be an early sign of diseases associated with pregnancy like anemia, and pre-eclampsia. Ensuring taking adequate rest, monitoring the weight gain and re-assurance will help. In certain cases medication may be necessary.

Swelling in the Feet and Legs

Pressure from the growing uterus on the blood vessels carrying blood from the lower body causes fluid retention that results in swelling (edema) of the legs and feet. Taking adequate rest will help reduce swelling. However persistent swelling and complaints of tightening ring or blouse must be investigated.

Bleeding and Swollen Gums

Because of the increased circulation and action of certain hormones in the body, the mucous membranes of several organs become swollen and painful. In some women most predominantly the gums are affected resulting in swelling, pain and at times bleeding of gums. In certain forms a dental checkup ensure that no tumor is developing. Avoiding vigorous brushing and taking vitamin C and B complex might reduce pain and swelling.

Dizziness

Fainting attacks (dizziness) are the common occurrence in every pregnancy. The pregnancy hormone progesterone dilates blood vessels and blood tends to pool in the legs with less amount returning to heart. In addition, more blood is going to the growing uterus reducing the blood pressure, especially when changing positions, resulting in dizziness. It can also occur with poor eating habits, when blood sugar levels fall below normal. By consuming adequate diet, liquids and nutrients and avoiding brisk movements will help and also prevent low blood sugar. When taking rest one should lie on left side.

Heartburn and Indigestion

Heartburn is a burning feeling that occurs in the upper abdomen and throat. This is because, the digestive system works more slowly due to changing hormone levels and the growing uterus pushing the bowels upwards. Avoiding large meals, eating slowly, drinking warm liquids, avoiding fried and spicy foods, or any foods that the patient has noticed in the past giving rise to heartburn like tea, coffee, tomatoes, citrus fruits etc., and ensuring walking after meals reduce heartburn and promotes digestion.

Constipation

Some women at one stage or the other during pregnancy feel difficulty in passing stool, incomplete evacuation or infrequent passage of hard stools. Pressure on the rectum by the growing uterus may also cause constipation. Consuming plenty of water (6-8 glasses) and juices of fruits and prunes (1 to 2 glasses) every day will prevent constipation. As a routine the diet should contain more fibre (such as whole grain foods, fresh fruits and vegetables). Further warm liquids, exercising daily, regular time for bowel movements will also help.

Varicose Veins and Hemorrhoids

An increased volume of blood and the pressure of your growing uterus can slow the circulation, causing veins of the legs to become larger or swollen usually causing pain in the calf muscles. One will get relief by avoiding standing or sitting in one place for long periods. Pregnant women also feel swollen veins appearing as painful lumps on the anus.

It is again due to pressure of the pregnant uterus on the rectum resulting in hemorrhoids, called piles. Having regular bowel habits and avoiding constipation may reduce the incidence. Applying ice packs or cold compresses to the area and local application of pain relieving ointments provide relief.

Stretch Marks

When the normal elasticity of the skin is overcome by the growing uterus the elastic fibres stretch leaving permanent scars resulting in pigmentation and these stretch marks are peculiar to pregnancy. They usually appear on the abdomen and can also appear on the breasts, buttocks or thighs. They are of permanent nature. However gentle massaging of the abdominal wall with few drops of olive oil can prevent permanent scarring.

Vaginal Discharge

In pregnancy due to increased blood supply and hormonal effects vaginal secretions become copious. Normal vaginal discharge is clear, non-irritating, and odourless and may look yellow when dries on undergarments. But sometimes infection might cause burning, itching, irritation or swelling of the genital with bad odour, bloody discharge, or bright yellow or green discharge.

Preventing Urinary Tract Infection (UTI)

As the uterus grows it presses against the bladder and also pulls up the bladder and urethra with stasis of some amount of urine. Pregnant women will have frequency of urinations, which normally disappears in course of time but as a result of incomplete voiding of urine end in infection. However, when women suffer from UTI one should also exclude any local conditions. It is important for the pregnant women to know that UTI is a common occurrence in many. However, if not prevented or inadequately treated it can affect kidneys, ureters, bladder and urethra. Bacteria are responsible for the infection and the source is usually from the skin around, lower bowel and stool. Sexual intercourse, passing of catheters, unhygienic practice while going to toilet, are some of the causes for UTI. But in some cases pre-existing infections of the kidney might precipitate UTI. Common symptoms of UTI are urgency and frequency to void and difficulty during urination. In severe cases burning sensation or lower abdominal pain while voiding. Routine periodic urine examination including culture to confirm the type of infection and taking appropriate antibiotics will help prevent complications like, anemia, toxemia, premature onset of labour and low birth weight of the baby.

Anemia is Preventable

A deficiency of red blood cells, which carry oxygen around the body during pregnancy is called anemia. It is one of the commonest complications that affect more than one third of the pregnant, women, especially belonging to the low socio-economic group and adolescents. In addition to nutritional deficiency women suffering from chronic blood loss (from piles) or hereditary illnesses such as sickle cell disease may also suffer from anemia.

During the first half of pregnancy, normally the diet contains enough of minerals and vitamins, unless their intake is poor. But during the second half of the needs of the mother and the growing baby must be met by taking additional quantities. Nutritional anemia where there is iron and folic acid deficiency is the most common type in about 80% of the pregnant women. Those who are suffering from anemia in pregnancy may be asymptomatic. Common complaints include breathlessness, tiredness and fainting attacks and in severe cases complain of palpitations, nausea, headaches and fever due to mostly because of respiratory and urinary tract infections. On examination they are pale, tongue is inflamed and sore and puffy a face and swollen legs and body.

Preventive measures include advising women to take good nourishing food rich in iron, such as leafy vegetables, whole grain foods, eggs etc. supplementing with iron, folic acid, vitamin C and other B-complex help prevent women developing anemia. However in severe cases these vitamins are given by injections to prevent complications like premature labour, small babies as a result of extrauterine growth retardation, increased blood loss during labour, requiring blood transfusions and increased susceptibility to infection to mother and baby.

Pre-eclampsia (Toxemia of Pregnancy)

It is a condition, which is marked by three specific symptoms: water retention (swelling particularly in the feet, legs and hands), high blood pressure (more than 130/90 mm. Hg) and protein in the urine. If any of these two symptoms are present they are diagnosed as suffering from 'pre-eclampsia' which normally occurs during the second half of pregnancy.

Eclampsia

Pre-eclampsia when it is neglected and left untreated might lead to eclampsia. Women with eclampsia have seizures, go into coma resulting in the onset of labour and might lead to even death of the foetus and mother at any time of the course of pregnancy and labour. Pre-eclampsia when associated with upper abdominal pain; severe headaches; blurring vision, reduced urine output, dizziness, nausea and vomiting are warning signs of impending eclampsia which can be prevented and difficult to treat.

Gestational Diabetes

Pregnancy as such can precipitate diabetes when high level of blood sugars are found. Normally mother's pancreas is able to produce more insulin to combat the increase of glucose levels in pregnancy, which could occur as a result of increased levels of insulin as a part of increase a production of placental hormones. When the maternal insulin is unable to cope up with the increased levels of glucose due to insulin resistance, sugar levels will rise, resulting in gestational diabetes. Gestational diabetes occurs because of these hormonal changes affecting transfers of nutrients from the mother to the body, interfering with the ability of insulin to manage glucose. This condition is called "insulin resistance". As the placenta grows larger during pregnancy, it produces more hormones and increases this insulin resistance. Therefore monitoring glucose levels is mandatory in suspected cases of diabetes or where there is family history, obese women or if the foetus is expected to weigh more than average.

Premature Labour and it's Prevention

Premature labour is also known as pre-term labour, which can occur 3 weeks earlier than the expected date of delivery. Adopting and honouring many of the traditional practices can prevent it. Avoiding travelling early and late in the pregnancy, avoiding intercourse during pregnancy etc. Signs include contractions of uterus resulting in dilatation of the neck of the womb. It can be predicted in many who show warning signs. Some who have medical conditions like diabetes, multiple pregnancy, excessive amniotic fluid surrounding the fetus, pre-eclampsia etc. Other signs of premature labour include mild to moderate low abdominal pain, increased pressure in the lower abdomen and vagina with blood stained vaginal discharge.

Breast Feeding and Health Education

Most pregnant women will feel some changes in their breasts. They increase in sizes due to enlarging milk glands and increased fat deposition causing breast firmness and tenderness in the first and last few months of pregnancy. Nipples become darker if one tries to express a thick milky fluid (colostrums) may escape. These are normal changes that occur in preparation of successful breastfeeding. However one should take care of a retracted or a cracked nipple. It is to be warned that excessive stimulation of nipples might initiate premature onset of labour. Patients must also be told that during breast feeding one could conceive.

Pregnancy and Counselling

Other common complaints most pregnant women have are: Backache which is caused by anemia, strain on the back muscles due to changing posture as a result of growing uterus. Leg cramps are mainly due to stasis of the blood in the limbs. Shortness of breath occurs as a result of upward pushing of the abdominal contents due to growing uterus. In take of adequate nourishing diet, supplements of vitamins and minerals, calcium, taking adequate rest, performing regular prescribed exercises may prevent most of the common complaints. Exercise in pregnancy will keep one fit and prepare well for the delivery. It must be remembered that intercourse during pregnancy may precipitate infections and premature onset of labour. Communicating with the partner may help prevent adverse changes in the attitude of the husband towards her and her pregnancy.

Women's Health and diseases

Women staying healthy and women developing diseases is a complex phenomenon to understand in the light of the socio-economic conditions of the family. The women apart from being a woman have to deal with the members of the family. She is usually the first to get up and the last to sleep. Her priorities are male and older members of the family and children. She is a victim of the torture in the family and suffers from psychological brunt. This is in addition to her reproductive functions that are again complex and filled with patho-physiological ups and downs. Therefore dealing with women's normally it pertains with that of the reproductive tract.

Physician while assessing the health status of the women deal with the problems of the genital tract in the last, although the malfunction of the reproductive system could be the main reasons for her present physical and psychological ailments. Therefore, it is stressed that the female reproductive system is an area that has a major impact on her health. In order to remain healthy, women must in addition to undergoing screening programs for detecting genital tract infections, common cancers (like breast and cervix) obtaining health education periodically and most importantly involving them in the process of self-care.

Menstrual Cycle and Regulating Fertility

Making the women understand normal and abnormal menstrual cycle is an important step to involve them to regulate their own fertility. Female reproductive cycles have two integrated cycles called the ovarian and the menstrual cycles. While the first half of the ovarian cycle is preparing to liberate the egg, the second phase is preparing the bed for receiving the fertilized egg, should it occur. Simple knowledge of testing the stretching strength of the cervical mucus which becomes, clearer, thinner and threadlike indicating the liberation of egg will help prevent pregnancy by avoiding intercourse for a period of 2-3 days during that *safe period.* Educating the women to understand about the functioning of their reproductive system will form the basis of preventing unwanted pregnancies and also protection from diseases like infections and cancer. It will help them prepare to undergo screening programs by undergoing gynaecological examinations and follow family planning measures.

Infections and it's Evolution, Ecological and Cultural Elements

It is important to understand, here, as to what we mean by infection. The basic definition is 'presence and growth of micro organisms that produce tissue damage. Some common infections that occur in women are the main cause of morbidity in the women who suffer from prolonged illness with less productivity. Infections can be caused by the entrance and growth and multiplication of bacteria, protozoan, fungi and viruses. Technical advances since the time of Louis Pasteur (1822-95) lead to the explosion of knowledge in the 19th century on the etiology of microbial etiology of infections. This scientific advances lead to think that, 'it's time that we close the book of infection' (*Rob Desalle,* 1999). However it was disappointing to see that it not only remained opened but additional burdens are surfacing in combating.

The *evolutionary, ecological and cultural* elements place, vis-a-vis human beings at the centre of the discussion of infections that is causing widespread diseases (*Rob Desalle,* 1999). In order to explain that the infection occurs, in *evolution* context, in which all the Earth's Organisms are bound by the same rules and the major rule is that of natural selection. The more efficient the organisms are at reproduction, the more successful they will be in the evolutionary sense. The second main concern is the understanding of the *ecology and ecosystem.*

The classical definition of *'ecosystem'* is a 'bounded system where living organisms coexist in a constant state of interaction and interdependency.' The human body is the habitat of a community of microbes that mutually interact and remain in specific parts of the body. One classic example is *E. Coli.* Many strains of *E. Coli* have evolved a mutually beneficial relationship with human digestive tract. When it begins to grow in areas other than the digestive tract it becomes dangerous and potentially deadly—a pathogen.

And the final key is *culture.* It is a historical fact that several cultural groups define 'disease' in different manners. While many Western cultural groups treat measles as a debilitating disease, the Chinese and other cultures of the far East think that the infection of measles is a rite of passage from childhood to adulthood and is not perceived as a disease.

The infections that commonly occur in women are in the genital tract. The normal flora of the vagina is greatly influenced by sex hormones. In women two factors help to maintain the self-cleansing action of vagina in order to defend from infections. Mainly the acid-base balance that is maintained by the normal inhabitant of the vagina, *Lactobacillus acidophilus,* which keeps the pH of the vagina on the acidic side discouraging the pathogens from invading. The second factor is the thickness of the vaginal epithelium, which is stronger from puberty until menopause (cessation of menstrual cycles). Sexually active women defend themselves contracting infections but are vulnerable during puberty and around menopause. In women this ecosystem is disturbed due to variety of reasons like changing pattern of hormonal levels, being on oral contraceptives and antibiotics etc. and pregnant with resultant pH variations.

Reproductive Tract Infections (RTI)

Reproductive tract infections (RTI) is defined as any infections of the genital tract. However, in this chapter we will deal with common infections that are encountered in women, commonly described as suffering from white discharge per vaginum. Discussion on the other major sexually transmitted diseases called STDs and infections affected by the Human Immune Deficiency Virus are avoided since they are being separately dealt with in another chapter. Most of the causative organisms occur due to overgrowth of the bacteria and other organisms that are normal habitats in the vagina. Women are more susceptible to reproductive tract infections compared to men. It is mainly because of the anatomical and physiological reasons. They are also less likely to be treated because of socio-cultural factors hence the ultimate suffering and morbidity in women as a result if these infections are heavy.

Common Symptoms of Reproductive Tract Infections

Many women who have RTI by sexual contact may not have severe symptoms to begin with. However, ultimately it may lead to serious complications if they are left untreated. They are also at a higher risk of acquiring or transmitting HIV infection, the virus that causes AIDS. Usual vaginal discharge may be as a result of common infections from bacteria or yeast. When there is excessive and abnormal vaginal discharge, painful urination, itching and burning sensation in the genital region, sores, blisters, warts, ulcers low abdominal pain, back ache, painful intercourse, bleeding following intercourse it may be because of more severe organisms like Gonococcus, Chlamydia, Trichomonas, etc. In addition another common infection could be that of Herpes caused by herpes simplex virus (HSV), and it can cause ulcers on the genitalia, around anus, mouth, face etc. Human Papilloma virus is type of infection that is much researched recently as a causative organism for carcinoma of the cervix (neck of the womb).

Pelvic Inflammatory Disease (PID)

Women who suffer from recurrent reproductive tract infection or infection of longstanding duration may develop a condition called PID. The long-standing infection ultimately involves the internal reproductive organs including uterus, fallopian tubes, ovaries and the surrounding pelvic tissues. When these organs get infected they are inflamed, become swollen and has deleterious effect on the entire health. Pelvic Inflammatory Disease is one of the common causes of women suffering from backache, menstrual irregularities, and inability to conceive, fever with rigors, urination problems, and the other psychosocial problems to sexual dysfunction. Therefore women who have symptoms of RTI must immediately get treatment. If left alone it can lead to further complications like developing abscess in the fallopian tubes, ovaries and in the pelvis often requiring major surgery. If and when they conceive, it is that they suffer from abnormal pregnancy occurring in other than the normal site i.e. outside the womb resulting in dangerous sequels.

Trichomoniasis

It is a common infection caused by *Trichomonas vaginalis*, which can be sexually transmitted from person to person. The symptoms of trichomoniasis are usual abnormal vaginal discharge, which is typically described as frothy, yellowish with an unpleasant characteristic odour. In addition the infected women suffer from itching of the genital region, and burning sensation while voiding urine. If not treated, it could become a cause of pelvic inflammatory disease (PID). Once diagnosed, the treatment is simple but both the sexual partners must take medication. Avoiding sexual intercourse until the treatment has proven effective is advisable. A healthy sexual practice and maintaining personal hygiene are important in order to prevent the disease otherwise recurrence is common.

Bacterial Vaginosis

Bacterial Vaginosis occurs when the normally inhabited bacteria in the vagina overgrow due to various reasons. It could be associated with sexual activity. It may also be because using certain substance as a douche and other medications. Avoiding douches, practising safe sex and other hygienic methods might reduce the occurrence of Vaginosis. Women who suffer from this kind of infection often have excessive vaginal discharge with a peculiar smell and irritation and itching of the genital region. The risk of developing Vaginosis is higher after delivery and abortions. The infection is treated with appropriate antibiotics and practising hygienic methods of self-management.

Monilial or Yeast Infection

It is also called candidasis, which is caused by an overgrowth of the fungus *Candida albicans*, which are normally found in the vagina in small numbers. The precipitating factors for this overgrowth could be pregnancy, usage of antibiotics, using of hygiene products, spermicidal gels and creams and it can also occurs in patients who are on steroids for some other medical conditions like asthma. Patients suffering from diabetes and the blood sugars are not controlled properly can get fungal infection. Therefore women must take care when resorting to use of hygiene products, resorting to safe sexual habits, avoid wearing under wears made of synthetic material.

Common symptoms in most women due to yeast infection (candidiasis) are vaginal itching and irritation, excessive vaginal discharge that is described as thick and curdy with burning and painful intercourse. It is diagnosed because of its characteristic discharge and whitish flakes adherent to vagina. It is best treated by anti-fungal suppositories, creams and sometimes in severe case using oral anti-fungal tablets. Although they might disappear with the treatment but can recur. Therefore it is essential to follow hygienic practices and appropriate medications. In women who get recurrent infection should also be investigated for pre-diabetic condition.

Urinary Tract Infection (UTI)

In women due to anatomical reasons urinary tract infections are much more common. An untreated UTI can lead to various complications. It involves infection of the kidneys, the ureters, the bladder, and the urethra. In women, UTI can occur mainly because the urethra opens just in front of the vagina. And as discussed, vagina is a storehouse for several organisms, which can make entry in to the urinary tract causing infections. Although urine is normally sterile and doesn't contain bacteria. Unhygienic practices may become one of the major cause of entry of bacteria. However bacteria entering the kidneys from the bloodstream can also infect from the above urinary tract. In newborn and infants usually the infections are due to generalized infection and sepsis. Usage of diapers can lead to infection from stools, which are pool of bacteria, and the urethral opening is in close proximity. Older girls may become prone to UTI's through wiping back-to-front when they are first toilet-trained, which pulls stool into the vaginal/meatal area. Sexually active women may develop because of injury to the urethra.

Urethritis which is a form of infection the urethra, *Cystitis, i.e.* infection of the bladder and *Pyelonephritis* i.e. infection of the kidney itself are some of the pathological conditions that occur when we talk about UTI. Patients suffering from UTI have a variety of symptoms like burning on urination, fever, lower abdominal pain, smell and altered colour including blood stained urine. When the kidneys are involved, *Pyelonephritis,* severe pain in the back or in the abdomen resulting complications due to malfunctions of the kidneys.

Understanding Cancer

It is a disease where the cells of a particular organ in the body over grow, invade and destroy the neighbouring normal structure out of proportion. The main factor could be a deranged gene. The damage to gene could be due to infections, environmental and the other such factors. Different types of cancers can affect practically any part of the body. However we will deal with the most common cancers that affect the women. By far the most common cancer in the female genital tract is that of neck of the womb (cervix).

Preventing Cervical Cancer

Cancer of neck of the womb (cervix) and breast are the commonest forms of the cancers that a woman might suffer from and are the main killers. While in developed countries it is the breast cancer is the number one killer, in developing countries death from preventable cancer of the neck of the womb is the chief killer. Every year millions of middle aged women die, which otherwise could have been prevented, if only appropriate health education is imparted. The cervix is the narrowed portion of the uterus (womb) that opens into the vaginal canal. It is ironical that on the one hand the scientists all over the world have accepted the WHO definition that the cervical cancer is preventable, yet many gynaecologists see women coming to their clinics in advanced stage of malignancy. Mostly it is lack of initiative for taking preventive measures on the part of health care workers that is responsible for the women to suffer from cancer cervix. It mainly affects the women who are about to complete their childbearing period and are about to take over the rearing of their adolescent children.

In order to prevent occurrence of this cancer, it is necessary for all the women who have become sexually active and active at an early age to seek a periodic evaluation by way of a gynaecological examination and also undergoing a Pap test. This will help prevent occurrence of the cancer of the neck of the womb and also help detect in early stages so that the treatment carried out is effective and becomes curative. For women who are under 30 years must get a checkup done at least once in five years while those who have crossed 30 and also have had many children to undergo this examination at least once in 2 years. In addition, women who have vaginal discharge, abnormal vaginal bleeding, and bloodstained discharge following intercourse must seek the opinion of gynaecologist immediately, since these could be early signs of malignancy. In developing countries it is important for the women who marry young and also who resort sexual activity early must be careful since they are more prone to suffer from cancer.

Cancer of the Body of the Womb

Another common form of cancer that might effect is the body of the womb occurs in women who are above the age of forty, have had no children or less number of children, obese and are suffering from hypertension and diabetes. In addition these women are also likely to suffer from abnormal menstrual patterns, white discharge etc.

Breast Cancer and it's Prevention

The incidence of breast cancer is increasing in the developing countries mainly because of the increased awareness. Normally women with a family history of breast cancer, women who have attained their menstrual cycles early and those who have reached their menopause late, and have suffered from fibro-cystic disease of the breast are more likely to be affected by breast cancer. Therefore, women must be taught for self-breast examination to detect any warning symptoms, including a lump in the breast or discharge from their nipple, who should seek the advise of their doctor immediately. Recent research have shown that there is an increased incidence of breast cancer in women who were on hormonal replacement therapy (HRT) and also obese.

Teaching self-examination of the breast in women, especially in high-risk patients and periodic routine mammogram has shown excellent results in detecting breast cancer in it's early stage. In recent studies it has been shown that women who undergo routine mammography after the age of 40 are less likely to suffer from breast cancer compared to those who did not undergo screening. It is also to be emphasized that the women may not have any symptoms until it has been diagnosed. Therefore it allows the doctors to perform simpler and less radical treatment. (Self-examination discussed elsewhere above.)

Ovarian Cancer

Ovarian cancer is also equally one of the commonest cancers in women perhaps after that of neck of the womb, breast, and body of the womb. Ovaries liberate eggs and the hormones control the menstrual mechanism are located on either side of the womb and primary cancers develop from it's cells. The major risk factor is age. The risk of ovarian cancer occurs mostly in women who have attained menopause and well past the age of 60. The familial factor of it's occurrence has not been established. However parity might play a role. Women who have never been pregnant are more likely to develop ovarian cancer than women who have had children. There is no screening that could help predict occurrence of ovarian cancers.

However, women who have vague swelling and unexplained pain of the abdomen over a long period, digestive problems, loss of appetite, constipation, weight loss, frequency of micturition (urination), unexpected and unusual abnormal bleeding per vaginum warrants for an examination and investigations. If detected earlier ovarian cancers may be easier to treat.

Obesity and Cancer

Recently, after reviewing the scientific evidence, researchers at the American Institute for Cancer Research (2003) concluded that additional weight on the body means additional risk for cancer. There is a definite relationship between obesity and cancer. Therefore it is necessary to raise awareness among the women especially since they are more prone to be on other side of the scale. Obesity is commonly defined as having at least 20% more body fat than is appropriate for a person's age, height, sex, and body build. Although most people know that obesity plays an important role in the development of diabetes and cardiovascular disease the relationship between obesity and cancer must be emphasized. Obese women are likely to suffer from colon, kidney, the breast cancer after menopause, and the lining of the uterus (endometrial cancer).

Therefore, in order to reduce the risk of developing a cancer, women must be recommended to eat food rich in vegetables and fruits (detailed elsewhere) and whole grains less in red meat instead choosing fish, poultry, and beans as alternatives. As a general rule restricting weight gain during the adulthood to about 5 kg. will help prevent many diseases. In addition moderate physical activity everyday or vigorous exercise periodically might help check the weight gain.

Conclusions

Woman must understand the important role she has in the family and society. Understanding her body must be the objective of every woman. Pregnancy is a physiological phenomenon but pregnancy complications can lead to deleterious effects on the health of the individual and the outcome of the pregnancy can keep the health of mother and baby in jeopardy. In addition health education plays an important role in making the women especially from poorer segments of the society and those who are illiterates in preventing or detecting, reproductive tract infections, some common cancers like that of breast and neck of the womb. Obesity is one single factor that is emerging as the major cause of many diseases. Becoming conscious about the diet and managing their weight, practising perfect personal hygiene and involving themselves in the care of their health will prevent common diseases like hypertension and diabetes and genital tract infections and then will be able to regulate their own fertility for achieving safe motherhood.

References

1. World Health Organization, 1947. Chronicle of WHO 1: p. 1.
2. *Webster's Ninth New Collegiate Dictionary*, 1990. Meriam-Webster Inc, Springfield, Massachusetts, USA, and pp. 1118.
3. World Health Organization, 1986. A discussion document on the concept and principles of health promotion. *Health Promotion*, 1: 73-78.
4. Hanlon, J.J. 1960. *Principles of Public Health Administration*, St. Louis, CV Mosby. 3rd edin. p. 23.
5. American Institute for Cancer Research, 2003. Published: Spring 2003, CNN Report.
6. Rob Desalle, 1999. 'Epidemic: The world of Infections, Ed., The New Press, New York, USA, pp. 1-7, 1999 as told by William S., Surgeon General USA (1967).

11

HIV Infection in Women—Prevention of Mother to Child Transmission (PMTCT)

Dr. G. Sunitha Subramanyam

The human immuno deficiency virus (HIV) infection a global pandemic has had devastating effects throughout the world, with the developing countries being the hardest hit socially and economically. It was first noticed in 1981 in U.S.A. The incidence has been rapidly increasing mostly in developing countries.

HIV infection is transmitted by sexual route, injections including blood and blood products, vertical route (infected mother to child), Breast feeding and Organ transplantation. Heterosexual contact represents the dominant mode of transmission of HIV infection in women in India.

Incidence

WHO (1995) estimates that all over the world there were 25 million HIV infected persons and out of them 50% were females. 10,000 new infections occur in each day and out of all 90% are in developing countries.

Globally HIV ranks 30th cause of death.

India takes second place globally for HIV infection and first being South Africa. Andhra Pradesh takes second position in India, first being Maharashtra.

In 1998 there were 3.5 million cases where as in 2003, 4.5 million and in 2004 expected 5.3 million cases and over all prevalence is 0.8%.

There is spread from urban to rural areas.

Incidence of AIDS

Infected males are 30,643 and females 10,065. Tamil Nadu, Maharashtra, Gujarat, Andhra Pradesh and Karnataka are having generalized epidemic. The seven northeastern states together have 1,704 AIDS cases.

Host Factors

Age and Sex

The spread of HIV infection occurs most frequently in the age group of 20 to 50 years. Globally at the end of 1998, out of 5.8 million newly infected cases, 50 per cent were females.

Susceptibility of Infection vis-à-vis Sexual Practices

* The receptive partner is at a great risk than the insertive or active partner, in both vaginal and anal intercourse. Thus the risk of transmission from male to female is higher than transmission from female to male.
* Anal sex carries a higher risk than vaginal sex.
* Oral sex and deep kissing carry relatively low risk.
* A good degree of protection is provided to persons using condoms. The safety depends upon the quality of condom and its correct and regular use.

High Risk Behaviours

Based on the epidemiological characteristics of HIV infection certain high risk behaviour groups, who are likely to be harbouring infection more frequently that the general population have been identified.

* People with multiple sex partners (commercial sex workers, men who are away from their families for long periods, as they are likely to seek extra-marital sex).
* Injection drug user, because they share needles and syringes.

* People requiring frequent transfusions of blood e.g. haemophiliacs, thalassemics etc.
* Truck drivers because of their sexual practices.

Natural History of HIV Infection/AIDS

The natural history of any disease refers to the stages through which a disease passes, in the absence of any intervention. Clear knowledge of natural history of a disease helps in identifying the stages vis-à-vis appropriate intervention to prevent or control the disease.

The natural history of HIV infection begins as soon as virus enters the body of a susceptible host through any of the routes of transmission as discussed earlier (sexual, parenteral and perinatal).

Antibody test at this stage does not reveal the true status as it takes some time for formation of antibodies. Therefore, a person during this stage is not aware (even after testing) that he is infected and is capable of transmitting the virus to others. Even after the test becomes positive the person still continues to look and feel healthy and remains asymptomatic for a number of years. Also, such a person continues to transmit infection to others, who may be unsuspecting i.e., he/she is a HIV carrier. The infectivity of the virus is thus lifelong, though it may vary with time, being high:

* In the initial stages of infection, and
* In the late stages when clinical manifestations appear.

Progression to AIDS is variable. Evidence today suggests 20% of those infected will develop AIDS in 5 years, and 50% in 10 years and a decreasing proportion even after 10 years.

Because of this long latent period in development of clear-cut clinical manifestations it is estimated that for every full blown case of AIDS, there are 3-5 with ARC (AIDS Related Condition) and 50-199 infected with the virus, but who are asymptomatic. AIDS is therefore often termed "The Hidden Epidemic".

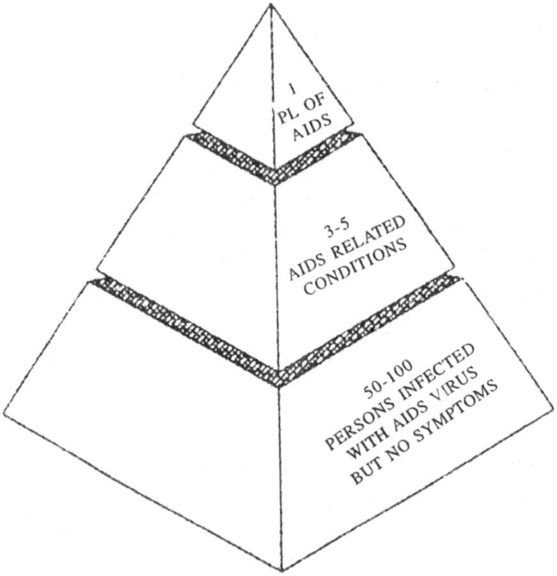

Thus, based on the clinical signs and symptoms, four distinct stages of the spectrum of HIV infection has been identified, in addition to the earliest stage of acute prodromal manifestations.

Acute Prodromal Manifestations

Acute illness can occur as early as a few weeks after the infection is acquired, and usually precedes sero-conversion, which occurs at about 6 - 12 weeks. This presents typically as a glandular fever-like illness with fever, lymphadenopathy, headache, night sweats and cough which may be accompanied by a skin rash and diarrhoea. This stage being similar to so many bacterial and viral infections often tends to go unnoticed and does not arouse suspicion of HIV infection but is present in 70-80 per cent of infected people.

Stages of Progression

There are 4 stages of progression as shown in the figure.

Stage - 4

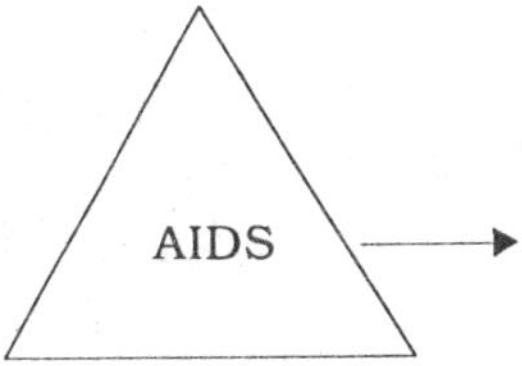

Pneumocystis carinii Pneumonia

Toxoplasmosis
Kapasi's sorcoma

- Persistent diarrhoea
- Weight loss more than 10%
- Fever

- Kaposi's sorcona
- Alveolar pneumonia
- Isosporiasis
- Labial/Genital herpes
- Oral candidiasis

ARC (AIDS Related Conditions)

- Weight loss
- Fatigue
- Anorexia

- Oral hairy leukoplakia
- Aphthous ulcers
- Herpes zoster
- Recurrent URI

Persistent Glandular Lymphadenopathy
(PGL)

Frequently first sign of HIV infection. Presence of enlarged nodes, at least 1 cm in diameter in two or more extrainguinal sites for at least 3 months.

Asymptomatic

Diagnosis on Laboratory results alone.

Acute Infection

Usually asymptomatic. Seroconversion at 6-12 weeks, sometimes accompanied by glandular fever-like illness (fever, malaise, lymphadenopathy, rash).

Mode of HIV Transmission

Epidemiological studies throughout the world have shown three modes of HIV transmission.

Sexual intercourse

Whether heterosexual or homosexual, is the major route of transmission. HIV can be transmitted through any individual act of unprotected sexual intercourse that is any penetrative sexual act where one partner is infected with HIV. The risk of becoming infected through an act of unprotected sexual intercourse depends on four main factors:

(a) *The likelihood that the sex partner is infected*

The probability that a person has become infected with HIV is in general proportionate to the number (frequency) of unprotected sex acts and the number of high risk partners with whom the person has had sexual contact in recent years.

(b) *The type of sex act*

All unprotected acts of sexual penetration (anal, vaginal, oral) carry a risk of HIV transmission because they bring sexual secretions directly into contact with exposed mucous membrane. Injury to the mucous membrane of the rectum, the vagina or the mouth may help the virus to enter into the blood stream. "Receptive" partners are thus at a greater risk than "insertive" partners in acts of intercourse. However, HIV can be transmitted even through unbroken mucous membrane.

(c) *The amount of virus present in the blood or sexual secretions (semen, vaginal or cervical secretions) of the infected partner*

Individuals with HIV infection become more infectious as they progress to HIV related diseases and AIDS. There is also an early period of high infectiousness around the time of seroconversion.

(d) *The presence of other sexually transmitted diseases and/or genital lesions in either partner*

HIV can be transmitted sexually even when either partner has any of the other sexually transmitted diseases.

However, there is strong evidence that men and women with genital ulcer disease or urethral discharge are at increased risk of acquiring and transmitting HIV.

Blood Borne Infections

HIV infected blood, blood products, transplanted organs or tissues and the use of improperly sterilized needles and syringes that have been in contact with infected blood can transmit HIV. This is the most efficient way of transmission of HIV. Even a small transfusion of infected blood results in virtually 100% seroconversion.

HIV infected woman can transmit HIV to her foetus or infant before, during, or after birth:

A pregnant woman with HIV infection has an approximately 30% chance of passing the virus to her foetus or new born baby. There is evidence that infection can occur as early as the first 12 -15 weeks of gestation. 60% perinatal infections are perinatal occurring during labour, or even after birth through breast milk. It is estimated that 40% of perinatal infections occur through breast feeding.

Diagnosis

The diagnosis of HIV infection is by serology, virus culture or by detection of viral DNA or RNA using polymerase chain reaction (PCR). The screening procedure is an enzyme-linked immunosorbent assay (ELISA) test that is very sensitive, inexpensive, and easy to perform. The ELISA test may show false-positive results. All positive tests must be followed by Western blot detects antibodies against the glycoproteins. The results of the Western blot are given as positive, negative, or indeterminate. The probability of a false-positive diagnosis is almost absent if two ELISAs and one Western blot are positive. Once the presence of infection has been demonstrated, it is possible to use CD4 cell count to assess the severity of the disease.

Viral cultures and PCR are used for the diagnosis of HIV in special circumstances. Cultures are labour intensive, expensive, and less sensitive than serology. PCR is a very sensitive technique that has the potential to become the test of choice for the diagnosis of HIV infection.

Clinical Case Definition for AIDS

(Acquired Immuno Deficiency Syndrome): According to National Aids Control Organization(NACO), India.

Acquired Immuno deficiency in an adult is defined as an individual who has been identified as meeting the criteria as explained in A and B below:

A. Positive test for HIV infection by two tests based on preferably two different antigens.

B. Having one of the following clinical criteria:

- Weight loss of 10% body weight or cachexia, not known to be due to condition unrelated to HIV infection.
- Chronic diarrhoea of more than one month duration intermittent or constant.
- Disseminated, miliary or extra pulmonary tuberculosis or bilateral pulmonary tuberculosis.
- Neurological impairment restricting daily activities, not known to be due to conditions unrelated to HIV (e.g. Trauma).
- Candidiasis of the esophagus, diagnosable as dysphagia and oral candidiasis.
- Kaposi's sarcoma (a type of cancer).

Screening

There are two types of screening:

1. Universal Screening

   If prevalance is more than 1% screening of all women including pregnancy is to be done.

   This is controversial in view of confidentiality and legal problems.

2. Screening in high risk patients

   Such as prostitutes, IV drug abusers, women with HIV positive husbands, husbands with homosexual experiences.

   The disadvantage of this is failed to identify 50% of sero positives.

Treatment

Treatment consists of therapy of opportunistic infections and malignancies. Anti retroviral treatment is the corner stone in the management of HIV infection.

Highly Active Anti Retro Viral Therapy (HAART) has advantage of long-term Viral Suppression with synergistic action at different sites. But the side effects, expensive therapy with poor patient compliance, drug interactions and toxicities are the draw backs with this.

Prevention is better than cure holds good for HIV infection than any other disease. Prophylaxis in the form of safe sexual practice, IV drug use restriction, screening of blood products with universal precautions. Secondary prophylaxis for opportunistic infections and post-exposure prophylaxis to health care professional are the aims of management.

Concept of no cure to HIV infection should be replaced with there is always something. We can do because HIV infection needs no longer be equated with an inevitably fatal disease.

Factors Increasing the Vulnerability of Females for HIV Infection

* Marriage with older man more likely increases HIV infection in women, because of the sexual experience of the older man.
* Economic dependence on man also increases the infection rate in women because of lack of personal protection.
* Infection transmission from male to female is more because of the bigger surface area in the female and the passive partner is being suffered more than the active partner.
* Reproductive Tract Infections and Sexually Transmitted Infections go unrecognized in women making them more susceptible.
* There is need for more blood transfusion in women because of the pregnancy problems and child birth increasing the vulnerability for HIV infection in women.
* Adolescents are the biggest segment indulging in unsafe sex practices.

Transmission of HIV Infection to the Child-Prevention

PMTCT means Prevention of Mother to Child Transmission was started in 2001 (WHO) and wide implementation has taken place from 2002 onwards.

PPTCT means Prevention of Parent to Child Transmission. Recently PMTCT is changed to PPTCT because mother is not only the responsible person for infection and both parents are responsible for the infection to the child. Prevention of perinatally acquired HIV was become critical component of public health strategies towards HIV.

Vertical transmission of HIV is estimated to account for 90% of paediatric Aids cases and almost all newly diagnosed HIV infection in children.

The burden of perinatal transmission also has differed geographically.

The transmission rate in developed countries is 14-33% and in developing countries 43-50%.

Routes of Transmission Mother to Child

* Transplacental—Through placenta infection is transmitted during pregnancy and during delivery
* Contact with infected secretions and blood during delivery
* Breast feeding—The infection is transmitted to the baby after delivery through this route.

Timings

HIV can be transmitted from Mother to Child throughout pregnancy. This includes all three trimesters of pregnancy, Intrapartum, Post Partum within 48 hours.

Obstetrics Factors

1. Intervention procedures such as Amniocentesis. (Removal of Amniotic fluid both theraputic and diagnostic procedures).
2. Prolonged rupture of membranes.
3. Operative procedures such as forceps delivery, vacuum extraction and emergency caesarian section.
4. Viginal deliveries.

Placental Factors

* Infection may occurs through placental route
* Infection of membranes—Chorio amnionitis.

Breast Feeding

Lactation causes risk of transmission by 14%.

Vitamin A Deficiency

Leads to weakening of the already weakened immune system leading to 3 to 4 folds increase in vertical transmission.

Anaemia—Increased Rate of Infection

HIV epidemic in India has entered to 3rd phase where in significant transmission has occurred through prenatal route. This has created two problems.

1. Public Health Problem
2. Social Problem.

Public Health Problem involves: Increased disease burden of morbidity among infants and children such as

* Recurrent infections
* Malnutritions
* Repeated hospital admissions

Treatment requires costly drugs taking away the bigger share of the hospital money.

Social Problems

* Emergence of orphans following death of the one or more of parents due to AIDS.
* School dropouts.
* Low educational oppurtuinity due to descrimination.
* Child labour.
* Social out caste.
* Child abuse.

Anti Retroviral Therapy has certainly proved to be a boon in developed countries. UNICEF and NACO had decided to work together to upscale the prevention of Mother to Child Transmission of HIV in India.

Preventive Aspects

In most instances of paediatric AIDS, vertical transmission is the predominant route of infection. Hence strategies aimed at preventing infection among women will also help in reducing the infection among children.

Behavioural change

Development of programmes with an integrated approach to induce behavioural change, promoting condom use, and controlling STDs is likely to reduce the infectivity of the transmitters as also the susceptibility of HIV exposed persons. Needle exchange programmes have helped in stabilizing and in some instances even reducing HIV incidence among IDUs.

Some potential means of reducing the risk of vertical transmission

1. The use of Zidovuaine by asymptomatic infected women with CD4 cell count of more than 200/cmm has been shown to reduce transmission by two-thirds. These women were treated with Zidovudine orally during pregnancy, and intravenously, during labour infants received oral Zidovudine for six weeks after birth. The approach may be feasible in countries where Zidovudine is available and affordable. For countries where the cost of this regimen is prohibitive, trials of modified timings does of antiretroviral drugs (as in the Thailand study) are needed to find most cost-effective methods for reducing perinatal transmission.
2. The observation that the risk of transmission from mother-to-child increases when foetal membranes rupture more than 4 hours before delivery may lead to simple precautions so as not to intentionally rupture membranes. Though every effort should be made to shorten the time between rupture of membranes and delivery. This should not be taken to mean using interventions that could increase morbidity for the mother or her infant.

3. Vitamin A stores are depleted during birth and pregnancy, it is known that vitamin A deficiency leads to weakening of the already weakened immune system. Vitamin A deficiency has been shown to be associated with a three to four folds increased risk of vertical transmission. This temporal relation may suggest that supplementing vitamin A intake during pregnancy may lower the vertical transmission of HIV.
4. A critical and much debated issue has been whether to advise mothers in developing countries against breast-feeding because of the risk of HIV transmission through breast milk. This potential risk can be eliminated in a population with access to breast milk alternatives. Breast feeding by HIV infected mothers is not recommended in the US and other industrialized countries.
5. The study on the role of other potential interventions, i.e., vaginal microbicides has not reached anywhere.

   There are different protocols for PMTCT by ARV drugs. Out of this HIV net 012 study is important in which Nevirapine 200 mg orally at the onset of labour is given for the mother.

   2 mg/Kg to babies with in 72 hours of birth.

   The simple single dose to mother and child of Nevirapine reduced maternal Transmission by 47%. This regimen is more practicable for use in developing countries.

FACTS-NACO (National Aids Control Organisation) to Summarise

* 3.87 millions people with HIV infection in India.
* 40,308 Aids cases in India.
* Survellance report of 2002.

  Tamil Nadu, Maharashtra, Gujarat, Andhra Pradesh and Karnataka are having generalized AIDS Epidemic.
* The seven northeastern states together have 1,704 AIDS cases.
* 43% of affected population are female.
* Less access to treatment.

* Care provider for family (neglects own health).
* Rejection by family more likely.

Future

* No vaccine developed yet
* Safe drugs for pregnant women awaited till then minimize blood transfusions and usage of blood products
* Strengthening of information, education and communication.

Universal precautions such as Disposable Gloves, Protective carriers, Eye glasses, Disposable Approns, Avoiding contacts with all secretions, Blood, Liquor and body fluids, Handling properly the needles and scalpels and disposing the infected materials properly.

Believe in Yourself and Others!!!

To believe is to know that every day.

It is a new beginning.

It is to trust that miracles do happen and dreams really do come true.

But for that.

"Do whatever it is that calls to you".

Do it with all your might.

With all your Strength.

And with all your heart.

The call is to fight against.

Let us do it now !

We will do it together.

Part - III

SEXUAL BEHAVIOUR

12

Human Sexuality and Reproductive Health: A Model and Policy Implications

K. Mahadevan, Lory Laing, Iqbal Shah, S. Siva Raju, V.M. Sandeep, N. Murugesan, V.K.R. Kumar, C. Deepak & P. Ganesh

Introduction

Traditionally sexual behaviour in India, Asia and the Western countries, was regulated by certain norms and values. However, such normative behaviour varied among different groups and communities. It ranged from simple to complex and a prolonged procedure through rigorous socialization or the absence of such normative restrictions. In addition, sexual behaviour in the past was conservative and confined to certain particular periods of one's life, like post-puberty and marriage duration, but such restrictions tended to give rise to sexual liberalism. At present the diversities and complexities of sexuality depend largely on the culture, social development, impact of the mass media and modernization of a given society. While sexuality was personal and an affair between married couples exclusively in the past, now-a-days it has assumed several social forms thanks to the spread of night clubs, the mass media, family planning and the alarming spread of a fatal disease like AIDS. Therefore, sexuality has assumed very great significance for the very survival of our society and its future.

There was diversity of sexuality among most communities in India and elsewhere in the past. Such diversities, however, are disappearing in the western societies. Interestingly, fascinating and healthy sexuality continues to prevail among certain tribals and developed communities in India. For instance among the Kurichia tribals inhabiting in the Wyanad districts of Kerala, chastity and virginity have very great significance. Among them there is no premarital and extra-marital sex. If at all any such case ever occurs, the boy and girl will be excommunicated and tortured. As a result, there is no STD and related communicable disease, so far, noticed among them [Aiyappan and Mahadevan, 1985]. Among the Juvangs, a tribe in Madhya Pradesh, there is an institutionalised training in marriage and family formation through the Ghotul, which is a residential club of the adolescents and youth of the Juvangs. Among the Brahmins, sexuality is not automatic after marriage as it is among several other forward communities. For Brahmins, initiation of the first sexual act is a sacred and auspicious one. Therefore, with the help of an astrologer or the elders, auspicious date for the marriage and couples cohabitation is fixed, which may take place a couple of days after the marriage or weeks or even months after it. Such occasion of consummation is popularly called "Shanthimuhurtham". Therefore, among the Brahmins, premarital sex is negligible and as a result STD, HIV and such communicable diseases are either rare or altogether absent.

The Concept of Sexuality

Generally sexuality manifests a complex of several concepts. It may begin with or without romance, and may lead to marriage followed by honeymoon during which contraception may or may not be used and sex is indulged in either for its pleasure or to beget a progeny and thus for leading a healthy sexual life. But it can face the risk of sex linked disease on the personal background of the man and woman, if they have pre-marital sex experience. Sexuality comprises, emotional and sensitive behaviour for physio-psychological satisfaction. Sexual act can be heterosexual or homosexual by mutual consent or it may culminate in rape. Major aspects of sexuality undergo change and are influenced by both the traditional and changing variables. The concept of sexuality can be framed only after taking into consideration several influential and interacting factors and variables which are cultural, religious, situational, environmental, and others, which take place through education and socialization. The process of sexuality begins with childhood and progresses through adolescence and fructifies during the adult period. The concept of sexuality therefore has to include not just the terminal act of sex but all associated and allied features of romance, values and attitudes to sex, and all those factors which influence the sexual urge, its degeneration and rectification.

The traditional and conservative pattern of sexuality has been changing in most urban areas as a result of urbanization, migration and prolonged separation of married couples. Several other factors causing cohabitation have emerged during the last half a century promoting liberal sexuality during the premarital period and development of a promiscuous life-style. In recent times, premarital sex has become widespread in several developed countries of the West, particularly in the Scandinavian countries, the USA and Europe. Even there, though, sexual relationship exists after marriage between the couples, frequent divorces, separation and migration of one of the spouses has led to extra-marital sex.

The determinants of the concept of sexuality are diverse and interdisciplinary. In the pages that follow, discussion is focused mostly on the factors that affect the sexuality of diverse population. They range from physiological urge for sexual gratification of personal interaction variables, educational exposure, mobility, opportunity for sex in different places (work place) and institutions, excitement and provocation by the TV, cinema and such entertainment, pornography and similar popular titillating literature, perceived safety from conception and availability of different kinds of contraception. Of course, age, health, harmony and its absence in married life, addiction to liquor, medication, use of stimulating food and so on are some of the other major factors influencing sexuality. Moreover, values of virginity and chastity were two powerful traditional factors that provided a normative pattern of sexual restraint in the past. These along with the other factors regulated sexuality and influenced it in different ways, as can be seen in the following discussion.

Oxford dictionary defined "sexuality according to the strict biological definition, is the characteristics of the male and female reproductive elements (genoblasts) and sex of the individuals in which the reproductive elements arise. It also includes possession of sexual powers or capability of sexual feelings. Another attribute of sexuality is the recognition of or preoccupation with what is sexual, allusions to sexual matters and appearance distinctive of sex" (*Oxford Dictionary*, 1978).

However, Encyclopaedia Britannica (1973) expanded the concept of sexuality as follows "the anatomical, physiological and behavioural characteristics of organisms that are involved in the process of sexual reproduction. The text article covers sexual and non-sexual reproduction, the adaptive significance of sex, the origin of sex and sexuality, sex patterns, and sex determination. The text article also covers types of behaviour, physiological aspects, psychological aspects and social and cultural aspects, including permissiveness and social control, socio-economic factors and legal regulation". Studies indicate that young married couples have coitus on the average of three times a week. This figure drops to twice a week by the age of 30, once every 4 days by the age of 40, and once every 12 days by the age of 60. Because these figures are averages, they tend to obscure the wide range of variation that exists from couple to couple (*G.A. Encyclopaedia*, 1983: 231).

The Conceptual Model

Studies of sexuality were restricted hitherto because of the taboo attached to it and preventing a frank and open discussion of it. As a result, funding for research on sexuality was not liberal. Hence, studies of sexuality could not develop for a long time. However, the emergence of family planning during the last fifty years and the spread of AIDS in epidemic proportions during the last two decades have not only

A CONCEPTUAL MODEL ON SEXUALITY AND IMPLICATION

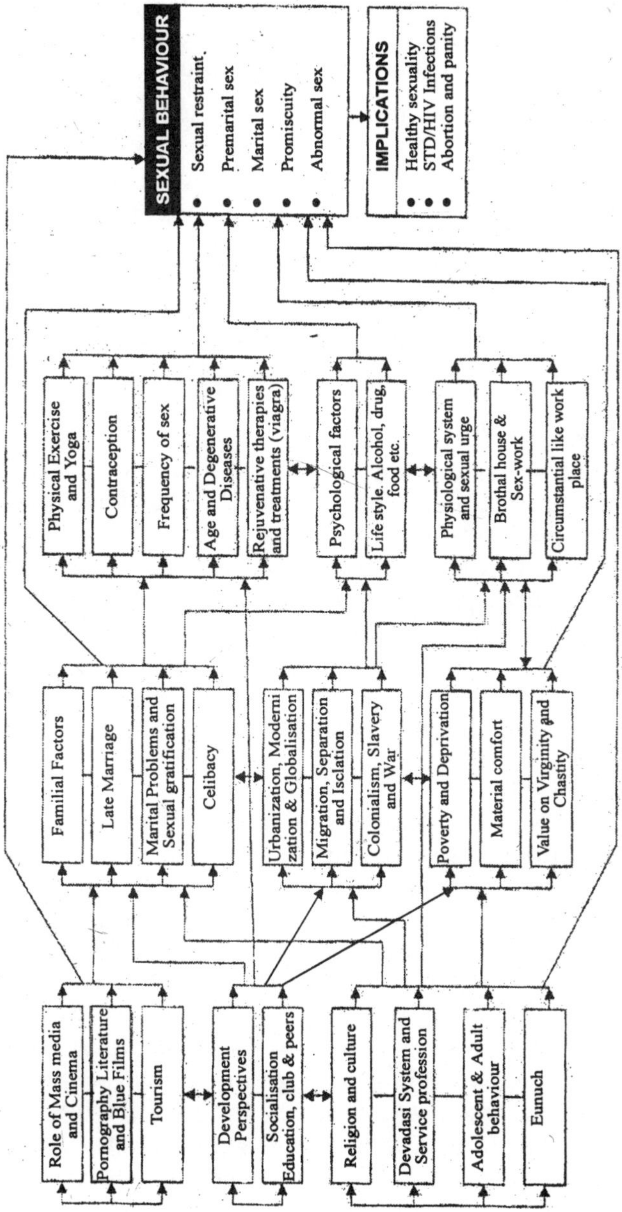

K. MAHADEVAN

weakened the taboo against it but the urgent need to give high priority for empirical research on it has begun to be realised. Even the sufficient literature has not been generated, so far, on this subject in India.

This conceptual model presented here has been, however, formulated on the basis of the meagre literature available and interaction with behavioural scientists and peripheral health and family planning workers, besides depending on certain evaluative studies carried out among sex-workers. On the basis of the available scientific evidence on the determinants of sexuality, most of the causal factors have been critically considered on their direct and indirect relationship with the dependent variable.

Dependent Variables

Sexual behaviour has several dimensions, since it is diverse and complex. The commonly accepted form of it is sex with ones spouse. But the less accepted but practised one is sex with commercial sex-workers. These two types may be pre-marital or during the marital period. Of course extra-marital sex can also be there with the other women in addition to commercial sex-workers. Yet there is another type of sexual behaviour which is called abnormal sex. It may take the form of homosexuality, masturbation, oral sex, and bestiality.

Pre-marital Sex

Although pre-marital sex is not approved in traditional societies, under the changing social institutions in several countries, pre-marital sex persists in a surreptitious manner. However, in the Scandinavian countries, Europe and North America, no longer pre-marital sex is frowned upon or disfavoured. In fact, some parents encourage their children to have dates before marriage. In Asian countries, brides and grooms and their parents frown upon dating. In fact, virginity shall enjoy very great respect among most communities. The major causes for pre-marital sex are westernization, industrialization, co-education, the impact of the spreading commercial mass media, entertainment, and social changes taking place in the institutions of family marriage, and religion.

Extra-marital Sex

Extra-marital sex has persisted and reached the present level because of social change. Historically there was free sex, before the evolution of the institution of marriage and family. However, social control of family and kinship led to the decline of extra-marital sex for several centuries. But, industrialization, colonialism, slavery, warfare, globalisation etc. have brought back into vogue extra-marital sex. In addition, to these factors, there are several other variables mentioned in the conceptual model given here, which are responsible for extra-marital sex. In recent times, commercial sex workers are organising themselves to institutionalised prostitution as a way of life under the emerging socio-economic and technological change both in the developed and developing countries. But the imminent threat of AIDS may arrest this trend, and commercial sex workers will be made at least regulate to their activity using condom and the other safety measures. Abolition of prostitution seems an impossible task, though desirable.

Independent Variables

Several independent variables are plotted here based on their expected relationship, direct or indirect like psychological variables and life-style variables have very great and immediate influence on sexuality. The other categories of possible variables are the physiological growth factors and age. These bio-demographic factors have direct influence over the years. Physiological factor like hormonal change and nervous debility have profound influence on even desire for sex and potency and the psychological desire itself. As age advances a corresponding decline in sexual frequency and ability is well established.

Parallel to these factors lies the frequency of sex, which is related to the bio-demographic factors and they influence sexuality either independently or jointly. Life-style factors and age can cause the degeneration of sexual organs and associated aspects, which in turn can adversely affect the efficiency and even the functioning of the sexual act. Such degeneration can be partially or fully corrected using medicines of different systems listed later on in this paper.

Infections, HIV and the other morbidity conditions can affect the sexual act, and so also the side effects of certain rejuvenating and aphrodisiac medicines. Along with these, possible variables are the concepts of virginity and chastity. They are in fact powerful sexual restrains. They are apt to change with changes taking place in society, mostly under the influence of urbanization, industrialization and globalisation and feminist movements. Historical factors like colonialism, warfare and the other independent factors listed earlier can also affect their influence. Therefore, some of these possible and probable variables may directly and proximately affect the sexual act [see figure on conceptual model].

Behind the imminent variables mentioned above there are two other sets or blocks of independent variables. One of them consists of variables such as social, circumstantial, brothel house and commercial sex workers, psychological and life style factors, which are behavioural and economic in their character. At the beginning lies two blocks of communication, entertainment (mass media and tourism) and pornographic literature variables. These materials and opportunity have a direct influence on sex and they may also affect indirectly through the subsequent variables like social opportunity, circumstantial situation and so on. Parallel to these factors are the familial, marital, institutional, individual factors and culture of adolescence, eunuchism and so on. These lists of variables are not complete and future research may unravel the other variables. The nature and extent of the influence of these known variables can be established on a cross-cultural and national basis after further investigation. A holistic understanding of the influence of these independent variables on the dependent variables of sexual act and their implications has become urgent and must be given very high priority now also in the context of the need for expanding family planning and preventing the impending dangers of AIDS epidemics.

Religion and Sexuality

Among the several religions of the world, Hinduism has several myths and legends about romantic and glamorous episodes in the lives of Gods and Goddesses. No other religion has in its myths so many divine and semi-devine being livings such a colourful life.

Of the three gods, Brahma, Vishnu, Shiva, who form the Trinity or Trimurtis. Shiva is projected as a foremost romantic deity. In fact the very worship of Shivalingam (Phallus) is based on a recognition of the power of his physiology and his procreative power. Interestingly his famous rhythmic dance the *Tandava*, itself manifests his romantic life. According to one myth he obtained progenies in three different ways. Of course Lord Muruga (Subrahmanya) was born to him through his wife, Parvathy. He begot another son, Lord Aiyappa in a charming lady, who was incarnated through the power of Lord Vishnu. He also adopted Ganesa as his son. Lord Krishna, the eighth incarnation of Lord Vishnu, was an equally romantic divinity, whose life was full of several romantic episodes of love, music and dance. Therefore, religious art, life-style and values of Hinduism permit the Hindus to take a flexible and liberal view of sex and reproduction. But it is not the case with the other religions. For instance, Buddhism lays, emphasis on a pious religious and non-romantic life and so do Jainism, Sikhism, and Christianity. However, Islam presents a different picture. The very fact of Nabi marrying a lady far older than himself and the practice of universal polygamy reveal a very liberal sexuality. Therefore. Religion has a commendable influence on sexuality of the followers of different faiths.

The institution of Devadasis, (Servants of God) were dancers got attached to temples for entertainment during festivals and ritual functions. The Devadasi formed a part of the functionaries of temple duties. The stone carving of Khajuraho and the temple at Konark in Orissa, depict several manifestations of complex sexual behaviour. Similarly ancient Hindu temples such as the Lingaraj temple in Bhubaneswar and Padmanabhaswamy temple in Trivandrum depict several scenes of sexuality. They indicate a healthy recognition and acceptance of the sex urge and sexuality.

Not only the famous temples mentioned, but many other temples, big and small, all over India have sculptures about the intimate relationship between man and woman. This means that the carvings were originally inspired by *Tantric* worship in which sex is carved as a means to salvation and closely followed the *Kamasastra* of *Vatsyayanan* with regard to details. One explanation for the presence of the such 'sex' figures on the walls of temples is that they separately and together suggest the enormous and boundless creative energy of the creator who presides on the sanctums of each temple. In addition to human 'romantic' figures, a variety of flora and fauna are also carved in the temple walls, because they also are a part of the plenitude of creation. The erotic sculptures in temple do not reflect the sex practices in everyday life, but indicate the attitude to sex to which a certain sanctity is expected to be attached because of their depiction in temples.

Chastity

However, the major deterrent that restricts aberrant sexual behaviour stems from the cultural value of chastity. During the prehistoric and early historical periods promiscuous life was the order of the day. Data is not available to establish when the value of chastity developed in our society. Chastity was deep-rooted in most countries of Asia, but it started losing its hold during the second half of 20th century with the impact of frequent urbanization, migration, international interaction and globalisation. Nevertheless, chastity remains even now as a strong deterrent to regulate sexual behaviour in several communities and sub-cultural groups in the Asian countries. In fact chastity is very dear to most bridegrooms and their parents as a major determinant of selection of a bride no matter whether the bride observed it during her adolescent and early adult periods.

In addition to chastity, celibacy, resulting from its religious institutionalization mostly among the Hindus, Buddhists, Jains and Christians, continues to be a major restraint against sexual permissiveness. Of course, one may practice celibacy as a personal philosophy. Apart from chastity as a value and institutional control of sexuality by monk/priest/nuns, social control stemming from familial interactions have controlled sexual behaviour considerably. Morphological manifestation, resulting from dress patterns of ghosa/veil, in fact, is intended to serve as a major barrier against pre-marital and extra-marital sex. When chastity was very dear to most people there used to be a saying in Kerala that when a woman is alone even in the Kitchen, man should not enter alone. Such restrictions and taboos in movements have been slowly given up with the impact of modernization/ westernization and the other facets of social change.

Familial and Marital Variables

Familial and social control has very great influence in socializing people during childhood and adolescence to develop chastity and celibacy. As a result of social control in family, sexual restraint may be inculcated among the adolescent and youth population. However, broken families cannot have hold over the members of kinship network and consequently people may not follow normative behaviour. Normative behaviour is enforced generally in joint and extended families.

Institution of marriage normally progresses in the family environment. In fact late marriage and celibacy cannot be followed without the role of the other family members. Therefore, family and marriage together have considerable influence to regulate sexuality. In fact delay in marriage may lead to indulgence in pre-marital sex. Similarly marital problems lead to extra-marital sex. Therefore these four facets of related variables may contribute to different types of conjugal relationship depending upon the situation and circumstances.

Poverty and Prostitution

According to recent study of sex workers near the Theni District in Tamil Nadu the single most important factor for the sex workers to follow their present avocation is poverty. As a result of poverty some times widows, divorced and separated women are forced to seek sex work to make a living. They are compelled to take up this unhealthy profession sometimes by the pressure of their own poor husbands to look after their poor children and their development.

In fact prostitution also developed under colonialism and slavery. The Anglo Indian community in India is an off shoot of colonialism. The negros slaves immigrated to North America produced the mulattos (Hybrid population). When the Americans fought the war in Vietnam several hundreds of parentless children were born. They may be circumstantial, situational and also due to the prevailing work culture. In any case these factors individually and together promote extra-marital sex and sex workers on a universal basis.

Culture and Sexuality

Already the role of religion as a cultural variable and its influence on sexuality has been discussed. There are other cultural variables also for different stages of life. In fact the culture of the adolescent population is a very uncrystallised state of affairs. Similarly the Eunuchs have their own culture and sexuality. In fact they are found to be a major source of infection of HIV according the field experiences of voluntary Health Services (VHS), an important, NGO working in Adayar in Chennai city (Krishnamoorthy, 1998).

Different types of clubs located mostly in urban and industrial areas have their own culture. First instance, they have a liberal life style and cosmopolitan culture, use of alcohol and drugs and dance of both sexes together are a part of the life style in night clubs. In fact under the impact of alcohol, extra-marital sex is likely to take place, wherever there is feasibility. These factors together differentially affect sexuality.

Mass Media and Sexuality

Mass media notably the cinema, blue films, the television, radio, pornographic literature, and the other print media like romantic novels, poetry, songs, drama and so on are powerful media, which sprout ideas and desire for sexuality. Sexologists have reported that after seeing a romantic feature film or after seeing a blue film, or reading a romantic novel or after listening to music over tones of love, youngsters and couple resort to courtship, cohabitation and connubial relationship. It is well-known that blue films are intended for providing enjoyment with or without subsequent sex. However, feature films in the past were not generally intended to provide vicarious satisfaction of sex. But the feature films produced during the last half a century in English, French, German, Spanish and in Asian languages have begun to have a pronounced overtone of love themes, music and dance. In India, Hindi and Tamil projects excessively love making scenes in them, and film songs have begun to have sexual suggestions. In fact the Tamil word *Kathal* (love) has become a byword to teenagers and youths for permissive, loose pre-marital sex now. Western societies have become a model for them to imitate. However, classical romantic films produced in Bengali and Malayalam are of a higher order and are intellectual feasts.

Modernisation and Migration

As a result of modernization several sequential change have taken place in ecology, residential set-up, employment and trade. When people become modern they migrate from rural to urban areas and then migrate further to far off places like the Punjabis and Keralites migrating to Canada and the Gulf countries. As a result of migration urbanisation will grow, urbanisation and migration for employment take place, familial separation and isolation takes place. Prolonged separation leads to both husband and wife resort to extra-marital sex to get the basic gratification of sex. In urban areas, separated or migrating husbands may be tempted or induced to go to brothel house, when liquor/drug add to their pleasure seeking pursuits. This is how sequentially social change either directly or indirectly affects sexuality.

Migration, Separation/Isolation

Generally migration whether it is temporary or long-term, local or to a far away place leads to temporary or prolonged separation of married couple and also may give rise to a sense of isolation, loneliness and large scale and long-term employment of men from Kerala in several Gulf countries has paved the way for extended separation of men from their spouses. When their wives are young or middle aged and have to live in isolation, opportunities and temptations for clandestine cohabitation are plenty. Added to this, changed residential living, better intake of food, and viewing romantic TV serials and cinemas, and availability of bachelors and poly cohabitating married men, facilitate extra-marital relationships. Incidence of such relationships is on the increase, as there is a parallel weakening of the value of chastity. This obvious multiple factors simultaneously operate for the increased incidence of promiscuous sex.

Temporary/short-term migration resulting from travel in transport, particularly among truck drivers, either under the influence of liquor or without it, promotes sex with sex-workers, when they are on their way. In fact it has been well established that truck drivers constitute a major category of high-risk group, who promote HIV infections, according to the study of AIDS awareness projects in India (Krishnamoorthy, 2000).

Separation of couple, whether it is long or short, affects the basic biological need of both men and women. However, women overcome such needs through their inherent self-control and the hold of convention. However, men are relatively weak in self-control. Such men succumb to situational attractions and chances leading to extra-marital sex including sex with sex workers. Therefore, during the socialization process measures to develop self-control have to be developed to overcome the weakness of couples resulting from separation and isolation.

Alcohol and Sex

Moderate use of alcohol mostly practised by men folk is believed to encourage gratification in cohabitation. In fact such sexual inducement, plasibo effect very often result in extra-marital sex and increase in frequency of sex. In fact alcoholism paves the way for indiscriminate sex and prostitution. When men are separated from their wives or the relationship between couples is strained, alcoholism promotes extra-marital sex including prostitution. Among labourers, alcoholism increases frequency of sex. For instance near Gorakhpur (UP state) an illiterate labourer who was habituated to taking liquor frequently, invariably resorted to sex with his wife, irrespective of her willingness and convenience, including during the menses period. Whenever the wife resisted she used to be beaten by the husband and raped. Such instances are very common among the poor and less educated/illiterate population.

Aphrodisiac

In many communities, conscious efforts are adopted to consume certain food items that stimulate sex and to avoid some others to resist stimulation. For example certain food items are avoided by the Brahmins to avoid sex stimulants. It is believed that drumsticks can stimulate the sexual urge. Similarly, dates and cashew nut are also considered to be such stimulants. Anthropological and Home science literature provides a list of several other food items, which have sex stimulants.

Sexual Degeneration

Generally sexual degeneration takes place slowly with ageing. But when people over-indulge in sex during the period of youth, later on sexual disinterest may develop and degeneration can take place as age advances. In addition, physiological and psychological factors can also cause different associated factors with sexuality. For instance, any reduction or blockade of blood flow into the sex organ and nervous trouble, to sex organs etc., can affect the sexual urge and ability in due course. Gender-wise, sexual urge varies considerably. For women, with the onset of menopause sexual urge may decline but for men normally the urge goes on not up to the 45th year as in women and may decline after sixty years and in exceptional cases, it can occur even earlier. Among women, testosterone, male hormone and its quantity can affect the sexual urge. Yet another factor that creates the mood for sex is the endofinse hormone secreted in the brain. Psychological factors like anxiety, fear, wrong perception of wife and close consanguineous relative with whom sex is forbidden can also adversely affect sexual disinterest and disfunction. According to Pramod, a serologist and sex therapist in Kerala, the single most important cause for various sex problems are the above-mentioned psychological problems (Vanitha, 2001). This expert attributes up to 80 per cent of the difficulty to indulge in sex to various psychic problems. Morphological attraction of either party like beauty, display of sex stimulating dress also can instantly increase the sexual urge. In fact more research is needed to explore further crucial factors associated with sexual behaviour. Thus mental condition, physiological health and growth, hormonal secretion, physical attraction and several other factors individually and collectively can affect the sexual urge or its absence for different people.

Sexual Regeneration/Rectification

Appropriate counselling by a competent sexologist is the primary therapy recommended by an endocrinologist, Jayakumar (Vanith, 2001). Because the single most causal factor for the lack of sexual urge, are various psychological problems. He holds that 80 per cent of such problems are due to psychic factors. Today the most popular drug widely used to increase sexual potency is Viagra. In recent times several other Viagra type Indian drugs namely Juan, Edega, Andros, Caverta, Erix, Penegra, are marketed to improve sexual potency. However, even Viagra may not be fully effective if anxiety and fear persist in the couple. However, several attractive/advertisements projected to improve sexual desire and ability are reported to be defective. The hormone namely Prolactin produced by the pituitary gland of the brain can stimulate sexual urge, however, its increase in production can reduce sexual interest. In fact regular physical exercise giving rise to health fitness and can rejuvenate normal sexual health.

Certain medicines particularly of Ayurveda, Siddha, Unani and Yoga exercises, certain food habits mentioned elsewhere in this paper, can improve the sexual urge and interest. Certain diseases particularly diabetics mellitus, blood pressure and heart disease can reduce the sexual urge due to degeneration of the nerves and poor physical health. Similarly the side effects of certain medicines used to cure certain diseases can also reduce the sexual urge.

Ayurveda and Siddha systems claims to have certain therapies for rejuvenation. For instance, the Kizhi and the ppu, two types, of massage with a medicated ball soaked in lukewarm oil and exclusive oil receptively used for massage certainly rejuvenate overall health. Normally they are done for 7 to 9 days and repeated annually and at least for three consecutive years. Such rejuvenating therapies are effective not only for toning up over all health but also for the regeneration of sexual potency. In addition to these measures Ayurveda recommends certain oral therapies. Chaturjatha Rasayanam, Narasimha Rasayanam and Aswaganthaam are recommended. Dabur company market Shilajit for sexual potency, an Ayruvedic medicine. In addition, certain roots, fruits and minerals are also prescribed for strengthening sexual efficiency and health. They are, roots of palm tree, drumstick, trace elements of gold etc. In fact Ayurveda has several well-developed therapies for physical rejuvenation. It has also well-established erotological rehabilitative therapies. However, metallic trace elements used in them may have side effects, if they are not processed properly by the Physicians. Siddha is only a derivative of Ayurveda. This indigenous system recommends a number of medicines without any side effects. They are Sanjeevi Lehyam, Dhathupushti Rasayanam etc. However, according to Siddha concept, these medicines have only a limited effect to improve the sexual efficiency in old people.

Ageing and Sexual Ability

Adolescents and adults have generally very great desire for sex and sexual potency. It varies according to gender after middle age. A person can look back and evaluate how he/she has changed the frequency of sex, a decade after marriage can be noticed. For example during the first decade of married life frequency of sex is at its highest. It may range from daily and alternate days, to a couple of times during every week and so on depending upon the social situation, mindset, social background, health and situational feasibility.

However, in the case of women as age advances and after a few conceptions, some of them lose their interest in sex. It might be due to loss of health, degeneration of the reproductive system including overwork, physical exhaustion, changes in the hormonal level, early onset of menopause and sex-linked diseases. In fact after menopause, which results around the age of 44, sexual urge declines in women. However, a study conducted at Tirupati revealed that mean age at menopause was around 36 years and not 44 years (Mahadevan *et al.*, 1982). However, for men normally deterioration of sexual desire and ability declines after 60 years. For them, decline and absence of erection during early morning is a symptom of degeneration of sexual potency. However, such problem may be temporary and can be corrected to a certain extent, if suitable interventions are timely adopted.

Operationalisation of this Model

Although the dependent variable has several dimensions all of them cannot be covered in a single study. In fact one of the facets of sexuality may have to be considered individually or separately based on the population choose for study based on the priority and gravity of the problem and the background of the research undertaken. Similarly the independent variables also must be carefully chosen for study based on the characteristic of the dependent variable (sub-variable) and the hypothesis has to be considered on the basis of the dependent and independent variables and the expected causal relationship based on logical reasoning, professional experience, exploratory and case studies, field experiences, discussion with resource persons and so on. In addition to the dependent variables plotted on the conceptual model, certain independent variables listed are to be considered judiciously for different studies. Normally the variable that is very close to the dependent variable have mostly direct relationship. Of course, other independent variables that lie behind the imminent variables may have either direct or indirect relationship with the dependent variable. When this model is used in future research, the order of importance of the causal factors can be established.

Implications

In the twenty first century, sexuality will have to be given very great priority in research, education and the other interventions. Because the sexual restraint that existed in the past, the importance attached to virginity, chastity and celibacy are fast declining. The casual factors for such change can be seen in the conceptual model. Variables that lie ahead and above virginity and chastity in the conceptual model have both direct and indirect influence on the value systems, which of course formed the safety value of sexuality itself. A holistic understanding of this conceptual model can help in identifying and devising suitable policies and interventions to promote permissible and safe sex in future.

References

1. Aiyappan, A. and Mahadevan, K. 1985. Ecology, Economy, Matriliny and Fertility of Kurichias, Mittal Publisher, New Delhi.
2. Encyclopaedia Britannica, Vol.14, 1973. William Berton Publisher, Chicago.
3. Grolier Academic Encyclopaedia, 1983. Grolier International, USA, 231.
4. Jayasree, R. and Parvathy, K.A. 2000. Sex workers, sexual behaviour and risk in reproductive health, (Mimeo).
5. Kanhaiah Bhelari, 2001. Viagra Falls. *The Week*, Feb. 4, 2001, pp. 50-51.

13

Analysis on Frequency of Sexual Intercourse among Married Women of Reproductive Age in China

Gao Ersheng, Wu Junqing, Chen Tikuwan and Zhang Zibao

Introduction

Sexual behaviour serves not only as the means of propagation, but also as an instinct of human beings. Physiological, social and psychological factors, such as physical status, social conventions, self-power, knowledge level and personal character can all have effects on sexual behaviour. Sexual intercourse, perhaps an indispensable component of life, is of vital importance in sexual behaviour patterns. The harmony and perfection of sexual intercourse also contribute to the stability of marriage and family. However, sex-related problems have seldom been widely recognized among Chinese women yet. Few study was concerning about the frequency of sexual intercourse among married women in China. The data of National Demography and Reproductive Health Survey (NDRHS) conducted in November 1997 were analyzed to quantify the frequency of sexual intercourse in married women of reproductive age as well as to investigate the possible affecting factors.

Methods

Sample Selection

National Demography and Reproductive Health Survey (NDRHS) in 1997 was organized by State Family Planning Committee (SFPC). The sampling was completed in two steps. In the first step, a total of 31 strata were set according to 31 provinces, municipalities and autonomous regions respectively. Each stratum was regarded as a sub-population in which multistage sampling including stratified, random, cluster sampling was applied to allocate the sampling unit. Villager or citizen groups were the smallest sampling unit in all the provinces, municipalities and autonomous regions except in Tibet where village served as the smallest sampling unit. The inhabitants in the selected groups or villages amount to 180,000 in total, their demographic characteristics and related information were all acquired. In the second step, all the women of reproductive age enrolled in the first step were considered as the population, then the sampling probability and the number of the women to be further inquired in every sampling unit were calculated. After the sampling probability was set, systematic sampling was employed to determine the subjects for further survey, the sample size here was 15,213 including married and unmarried ones. Actually, a total of 12,305 married women of reproductive age were surveyed, in which 10,948 responded. The data of these 10,948 subjects were analyzed to quantify the frequency of sexual intercourse and to investigate the possible affecting factors.

Statistical Analysis

All the data had been censored by SFPC before statistical analysis with SAS software. Non-parametric test was applied to analyze the possible affecting factors at first, then we select multi-category ordered non-conditional logistic regression analysis to evaluate these possible affecting factors. According to sexual intercourse frequency, three categories were classified: equal to or greater than 6 times per month, 3 to 5 times per month and 0 to 2 times per month.

Results

A total of 12,305 married women of reproductive age were surveyed using self-completion questionnaire, in which 10,948 finished the investigation. The response rate was 88.97 per cent. Because the frequency of sexual intercourse didn't fit the normal distribution, non-parametric analysis was applied instead. The median frequency of sexual intercourse of married women was 4 times per month with the quartile interval of 2 to 6 times, and the 90% confidence interval (CI) was 1 to 12 time(s) while the range was 0 to 30 time(s).

Frequency of Sexual Intercourse in Married Women of Reproductive Age with Different Characteristics

Frequency of sexual intercourse among married women with different demographic characteristics

The women with different residence registration type, dwelling area, age, nationality and education level had different frequencies of sexual intercourse ($P<0.0001$). Rural women had a higher frequency than urban ones. As far as residence region was concerned, those living in Northeast China were the most active, whereas those in Southern China the least. The frequency of sexual intercourse decreased as age went up. Women with the education level of junior high school showed the highest frequency of sexual intercourse while the illiterate the lowest. Minority women had a higher frequency of sexual intercourse than Han women did (Table 1).

Frequency of sexual intercourse among married women by husbands' demographic characteristics

The frequency of sexual intercourse in married women varied if their husbands' nationality or education level was different ($P<0.0001$). Those women with minority husbands had a higher frequency of sexual intercourse than the women whose husbands were Hans did. As to husbands' education level, the women whose husbands had the education level of junior high school had the highest frequency while those with illiterate husbands had the lowest (Table 2).

Table 1: Frequency of Sexual Intercourse among Married Women with Different Demographic Characteristics (Times Per Month)

Variable	N	Median	Quartile interval	Mean score	χ^2	P
Residence registration type						
Rural	8453	4	2-6	5579.70	41.70	0.0001
Urban	2495	4	2-6	5118.09		
Residence region						
Northern China	1577	4	2-6	5447.37	45.89	0.0001
Northeast China	1032	4	2-7	5839.07		
Eastern China	3288	4	2-6	5361.87		
Southern China	2842	4	2-6	5298.48		
Southwest China	1544	4	2-7	5821.30		
Northwest China	665	4	2-6	5462.18		
Age (years)						
15~	900	6	3-10	6816.87	1309.10	0.0001
25~	2373	5	3-8	6485.84		
30~	2433	4	3-7	6110.13		
35~	1645	4	3-6	5514.44		
40~	1959	3	2-5	4493.87		
45~49	1638	2	1-4	3562.88		
Nationality						
Han	9962	4	2-6	5423.17	20.13	0.0001
Minority	986	4	3-7	5909.19		
Education level						
Illiterate	2596	3	2-5	4608.84	280.81	0.0001
Primary school	3515	4	2-6	6556.10		
Junior high school	3264	4	3-7	5936.33		
≥ Senior high school	1575	4	2-6	5539.18		

Variable	N	Median	Quartile interval	Mean score	χ^2	P
Marital status						
In first marriage	10661	4	2-6	5483.46	3.313	0.0687
Remarried	287	4	2-6	5141.85		
Financial aid						
Need	881	4	3-6	566.88	3.60	0.0577
Not need	10067	4	2-6	5457.66		

Table 2: Frequency of Sexual Intercourse among Married Women by Husbands' Demographic Characteristics (Times Per Month)

Variable	N	Median	Quartile interval	Mean score	χ^2	P
Husbands' nationality						
Han	10048	4	2-6	5430.06	24.52	0.0001
Minority	900	4	3-8	5970.61		
Husbands' education level						
Illiterate	718	3	2-5	4482.01	107.77	0.0001
Primary school	3130	4	2-6	5375.77		
Junior high school	4696	4	2-7	5731.04		
≥ Senior high school	2404	4	2-6	5398.34		

Frequency of Sexual Intercourse among Married Women by Marital Characteristics

The frequency of sexual intercourse varied with many factors. Duration of marriage, length of living together with husband and satisfaction degree in sexual behaviour could influence the frequency. At the same time, the capability of proposing or refusing a sexual intercourse affected the frequency too. Besides, gynaecological symptoms, regular gynaecological examinations, visiting the family planning service centre and participating in antenuptial education also had their impacts on the frequency of sexual intercourse.

The frequency of sexual intercourse declined when years of marriage increased. The longer did they live together with husband, the higher was the frequency of sexual intercourse. Those who thought it possible for a woman to propose a sexual intercourse had a higher frequency than those thinking it impossible did. Those who thought it possible for a woman to refuse a sexual intercourse also had a higher frequency than those who thought it impossible or remained uncertain to the question did. The frequency of sexual intercourse decreased if a woman had some mild or severe gynaecological symptoms. Those never attending gynaecological examination had a higher frequency than those attending irregularly or regularly did. Visiting family planning service centre or participating in antenuptial education would increase the frequency of sexual intercourse (Table 3).

Frequency of Sexual Intercourse among Married Women and History of Pregnancy or Abortion

The frequency of sexual intercourse differed with having or having no pregnancy or induced abortion ($P<0.05$). Those who had no pregnancy had more sexual intercourse than those having experienced pregnancy did. The women with induced abortion had a higher frequency of sexual intercourse than those without such a history did (Table 4).

Table 3: Frequency of Sexual Intercourse among Married Women by Marriage Information (Times Per Month)

Variable	N	Median	Quartile interval	Mean score	χ^2	P
Duration of marriage						
0~	2084	5	3-8	6535.48	1059.5	0.0001
6~	2852	4	3-7	6215.74		
12~	2799	4	3-6	5561.25		
18~	3213	3	2-4	4052.81		
Weeks living together with husband in the last month						
<1	365	2	1-3	3097.97	250.28	0.0001
1~	402	3	2-5	4694.83		
2~	259	4	2-6	5530.96		
3~	197	4	2-6	5281.08		
4	9725	4	2-6	5598.35		
Satisfaction degree in sexual behaviour						
Perfect	6427	4	3-7	5830.80	357.46	0.0001
Good	1982	4	2-6	5558.97		
General	1589	3	2-5	4776.80		
Bad	950	3	1-5	4054.77		
Proposing a sexual intercourse by woman						
Impossible	3224	3	2-6	4964.01	214.43	0.0001
Uncertain	879	3	2-5	4800.92		
Possible but impracticable	1991	4	2-6	5578.18		
Possible and practicable	4854	4	3-7	5893.02		

Variable	N	Median	Quartile interval	Mean score	χ^2	P
Refusing a sexual intercourse by woman						
Impossible	2166	4	2-6	5306.22	95.36	0.0001
Uncertain	630	3	2-5	4654.05		
Possible but impracticable	1283	4	3-8	6067.47		
Possible and practicable	6869	4	2-6	5492.06		
Gynaecological symptoms						
No	7465	4	2-6	5598.49	43.38	0.0001
Mild	2793	4	2-6	5277.35		
Severe	690	3	2-6	4931.09		
Gynaecological examination						
Never	7474	4	2-6	5573.71	37.17	0.0001
Irregular	1417	4	2-6	5497.77		
Regular	2057	4	2-5	5097.99		
Visiting family planning service centre						
Yes	4408	4	3-7	5860.19	111.53	0.0001
No	6540	4	2-6	5214.54		
Participating in antenuptial education						
No	9852	4	2-6	5371.55	105.98	0.0001
Yes	1096	5	3-8	6399.96		

Table 4: Frequency of Sexual Intercourse among Married Women and History of Pregnancy or Abortion (Times Per Month)

Variable	N	Median	Quartile interval	Mean score	χ^2	P
History of pregnancy						
Yes	10655	4	2-6	5418.23	128.08	0.0001
No	293	6	4-10	7520.86		
History of induced abortion						
Yes	3631	4	2-6	5373.32	4.54	0.0331
No	7024	4	2-6	5240.33		

Multiple Analysis on Frequency of Sexual Intercourse in Married Women of Reproductive Age

The frequency of sexual intercourse was set as the dependent variable, and the demographic characteristic of the subjects or their husbands, antenuptial education, times of induced abortion and contraceptives were set as independent variables in multi-category ordered logistic regression model. The three categories of frequency involved were equal to or greater than 6 times per month, 3 to 5 times per month and 0 to 2 times per month according to the frequency of sexual intercourse.

Our results showed that those having urban residence registration, being older, living shorter together with husband in the last month, showing general or no satisfaction toward sexual behaviour, never hearing of sexually transmitted disease had less times of sexual intercourse per month. In contrast, those living in Northeast or Southeast China, being minority, having a higher education level, living together with husband all the month, thinking it possible for a woman to propose a sexual intercourse or using contraceptive had a higher frequency of sexual intercourse (Table 5).

Discussion

All the investigators of this study were female of grassroots family planning service centres, and they all received stepwise training by SFPC. The response rate of the study was about to 90 per cent, so the subjects were representative to the frequency of sexual intercourse in married women of reproductive age in China.

Our results showed the median frequency of sexual intercourse was 4 times per month, and the quartile interval was 2 to 6 times while the range 0 to 30 time(s). Another study in Zhongshan, Guangdong Province showed the frequency of sexual intercourse in married women of reproductive age was 4.18 times per month through a survey of 3,340 subjects in 1995.[1] However, a survey of 104 married women in Guilin, Guangxi Province revealed that the frequency of sexual intercourse in married women was 8.8 times per month with the range of 0 to 28 time(s).[2] Although differing from the results in Guilin, our results were similar

Table 5: Multivariable Logistic Regression Analysis on Frequency of Sexual Intercourse in Married Women

Variable	Comparison group	Reference group	Regression coefficient	Standard error	P	OR	95 per cent CL[#]	
							Lower	Upper
Residence registration type	Urban	Rural	-0.4269	0.0569	0.0001	0.653	0.584	0.729
Dwelling area	Northeast China	Northern China	0.2216	0.0653	0.0007	1.248	1.097	1.420
	Southeast China	Northern China	0.3239	0.0566	0.0001	1.382	1.236	1.547
Age	25-29	15-24	-0.3768	0.0782	0.0001	0.686	0.587	0.802
	30-34	15-24	-0.6308	0.0806	0.0001	0.532	0.453	0.625
	35-39	15-24	-0.9401	0.0872	0.0001	0.391	0.329	0.464
	40-44	15-24	-1.4531	0.0858	0.0001	0.234	0.197	0.277
	45-49	15-24	-1.8805	0.0883	0.0001	0.153	0.128	0.182
Nationality	minority	Han	0.2538	0.0676	0.0002	1.289	1.128	1.473
Education level	Primary school	Illiterate	0.2512	.0.0535	0.0001	1.286	1.157	1.428
	Junior high school	Illiterate	0.2826	0.0606	0.0001	1.327	1.178	1.494
	≥ Senior high school	Illiterate	0.2509	0.0792	0.0015	1.285	1.101	1.500
Weeks living together with husband in the last month	<1	0	-1.5125	0.1443	0.0001	0.220	0.166	0.292
	1-2	0	-0.4681	0.133	0.0004	0.626	0.482	0.813
	4	0	0.2662	0.0932	0.0043	1.305	1.085	1.570
Satisfaction toward sexual behaviour	General	Perfect	-0.3800	0.0541	0.0001	0.684	0.615	0.760
	Never	Perfect	-0.7241	0.0703	0.0001	0.485	0.421	0.557
Woman propose a sexual behaviour	Possible but impracticable	Impossible	0.1722	0.0546	0.0016	1.188	1.067	1.322
	Possible and practicable	Impossible	0.3101	0.0443	0.0001	1.364	1.250	1.487
Current Contraceptive	Sterilization	Not use	0.6248	0.0646	0.0001	1.868	1.642	2.125
	IUD	Not use	0.5542	0.0626	0.0001	1.740	1.535	1.974
	OC[##] or spermicide	Not use	0.4899	0.0940	0.0001	1.632	1.357	1.964
Sexually transmitted disease	Hadn't heard	Had heard	-0.2628	0.0443	0.0001	0.769	0.705	0.839

[#] Confidence limits [##] Oral contraceptive.

to that in Zhongshan, season difference or sample characteristics might account for the discrepancy.

It is showed that urban females had a lower monthly frequency of sexual intercourse than the rural ones did (OR=0.653, 95% CI was 0.584 to 0.729). Minority women had a higher frequency than Han women did (OR=1.289, 95% CI was 1.128 to 1.473). Perhaps it was related to the physical conditions and amateur culture amusement which differed in the rural or minority area and urban or Hans' inhabitance area. Also it was found that the frequency of sexual intercourse tended to decline while the age and years in marriage going up, perhaps it was because of the increasing of physiological, psychological and family burden.

Gynaecological sickness also affected the frequency of sexual intercourse. Those without gynaecological symptoms showed a higher frequency than the women with these symptoms did. Participating in gynaecological examination or visiting family planning service centre had increased the frequency of sexual intercourse, perhaps it was because of the timely treatment of gynaecological diseases. Age, physical status and psychological factors were considered to contribute to the decrease of the frequency of sexual intercourse in women with a history of pregnancy or induced abortion. The longer one lived together with his husband in the last month, the more times she had sexual intercourse. It was concluded that improving the women's health and treating their gynaecological disease would influence the frequency of sexual intercourse.

Our results also showed that those who were satisfied with sexual life had more sexual intercourse than those who were not satisfied did. With the decrease of satisfaction degree in sexual life, the frequency of sexual intercourse descended too (general satisfaction versus perfect satisfaction, OR=0.684, 95% CI was 0.615 to 0.760; no satisfaction versus perfect satisfaction, OR=0.485, 95% CI was 0.421 to 0.557). Those who answered "possible and practicable" to the question whether a women can propose a sexual intercourse showed a higher frequency of sexual intercourse than those who answered "impossible" did (OR=1.364, 95% CI was 1.250 to 1.487). Similarly, those who answered "possible and practicable" to the question whether a women can refuse a sexual intercourse showed a higher frequency of sexual intercourse than those who answered "impossible" did. It was inferred that the satisfaction degree toward sexual intercourse and the role of women in sexual behaviour directly influence the frequency of sexual intercourse.

References

1. He, J.L. and Zhu J.M. 1996. An investigation on the frequency of sexual intercourse in 3340 married women of reproductive age and its affecting factors. Sexology, 5 (4): 3-4.
2. He, Z.P., Yu, Y.G., and Chen, Y.P. *et al.* 1991. A sexual psychology and sexual behaviour survey in 104 married women. J Chinese Psychological Health, 5 (3): 128-129.

14

Attitudes towards Antenuptial Sexual Behaviour among Chinese Women of Reproductive Age

Chen Tikuwan, Wu Junqing, Tao Jianguo and Gao Ersheng

Introduction

Antenuptial sexual behaviour in China has been rising since the last decades. The pregnancy of unmarried women and induced abortion not only do harm to their health, but also make negative impact on the family and society. It has aroused general concern in various circles. Although many factors are involved, the attitudes of the women themselves to antenuptial sexual behaviour play an important role in it. Few studies had been concerned with the attitude to the antenuptial sexual behaviour. Based on the data of national "Demography and Reproductive Health Survey" conducted by the State Family Planning Commission (SFPC) in 1997, the attitudes to and the influencing factors of antenuptial sexual behaviour were analyzed so as to provide some recommendation for decreasing and preventing antenuptial pregnancy and abortion.

Materials and Methods

Data employed in this paper were derived from "Demography and Reproductive Health Survey" in 1997, executed by SFPC. The whole survey was divided into two stages. A stratified, three-phase, cluster and probability proportional sampling method was adopted in the first stage to select subjects from thirty-one provinces/municipalities in China. All of registered and emigrant population at the sampling sites was surveyed about the basic information. Childbearing women registered in the first stage were used as sampling frame in the second stage. 15,213 woman of childbearing age were interviewed using the questionnaire. The collected data were entered into the computers first, and then issued by SFPC after being checked and pooled together. The attitudes of childbearing women to antenuptial sexual behaviour (ASB) were analyzed with one way analysis and multi-variable analysis by SAS software.

Results

Whether the ASB was acceptable was analyzed. Among 15,213 surveyed women, 12.6% agreed with it, 7.1% were uncertain about it and 80.3% disagreed with it.

The Attitudes of Women to Antenuptial Sexual Behaviour

The attitudes towards ASB by different characteristics of women

Registered permanent residence, residence area, age, education level, marital status of women are influencing factors of the attitude to ASB, statistically significant ($P<0.05$) (Table1).

The proportion of agreement (PA) in women of urban resident area was higher than that in women of rural resident areas. The proportion was the highest in East China, and that was the lowest in North China. The PA tended to increase with the rising of education years. As to the marriage status, the PA was the highest in divorced women, and that was the lowest in unmarried women.

The attitudes towards ASB among women whose husbands with different characteristics

The proportion of agreement in the women whose husbands were Han nationality was significantly higher than that of the minorities (Table 2).

The attitudes towards ASB among women with different knowledge of sexual health

Whether they had ever heard of STDs and AIDS, the score in the knowledge about the transmission of AIDS and

Table 1: The Attitudes Towards ASB by Women With Different Geographical Characteristics (%)

Variable	N	Agree	Uncertain	Disagree	$\chi^2_{M\text{-}H}$	P
Registered permanent residence						
Urban	11668	12.06	6.80	81.14	20.41	0.001
Rural	3545	14.41	8.04	77.55		
Area of residence						
North China	2215	8.76	4.92	86.32	107.97	0.001
Northeast China	1342	10.28	4.40	85.32		
East China	4467	15.58	7.39	77.03		
South China	3980	13.47	7.51	79.02		
Southwest China	2214	11.61	9.89	78.50		
Northwest China	995	9.75	6.33	83.92		
Age (years)						
15~	1620	6.17	11.48	82.35	5.17	0.023
20~	1944	13.07	7.61	79.32		
25~	2881	15.41	7.67	76.92		
30~	2776	16.17	5.76	78.06		
35~	1840	12.39	6.36	81.25		
40~	2223	11.11	5.22	83.67		
45~	1929	10.16	6.79	83.05		
Nationality						
Han	13797	12.74	7.06	80.20	1.74	0.187
Minority	1416	11.30	7.42	81.29		
Education level						
Illiteracy	3249	10.80	8.80	80.39	4.95	0.026
Primary school	4546	12.65	6.80	80.55		
Secondary school	4892	13.41	5.81	80.78		
>=High school	2526	13.30	7.92	78.78		
Marital status						
Unmarried	2695	8.42	1069	80.89	21.38	0.001
Firstly married	11977	13.47	6.20	80.33		
Remarried	328	11.89	7.32	80.79		
Divorced	213	18.31	11.27	70.42		

Table 2: The Attitudes Towards ASB Among Women Whose Husbands Have Different Geographical Characteristics (%)

Variable	No. of women	Agree	Uncertain	Disagree	$\chi^2_{M\text{-}H}$	P
Nationality of husband						
Han	11256	13.64	6.23	80.14	47.09	0.030
Minority	1049	11.15	6.29	82.55		
Husband's education level						
Illiteracy	866	12.12	10.39	77.48	1.00	0.316
Primary school	3589	13.04	6.77	80.19		
Secondary school	5222	13.06	5.23	81.71		
>=High school	2628	15.11	6.13	78.77		

Table 3: The Attitudes Towards ASB Among Women With Differential Knowledge of Sexual Health (%)

Variable	N	Agree	Uncertain	Disagree	χ^2_{M-H}	P
Know about STDs						
Yes	8674	14.19	6.44	79.36	28.09	0.001
No	6422	10.53	7.79	81.69		
Know about AIDS						
No	5482	10.67	8.50	80.83	10.58	0.001
Yes H not clearly	7933	13.66	6.10	80.23		
Yes H clearly	1681	14.16	6.48	79.36		
Knowledge about the transmission of AIDS (score)						
0	6458	10.90	8.33	80.77	7.00	0.008
1~3	2188	13.57	6.81	79.62		
4~5	3742	13.90	6.68	79.42		
6~7	2708	14.25	4.51	81.24		
Knowledge about sexual health (score)						
0	83	10.84	31.33	57.83	19.21	0.001
1~3	3376	15.28	7.73	76.98		
4	5851	12.61	5.18	82.21		
5	2878	13.13	5.46	81.41		

Table 4: The Attitudes Towards ASB Among Women With Differential Pregnancy and Induced Abortion Experience (%)

Variable	N	Agree	Uncertain	Disagree	$\chi^2_{M\text{-}H}$	P
History of pregnancy						
Yes	12517	13.53	6.19	80.28	0.65	0.417
No	361	12.74	10.80	76.45		
History of induced abortion						
Yes	4044	16.49	6.48	77.03	47.55	0.001
No	8113	12.05	6.04	81.91		

the score in the knowledge about sexual health affected the women's attitude to ASB. Although the proportion of agreement in the women who had heard of STDs and AIDS was higher than that of the women who hadn't heard, their proportions of disagreement were all so high to about 80% (Table 3).

The attitudes towards ASB among women with different pregnancy and induced abortion experience

The proportion of agreement in the women who had induced abortion history was higher than that of the counterparts (P<0.001) (Table 4).

The attitudes towards ASB among women in terms of the antenuptial sexual experiences of the people around them

The antenuptial sexual experiences of the people around them were significantly associated with their attitudes (P<0.001). The more people around them had antenuptial sexual experiences thought by them, the higher the proportion of agreement was. The proportion ran from 8.20% to 28.33% (Table 5).

Table 5: The Attitudes Towards ASB Among Women in Terms of the Antenuptial Sexual Experiences of the People Around Them (%)

The antenuptial sexual experiences of the people around them	N	Agree	Uncertain	Disagree
No	4696	8.20	3.92	87.99
Several	3563	10.75	6.01	83.24
Some	1784	16.70	9.75	73.54
Common	2206	28.33	6.48	65.19
Not clear	2946	7.66	12.28	80.06
Total	15213	12.60	7.10	80.30

$\chi^2_{M\text{-}H}$ =274.12 P=0.001.

The attitudes towards ASB among women in terms of their perception on the harm of induced abortion

There is no significant difference of attitudes towards ASB among women in terms of their perception on the harm of induced abortion (Table 6).

Table 6: The Attitudes Towards ASB Among Women in Terms of Their Perception on the Harm of Induced Abortion (%)

Perception of the harm of induced abortion	N	Agree	Uncertain	Disagree
No effect	1981	14.34	5.75	79.91
Uncertainty	1778	11.36	9.96	78.68
Some	6391	14.47	5.51	80.02
Much	1892	11.79	4.70	83.51
Total	12042	12.60	7.10	80.30

$\chi^2_{M\text{-}H}=3.39$ P=0.065.

Multivariable Analysis on the Attitudes

The dependent variable was the attitude, which had three categories (agreement, uncertainty, and disagreement). The independent variables were her conditions, her husband's, the antenuptial health examination, the number of induced abortion, the methods of contraception ever used. The multinomial ordinal logistic stepwise regression analysis (Table 7) shows that women who was uncertain to answer or who could refuse the demand of sexual activities from sex partners, who resided in Southwest China or who didn't know of what the experiences of the people around them tended to disagree. Meanwhile, women who residing in East China or South China, thinking that induced abortion impact on their health, staying longer with their husbands, were able to take the initiative in sexual activities, or considering it was common of the people around them to experience sexual behaviour tended to agree.

Discussion

The study showed that Chinese women adopted steady attitudes to the ASB, 80.3% of the surveyed women disagree with it. The proportion of agreement only accounted for 12.6%. The results were not consistent with other two studies carried out in Shanghai. The study, which analyzed the attitudes of the antenuptial health examination women to the ASB in 1998, showed that 60.69% of them agreed, and only 5.77% of them disagreed with it. Another similar study

Table 7: Multivariable Analysis on the Attitudes of Women of Childbearing Age to Antenuptial Sexual Behaviour (n=15096)

Variable	Comparison group	Reference group	β	SE	P	OR	OR 95%CI	
							Lower	Upper
Area of residence	East China	North China	0.1555	0.0535	0.0036	1.168	1.052	1.297
	South China	North China	0.1152	0.0554	0.0376	1.122	1.007	1.250
	Southwest	North China	-0.1777	0.0670	0.0079	0.837	0.734	0.955
Perception on the harm of induced abortion	Have some	No	0.1585	0.0438	0.0003	1.172	1.075	1.277
How long living together with husband week	1-	0	0.5005	0.1282	0.0001	1.650	1.281	2.117
	2-	0	0.5525	0.1548	0.0004	1.738	1.280	2.344
	4	0	0.2746	0.0506	0.0001	1.316	1.192	1.454
Taking the initiative in sexual activities	Uncertainty	No	-0.3959	0.0967	0.0001	0.673	0.556	0.814
	May & succeed	No	0.1728	0.0468	0.0002	1.189	1.085	1.303
Could refuse the opposite sex's demand for sexual activities	May & succeed	No	-0.6559	0.1085	0.0001	0.519	0.418	0.644
The antenuptial sexual experiences of the people around them	Some	No	0.1431	0.0670	0.0327	1.154	1.010	1.318
	Common	No	0.9271	0.0571	0.0001	2.527	2.256	2.830
	Not clear	No	-0.4847	0.0568	0.0001	0.616	0.551	0.688

conducted in medical students from 1993 to 1994 showed that the agreement proportion of the boys and girls accounted for 87.8%, 73.7% respectively. The great difference of these studies was mainly attributed to three factors, i.e. the study location, age and education level. The two studies carried out only in Shanghai, which was a well-developed city, and most of them were less than 30 years. In our study, the women aged 15-49 years were surveyed all over the country. The rural and urban proportion accounted for 76.7% and 23.3% respectively.

Attitude is related with the individual appraisal and tendency to a certain matter or activity. It is influenced by many aspects such as society, family and school. Our study shows that the influencing factors of the attitude to the ASB include the recognition of the harm of induced abortion, the experience of the people around her they thought, the local economic level, age, education level and so on. The agreement proportion of the women who thought it was occasional or common that the people around them involved in the antenuptial sexual behaviour was higher than that of those who thought it impossible (OR 1.154, 95% CI: 1.010, 1.318, and OR 2.527, 95% CI: 2.256, 2.830). It suggests that the attitudes and behaviour of the people around her have an impact on attitude. The agreement proportion was comparably high in those who live long together with their husbands or take the initiative in sexual activities. It suggests that matrimony impact on the attitude to ASB.

It needs various strata to make joint efforts to tackle such a formidable issue as to decreasing antenuptial pregnancy and induced abortion. On one hand, we should help the youth to acquire correct goals in life, to set up correct outlooks on courtship and marriage. On the other hand, education should be strengthened to increase the youth's knowledge level on reproductive health.

Results

Whether the ASB was acceptable was analyzed. Among 15,213 surveyed women, 12.6% agreed with it, 7.1% were uncertain about it and 80.3% disagreed with it. The proportion of agreement in women of urban resident area was higher than that in women of rural resident areas. The proportion was the highest in East China, and that was the lowest in North China. The proportion of agreement tended to increase with the rising of education level. As to the marriage status, the proportion of agreement was the highest in divorced women, and that was the lowest in unmarried women. The proportion of agreement in the women whose husbands were Han nationality was significantly higher than that of the minorities. Whether they had ever heard of STDs and AIDS, the score in the knowledge about the transmission of AIDS and the score in the knowledge about sexual health affected the women's attitude to ASB. Although the proportion of agreement in the women who had heard of STDs and AIDS was higher than that of the women who hadn't heard, their proportions of disagreement were all so high to about 80%. The proportion of agreement in the women who had induced abortion history was higher than that of the counterparts. The Antenuptial sexual experiences of the people around them were significantly associated with their attitudes. The more people around them had antenuptial sexual experiences thought by them, the higher the proportion of agreement was. There is no significant difference of attitudes towards ASB among women in terms of their perception level on the harm of induced abortion. In multivariable analysis, the dependent variable was the attitude, which had three categories (agreement, uncertainty, and disagreement). The independent variables were her conditions, her husband's, the antenuptial health examination, the number of induced abortion, the methods of contraception ever used. The multinomial ordinal logistic stepwise regression analysis shows that women who was uncertain to answer or who could refuse the demand of sexual activities from sex partners, who resided in Southwest China or who didn't know of what the experiences of the people around them tended to disagree. Meanwhile, women who residing in East China or South China, thinking that induced abortion impact on their health, staying longer with their husbands, being able to take the initiative in sexual activities, or considering it was common of the people around them to experience sexual behaviour tended to agree. Conclusions and policy implications: It needs various strata to make joint efforts to tackle such a formidable issue as to decreasing antenuptial pregnancy and induced abortion. On one hand, we should help the youth to acquire correct goals in life, to set up correct outlooks on courtship and marriage. On the other hand, education should be strengthened to increase the youth's knowledge level on reproductive health.

References

1. Gao, E.S. *et al.* 1999. Analysis on attitudes and influence factors of antenuptial checked women to antenuptial sexual behaviour. Population, 1:46-51.
2. Zhao, P.F. *et al.* 1994. Analysis on the sexual concept and sexual behaviour of Shanghai medical students. Corpus on sex education. 15 13-16.
3. Pan, B.L. 1997. Investigation on the psychological and physiological state of 400 men with pre-marital sexual behaviour. China psychological health, 11 3 151-153.
4. Wu, D.C. *et al.* 1989. Investigation on sexual experience, pregnancy and abortion of unmarried women in Shanghai. China public health, 6 11 481-483.
5. Wang, J.F. 1999. The sexual behaviour, contraception method and choice to their pregnancy of women with pre-marital pregnancy in Shanghai transient population. Population research, 23 1 50-55.
6. Liu, Y.R. *et al.* 1992. Investigation on the psychological state and behaviour of women with pre-marital pregnancy. China psychological health, 6 2 79-80.

15

Community based Sex Education and Reproductive Health Service Intervention among Unmarried Youths' in China

Gao Ersheng, Lou Chaohua, Wang Bo, Shen Yan and Tu Xiaowen

This paper examines the effects of community-based sex education and reproductive health service on improvement of reproductive health knowledge and attitude towards sex-related issues among unmarried young people. The intervention intended to build awareness and offer counselling and services relating to sexuality and reproduction among unmarried youth and existing programme activities in the intervention site were supplemented by awareness building, counselling and services providing. In the control site, comparable in socio-cultural-economic and demographic characteristics to the intervention site, continued to provide standard programmes and services. In order to test the feasibility and effectiveness of the intervention, base-line surveys were conducted in both sites prior to the implementation of the intervention, and similar surveys were conducted in both sites 20 months after the intervention had been initiated. Totally, 1220 unmarried young people from the intervention site, and 1007 from the control site consented to be interviewed, and about 92% of these were re-interviewed at follow-up. Results showed that a community-base intervention program, which provides sex education and reproductive health service, can indeed increase young people's knowledge on reproductive health. The average knowledge score, which was based on the answers to 80 questions on reproduction, contraception and STDs/AIDS in the questionnaire, was 36.8 for intervention group, and 36.4 for the control at baseline, and 72.3 and 43.6 respectively at post-intervention. The intervention also had positive influence on unmarried youths' attitudes towards pre-marital sex. More subjects in the intervention group expressed less favourable attitude to pre-marital sex and believed that pre-marital induced abortion can influence, even damage their health than those in the control group. Findings suggest providing sex education and reproductive health services in community is an effective public health strategy to increase reproductive health knowledge of unmarried young people.

In China today, young people's attitudes towards sex are becoming much more liberal. More and more young people have sex before marriage, and the age at debut is declining. As a result, there has been a marked increase in the number of unplanned pregnancy and induced abortion among unmarried young people. There is also an upsurge in the incidence of sexually transmitted diseases (STDs) and a rapidly spreading in HIV infection.[1-3] However, the sexual and reproductive health education of young people in China remains poorly provided. Although general sex education for adolescents has been available in China since 1986, it has remained, for the most part, focused on physiological and psychological development, and provides little information on contraception or reproductive health services. Moreover, being affected by the traditional culture and the competition for a high proportion of students entering key senior middle schools or universities, the education in middle school is actually ignored. A lot of teachers and leaders of schools don't think sex education is necessary or important to adolescents. Most of schools spend very limited time and paid little attention on it. Besides, sex education is not regularly provided for the students in colleges and universities, and no education is provided in the communities. So, current sex education in China falls greatly behind the adolescents' physiological and psychological development and can not meet the needs of young people. The government has in the recent past recognised this gap of education and services, and is committed to expanding access to the education, information, and services for young people. Unfortunately, few well-tested examples exist of successful interventions that expand access to sex education and reproductive health service for adolescents and unmarried young adults. The objective of this paper is to report the experience of one such example of an intervention intended to provide education, information and services to unmarried youth at community level, and to explore the extent to which exposure to this programme succeeded in influencing one aspect of sexual and reproductive health, namely, improvement of knowledge on reproductive health and attitude towards sex-related issues among unmarried youth.

The Intervention

A youth-friendly intervention intended to build awareness and offer counselling and services relating to sexuality and reproduction among unmarried youth was designed and implemented in a town in Songjiang district, Shanghai. In the intervention site, the existing programme was supplemented by awareness building, counselling and services providing. In the control site, comparable in socio-cultural-economic and demographic characteristics to the intervention site, continued to provide standard programmes and services. The intervention was intended for all unmarried youth (15-24) irrespective of whether they were in school and colleges or not. It lasted 20 months and comprised three main areas of activity.

The first activity focused on building awareness, and included the dissemination of educational materials, the viewing of instructional videos, lectures and group discussions. Totally, nine brochures or pamphlets and four books were disseminated to 1220 youths in the intervention group during the 20 months intervention period; these publications discussed sexual physiology and psychology, reproduction, sexual responsibility, relationships, love, marriage and family, consequences of pre-marital sexual behaviour, responsible and safe sex, contraception and condom use, and STIs/HIV. Information was also provided on how and where to access reproductive health services and contraceptive supplies as well as counselling. In addition, three educational videos—on topics ranging from anatomy and physiology to infection and health care—were developed and played at a local cinema, and were followed by the showing of popular movies. A lecture on sexual maturation and adolescent sexual and reproductive health matters was given by a professional educator. Finally, in a total of 36 group discussions, skills on sexual communication and negotiation were developed, particularly among youth who had partners—activities included short presentations which provided information on the risks of unprotected intercourse, methods of avoiding unwanted pregnancy, prevention of STIs and HIV/AIDS, and discussions. The activities were facilitated by research staff.

The second activity focused on the provision of counselling. A youth health counselling centre was set up in the town, where a full time female counsellor was trained and responsible for routine and telephone counselling.

The final activity focused on enhancing access to services, specifically contraceptive services. Contraceptives, including condoms, oral contraceptives, creams, tablets, diaphragms, and emergency contraceptive pills were distributed at no cost. Pregnancy testing papers were also supplied to those who suspected pregnancy. Services were provided through a variety of channels—local family planning units, the youth health counselling centre, and after group activities described above were held.

The intervention was implemented in cooperation with the local FP committee. This committee is part of a wide network, consisting of staff at different administrative levels. At grassroot levels are residence district, village and work unit service mechanisms. Routine services are usually provided through this network and rapport between local level providers and communities is generally close. Hence, one of the first activities of this intervention was to gain the support of local FP staff, provide them training in the youth-friendly aspects of the proposed intervention and familiarize them with the materials to be disseminated and activities to be conducted under this programme. Training focused on building skills to provide contraceptive/reproductive health services and counselling to adolescents and unmarried young people, expanding counselling skills, and sensitization with regard to interaction with young people in supportive, non-judgmental, friendly and confidential ways. Providers were also trained in how to assist young people deal with sex related issues, choose appropriate contraceptives and avoid high-risk behaviours.

At the same time, prior to the implementation of the intervention, efforts were made to gain rapport with the communities in which the programme would be implemented. Efforts included meetings with key community members and leaders, communication with parents, and displays of information to apprise people of the sexual and reproductive health situation and needs of young people and the rationale for the intervention.

Study Population and Data

In order to test the feasibility and effectiveness of the intervention, base-line surveys were conducted in both sites prior to the implementation of the intervention. A similar survey was again conducted in both sites 20 months after the intervention had been initiated. Data for this paper compare findings then at two points in time in the two sites. Totally, 1220 unmarried young people from the intervention site, and 1007 from the control site consented to be interviewed, including 1304 out-of-school youth and 923 high school students. Those intending to marry within a year of the initiation of the intervention were excluded. Of this group, 2042 participated in the post-intervention survey; this included 1148 and 894 youth from the intervention and control sites, respectively, and 1169 in-school and 863 out-of-school youth. In short, a total of 91.7% were successfully followed-up, including 94% from the intervention site, and 86% from the control site.

The survey comprised the administration of self-administered questionnaires. Efforts were made to ensure anonymity and privacy while filling out the questionnaires.

Trained interviewers assisted respondents, where necessary, in understanding questions with which they may have had difficulty. All filled-out questionnaires were reviewed by the research staff for completeness and consistency, and open-ended questions were coded after the survey.

Results

Profile of Study Participants

The socio-demographic profile of young people recruited for the study from intervention and control sites is presented in Table 1. At base-line, a total of 1220 young people were recruited in the intervention site and 1007 in the control. As Table 1 suggests, socio-demographic characteristics do vary somewhat between the two groups. Some characteristics are similar: no significant differences were observed, for example, in leisure-time activity, co-residence with parents, type of school, or relationship with classmates. Clear differences were observed in terms of age distribution and education and occupation profiles. Youth from the intervention site tended to be younger and more likely to be university students or have a higher education level than those in the control group. Gender disparities were also evident in both groups: females tended to be younger, more likely to be in school, and more likely to be engaged in administrative occupations than were males. With regard to leisure time activities, females were more likely than males to report studying and males more likely to report physical activity.

Exposure to Intervention Activities

Table 2 confirms that almost all young people in the intervention site were exposed to one or more activities of the intervention. Half or more read the materials with interest or were exposed to eight or more of them or watched 2 or more educational videos. Evaluations (not presented here) of activities were generally positive.

Effectiveness of Intervention

a. *Change of Reproductive Health Knowledge*

For each of 80 questions on the knowledge of reproduction, contraception and STDs/AIDS in the questionnaire, one score

Table 1: Socio-demographic Profile of Study Participants at Base-line: Intervention and Control Groups

Characteristics	Intervention group				Control group				
	Total n=1220	Male n=719	Female n=501	p*	Total n=1007	Male n=554	Female n=453	p*	p (Interv.-Control)
Type of subjects									
Out-of-school youth ⊕	57.3	61.3	51.5	0.0006	60.1	65.0	54.1	0.0004	0.1843
Middle school student	42.7	38.7	48.5		39.9	35.0	45.9		
Age									
≤ 17	27.8	24.3	32.7	<.0001	27.2	24.9	30.0	<.0001	0.0016
18~	38.5	35.2	43.3		39.0	34.7	44.4		
20~	29.3	35.6	20.4		25.7	29.8	20.7		
22~24	4.4	4.9	3.6		8.1	10.6	4.9		
Leisure-time activity@									
Study	35.9	30.8	43.2	<.0001	36.6	28.0	47.1	<.0001	0.1818
Physical exercise	18.6	27.2	6.4		15.0	23.7	4.4		
Enjoyment	38.8	36.3	42.4		41.4	43.0	39.4		
Others	6.7	5.7	8.0		7.0	5.2	9.1		
Live in home everyday									
Yes	76.0	79.8	70.5	0.0002	76.8	80.3	72.6	0.0037	0.6364
No	24.0	20.2	29.5			23.2	19.7	27.4	
Education □ (n)	699	441	258			605	360	245	
Junior high or below	39.9	48.8	24.8	<.0001	51.7	58.6	41.6	0.0001	<.0001
Senior high	52.4	44.9	65.1			44.4	38.9	52.7	
College or above	7.7	6.3	10.1			3.8	2.5	5.7	

Characteristics	Intervention group				Control group				p (Interv.-Control)
	Total n=1220	Male n=719	Female n=501	p*	Total n=1007	Male n=554	Female n=453	p*	
Occupation □ @ (n)	698	441	257		604	359	245		
University students	5.9	4.8	7.8	0.0003	1.8	1.1	2.9	0.0003	0.0006
Workers	61.0	63.5	56.8		66.6	64.1	70.2		
Job-waiting youth	19.2	20.4	17.1		21.4	25.6	15.1		
Shop/restaurant employees	6.5	7.0	5.5		4.1	5.3	2.5		
Administrative personnel	7.4	4.3	12.8		6.1	3.9	9.4		
Type of school # (n)	521	278	243		402	194	208		
Top	12.9	11.5	14.4	0.4936	14.2	13.9	14.4	0.5327	0.7418
Common	43.4	45.3	41.2		44.3	41.8	46.7		
Vocational school	43.7	43.2	44.4		41.5	44.3	38.9		
Grades of students# (n)	521	278	243		402	194	208		
Junior high	6.0	5.0	7.0	0.3455	17.2	14.4	19.7	0.1608	<.0001
Senior high	94.0	95.0	93.0		82.8	85.6	80.3		
Relationship with classmates# (n)	521	278	243		402	194	208		
Excellent	31.5	34.9	27.6	0.2949	26.1	21.6	30.3	0.056	0.0955
Harmonious	50.7	47.1	54.7		57.7	58.8	56.7		
Common	17.5	17.6	17.3		15.2	19.1	11.5		
Bad	0.4	0.4	0.4		1.0	0.5	1.5		

⊕ : Including university students. @:There are missing values. □ : Only for out-of-school youth. #:Only for middle school students. *Chi-square test between male and female; the same below.

Table 2: Participation/Involvement in Intervention Activities as Assessed from the Post-intervention Survey (%)

Participation & evaluation	Total	Male	Female
NUMBER#	1148	678	470
Exposure to the intervention			
Received educational materials	99.7	99.6	99.8
Attended at least one lecture	22.5	22.0	23.2
Exposed to at least one video	78.8	79.2	78.3
Participated in one or more group discussions	32.6	32.7	32.3
Intensity of exposure to intervention			
% exposed to 8 or more materials @	76.2	75.7	77.8
% who read most or all materials earnestly	76.7	75.4	78.7
% who watched 2 or more educational videos	50.2	50.0	50.6
% who participated in 2 or more group discussions	9.2	9.6	8.5
Distribution of contraceptive and other supplies (number)			
Condoms	4348		
Oral contraceptive cycles	137		
Diaphragms	146		
Creams	107		
Tablets	870		
Emergency contraception	106		
Pregnancy testing papers	93		
Person times of counselling provided	328		

#:Data drawn from post-intervention survey.@:There are missing value(s).

was given if answered correctly and zero to the other. Then the original score was converted into a new score, the average knowledge scores were 36.81 and 36.38 for the intervention and control group at baseline, and there was not significant difference between two groups (P=0.5853). After 20 months intervention, the average knowledge score for intervention group was 72.26, which was much higher than 43.63 in the control group (P=0.0001) (Table 3).

At baseline, there were about 31%-73% subjects in the intervention and control groups had correct answers to most sexual and physiological questions. With regard to questions of "Does masturbation do harm to health?" "In which period of a menstrual cycle are women most prone to be pregnant?" and "Where is the ovum fertilized?", the correct answer rates

Table 3: Comparison of Knowledge Score on Reproductive Health Between the Intervention and Control Groups

Knowledge	Baseline			Post-intervention		
	Interv. n=1220	Control n=1007	p	Interv. n=1148	Control n=894	p
Average score	36.81	36.38	0.5853	72.26	43.63	0.0001
1. Reproduction	39.57	39.13	0.6755	80.71	50.46	0.0001
2. Contraception	20.94	20.78	0.7818	57.57	28.01	0.0001
3. STDs	41.48	41.47	0.9068	79.97	48.54	0.0001
4. HIV/AIDS	66.80	65.33	0.1772	94.06	76.22	0.0001

Table 4: Proportion of Correct Answers on Questions of Reproduction at Baseline and Post-intervention, Intervention and Control Groups ÿ % K

Reproductive knowledge	Interv. group (n=1148)			Control group (n=894)		
	Baseline	Post-int.	Dif.	Baseline	Post-int.	Dif.
1. At what age do most boys have their first ejaculation?	45.99	72.39	26.40	38.70	49.89	11.19
2. Which organ produces sperm?	44.86	87.63	42.77	37.70	46.53	8.83
3. Will nocturnal emission 1-2 times a week do harm to unmarried males' health?	33.89	77.70	43.81	33.89	52.35	18.46
4. At what age do most girls have their first menstrual period?	48.17	85.63	37.46	49.78	58.05	8.27
5. How long is the general menstrual cycle?	48.61	81.79	33.18	45.64	55.82	10.18
6. Does masturbation do harm to health?	16.90	63.33	46.43	21.36	37.92	16.56
7. Which organ produces ovum?	44.51	90.24	45.73	42.73	54.14	11.41
8. In which period of a menstrual cycle are women most prone to be pregnant?	13.85	61.06	47.21	16.55	26.06	9.51
9. Where is the ovum fertilized?	7.06	59.23	52.17	10.74*	12.19	1.45
10. Where is the foetus develops?	55.14	94.86	39.72	56.38	68.79	12.41
11. How long is the full-term pregnancy?	70.73	98.61	27.88	72.60	81.77	9.17
12. From where is the foetus delivered by nature?	47.13	97.56	50.43	48.10	63.53	15.43
13. Can occasional sex lead to pregnancy?	40.33	83.01	42.68	37.81	55.93	18.12
14. What's the most important symptom of early pregnancy?	30.66	76.92	46.26	31.99	43.51	11.52

Note: Chi-square test for each question between baseline and post-intervention: $p<0.05$ except for the question with the note of "*" ($p>0.05$).

were lower (7-21%). After 20 months intervention, the proportions of the subjects who gave the correct answers in the intervention group to the same questions as the baseline survey increased 26%-52%, compared to 1%-18% only in the control group (Table 4).

For most contraceptive methods, the proportion of awareness of the methods and the use of the methods in the intervention group increased 17%-63% and 8%-60% respectively in the post-intervention survey, compared to 4%-24% and 1%-19% respectively in the control group (Table 5, Table 6).

Table 5: Proportion of Awareness of Contraceptives at Baseline and Post-intervention, Intervention and Control Groups Ӻ % K

Contraceptives	Interv. group (n=1148)			Control group (n=894)		
	Baseline	Post-int.	Dif.	Baseline	Post-int.	Dif.
Withdrawal	30.49	88.41	57.92	28.41	52.68	24.27
Rhythm	23.17	79.88	56.71	22.37	41.16	18.79
Oral contraceptive pill	62.72	99.22	36.50	62.08	83.45	21.37
Condom	58.10	98.69	40.59	55.93	80.31	24.38
IUD	34.84	90.42	55.58	36.80	55.82	19.02
Spermicide	8.01	47.56	39.55	9.17	12.98	3.81
Injection	13.15	45.21	32.06	14.21	22.04	7.83
Implant	4.97	21.86	16.89	4.03	8.50	4.47
Diaphragm	12.02	50.00	37.98	9.84	15.10	5.26
Vaginal ring	12.28	47.56	35.28	10.18	14.88	4.70
Sterilization	31.45	82.06	50.61	33.67	45.08	11.41
Emergency	19.86	82.49	62.63	20.47	29.42	8.95

Note: Chi-square test for each question between baseline and post-intervention: $p<0.05$.

Table 6: Proportion of Awareness of the Use of Contraceptives at Baseline and Post-intervention, Intervention and Control Groups Ӻ % K

Contraception methods	Interv. group (n=1148)			Control group (n=894)		
	Baseline	Post-int.	Dif.	Baseline	Post-int.	Dif.
Withdrawal	19.69	64.20	44.51	19.46	38.14	18.68
Rhythm	14.11	55.23	41.12	13.31	25.73	12.42
Oral contraceptive pill	42.94	86.93	43.99	39.82	57.94	18.12
Condom	37.02	86.93	49.91	35.35	54.81	19.46
IUD	15.59	60.54	44.95	13.98	26.29	12.31
Spermicide	3.14	21.95	18.81	4.14*	4.92	0.78
Injection	7.14	22.04	14.90	6.04	10.51	4.47
Implant	2.61	10.45	7.84	1.23	2.80	1.57
Diaphragm	6.36	28.05	21.69	4.14	6.38	2.24
Vaginal ring	5.57	21.43	15.86	4.59*	6.04	1.45
Sterilization	15.68	51.05	35.37	16.33	20.69	4.36
Emergency	8.97	68.82	59.85	8.61*	9.73	1.12

Note: Chi-square test for each question between baseline and post-intervention: $p<0.05$ except for the question with the note of "*" ($p>0.05$).

With regard to most questions on AIDS, the proportions of correct answers among subjects in the intervention group increased 14%-41% from the baseline to post-intervention, while 6%-17% only in the control group (Table 7). To questions on STDs, the increased proportions of correct answers in the intervention group were much higher than those in the control group, as assessed from the baseline and post-intervention survey (Table 7 and Table 8).

Table 7: The Proportion of Correct Answers on HIV/AIDS Related Questions at Baseline and Post-intervention, Intervention and Control Groups Ӂ % K

Questions	Interv. group (n=1148)			Control group (n=894)		
	Baseline	Post-int.	Dif.	Baseline	Post-int.	Dif.
1. Have you heard of AIDS?	86.41	100.00	13.59	86.35	92.06	5.71
2. What is the cause of AIDS?	52.35	91.03	38.68	52.80	58.61	5.81
3. What is the pathway for AIDS transmission?						
Shaking hands with an AIDS patient	59.84	94.86	35.02	56.38	70.58	14.20
Using same needles for injection with an AIDS patient	77.09	99.04	21.95	73.04	85.23	12.19
Having sex intercourse with an AIDS patient	80.14	99.48	19.34	77.52	87.47	9.95
Mother-infant vertical infection	70.99	98.87	27.88	69.57	81.66	12.09
General contact with an AIDS patient	53.22	93.73	40.51	50.11	66.44	16.33
Blood transfusion	79.62	99.39	19.77	76.06	85.79	9.73
4. Who are more likely to be infected with AIDS?						
Prostitutes	71.34	96.08	24.74	70.25	81.54	11.29
Homosexual persons	53.22	80.23	27.01	54.70	62.30	7.60
Drug abusers	45.99	83.10	37.11	46.20	63.53	17.33
Persons who have multi-partners	67.25	92.94	25.69	69.57	79.42	9.85

*: Chi-square test for each question between pre-intervention and post-intervention: $P<0.05$.

Table 8: The Proportion of Correct Answers on STDs Related Questions at Baseline and Post-intervention, Intervention and Control Groups Ӂ % K

Questions	Interv. group (n=1148)			Control group (n=894)		
	Baseline	Post-int.	Dif.	Baseline	Post-int.	Dif.
1. Have you heard of STDs?	77.18	100.00	22.82	77.74	82.89	5.15
2. Which of the following diseases is STD?						
Syphilis	69.25	99.83	30.58	64.88	78.30	13.42
Gonerrhoea	61.85	99.04	37.19	56.82	69.13	12.31
Nephritis	51.48	93.90	42.42	49.11	60.85	11.74
Chancroid	3.22	45.73	42.51	5.37	8.50	3.13
Uterine fibroids	46.25	95.21	48.96	47.65	60.74	13.09
Pointed condyloma	21.60	90.33	68.73	20.13	26.40	6.27
NGU	14.72	70.82	56.10	14.43*	14.21	-0.22
Genitals herpes	18.90	78.22	59.32	20.92	25.39	4.47
Haemophilia	39.20	90.94	51.74	37.58	45.75	8.17
AIDS	58.71	96.95	38.24	59.17	64.54	5.37
3. What is the pathway for STDs transmission?						
Sex intercourse	71.25	99.91	28.66	72.15	80.54	8.39
Kissing	39.46	84.84	45.38	36.47	47.09	10.62
Hugging	62.28	99.30	37.02	60.74	68.12	7.38
Shaking hands	62.37	98.95	36.58	60.29	68.46	8.17
Using same towels or basin	18.47	89.29	70.82	16.89	52.80	35.91
4. Which are the symptoms of STDs?	32.40	93.12	60.72	33.78	47.32	13.54
5. If a man/woman has a STD, can he/she always find it promptly?	34.76	82.23	47.47	40.27	48.77	8.5
6. If a woman has a STD, may this affect her fertility?	17.60	41.29	23.69	21.03	25.62	4.59
7. Can STDs be prevented?	69.34	98.00	28.66	68.34	72.82	4.48
8. Which of the following behaviours can reduce the risk of infecting STDs?						
Don't have sex with multi-partners	54.79	92.42	37.63	54.81	65.44	10.63
Using condom in the intercourse	41.72	89.90	48.18	39.37	55.70	16.33
Avoiding homosexual behaviour	27.00	61.50	34.50	29.42	41.61	12.19

Note: Chi-square test for each question between pre-intervention and post-intervention: $P<0.05$ except for the questions with the note of "*" ($p>0.05$).

b. *Change of Attitude Towards Sex-related Issues*

At baseline, there was no significant difference on attitudes towards male/female's pre-marital sex between the intervention and control group. After 20 months intervention, the proportion of subjects who hold favourable attitudes to pre-marital sex in the intervention group was lower than that of the control, i.e., more subjects in the control group thought young people could have pre-marital sex "if it based on love" or "they are willing to do so". Besides, at baseline, there was slightly but significantly higher proportion of subjects who thought induced abortion "does harm to women's health" and "influences women's fertility" in the control group than was that in the intervention group. In the post-intervention period, the situation was reversed—more subjects in the intervention group believed that pre-marital induced abortion can influence women's health and their fertility. When the two groups were asked "Who would you like to talk with when you have problem on love affair?", "friends of same sex" was first choice for most subjects of both groups. However, there was slightly higher proportion of subjects in the intervention group who would talk with health workers about their love affairs that was that in the control group (Table 9).

c. *Factors Influencing the Knowledge*

In order to assess the net effect of exposure to the intervention on reproductive health knowledge, a logistic regression was performed. The dependent variable was ordinal classified, set to equal zero, one and two if the knowledge score was less than 50, between 50-69 and more than 69 respectively. The independent variables included intervention or control group, age, gender, education level, in or out of school status, asked parents or provided by parents the knowledge or not, learnt actively and communication with other people on sexual matters or not. Result is presented in Table 10. Findings suggest that exposure to the intervention is the most powerful correlate of reproductive health knowledge. In comparison to the control group, the adjusted odds ratio for the participants of the intervention was 52.04 (95% CI: 39.51-68.54). Besides, participants, who were older, well-educated, in out-of-school,

Table 9: Attitudes and Perspectives of Subjects to Sex-related Issues at Baseline and Post-intervention, Intervention and Control Group (%)

Questions and answers	Baseline			Post-intervention		
	Interv. n=1220	Control n=1007	p	Interv. n=1148	Control n=894	p
Attitude to man's pre-marital sex						
It is OK if only based on love	16.97*	15.09*	0.431	13.15	15.21	0.004
It is OK if only they are willing	35.74	38.23		39.81	44.30	
It isn't good, but understandable	33.93	32.27		39.46	32.21	
It should be condemned by social morals	8.52	9.04		6.27	5.82	
It should be punished	1.64	2.48		0.96	1.23	
Others	3.20	2.88		0.35	1.23	
Attitude to woman's pre-marital sex						
It is OK if only based on love	16.39*	15.29*	0.227	13.41	16.46	0.000
It is OK if only they are willing	35.16	37.64		38.15	43.34	
It isn't good, but understandable	33.11	30.09		39.29	29.34	
It should be condemned by social morals	10.16	10.63		7.75	8.17	
It should be punished	1.64	2.88		1.05	1.46	
Others	3.52	3.48		0.35	1.23	
Influence of pre-marital induced abortion to women? (multi-choice)						
Do harm to women's physical and mental health	68.11*	72.27	0.033	81.36	73.60	0.000
Influence women's fertility	56.31*	61.43*	0.015	84.84	72.15	0.000
Damage women and their family's fame	31.89	34.49	0.193	31.79	32.10	0.882
Influence women's future	15.90	17.40	0.346	16.55	19.69	0.067
Other bad consequences	1.64*	1.39	0.635	0.00	1.57	0.000
No influence	4.10*	3.18	0.253	1.83	3.58	0.014
Who would you like to talk with when you have love affair problem?						
Friends of same sex	60.82*	71.37	0.000	71.08	73.38	0.008
Friends of opposite sex	7.87	7.65		6.62	7.05	
Father	2.21	1.49		1.92	1.68	
Mother	14.59	10.54		8.10	7.72	
Sibling	4.43	2.78		3.31	3.80	
Health workers	6.39	3.68		7.84	4.03	
Teachers etc.	3.69	2.49		1.13	2.35	

*: Chi-square test for each question between baseline and post-intervention in the intervention group and the control group: $p<0.05$.

Table 10: Logistic Regression Analysis of the Factors Related to Knowledge of Reproductive Health Among Unmarried Young People (n=2042)

Variables	Estimate	Standard error	OR	95% CI	p
Intercept	-4.9341	0.2197	—	—	<.0001
Intercept 2	-2.0497	0.1810	—	—	<.0001
Age (year)					
<18 (ref.)	—	—	1.00	—	
18~	0.5073	0.1299	1.66	1.29-2.14	<.0001
21~	0.7625	0.1887	2.14	1.48-3.10	<.0001
Gender					
Male (ref.)	—	—	1.00	—	
Female	0.0794	0.1039	1.08	0.88-1.33	0.4449
Interventions					
No (ref.)	—	—	1.00	—	
Yes	3.9520	0.1405	52.04	39.51-68.54	<.0001
Education					
Junior high or lower (ref.)	—	—	1.00	—	
Senior high or higher	0.2386	0.1177	1.27	1.01-1.60	0.0427
Type of subjects					
Student (ref.)	—	—	1.00	—	
Out-of-school youth	0.7211	0.1328	2.06	1.59-2.67	<.0001
Asked parents about sex-related problem					
No (ref.)	—	—	1.00	—	
Yes	-0.5352	0.3417	0.59	0.30-1.14	0.1173
Parents provided sex education initiatively					
No (ref.)	—	—	1.00	—	
Yes	0.1277	0.1252	1.14	0.89-1.45	0.3079
Learn RH knowledge actively					
No (ref.)	—	—	1.00	—	
Yes	1.0496	0.1020	2.86	2.34-3.49	<.0001
Communicated with others					
No (ref.)	—	—	1.00	—	
Yes	0.2527	0.1263	1.29	1.01-1.65	0.0455

ever learnt reproductive health knowledge actively, and could communicate with other people on sexual matters, were more likely to have a higher knowledge score. Surprisingly, neither asking parents about sex-related problem nor being provided sex education by parents were as likely to influence reproductive health knowledge as was exposure to the intervention. Education came from parents seems not so effective.

Summary and Conclusion

This paper examined the effectiveness of a youth-friendly intervention on improvement of knowledge on reproductive health among unmarried youths of sub-urban Shanghai. Findings strongly supported the hypothesis that a community-based intervention program, which provides sex education and reproductive health service, can indeed increase young people's knowledge on reproductive health, including knowledge on reproduction, contraception, and STDs/AIDS. Besides, age, education level, in or out of school status, learnt actively and communication with other people on sexual matters were also likely to influence the knowledge. Results are consistent with a growing body of evidence that suggests that reproductive health education and service program can build awareness of reproductive health knowledge among unmarried youth.[4,5]

Young people lacked the knowledge on contraception according to baseline survey is caused by the situation that sex education in China don't provide the knowledge on contraception and information on reproductive health services in school, and don't cover the out-of-school youth in communities. The intervention was designed and implemented in consultation with key community members and implemented in cooperation with local family planning authorities. Appropriate training to personnel, distribution of free contraceptive supplies and the establishment of a "youth health counselling centre" were important features of the intervention; at the same time, information was provided in a variety of ways including reading and viewing materials, group discussions and telephone hotlines. The increase in reproductive health knowledge may thus be attributed to both the intervention through the above mentioned IEC activities, and through youth friendly services and distribution of contraceptive supplies.

The intervention also had positive impact on unmarried youths' attitudes towards pre-marital sex. In the Chinese context, pre-marital abstinence is unavoidable encouraged, and it is indeed the safest method to prevent pregnancy and STDs/HIV. So, the evidence from the study that there are increasing numbers of subjects who hold less favourable attitude to pre-marital sex because of the intervention are more acceptable by public, which also enhance the feasibility of the programme if extended. The results are similar with other studies that suggest reproductive health education and service programme have positive influence on adolescent's attitudes towards pre-marital sex and contraceptive use through increasing their knowledge on reproductive health.[6,7]

However, the study has limitations. The most significant one was the lack of a longer-term follow-up to determine whether the observed differences are sustained. Limitations of the evaluation include loss to follow-up of some participants, although more than 90% of eligible subjects were successfully followed up at the post-intervention survey. One main reason for the drop from follow-up is that some of subjects got married or joined the army during the research period. The follow-up rate in the control group is lower than that in the intervention group, as subjects in the control group received no direct benefit from the program.

Nevertheless, findings strongly suggest the need to incorporate within existing family planning programmes youth friendly interventions directed to provide information, counselling and services to the unmarried. Current sex education is not provided to unmarried youth by family planning program in China. Young people themselves are inhibited to get the knowledge and information for family planning staff, for feeling embarrassment or the hostile attitudes of providers. Providers not only hold relatively conservative attitudes to sex education, but also consider that the unmarried do not fall within the population they are expected to serve. Youth friendly interventions need to reverse these provider attitudes, and encourage knowledge, information and service delivery in a supportive, friendly and confidential manner. The experience of this intervention suggests that such a youth friendly programme tends to be welcomed by unmarried youths and might substantially increase safe sexual behaviours including contraceptive use. The experience of this intervention—conducted in conjunction with existing facilities—suggests the feasibility of youth friendly models and suggests that such a model can be cautiously replicated in additional sites.

Acknowledgement

The authors thank RHR/WHO for its generous financial and technical support, which enabled the conduct of this study. We would also like to thank the field staff in the Shongjiang family planning site for their enthusiastic work in the field.

References

1. Gao, Y., Lu, Z.Z., Shi, R., Sun, X.Y. and Cai, Y. 2001. AIDS and sex education for young people in China. Reprod Fertil Dev, 13 (7-8): 729-37.
2. Li Zhiping. 2000. Investigation on adolescent sex-related issues in Guangzhou. Chinese Journal of school health, 21(2): 105.
3. Zheng Zhenzhen and Zhou Yun, etc. 2001. Sexual behaviour and contraceptive use among unmarried, young women migrant workers in five cities in China. Reproductive health matters, 9(17): 118-127.
4. Lou Chaohua, Ding Yonggang and Gao Ersheng. 2002. Effects of sex and reproductive health education among high school students. See Gao Ersheng (editor)—adolescent and unmarried youth reproductive health: status, perspectives and strategies. Shanghai: the press of Shanghai Second Army Medical University, pp. 257-263.
5. Chen, J. and Ye, G. 1997. Sex education in 6th and 7th grade girls. Zhonghua Yi Xue Za Zhi, 77(1): 11-4.
6. Brieger, W.R., Delano, G.E. and Lane, C.G. *et al.* 2001. West African Youth Initiative: outcome of a reproductive health education program. J. Adolesc Health, 29(6): 436-446.
7. Shrier, L.A., Ancheta, R. and Goodman, E. *et al.* 2001. Randomized controlled trial of a safer sex intervention for high-risk adolescent girls. Arch Pediatr Adolesc Med., 155(1): 73-79

Part - IV

COMMUNICATION STRATEGIES

16

Effective Communication Strategies for Promotion of Health and Family Planning: An Interdisciplinary Perspective

K. Mahadevan, K.A. Pisharoti, S.L.N. Rao, K.V. Ranganathan, Lory Laing, N. Murugesan, M. Ubaidulla and P. Ramalingam

Introduction

Information technology has revolutionized the communication of all message towards the end of 20th century. As a result message can be sent to any distant place all over the world during a fraction of a second. For instance, E-mail communication has become the speediest transmission of message during the last one-decade. In addition, electronic communication through TV has become another expeditions transmission of message visually to common man, which is more resourceful and effective than communication through radio. Therefore, thanks, to information and electronic technology, communication has become instantaneous, extensive and very fast throughout the world.

However, such facilities and their impact are confined to relatively more among the educated groups and their users. Today such users are restricted to less than one tenth of rural people but over fifty per cent of urban people. When rural people constitute more than 75% of population in most of the developing countries, the role of electronic media and information technology has limitation to reach majority of the population in a country. Of course, their role can be made extensive, when their availability to most people are facilitated, literacy of people are increased, and their purchasing power developed, which will take several years more. This does not mean that, we should underestimate the potentiality of information technology and electronic communication revolution for the promotion of health and family planning innovations. Under such existing constraints and limitations of these communication facilities, the other successful communication strategies are to be explored and supplemented for developing. The high priority health and family planning welfare programmes, since these programmes cannot any longer wait for universal availability and use of information technology for dissemination of ideas and message. In this context we present here the unique and successful communication strategy followed in the state of Andhra Pradesh, in India for the benefit of their adoption elsewhere in India and in the other countries.

The Concepts of Communication

Everett M. Rogers (1993), defined "Communication as the process by which an idea is transferred from a source to receiver with the intent changes his behaviour. The source transfers the idea with intent to modify the behaviour of a receiver. The purpose of communication is to bring about certain desired effects on the part of the receiver. These effects may consist of an alteration in the receiver's knowledge of some idea, change in his attitude towards the idea or a change in his overt behaviour". Communication in the present context refers to health and family planning innovations.

The major components of communication system consists of sources, channels, messages and effect. Till 1950s theoretically communication was conceptualized and studied as a linear model. However, since 1960s communication, like the other social sciences, adopted systems approach for theoretically explaining the entire concept on a holistic basis, which is more scientific and appropriate. Therefore, we treat communication here using the systems model of input-

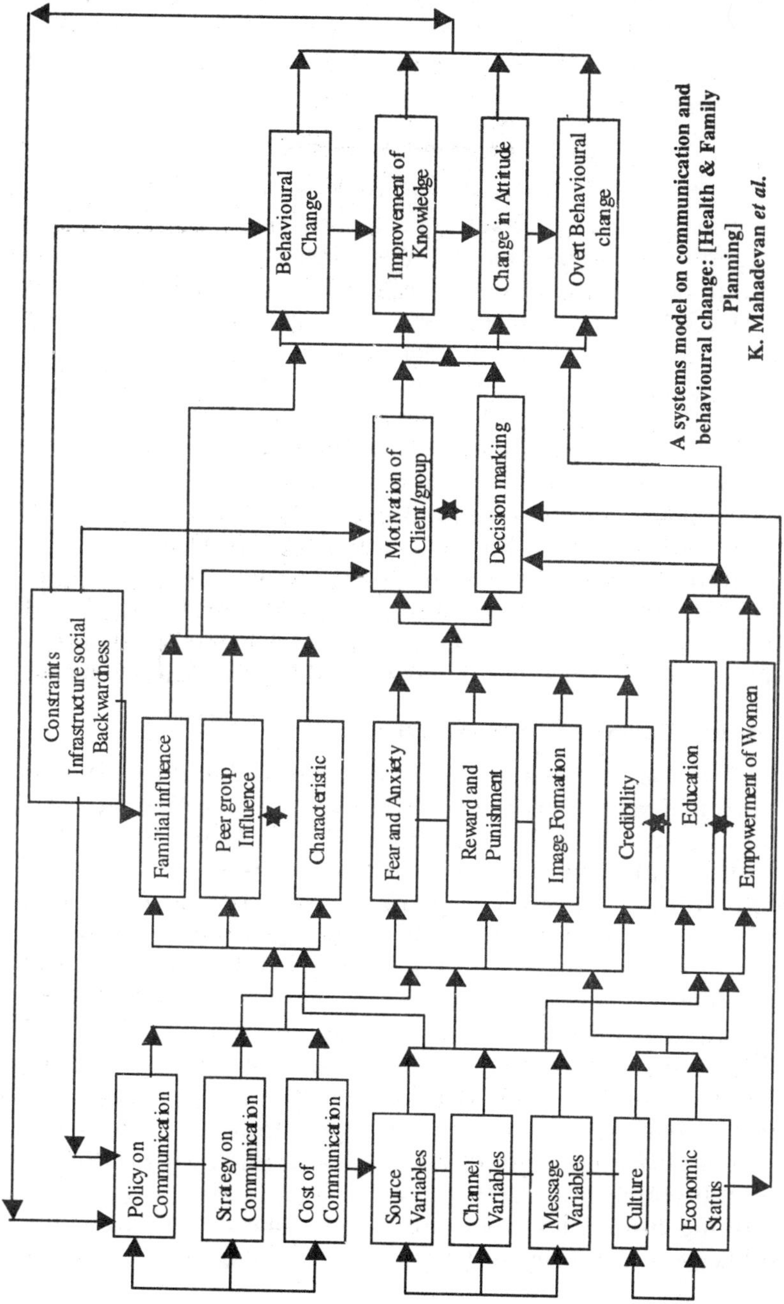

A systems model on communication and behavioural change: [Health & Family Planning]
K. Mahadevan *et al.*

process and output. In fact most of the concepts of communication can be systematically classified and suitably linked to these tripartite dimensions of communications (see diagram enclosed).

Input-Output Model of Communication

A holistic approach for understanding the entire communication for developing health and family planning programmes can be conceptually devised following the input-output model. In the absence of adopting such comprehensive methodology in communication, very often one-sided approach based on the background and orientation of the communicator, the overall strategy has been devised. As a result, the technology of communication namely the inputs are given overemphasis and less priority given tc the process and least cognizance given to the clients; back group. Such piecemeal approach in communication very often leads to partial or complete failure of communication. Therefore, very rightly we discuss here communication on a holistic basis using the systems model of input, process and output and then proceed to the successful case study of communication experiment successful implemented in Andhra State of India.

Communicatees Characteristics

For the success of communication, characteristics of communicatee form major component, however, the communicator does very often not visualize it. In this context, educational background of the clients and form the key factor. In common parlance, literacy of the communicatees has been taken for granted as equal to education. Several studies have confirmed that literacy upto tenth class has very negligible, importance to accept health and family planning innovations (Mahadevan *et al.*, 2002 and 2003). In reality acceptance of these innovations, without incentives and correction takes place among people, who studied beyond the tenth class level. However, it does not mean for instance, that all the graduates and post-graduates spontaneously and voluntarily accept health and family planning innovations without much time lag. In fact, the reality is surprising and strange. For instance, when Air

India pilots requested Government of India to suspend flight temporarily to Hong Kong and Singapore in April 2003 to avoid the risk of spreading SARS through incoming tourists, and passengers, who are likely to spread it fast across India. Unfortunately, even WHO also did not take any measure to reduce people's travel to SARS infected countries from the other vulnerable and non-infected developing countries at least for a limited period. These unimaginative policies are likely to spread SARS to the other developing countries, who are vulnerable for mass infection of SARS leading to unpredictable mortality.

In India, except Kerala and Goa even literacy level is on an average around 65% by 2001. Out of the literates those who studied up to intermediate (12th class plus) level and beyond are less than 25 per cent. Thus, at least 75% of people are fully or partially ignorant and/or not well informed about scientific aspects of life. In other words, cognition of health and family planning innovations by majority of people takes more time difficult to comprehend, and need repeated exposure to education and multiple media exposure needed to communicate effectively for their behavioural change. These realities of recipients characteristics in communication process are generally overlooked or under estimated very often on health population education programme. Therefore, failure or partial success in communication can be attributed to these neglected poor understanding of the clients and their inadequate scientific educational background by the communicators. In addition to general education several other characteristics of the clients are to be kept in mind to design a communication strategy.

There are several other background characteristics of the clients that determine free and effective communication. Unless they are visualized by the communicator/educator, the efforts of communication will misfire. In this context, cultural background like, caste, tribe, religion and ethnicity have several barriers/facilitating characteristics for rejection and acceptance of innovations. In addition, the level of autonomy empowerment and modernization of the clients also determine the free flow of communication and outreach of communication. A step further in this context to visualize communication is to familiarize with the decision making pattern among the couple to design the appropriate target group of communication and the strategy of communication. More than all these personal attributes, several other clients need group pressure or their credible peer groups support for acceptance of innovations have to be kept in mind by the communicator. Generally, these aspects of clients are given only negligible importance in communication strategy and focus is given largely to the method, process and technology of the inputs in communication. As a result, communication strategy very often partially succeed and not fully.

Communication Strategies

Communication strategies followed till 1980s were mostly interpersonal in nature and mass communication had only a subordinate role. However, during 1990s mass communication gained a prominent role in development communication. Nevertheless, most of the space and time in several mass communication devote for entertainment and political purpose, and very negligible time devoted for development communication, particularly, health and family planning programmes. Therefore, a thorough reorientation in policy and mass media by the government and private sector are urgently needed now. In the absence of such proper policy on utilization of mass media, full potentialities of mass media could not be tapped hitherto for health and family planning programmes.

Even appropriate and effective utilization of interpersonal strategy for promotion of welfare communication has not been exploited. As a result on a stereo typed manner peripheral workers are over dependent on promoting welfare communication particularly health and family planning. Earlier studies have fully confirmed that peripheral workers communication and education alone cannot deliver the goods (Mahadevan, 1997). It is because, decision making process by the clients are largely on multi-personal basis and not on uni-personal basis (Mahadevan, 1997). In addition, their stereo typed strategies are not effective to convince the clients to make the difficult behavioural change. (Kivlin *et al.*, 1968; Rogers, 1973; Mahadevan *et al.*, 1997 (a), 1977b, 1984).

A Successful Diffusion Strategy

However, an exceptional success in interpersonal communication was discovered and operationalised using an action research in 1970s in Gandhigram Institute (Mahadevan *et al.*, 1977, 1984), which has received national and international recognition. However, this powerful communication strategy has not been extensively and regularly adopted by most peripheral workers, though it has been approved by Indian government as a job function of peripheral workers. The above mentioned action-research using satisfied family planning adopters interaction in group meetings with non-adopter during three and more occasions, rapidly helped the clients to change their indifference and negative attitude and adopted family planning expeditiously. The secret of success of this diffusion experiment was the credibility attached to the satisfied adopters of family planning (change agent) and reinforcement opportunity provided to develop knowledge, facilities extended for clarifications without delicacy, group pressure and free flows of interpersonal communication. Interestingly this successful strategy of communication within one year increased the couple protection rate by leaps and bounds in the action-research population. After this epoch-making successful communication experiment, no other innovative and effective strategy of communication has been evolved so far. However, this diffusion experiment was parallelly promoted in Thailand (1996), USA (Palmore, (1967)), Germany (Based on Mahadevan's Model). For more details readers may refer to seven papers published on satisfied adopters of communication and particularly "Successful diffusion through satisfied adopters: An action research design" (Mahadevan, 1993).

For the success of communication in education, effective strategy may be adopted. Mechanical promotion of communication without vision and holistic perspectives, the efforts of communication cannot succeed. According to Rogers (1992), "A communication strategy is a plan or a design for changing human behaviour on a large-scale basis through the transfer of new ideas. The purpose or intent of any communication event is to change the behaviour of the receivers. A strategy is thus implied in every communication act. The source always wishes to alter the knowledge, attitudes or overt behaviour of the receiver. However, in many communication situation little explicit attention is paid to the strategy or strategies that are involved. The source may not even be consciously aware that he is utilizing a strategy, although one must be involved, whenever the source selects the most appropriate channel, designs the message, aims at certain receivers, and so forth. Thus, the planning and assembling of the elements in the communication process necessarily involve strategies".

Community Mobilization Model for Successful Communication

Communication through community mobilization was an integral part of integrated and holistic development model expeditiously and successfully promoted in the state of Andhra Pradesh (Mahadevan, 2002). This state lies in the south-central region of India. It was a moderately developed state till 1996, out of all the states in Indian union. However, this state poised for very fast development ever since the following two Chief Ministers, namely Mr. N.T. Rama Rao and Mr. Chandra Babu Naidu assumed power from 1996 onwards. Their commitment, visionary efforts, holistic approach and periodic mobilization of the entire administration, community, NGOs and people's representatives for implementing several high priority programmes really became an exceptional success story among the Indian states. They adopted community mobilization continuously for a week to ten days during every third month and focused one after the other on different developmental themes. Such themes included programmes like family planning, reproductive health, immunization of children, empowerment of women through self-help groups, clean and green environment, marketing of farm products by farm without middlemen, self-employment of youth and so on. These programmes together came under a local and popular terminology called Janmabhoomi (birth place) to denote development on an emotional and sentimental basis. The details of all Janmabhoomi programmes can be seen in two of our recent books (Mahadevan *et al.*, 2002 and 2003).

Repeted Group Meetings and Success in Communication: The Case Study from Andhra Pradesh

The community mobilization-cum-self-help group model of development successfully experimented in the state of Andhra Pradesh, India emerged as a replicable strategy for expeditious development of any backward region in a developing country. Out of the package of development included under this model, periodic group efforts, consisting of administrators, extension educators, NGOs, people of the locality and elected representatives, paved the way for rapid decision making, paving the way for appropriate selection of priority for development in an expeditious manner.

These group meetings facilitate free flow of two-way communication without any barrier of status and hierarchy among people, elected representatives, bureaucrats and one and all. In addition, the prevailing large scale illiteracy (literacy for males 65.5% and females 54% according to 2001 census) and low level of education (< 10th class) among most of the people, did not adversely affect communication in the group meetings because face to face periodic interaction facilitated clarification, removal of fear and effective education of various programmes. Some of these high priority health and family planning programmes rapidly succeeded in this educationally backward state.

Empowerment of Women Through SHGs Facilitated Communication

In Andhra Pradesh, prior to 1996 women were not socially and economically empowered, except in the districts of Guntur, Krishna, East and West Godavari. In these districts most of the people are agriculturally prosperous and women enjoy high degrees of autonomy. Their autonomy is largely a cultural characteristic particularly among the Kamma Naidu caste. In addition literacy level in these prosperous districts are far higher than in AP and India level except in the state of Kerala. However, in most of the other districts in Andhra Pradesh, literacy is very low and people are economically not prosperous. Under these circumstances very rightly the present government gave priority to empowerment of women through organised Self-Help Group (SHGs) and the DWCRA. Each of these groups consisted of 10 to 15 women members from each ward of village and urban areas. They elected a President and Vice President among them and monthly once meet and discuss all their common family and local problems. They have been liberally and without red-tapism given loan by credit societies and banks to promote economically productive work and save money in their own names. As a result, through thousands of SHGs, women promoted economically productive and profitable ventures and saved thousands of rupees without the interference of their husbands. This silent revolutionary economic empowerment of women throughout Andhra Pradesh enabled them to gain autonomy, capacity to move freely in and around and promote diverse knowledge on several aspects of welfare programmes. Interestingly, health and family planning programmes figured as a major items of every monthly meeting of the SHGs/DWCRA. In addition, adoption of family planning and immunization of children against communicable diseases formed a major priority of the members of these groups. Whoever did not adopt these welfare programmes were pressurized by the group member to accept them without delay. These groups periodically invite and involve peripheral workers/doctors and the other resourceful persons to interact and communicate with their members for expert advice and clarifications. In other words free flow of repeated communication in the group meetings gave a new dimension to the strategy of successful health and family planning programmes.

Homophyly and Diffusion

When communication on health and family planning theme facilitated among the familiar and similar (Homophilous) people of the SHGs and allowed subsequent diffusion among members of the same group and to other local people, communication succeeded very fast without any barrier. Further, repeated communication and interaction in the same group with and without resourceful persons, eminently facilitated excellent learning situation even among the illiterate, fatalistic and backward women. It is fascination to see several successful case studies on DWCRA in our two books, (Mahadevan, 2002 and 2003), where illiterate and Muslim women adopted family planning expeditiously. The secrets of such fast flow of communication and adoption of health and family planning innovations stem out of the repeated communication and education during every monthly meetings of SHGs on a regular basis and also through tri-monthly community mobilization for a period of one week to ten days throughout the state. These programmes are regularly and effectively happening all over Andhra Pradesh, which cannot be guaranteed similarly in the ongoing interpersonal communication and education from peripheral workers to the clients. Further, impact of the homophilous and credible groups of satisfied few adopters in every SHGs/DWCRA motivated non-adopters expeditiously. No such impact and influence exists in the efforts of solitary and heterohilous (strange) peripheral workers communication and education with the illiterate and traditional clients in rural areas. The details of several success case studies of SHGs/DWCRA in communication revolution and expeditious adoption of health and family planning can be seen in our two recent books (Mahadevan *et al.*, 2002 and 2003).

In conclusion, communication efforts can lead to success, when it is carried out with vision and holistic understanding of all aspects of the system of communication. Conventional communication efforts, do not give due consideration to the diverse background of the communicatee and for selection of suitable strategies in communication. In addition, one time or two times communication may not be adequate to educate socially backward people, particularly on technical subjects on health and family planning. When rumour and the other barriers create fear among the clients, group approach and credible strategies are to be adopted to make communication successful. More than all these considerations communication must be approached holistically and as a system consisting of various inputs, process and output to achieve complete success. Thus, Andhra Pradesh's successful communication in family through group meetings made a historical success in rapidly reducing annual growth rate of population from 2.4 to 1.3 during a short period of six years. It is a world record.

References

1. Mahadevan, K., Ito Youchi, Vijayan K. Pillai and Kiran Prasad, 2003. "Communication, Modernization and Social Development, Vol. I & Vol. II, BRPC, New Delhi.
2. Mahadevan, K. 1997. "Communication Through Satisfied Adopters of Female Sterilization. In such in Family Planning", The Population Council, Vol. 8, New York.
3. Mahadevan, K. *et al.*, 2002. "Expeditious Empowerment of Women through Innovative Strategies in Andhra Pradesh", BRPC, New Delhi.
4. Mahadevan, K. *et al.*, 2003. "Participatory Experiment in Holistic Rapid Development" BRPC, New Delhi.
5. Mahadevan, K. 1993. "Successful Diffusion through Satisfied Adopters: An Action Research Design in Mahadevan and P. Krishnan, SAGE, London.
6. Mahadevan, K. 1997. "Satisfied Adopters for Diffusion of Family Planning: A Strategy for Improving Programme", JPR, New Delhi, 4 (2).
7. Mahadevan, K. 1974. Determinants of Non-Contraception: An Exploration in The Process of Decision Making Among Non-Adopters. Bulletin GIRHW & FW Vol. IX. No. 2.
8. Everett M. Rogers, 1997. "Communication Strategies for Family Planning", The Free Press, New Delhi.
9. Joseph Kivlin, E. 1996. "Communication in India: Experiments in Introducing Change", NIRD, Hyderabad.
10. Palmore James, 1967. "The Chicago Snowball: A Study of the Flow and Diffusion of Family Planning Information". In Bogue, Sociological Contribution to Family Planning Research, University of Chicago, Chicago.

17

Communication Strategies for Health Education in the USA: HIV/AIDS and Educational Resistance in the United States

Carol Key

Introduction

The United States through the promotion of sexual education has acquired resistance with certain groups. This period of rapid globalization, while homogenizing also may be instrumental in the fragmentation of trust in expert systems albeit education. As economic and political actions between countries increase and individual national sovereignty diminish, resistance and the lack of trust in expert systems allows the ability of certain groups to influence the state system. According to Giddens (1990) trustworthiness is composed of two types. First is what I will call familiarity or re-embedding of social relationships where trust or facework commitments develop on a personal level between individuals over a period of time and is sustained by credentials which have been proven reliable in another's eyes. The trust that develops in disembedded social relationships links local practices with globalized social relations, is based on faceless interactions and concerns the development of faith in experts or abstract systems.

Simmel's essay on The Stranger (1972), makes a sociological observation that in a modern society which of course ensues a modern social life, people for the most part interact with strangers unfamiliar to themselves. In pre-modern societies where the local community is the social organization the "stranger" although mistrusted until proven otherwise is seen as a whole person. However, in modern societies we do not necessarily interact with strangers as whole people especially in urban areas we interact with others that we do not know well or have never met before. But in order for modern institutions to operate there must be "trust bound up with the mechanisms of trust in abstract systems, especially in expert systems" (Giddens, 1990: 83). Anthony Giddens discusses the notion of dis-embedding with one of re-embedding. "By this I mean the reappropriation or recasting of disembedded social relations so as to pin them down (however partially or transitorily) to local conditions of time and place" (Giddens, 1990). Thus dis-embedding mechanisms interact with re-embedding mechanisms and may act to either support or to undermine them. In rural areas where the stranger is part of an expert system such as medical health professional can and may be seen as untrustworthy. It is within this juxtaposition of dis-embedding and re-embedding that trust in modern institutions is most salient. The abstract system (expert system) has encounters through face-work or faceless commitments. For example, representatives of abstract systems can attain characteristics of trustworthiness that contain friendship and intimacy as may be the case of a doctor, dentist, veterinarian or a travel agent. The Delia however is that in some abstract systems the contact is irregular and unreliable. Expert systems while many times contain face-work commitments also may contain face-less commitments. Thus the rise of abstinence only education is a form of distrust (disembedded social relationship) in modern expert systems and resistance is salient in the form of abstinence education through local communities. Thus abstinence as a form of sexual education acts as a re-embedding social relationship at the local level.

The abstinence only programs are more numerous in the southern regions of the United States and are a form of resistance to the unequal distribution of resources. Globalization and the dialectical nature involved in push and pull factors in the centralization of states have also contributed toward resistance toward programs such as the sexual abstinence programs in the United States. While poverty in inner cities has been given a lot of media attention, little attention has been given to rural areas and poverty. One fourth of the rural poor live in the Midwest, one third live in the South, 14.5 per cent live in the West and 7 per cent live in the Northeast. Of the rural poor 44% are African Americans. The farm population is only 10 per cent of the rural population so the rural poor are mostly non-farmers (Ropers, 1991). The decline in non-agricultural industries in rural America relates directly to poverty in rural communities. Most of the rural populations rely on non-agricultural industries to support the economy, therefore there is few retail and manufacturing industries to support the economy. The results are dwindling incomes, rising unemployment and populations leaving rural areas. Though unemployment is high, the rural poor do not rely on public assistance to the degree the urban poor use assistance. The lack of information and access to services, fear of stigmatism and reliance on informal employment as a means of earning money are some of the traits rural populations share.

> He is no stranger to hard times. He lived through the dust bowl on a farm in Kansas and then moved to Iowa and scrapped together the cash to buy a 35 acre farm. He sold the land years ago and moved to town, and when times got tough he went to work in nearby family owned business. In 1985, when the farm economy went completely bust and the company laid off anyone who wasn't immediate family, he took to scouring the roads that crisscross the flat treeless land just west of the Mississippi, in search of cans. His children moved away, a daughter to a good job out east, a son to Des Moines, where he is still looking for work.
>
> "But what good does complaining do?" the old man says. "You do whatever you have to, to get by, that's all. Say, be careful picking those things up", he adds, deadpan, when I hand him a can. 'You might catch AIDS."
>
> (Davidson: 1996: 70).

History of the AIDS Epidemic in the United States

In 1981 the United States Centre for Disease Control quietly released a small report on five cases of an unusual disease in gay men. Public fear escalated as the realization that there were no cures and the potentiality of becoming the largest epidemic and the plague of the 21st century mounted. However while AIDS was recognized in 1981, HIV, the human immuno-deficiency virus that causes AIDS, was not identified until 1983. HIV is a virus and is different than many other viruses in that it directly attacks the cells of the immune system, the body's defence system. HIV directly attacks the cells of the immune system and goes after a type of immune cell called the CD4 lymphocyte. CD4 cells are important in the immune system because they coordinate the attack by white blood cells and antibodies on viruses and other body invaders. Yet the HIV virus has the ability to escape detection by CD4 cells. Thus once inside, the virus's genetic material takes command of the CD4 cell and forces it to make copies of the virus.

In the 1980's, gay rights organization and public health professionals began campaigns to provide those most at risk with direct advice on how to prevent AIDS through the use of the condom. Information also was targeted at intravenous drug users another high-risk category. Some of these campaigns were controversial for example making needles available for intra-venous drug users and easy accessibility to condoms. These campaigns helped to slow the spread of the disease both within at risk groups and outside groups.

In 1987 the first drug to treat AIDS was (zidovudine) and, was approved by the FDA in the United States. AZT was pronounced as a miracle drug and was the first drug to show promise in keeping the virus in check. At this point, AIDS patients and advocates began to demand the drug even when it was in clinical trials. Consequently the FDA shorten the approval process to help get the drug to those who needed it while simultaneously ensuring its safety.

AZT belongs to a group of AIDS drugs known as nucleoside analogue reverse transcriptase inhibitors

(NRTIs). NRTIs were the first group of drugs developed to fight the virus, however AZT and the other NRTIs were not a cure. While they seemed to lower the amount of virus in the blood or for a time keep it in check they were not able to eradicate the virus completely. Also AZT which seemed to hold the most promise began to lose its effectiveness as the virus began to change. Other drugs were developed such as the protease inhibitors in 1995 and the non-nucleoside reverse transcriptase inhibitors (NNRTIs). None of these drugs proved to be the solution, however scientists began to realize that by combining the drugs together the rate of mutation declined. These drugs became known as "Cocktails". Between 1996 and 1997, the number of AIDS-related deaths dropped 42 per cent with another decline of 20 per cent between 1997 and 1998.

New drugs are currently being produced and moving ahead at a rapid pace along with research on potential vaccines. Since 1987, more than 40 vaccines have been tested on a limited basis. Only one, AIDSVAX has been promising enough to be tested in humans. One major issue at the heart of AIDS treatment has been the expense. Treatment for HIV and AIDS patients cost the United States government $6.9 billion in 1999, up from 4.5 billion two years before.

With the innovation of the new drugs many physicians and AIDS advocates began to notice that the prevention message, the call for safe sex and drug practices became less noticeable. Thus HIV infections began to climb in the late 1990's.

Social History of an Epidemic

When examining AIDS as an epidemic in the United States we must place it in a historical social context and understand the overarching social processes and changes that have affected American Society. The 1960's and 1970's brought dramatic changes in the dynamics of American Society, such as the Black civil rights movement, the women's movement and the gay civil rights movement. It is the later movement, which is the most relevant in the AIDS epidemic. The roots of the gay movement in the United

States began in the 1920's, however the movement never fully attracted public attention until the Stonewall Riots of June 28, 1969. In New York's Greenwich Village the gay population rebelled against police harassment. This is the first large publicized attack on gays and was the birth of the "gay rights" movement. The movement emerged as a form of resistance at the state level. During this period of rapid transformation occurring over two decades and the changing social milieu brought about changes and spin-offs in opposition to the various changes in institutional arrangements. Looking for answers and a growing disparity between rural and urban due to corporate agricultural conglomeration, farmers are loosing subsidies on crops. Thus, there are basic stratification issues involved in the accumulation and distribution of resources across time and space. It is within the spatial interaction of rural/urban where the distribution of resources is most salient. In the past decade, rural areas in the United States have felt the change in economic restructuring at an unusual pace. A basic indicator in human development such as food security is indicative of a country's unequal distribution in resources but is a spatial arrangement of un-even development and is the most basic indicator of a country's level of development. Food security, food insecurity and hunger vary by metro versus non-metro regions in the United States. For example Nord (2002) found that a large majority of non-metro households were food secure. However within a spatial distribution of access to resources rural areas are most at risk. Rates of food insecurity and hunger were unchanged from 1998 to 2000 in non-metro areas, while declining in metro areas. The USDA monitors food security and hunger in the United States through a nationally representative food security survey, conducted annually since 1995 by the US Census Bureau as a supplement to the Monthly Current Population Survey. Food insecurity and hunger declined from 1995 to 1999 in both non-metro and metro areas. The result of the survey indicates the rate of food insecurity was higher in non-metro areas. Food security is not the only resource that enhances the lack of trust in expert systems.

Cumulative AIDS cases in 2001

Age	# of Cumulative AIDs Cases
Under 5:	6,975
Ages 5 to 12:	2,099
Ages 13 to 19:	4,428
Ages 20 to 24:	28,665
Ages 25 to 29:	105,060
Ages 30 to 34:	179,164
Ages 35 to 39:	182,857
Ages 40 to 44:	136,145
Ages 45 to 49:	80,242
Ages 50 to 54:	42,780
Ages 55 to 59:	23,280
Ages 60 to 64:	12,898
Ages 65 or older:	11,555

Source: Centres for Disease Control 2001.

The availability of medical care and education along with the transformation of religious institutions has changed the educational approach of AIDS and sexually transmitted diseases. Medical education reaction to AIDS is being challenged through programs such as abstinence.

Education

Prevention is the most important instrument for fighting against HIV and AIDS. In the 1980's gay political organizations and public health professionals initiated campaigns to those most at risk for sexual transmission of the disease with direct advice on how to prevent it with the use of condoms. Other information was aimed at intravenous drug users who can acquire the virus by sharing needles with someone who is infected with HIV. These campaigns were controversial.

Overall the incidence of AIDS among US populations declined in the 1990's, but comparatively there has not been a decline in new cases among young people. Many government institutions that are responsible for public health education have consistently and repeatedly urged providing complete and accurate information to adolescents about HIV/AIDS prevention. The information includes the proper use of condoms to be an important part of the government's prevention programs. Federal health agencies share the broad scientific consensus that if used correctly, condoms are effective in preventing the transmission of HIV. However under the Bush administration the US government spends more than $100 million each year on "abstinence only-until-marriage programs". These programs cannot by law endorse or promote the use of condoms or even provide instruction in regard to their use. Medical education programs must provide abstinence education as defined by Section 510(B) of the Welfare Reform Act. "Abstinence education" means an educational or motivational program which:

(A) has as its exclusive purpose, teaching the social, psychological and health gains to be realized by abstaining from sexual activity;

(B) teaches abstinence from sexual activity outside marriage as the expected standard for all school age children;

(C) teaches that abstinence from sexual activity is the only certain way to avoid out-of-wedlock pregnancy, sexually transmitted diseases, and other associated health problems;

(D) teaches that a mutually faithful monogamous relationship in context of marriage is the expected standard of human sexual activity;

(E) teaches that sexual activity outside of the context of marriage is likely to have harmful psychological and physical effect;

(F) teaches that bearing children out-of-wedlock is likely to have harmful consequences for the child, the child's parents and society;

(G) teaches young people how to reject sexual advances and how alcohol and drug use increase vulnerability to sexual advances; and

(H) teaches the importance of attaining self-sufficiency before engaging in sexual activity.

The Bush Administration is advocating for an increase in funding for the "abstinence only until marriage" programs that basically promote abstaining from sexual activity until marriage as the only acceptable behaviour for youth, where marriage is defined as heterosexual marriage in a traditional nuclear family. These programs of abstinence until marriage cannot provide education that is sensitive to the rights and needs of gay, lesbian and bisexual adolescents. In sum these programs deny young people basic information that could prevent the spread of HIV/AIDS.

> Federally funded abstinence programs negate the fundamental rights guaranteed by international law, including the right to seek, receive and impart information and ideas of all kinds and the right to the highest attainable standard of health, and, indeed may have dire consequences of the right to life (Human Rights Watch, 2002).

The Bush Administration has not limited the promotion of abstinence-only programs to the United States. At the UN General Assembly Special Session on Children in May 2002, the US delegation, along with Iran, Libya, Pakistan, Sudan, argued that the summit declaration should endorse sexual abstinence before and during marriage as the only way to prevent HIV/AIDS transmission (Sanders, 2002). The Secretary of Health and Human Services, Tommy Thompson, addressing the Special Session on Children, stated, "As President Bush has said, abstinence is the only way of avoiding sexually transmitted disease, premature pregnancy and the social and personal difficulties attendant to non-marital sexual activity". The United States efforts "include strengthening close parent-child relationships, encouraging the delay of sexual activity and supporting abstinence education programs" (Sengupta, 2002: A14).

Several US states have enacted legislation promoting or mandating abstinence education. For example in 1995, North Carolina, as part of a comprehensive health program enacted a law requiring public schools to offer an abstinence-only-until marriage program and to offer sex education only after the local board of education has held a public meeting and reviewed instructional materials (Dellinger, 1997). After 1995 several states have passed legislation incorporating some or all of the federal definition of abstinence education.

Several US federal government organizations are in direct opposition to the abstinence only programs. The Institute of Medicine, the National Institutes of Health and the Centres for Disease Control all assert that providing accurate information to young people is an essential tool to fight HIV. Another US Organization such as the Department of Health and Human Services has placed as one of its objectives to increase the proportion of adolescents who use condoms if sexually active. Federal funding for abstinence-only education has not provided evidence that abstinence-only education delays adolescent (or extra-marital) sexual activity, nor changes in sexual behaviour that puts adolescents at risk for pregnancy, HIV/AIDS, and sexually transmitted diseases.

Young people are at risk for a number of serious health problems according to The Centres for Disease Control and Prevention's (CDC), Youth Risk Behaviour and Surveillance System (YRBSS). One of the more serious health problems includes sexually transmitted diseases and HIV/AIDS. In the most recent survey of high school students (Kann *et al.*, 1966) reported 53% of students have had sexual intercourse and 38% of students are sexually active. Of these students over half reported using a condom during their last sexual intercourse, with African American students significantly more likely than Hispanic or white teens to report condom use at last intercourse. Experts have reported that in recent years, the median age of HIV onset in the United States is lowering. While the overall decline in the incidence of AIDS among all the US populations declined during the 1990s, there has not been a comparable decline in young people. Medical care experts have found one of the most important ways to combat the transmission of HIV and AIDS is through education and this education must begin before young people engage in sexual activity and no later than seventh grade (Black and Jones, 1988; Kirby, Barth, Leland and Fetro, 1991;

White and Ballard, 1993). Since education is mandatory in the United States for children schools offer an appropriate setting for HIV/AIDS education.

The Institute of Medicine and the federal body of experts charged with the responsibility of advising the federal government on issues of health care, research and education assert the scientific literature shows that comprehensive sex and HIV/AIDS education programs along with condom availability can be effective in reducing high-risk sexual behaviour, however no evidence exists for abstinence-only programs. The Institute of Medicine concerned with the lack of scientific evidence of the effectiveness for the program, has asserted that "investing hundreds of millions of dollars of federal, state and local funds constitutes poor fiscal and health policy" (Medical Health Institute, 2001). The Institute of Medicine also recommended that Congress at all political levels, federal, state and local eliminate requirements that public funds be used for abstinence-only education but also, states and local school districts to continue to support or implement comprehensive sex education and condom availability programs in schools.

Kirby (2001) found analyzing methodologically rigorous outcome evaluation studies of HIV prevention and sexuality education programs that not only included abstinence but also the use of condoms and contraceptives can successfully delay the onset of sex and increase the use of condoms among sexually active teens. Another finding of this report concludes that there is little if any rigorous of abstinence-only program evaluations. This report also found very few rigorous evaluations of abstinence-only programs and among the few high quality studies that had been conducted did not show that abstinence-only programs had any effect on sexual behaviour among sexually active teens. At least one study (Jemmott *et al.*, 1998) compared the efficacy of educating teenagers about safer sex with an abstinence-only intervention found while both approaches affected sexual behaviour short-term, over time the safer-sex program proved more effective in reducing unprotected sexual intercourse. Thus the safer-sex strategy may be more effective with teens that are already sexually active. In 1997, Congress authorized an evaluation of the impact of abstinence-only programs funded by the Welfare Act of 1996, yet six years later there is no evidence to prove that the abstinence-only program to be effective in reducing teen sex, pregnancy of transmission (Mathematics Policy Research Institute, Inc., 2002). The Adolescent Family Life Act (AFLA) also concluded that to date there no adequate evaluations of the effectiveness of abstinence-only programs. The Joint United Nations Programme (1997) on HIV/AIDS (UNAIDS) found evidence that sexual health education for children and young people that included condom use promoted safer sexual practices and did not increase their sexual activity.

Non-metro areas in the US and AIDS

The Centres for Disease Control and Prevention (CDC) has monitored the AIDS epidemic since 1981 in the United States. The total of AIDS cases reported through December 1996 was 581,429. Of the AIDS cases reported, 32,043, or 5.5 per cent were from non-metropolitan areas (non-MSA's). The Office of Management and Budget defines a metropolitan statistical area (MSA) as a county or group of counties that includes a city of 50,000 residents or an urbanized area with at least 50,000 people that is part of a county or group of counties with at least 100,000 people. Non-metropolitan counties are all remaining counties. The cumulative deaths for the same period are 362,004. Other than the total from non-MSAs, the CDC does not publish rural statistics in their surveillance report.

The epidemic first appeared in urban areas and efforts to fight the disease were concentrated. Recently, the spread of AIDS in rural areas has become acknowledged by public health officials. Between the years of 1991 and 1992 according to the CDC, the number of AIDS cases in non-MSAs increased 9.4 per cent as compared with 3.3 per cent in MSAs with a population of 50,000 to 500,000. As a group non-MSAs have experienced a 69 per cent increase in the rate of AIDS among men who have sex with men between 1989 and 1994. Yet in comparison, the MSAs with more than 2.5 million people experienced only a 19 per cent increase (CDC, 1995a). The 25 counties with the highest rate of increase in AIDS during the period from 1988 and 1990 were primarily rural counties with an average county population of 73,000. Most of the women with HIV/AIDS reside in urban areas, 6 per cent of the female AIDS cases reported to the CDC in 1994 were residing in non-MSAs at the time of diagnosis. The number of HIV/AIDS cases in rural areas of the United States are increasing but not as rapidly as previously thought (Stephenson, 2000). According to CDC researchers, there has been a statistically significant trend of increasing AIDS rates in rural areas relative to urban areas. This trend points not so much to a large AIDS epidemic in rural areas, but to a slow infiltration of the virus into some smaller communities in the United States.

In the spring of 1991 the CDC began reporting AIDS by non-metropolitan area. Most states' information on rural areas is based on public health reporting. The data collected by a state may be influenced by the test itself. Another factor that may affect calculations of AIDS cases is that resident in rural areas may be more likely to travel to urban areas for HIV testing to protect their confidentiality. Also rural residents are less likely to seek HIV testing. Compared to their urban counterparts, rural residents had a lower perception of their risk for HIV (Mainous, Neill and Matheny, 1995).

Studies indicate that HIV/AIDS patients tend to be diagnosed in later stages of the disease because many time the physicians do not consider them to be at risk for HIV (Calonge, Peterson, Miller and Marshall, 1993; Miller *et al.*, 1995). Other issues in the accuracy of data include how many patients are infected in urban areas and return home along with those acquiring AIDS in rural areas then travelling to urban areas for treatment.

Studies of HIV/AIDS patients at university medical centres in eastern North Carolina and southeast Iowa reveal that 43 per cent to 46 per cent had migrated to these states and that 13 to 17 per cent had been diagnosed with AIDS before moving (Davis, Cameron and Stapleton, 1992; Rumley, Shappley, Waivers and Esinhart, 1991). Researchers have also asserted rural HIV/AIDS patients often travel several hours to procure medical services without changing their place of residence (Mainous and Matheny, 1996).

Rural HIV/AIDS patients are less likely to have public and private health insurance and they may delay seeking care until they are in the advanced stages of the disease. Service gaps exist and include an inadequate supply of mental health, counselling services and discriminatory attitudes.

The South has experienced the most rapid growth in AIDs cases. Between the years of 1988 and 1995, the southern states reported the largest and the greatest proportionate increase 31 per cent in AIDS cases. The South has also led the nation in the percentage of adolescent and young adult AIDS patients who reside in MSAs (50,00 to 500,000 population) and rural areas (CDC, 1995b). According to the Centres for Disease Control at the end of 2001 more than 1,822 adolescent 13 to 19 years old were known to be living with AIDS in the United States. From the 37 areas that conducted adult/adolescent name-based HIV infection case surveillance, 1,244 persons aged 13 to 19 years living with AIDS were reported representing 68% of all adolescents living with AIDS in the United States. These 37 areas reported an additional 1,926 adolescents living with HIV infection. The HIV data underestimate the population of infected adolescent as some states do not report HIV-infected person to CDC, and only persons who have been tested confidentially are reported. The South compared to the other regions in the United States also has the largest number of reported adolescents 13-19 years of age living with HIV infection and AIDS as of 2001. For example the state of Florida reported 287 cases of AIDS and 343 cases of HIV. Regional analysis in the United States indicates that the South is experiencing the most rapid growth of AIDS/HIV cases and a rapid growth in adolescent HIV/AIDS cases.

In conclusion, AIDS/HIV infection is a global epidemic. The disease first made its appearance in the homosexual population but now is entering new populations in the United States. Distrust of social institutions and the unequal distributions of resources by region in the United States has led to the politicization of morality through the abstinence-only programs sexual education programs. The strategies for communication for the prevention of HIV infection in the United States appears to be influenced by strong ideological and moral value systems rather than by empirical evidence on efficiency of available communication strategies for prevention. The focus on ideological and moral values is likely to reinforce unscientific notions and knowledge about HIV transmissions. In the long-terms these strategies may contribute to increasing the pace of the epidemic. Unfortunately, the measures supported by the United States Government to prevent HIV infection have powerful demonstration effects in the developing countries where HIV incidence rates are already high. The potential cost of misinformed communication strategies are too high to be borne silently anymore.

References

1. Black, J.L. and Jones, L.H. 1988. "HIV infection: Educational Programs and Policies for School Personnel". *Journal of School Health*, 60(6), 262-265.
2. Calonge, B.N., Peterson, L.R., Miller, R.S. and Marshall, G. 1993. "Human Immunodeficiency Virus Seroprevalence in Primary Care Practices in the United States." *The Western Journal of Medicine*, 158(2), 148-152.
3. Centers for Disease Control and Prevention, 1995a. "Update: Trends in AIDS Among Men Who Have Sex With Men-United States, 1989-1994". *Morbidity and Mortality Weekly Report*, 44(21), 401-404.
4. Centers for Disease Control and Prevention, 1995b. "First 500,000 AIDS Cases-United States, 1995." *Morbidity and Mortality Weekly Report*, 44(46), 849-853.
5. Centers for Disease Control and Prevention, 1996. *HIV/AIDS Surveillance Report*, 8(2), 9.
6. Committee on HIV Prevention Strategies in the United States, Institute of Medicine, 2001. *No Time to Lose: Getting More from HIV Prevention*, pp.118-20. Washington, D.C.: National Academy Press.
7. Davidson, Osha Gray, 1996. *Broken Heartland: The Rise of America's Rural Ghetto*. Iowa City: University of Iowa Press.
8. Davis, K.A., Cameron, B. and Stapleton, J.T. 1992. "The Impact of HIV Patient Migration to Rural Areas". *AIDS Patient Care*, 6(5), 225-228.
9. Dellinger, Anne, 1997. "Parental Rights and School Health: North Carolina's Legislation," *School Law Bulletin*, Winter 1997 pp. 1-9.
10. Giddens, Anthony, 1990. *The Consequence of Modernity*. Stanford: Stanford University Press.

11. Gwinn, M. and Wortley, P.M. 1996. Epidemiology of HIV Infection in Women and Newborns. Clinical Obstetrics and Gynecology, 39(2), 292-304.

12. Human Rights Watch, 2002. Ignorance Only: HIV/AIDS, Human Rights and Federally Funded Abstinence-Only programs in the United States. Vol.14, No.5(G), September 2002.

13. Jemmottet, *et al.*, John B. Abstinence and Safer Sex HIV Risk-Reduction Interventions for African American Adolescents," *Journal of the American Medical Association.* Vol. 279 no. 19, May 20, 1998, pp. 1529-1536.

14. Joint United Nations Programme on HIV/AIDS, Impact of HIV and Sexual Health Education on the Sexual Behaviour of Young People: A Review Update. p. 15, Geneva: UNAIDS, 1997.

15. Kann, L., Warren, C.W., Harris, W.A., Collins, J.L., Williams, B.I., Ross, J.G. and Kolbe, L.J. 1996. Youth risk behaviour surveillance—United States, 1995. Morbidity and Mortality Weekly Report. CDC Surveillance Summaries, 45(No. SS-4), 1-83.

16. Kirby, Douglas, 2001. *Emerging Answers: Research Findings on Programs to Reduce Teen Pregnancy.* p. 5, 88-91. Washington, D.C. National Campaign to Prevent Teen Pregnancy.

17. Kirby, D., Barth, R.P., Leland, N. and Fetro, J.V. 1991. "Reducing the Risk: Impact of a New Curriculum on Sexual Risk-Taking". *Family Planning Perspectives,* 23, 253-262.

18. Mainous, A.G., Neill, R.A. and Matheny, S.C. 1995. "Frequency of Human Immunodeficiency Virus Testing Among Rural U.S. Residents and Why It Is Done". *Archives of Family Medicine,* 4, 41-45.

19. Mainous, A.G., Neill, R.A. and Matheny, S.C. 1996. "Rural Human Immunodeficiency Virus Health Service Provision: Indications of Rural-Urban Travel for Care". *Archives of Family Medicine,* 5(9), 469-472.

20. Mathematica Policy Research, Inc. 2002. *The Evaluation of Abstinence Education Programs Funded Under Title V Section 510: Interim Report.*

21. Miller, R.S., Green, L.A., Nutting, P.A., Peterson, L., Stewart, L., Marshall, G. and Main, D.S. 1995. "Human Immunodeficiency Virus Seroprevalence in Community Based Primary Care Practices, 1990-1992: A Report from the Ambulatory Sentinel Practice Network". *Archives of Family Medicine,* 4(12), 1042-1047.

22. Nord, Mark, 2002. *Rates of Food Insecurity and Hunger Unchanged in Rural Households Economic Reasearch Service, U.S. Department of Agriculture.*

23. Ropers, Richard H. 1991. *Persistent Poverty.* New York: Insight Books.

24. Rumley, R.L., Shappley, N.C., Waivers, L.E. and Esinhart, J.D. 1991. "AIDS in Rural Eastern North Carolina-Patient Migration: A Rural AIDS Burden". *AIDS*, 5(11), 1373-1378.

25. Sanders, Doug, 2002. "Birth Control No Solution for AIDS," *Globe and Mail*, May 8, 2002, p. A7.

26. Sengupta, Somini, 2002. "U.N. Session Begins to Tally The Perils of Being Young," *New York Times*, May 9, 2002, p. A14.

27. Simmel, Georg, 1972. *Georg Simmel on Individuality and Social Forms: Selected Writings*, eds. Donalds Levine and Morris Janowitz. Chicago: University of Chicago Press.

28. Stephenson, Joan, 2000. "Rural HIV/AIDS in the United States: Studies Suggest Presence, No Rampant Spread". *JAMA: Medical News and Perspectives*, Vol. 284(2).

29. White, D.M. and Ballard, D.J. 1993. "The Status of AIDS/HIV Education in the Professional Preparation of Preservice Elementary Teachers." *Journal of Health Education*, 24(2), 68-72.

30. Wilcox, Brian and Wyatt, Jennifer, 1997. "Adolescent Abstinence Education Programs: A Meta Analysis", Presented at *The 1997 Joint Annual Meeting of the Society for the Scientific Study of Sexuality and the American Association of Sex Educators, Counselors and Therapists*, Arlington, Virginia, November, 1997.

18

Impacts of Clinic-based Informed Choice Program on Quality of Individualized Counselling Service in China

Wu Junqing[1,2,3], Chen Tikuwan[1], Gao Ersheng[2,3]

To evaluate the impacts of clinic-based informed choice program on quality of individualized service in family planning clinic in China. **Methods:** During the program, family planning service staffs in intervention clinic were trained on counselling skills, key points of individualized counselling service. Questionnaire surveys were conducted pre-and post-informed choice program to evaluate the impacts of the program. **Results:** Informed choice program had significantly improved the quality of individualized counselling service. The multivariate regression analysis showed that clients of the clinic were more likely to give the better evaluation of the service, the OR of evaluation score of individualized service is 1.712 (95% CI is 1.146 to 2.564) in experiment group of post-program in contrast with pre-program. The program also can satisfy the personal needs of clients and increase the satisfaction degree of the

1. Fudan University.
2. Shanghai Institute of Planned Parenthood Research.
3. National Laboratory of Contraceptives and Devices Research.
* Correspondence to: WU Junqing, Shanghai Institute of Planned Parenthood Research, #2140 Xietu Road, Shanghai, 200032, China. Email: *wujq@sippr.stc.sh.cn.*

service. **Conclusions:** Informed choice program is helpful for the improvement of the quality of individualized counselling service. It is necessary and imperative to improve the skills of service provided in counselling in family planning clinics.

The ideal family planning programs should satisfy the clients' needs, respect their value, protect their right and empower clients to make their own decisions about family planning based on full and unbiased information, that is informed choice. Informed choice is necessary for family planning program to achieve ideal situation, which was firstly proposed in the Act of International Conference on Population and Development in 1994. Because each client cherishes his/her own desire, live in special circumstance and have distinct background of culture and religion, this requires service providers tailor counselling and advice to each client's expressed needs and personal situation. Individualized service has become the core part and essential norm of informed choice program. This article aimed to evaluate the impacts of clinic based informed choice program on quality of individualized service in family planning clinic in China. It is expected to provide useful policy suggestion for the implementation and promotion of informed choice on contraceptives in China.

The data for the present study come from the projects entitled "The Intervention study of informed choice on contraception among married women in China", which was funded by UNFPA. The study was designed as a clinic-based intervention program. Two clinics were selected as field sites in Xuanzhou District, Anhui Province, China, one as the experiment group and the other as the control group. The duration of the intervention was 1 year. In the experiment clinic, informed choice program were implemented, which covered IEC program, training activities among service providers and follow up. Service providers were trained on counselling skills, which mainly include 6 principles, 6 subjects and 6 steps during the counselling process advocated by Centre for Communication Program, The Johns Hopkins University. While in control group, only regular family planning services were provided. Structural questionnaire surveys were conducted by exit interview pre-program and post-program respectively among clients to assess the quality of counselling service of the clinics. Before intervention, 357 clients of control clinic and 350 clients of experiment clinic were interviewed by specially trained interviewers respectively. In evaluation survey, 334 clients were interviewed in control group and 326 clients in experiment group. Some aspects of quality of care, as outlined in the Juidth Bruce framework could be adapted readily to the questionnaire form the clients perspective—for example, the choice of methods offered, the nature of client-provider interactions, and the extent to which information was provided to clients. The other main content of questionnaire included demography characteristics, KAP of contraceptives, evaluation of the service and so on.

Statistical Analysis

The data were analyzed using Statistical Analysis System (SAS) 8.12. The distributions of indexes were compared by Chi-square test. Multivariate Logistic Regression were applied to explore the related factors of clients assessment of the quality of counselling service received.

Results

Demographic Characteristics

The data collections of this study provide a wealth of information on women's perception of and experience with the informed choice program. As seen in Table 1, there were no significant differences of age distribution among different groups. The ages of most subjects are ranged from 26 to 40 years old. The distribution of occupations, education level and average income of subjects have no significant differences in the survey before the program. There are statistical differences in occupations, education levels and average income among control group and experiment group of post-program, control groups between pre-program and post-program, experiment groups between pre-program and post-program. Most of subjects are workers, which accounted more than 50%. About half of them are in or lower than middle school level or lower level.

Table 1: General Characteristics of Subjects (%)

Variables	Pre-program			Post-program			Pre and Post	
	Control group n=357	Exp group n=350	P_1	Control group n=334	Exp group n=326	P_2	Control group P_3	Exp group P_4
Age (years)								
20~	7.84	6.86	0.1024	5.39	4.91	0.9941	0.6185	0.0845
26~	29.13	36.29		30.54	30.67			
31~	41.74	40.86		41.62	41.27			
36~	21.29	16.00		22.46	22.70			
Occupation								
Worker	55.18	49.71	0.4678	66.47	51.53	0.0002	0.0182	0.0495
STM*	10.92	13.71		6.59	7.36			
Business/private/other	24.65	29.71		19.76	34.66			
Medical staff	9.25	6.87		7.19	6.44			
Education level								
Middle school or lower	49.58	46.86	0.5288	55.09	45.09	0.0215	0.2228	0.8983
High school	38.94	41.14		32.63	42.64			
College or higher	11.48	12.00		12.28	12.27			
Annual income per person (¥)								
~3000	6.72	7.71	0.9990	4.79	6.75	0.0006	0.0072	0.0001
3000~	25.21	23.43		17.96	19.02			
4000~	36.13	34.00		35.33	22.70			
5000~	11.49	16.57		20.36	17.79			
6000~	20.45	18.29		21.56	33.74			

* STM: scientist, teacher, manager.

The Quality of Individualized Counselling Service

In the structural questionnaire, 16 questions were set to assess the quality of individualized counselling service.

In the pre-program survey, the proportion of service provider who were polite to clients in control group was higher than that in experiment group. More service provider who were more likely to actively introduced the use, advantage and disadvantage of contraceptives to clients in control group than in experiment group, which is significant different. However, the proportions of both groups were still in a low level, below 50%. The availability and accessibility of contraceptives were higher in control group. As showed in Table 2, during nearly half of counselling activities, service providers didn't ask the desire of client, not understand the history of contraceptive use and introduce only one type of contraceptive method to clients. In more than 60% counselling, clients could not make clear the side effects and time limit of the contraceptives. IEC program were not effectively provided in clinic. Only 17.21% and 16.67% clients have ever gotten education material in control clinic and experiment clinic respectively. Only 40% clients were invited to return. About half counselling activities intended to induce the clients to choose a certain contraceptive in both control clinic and experiment clinic. Nearly 1/5 of the service providers had ever proposed the clients to choose certain contraceptive.

In the post-program survey, 12 out of 16 indexes were significantly different between control group and experiment group. In control group, most indexes have no significant difference between pre-program survey and post-program survey. While in experiment group, 12 out 16 indexes increased significantly.

In experiment group, the percentage of service providers who can understand the desire of contraceptive of clients increased from 45.24% to 55.38%, which was significantly different. The service providers who actively understand the history of contraceptives accounted for 52.68% in pre-program survey; it is 68.99% in post-program survey. Those who provide 2 or more types choices to clients increase from 49.20% to 58.23% in experiment group. The proportion of

Table 2: Assessment of Individualized Counselling Service (%)

Variables	Pre-program			Post-program			Pre and Post	
	Control group n=357	Exp group n=350	P_1	Control group n=334	Exp group n=326	P_2	Control group P_3	Exp group P_4
1. Whether they are polite	80.68	70.62	0.0248	72.79	72.11	0.8909	0.0994	0.7473
2. Whether they inquired desired contraceptive	50.15	45.24	0.2022	41.03	55.38	0.0003	0.0198	0.0096
3. Whether they inquired contraceptive experience	53.41	52.68	0.8487	46.79	68.99	0.0001	0.0921	0.0001
4. Whether they introduce two types or above of contraceptive methods	49.26	49.20	0.9697	46.15	58.23	0.0025	0.4289	0.0239
5. Whether introduce how to use	42.14	32.44	0.0093	38.78	53.16	0.0003	0.3845	0.0001
6. Whether they introduce side-effects of methods	39.17	35.71	0.3545	36.22	51.90	0.0001	0.4384	0.0001
7. Whether introduce time limit of methods	46.29	42.56	0.3300	44.23	55.38	0.0052	0.5984	0.0011
8. Whether they introduce advantages of methods	51.93	41.67	0.0076	42.63	57.59	0.0002	0.0178	0.0001
9. Whether they introduce disadvantages of methods	49.85	39.88	0.0093	36.86	51.90	0.0001	0.0009	0.0021
10. Whether they disseminate education material	17.21	16.67	0.8508	19.87	40.51	0.0001	0.3829	0.0001
11.Whether they explain the results of examination	60.53	54.17	0.0949	58.01	69.30	0.0033	0.5136	0.0001
12.Whether they induce client to choose certain method	50.45	44.05	0.0965	50.64	46.52	0.3014	0.9602	0.5263
13.Whether they confine client to choose certain method	21.07	18.75	0.4514	20.51	19.30	0.7044	0.8617	0.8571
14.Whether they invite to return	38.87	40.77	0.6144	25.32	40.19	0.0001	0.0002	0.8793
15.Availability of method	91.39	84.23	0.0045	89.10	93.04	0.0836	0.3244	0.0004
16.Accessibility of method	91.39	86.61	000471	89.10	94.62	0.0114	0.3244	0.0005

Note: 1. The proportion showed above is for "yes";
2. Statistical analysis method: Chi-square test.

service providers who can actively introduce the use, time limit, advantage and disadvantage of contraceptives to client are significantly different between pre-program and post-program in experiment group. The percentage of clients received education materials increased from 16.67% to 40.51%. After the intervention, more service providers can explain the results of examination to clients. The availability and accessibility of experiment clinic are significantly promoted.

Subjects' Satisfaction Rate of Counselling Service

The satisfaction rates of experiment group have significantly increased by 9.75% (from 49.11% for pre-program survey to 58.86% for post-program survey) ($P<0.05$). There was no significant increase of satisfaction rate in the control group between pre-program and post-program (Table 3).

Multivariate Regression Analysis

In this paper, score of clients' evaluation of individualized counselling service has been set as predicator of quality of counselling. Owing to the abnormal distribution of score, the score was divided into five categories—13~16, 10~12, 7~9, 4~6 and 0~3. The categories of score were used as dependent variable. The multi-category ordinal logistic regression model was applied to further examine the impacts of informed choice program. In the crude model, only groups of subjects were used as independent variables. In adjusted model, demographic characteristic of subjects were also added as independent variables. The results derived from the logistic regression analysis were tabulated in Table 4. It indicated that whether in crude model or adjusted model, the implementation of informed program is the significant variable explaining the magnitude of score of individualized counselling service. In crude model, OR is 1.712 and 95% confidential interval ranged from 1.146 to 2.564 in experiment group of post-program, in which experiment group of pre-program is selected as reference. While in adjusted model, OR is 1.668 and 95% confidential interval is from 1.106 to 2.520 (Table 4).

Table 3: Subjects' Satisfaction of Counselling Service (%)

Variables	Pre-program			Post-program			Pre and Post	
	Control group n=357	Exp group n=350	P_1	Control group n=334	Exp group n=326	P_2	Control group P_3	Exp group P_4
Satisfied	57.86	49.11	0.0739	55.13	58.86	0.5296	0.2032	0.0219
Partly satisfied	31.45	38.39		29.49	28.48			
Dissatisfied	10.68	12.50		15.38	12.66			

Statistic analysis method: Chi-square test.

Tables 4: Multivariate Regression Analysis of Individualized Counselling Service

Comparative Group	Reference group	Crude OR			Adjusted OR*		
		OR	95% CI		OR	95% CI	
			Lower	Upper		Lower	Upper
Control group of pre-program	Experiment group of pre-program	1.179	0.789	1.763	1.188	0.787	1.795
Control group of post-program		0.944	0.634	1.405	0.951	0.633	1.428
Experiment group of post-program		1.712	1.146	2.564	1.668	1.106	2.520

*Adjusted OR was calculated by controlling the distribution of personal characteristics of subjects among different groups.

Discussions

Decisions about contraceptive use are most likely to meet a person's need when they reflect individual desires and values, are based on accurate, relevant information and medical appropriate—that is, when they are informed choices. To make informed choice, people need to know about family planning, to have access to a range of methods and to have support for individual choice from social policies and community norms.

Individualized counselling is the heart of informed choice programs. It is face-to-face communication in which one person helps another make decisions and act on them. Face-to-face discussion with a family planning provider can be the crucial step for a person in deciding to use a family planning method and in learning how to use it correctly. Any family planning provider, at any level, at any time, can help a client make decisions.

In 1987, Centre for Communication Programs of The Johns Hopkins University, suggested the 6 steps in counselling new clients, that is, GATHER steps. GATHER steps include: G- Greet clients in an open, respectful manner. A-Ask clients about themselves. T- Tell clients about choices. H- Help clients make an informed choice. E-Explain fully how to use the chosen method. R- Return visits should be welcomed. In 1997, Murphy, E.M. and Steele, C. proposed the 6 principles and 6 topics of family planning counselling. 6 principles of counselling are: (1) Treat each client well. The provider is polite, show respects for every client and creates a feeling of trust. (2) Interact. A provider can help best by understanding the person's need, concerns and situations. At the same time, the provider encourages clients to talk and ask questions. (3) Tailor information to the client. Listening to the client, the provider learns what information each client needs. The provider gives the information accurately in language that the client understands. Also, the provider helps the client understand how information applies to his or her own personal situation and daily life. (4) Avoid too much information. The providers must avoid information overload. (5) Provide the method that the client wants. The provider helps the clients make their own informed choices and respects those choices—even if a client decides against using family planning or puts off a decision. (6) Help the client understand and remember. The provider shows samples family planning materials, encourages the client to handle them and shows they are used. If the client can be given print materials to take home, they help reminds client what to do. Most counselling about method choices cover 6 topics, which are: effective advantages and disadvantages, side effects and complications, how to use, STD prevention and when to return. In the training activity, all service providers of experiment clinic are trained on the above theory of counselling. In the evaluation survey, sixteen questions were put forward to assess the individualized counselling provided by family planning clinics.

The result of multivariate analysis showed evident improvements in the quality of individualized counselling skills among service providers in the experiment group, in which OR is 1.712 (95% CI is 1.146 to 2.564) in experiment group of post-program in contrast with pre-program. However, it is still in a low level, which is related to the traditional family planning management system in China. Traditionally, most family planning program concentrated on quantitative index. Less attention was paid to how to listen and respond to clients in an empathetic way, how to help them make decisions, and how to inform and instruct clients in ways that they will remember and follow.

In a good counselling situation the provider not only gives accurate, clear information but also establishes a relationship of trust and confidence with the client. This is done by expressing empathy, being respectful and telling the truth. Providers and clients must exchange information. The clients should be encouraged to think and talk about her or his concerns, circumstance and family planning need. The provider must describe appropriate family planning methods, their risk and benefits and, when a client chooses a method, how to use it. The results showed that half of service process can't effectively understand the desire of clients and give sufficient information to them.

From the experience of research, we recognized that

good and individualized counselling is not hard, but it needs skills. The service providers can counsel well if they learn to: show that they understand and care about clients—build trust; find out and understand how their clients feel; give useful and accurate information to clients; help clients to make their own choices, based on clear information and their own feelings, situations and need—individualized service; and help them remember what to do and follow it.

Acknowledgements

The project was supported by a grant from The United Nations Population Funds (UNFPA). The support of the State Famiiy Planning Commission, China and Xuanzhou District Family Planning Commission, Anhui Province, China are gratefully acknowledged.

References

1. Center for Communication Program, 1987. The Johns Hopkins University. For family planning providers: why counselling counts! Population Reports. Series J No:36.
2. Center for Communication Program, 1987. The Johns Hopkins University. Counselling make a difference. Population Reports. Series J No: 35.
3. Center for Communication Program, 1998. The Johns Hopkins University. New GATHER to counselling. Population Reports. Series J No: 48.
4. Center for Communication Program, 2001. The Johns Hopkins University. Informed choice in family planning: helping people decide. Population Reports. Series J No: 50.
5. Murphy, E.M. and Steele, C. 1997. Client-provider interactions in family planning services. In: Technical Guidance/ Competence Working Group. Recommendation for updating selected practice in contraceptive use. Vol. 2. Chapel Hill, NC, INTRAH, pp. 187-194.
6. Robert, A., Hatcher, Ward Rinehart and Richard Blackburn, 1997. The Essentials of Contraceptive Technology—A Handbook for Clinic Staff. Center for Communication Programs. The Johns Hopkins University School of Public Health, pp. 3-1-3-8.
7. Wu Junqing, Chen Xikuan and Gao Ersheng, 2001. The counselling skills of informed choice on contraception. Reproduction and Contraception (in Chinese) 21(5): 312.
8. Yang Lifang, 1999. The skill of counselling of informed choice on contraceptive. Chinese Journal of Family Planning (in Chinese) (7): 293.

19

Intensive Health Education for Leprosy Case Detection through Networking—A Model Replicated all over the Country

N. Murugesan

Introduction

Tamil Nadu was one of the hyper endemic states in India. National Leprosy Eradication Programme (NLEP) has been implemented since 1955. It contributed almost one third of the country's patients load in the early 1980s. Very few districts namely undivided South Arcot, undivided Salem, undivided Chengalpattu, undivided North Arcot contributed to more than half of patients' load in Tamil Nadu. Multi-Drug treatment (MDT) programme was introduced on pilot basis in 1983 in the undivided North Arcot district. On successful implementation of MDT in North Arcot, it was expanded to other districts.

The entire state was brought under MDT in a phased manner from 1983 to 1991. Before the introduction of MDT, treatment was given to leprosy using Dapsone tablets called Monotherapy. Patients were under long-term treatment and they were getting accumulated in the records and not discharged and because of its long-term nature, the patients were also not regular. With the advent of MDT, patients after getting adequate treatment were immediately discharged. But, in the endemic districts, the leprosy was still posing a problem because of its magnitude. Unless the burden of leprosy was reduced by detecting and treating all available cases in a short period, the chain of transmission of leprosy could not be arrested and the disease could not be eliminated.

Danish Assistance to NLEP (DANLEP) in Tamil Nadu

DANLEP, a bilateral agency has been supporting Tamil Nadu in the leprosy control programme. The support started in 1986 in the undivided Salem District. During 1991, DANLEP extended its support to the undivided South Arcot district a hyper endemic district and Chennai city. The undivided South Arcot has been a highly populated district with a population of 4.88 million and a vast stretch of area with a Sq Km of 10,898. It had 11 Government Leprosy Control Units (GLCUs), 2 Urban Leprosy Centres (ULCs) and 5 Non-Government Organisations. These Units were well located geographically to plan and provide services to the people who live in and around these institutions. But, the District Office for leprosy was located in an extreme corner of the district at Cuddalore and it became difficult to coordinate the sub-district level institutions. In order to facilitate better administrative functioning, the entire district was divided into three operational zones, keeping the geographical contiguity in view. The units falling under these zones became the zonal members. By taking membership of Medical Officers from each zone, priority committees were formed. The zonal members became priority committee members as per their own interest and choice.

The priority committees formed were

1. Case detection/holding/release
2. Prevention of Disability and Rehabilitation
3. Information Education and Communication-cum-Community Participation
4. Training and capacity building.
5. Monitoring and Evaluation.

These priority committees were given the following terms of reference to work:

1. To do situation analysis with respect to their own priority,
2. To identify problems, deficiencies, give feed back to the institutions concerned,
3. To design need based interventions, to be implemented and followed-up.

To illustrate one priority namely Case detection/ Holding/Release, brainstorming was done with the members of the committee of this priority in keeping with the terms of reference. The problem identified was: A gap existed between the New Case Detection Rate (NCDR) reported from the field and the NCDR found by Sample Survey and Assessment Units (SSAU). In order to bridge the gap between these two, it was decided to detect all the leprosy cases not detected so far in a shorter period. The outcome of the brainstorming was to identify various stake holders in the district, sensitize them on leprosy elimination and involve them in awareness creation through Interpersonal Communication and referring of suspected cases for diagnosis. It was decided to cover the entire district in a short period. Strategically, it was decided to cover half of the Govt. Leprosy Control Units in one month namely October 1991 and the next half of the areas in another month after few months.

Keeping the spark of the brainstorming in mind, a systematic planning, implementation and follow up were done, by analytically looking at the related factors.

They are described under:

1. Need and Rationale for the campaign,
2. Objectives,
3. Essentials and Prerequisites,
4. Planning,
5. Preparatory phase—District level/Sub-district/LCU level,
6. Implementation phase,
7. Follow up and Evaluation phase,
8. Actions on track,
9. Activities carried out at the district and in the field,

10. Post-campaign review and factors that contributed to the success of the campaign,
11. Independent Evaluation Team's observations and recommendations,
12. Efforts for replication—State and National level.

1. Need and Rationale for the Campaign

The Intensive Health Education-cum-Leprosy Case Detection Campaign (ICDC) was proposed in order to fulfil the following needs:

a) Bridging the gap between actual prevalence and recorded prevalence
b) Using an alternative methods of case finding with community participation
c) Accelerating case detection activity and treating the patients
d) Increasing awareness about leprosy among public and encourage voluntary reporting
e) Stimulating and enthusing the leprosy programme staff at all levels who have got into 'routine' mode.

2. Objectives of the Campaign:

a) To cover the entire state with Information, Education, Communication and Community Participation and thereby creating awareness about leprosy, through interpersonal communications.
b) To identify the hidden leprosy cases in the community, to reach the un-reached and put them on treatment to reduce the chain of transmission of leprosy in the community.
c) To involve Primary Health Care system and other health care systems in leprosy elimination work.
d) To involve various Govt. departments like Family Welfare, Public Relations, Education, Revenue, Nutrition and other Non-Govt. Organisations in Leprosy Elimination Campaign.
e) To train and involve community volunteers in creating awareness among public to ensure their support in leprosy elimination activities.

3. Essentials and Prerequisites

One knows that for any programme to succeed, the prevailing environment and the positive features of opportunities are highly essential. The following favourable features fostered the campaign since its conception stage.

- Political and bureaucratic support and commitment.
- Govt. departments' willingness, interest and cooperation.
- Strong support from bilateral agency DANLEP, Non-Govt. Organisations' help and support.
- People's interest, motivations and participation.

4. Planning

During the initial stages, the District level managers and the priority committee had a couple of sittings to review and analyze the leprosy situation. The purpose was to identify appropriate ways and means of conducting the campaign efficiently at all levels. Experience based suggestions on organizing campaigns to create awareness and detect case were put-forth.

The major emphasis and focus were intensive health education throughout the project area and thrust was on interpersonal communication with the support of mass media.

The project area would be covered by Intensive Health Education-cum-Case detection campaign in 30 days. It was proposed to have three phases namely Preparatory phase, Implementation Phase and Post-campaign follow-up-evaluation phase.

During planning phase, micro planning was developed for the areas to be covered. This was done jointly by the District Leprosy Officer, Medical Officers of GLCUs concerned in consultation with Joint Director of Health Services/ Deputy Director of Health Services (Public Health) and NLEP field staff, facilitated by DANLEP Advisor.

The overall campaign plan specified the following critical activities under each phase:

5. Preparatory phase

- IEC materials should be designed, produced and supplied. Adequate interpersonal communication materials should be made available to field staff and volunteers.
- The vehicles should be made road worthy to be used for the campaign and campaign related activities.
- Collaborative efforts should be initiated with other Govt. departments to get their support for the campaign. The help, support and cooperation of officials and staff of Primary Health Care, General Health Care Systems, Panchayat and Development, Revenue, Education, Social Welfare and other support of Distt. Collector can be used to a greater extent.
- Volunteers should be identified locally, briefed about the campaign and trained. In order to cover the entire area, the local volunteers like NSS, NCC, Scouts, Nehru Yuvak Kendra (NYK), Mahalir Mandram, Cine Fans Associations, Service Agencies, Welfare Organisation etc. can be identified, trained and used.
- Detailed activity plan should be prepared for training of PHC and other Govt. department staff and volunteers should be prepared in advance and training programmes should be organized prior to campaign.
- Training materials for medical officers, trainers and searchers should be designed before imparting training.
- Mass media should be fully harnessed to disseminate messages on early signs of leprosy with a specific focus on infectivity, multi-drug treatment services, drug delivery and other details of the campaign.
- Drugs should be procured and supply ensured.
- Development, printing and supply of special formats for reporting should be organised.

6. Implementation Phase

- The campaign should be carried out as per plans.
- Health Education-cum-Case Detection activity has to be conducted at the village level in rural areas/wards in urban areas. It should be essential to keep in mind,

the community participation and try to involve as many people as possible.

- Special focus should be laid on education of people on cases, especially cases of consequences and detection of these cases. The purpose of elimination of leprosy and breaking the chain of transmission in the community should be kept in mind.
- Formats designed for recording and reporting of field activities and findings are to be used. The cases are to be confirmed and put on treatment.
- Education of patients/family members should be done for regular drug compliance and self-care practices for disability prevention.

7. Post-Campaign follow up and Evaluation Phase

- All the cases detected should be put on treatment immediately.
- Patients requiring services for Prevention of Disability (POD) should be promptly attended to.
- A format designed for reporting on the campaign can be used for consolidation of district level findings.
- Based on the findings and experiences future, strategies and plans could be evolved and pursued through.

8. Actions on Track

District stretegies/plans thus finalised by the District Managers and Medical officers of the GLCUs were presented to the District Leprosy Eradication Society under the Chairmanship of District Collector.

It was suggested that intensive health education and case detection campaigns could be done in a phased manner throughout South Arcot District. To start with, it was also suggested to take up half of the GLCUs during October 2-31, 1991. As such 98 sub-centres were selected for coverage during Phase-I, throughout South Arcot District. The District Collector, Joint Director of Medical and Rural Health Services, Chief Educational Officer assured the District Leprosy Organisation of their help and co-operation in these campaigns.

The District Collector sent out letters to Tashsildars, Block Development Officers to extend their helping hands by deputing Village Administrative Officers, and Supportive staff and Noon Meals Organisors, Rural Welfare staff.

The Joint Director issued out letters to Medical Officers of PHCs to depute their Multipurpose workers supervisors and Block Extension Educators to get involved in Health Education and case finding campaign when it was conducted in their areas of work.

The Chief Education Officer sent out circulars to Head Masters of Higher Secondary Schools and High Schools to depute programme officers and NSS/NCC/Scouts students for training and involvement.

The District Adult Education Officer requested his Animators and supervisors for their orientation and involvement in leprosy work.

Service organisations, Banks, Youth Clubs, Voluntary Agencies, Welfare Associations, Women groups were identified and used.

Varieties of training and education programmes were organised. Lot of enthusiasm was seen from the field staff, other participants of the campaign and the community. The foci of health education were to create awareness on early signs, efficacy of Multi-drugs and service facilities available.

9. Activities Carried Out at the District and in the Field

A. *Back Drop Activities*

a) Specific strategy was shared with all NLEP staff of the district to arrive at common understanding for standardized quality of implementation.

b) Action plan was prepared of at each unit level based on rural and urban needs. This was done under the leadership of the unit Medical Officer of NLEP, involving PHC Medical officer.

c) Information on staff position of Primary Health Care from the Deputy Director of Health Services was collected.

d) District Collector and other members of the District Leprosy Eradication Society were involved in all stages of planning and preparation.

e) Planning was done with other local NGOs, Volunteers and interest groups.

f) Preparatory meetings of NLEP, Health and Development officials at district level were conducted.

g) Searchers—PHC, NLEP and local volunteers were identified and sensitised. The interested school teachers and students were involved as well.

h) IEC materials were designed, produced and procured whereever necessary and supplied to all the field units.

i) As per the mobility plan, vehicles were procured or diverted from various departments as ordered by the District Collector.

j) Inaugural function was conducted at district, sub-district level which created a healthy and conducive atmosphere at start of the campaign. Ministers, MPs, MLAs and Panchayat Presidents/Ward Members/Councillors participated in the inauguration and this added to the credibility and acceptance of the campaign and these ensured excellent publicity through Television, All India Radio, Press and other media as well.

B. *The Search through Rapid Survey*

The searchers visited house to house and conducted rapid survey. They examined the people with suspected lesions of leprosy. Those suspected by the SEARCHERS were entered into a format specifically designed for this purpose it had names of those examined and other demographic and clinical details. These suspected cases were seen by NLEP staff for final diagnosis.

C. *IEC and Community Participation*

IEC activities were found to be very crucial and extremely important for the campaign. Only effective IEC strategies and involvement of public, could motivate people to volunteer and acquire correct knowledge about the facts of leprosy. Hence IEC was done before and during the campaign to provide backup and support to achieve campaign objectives, since everything hinges around the qualitative and quantitative coverage of IEC.

D. *Monitoring*

At the HSC, PHC, sub-district and district level, the survey data collected were consolidated daily using the formats.

The consolidated data were sent to the district headquarters on the very same day. This helped in assessing the trend of the campaign in various units day to day and adopt mid-course intervention.

E. *Treatment and Drugs*

Availability of drugs were ensured with NLEP and Primary Health Care system so that people who were found to have leprosy were given treatment immediately on confirmation.

F. *Valedictory*

Valedictory functions were conducted at different levels namely Taluk, sub-district, and district level to share the campaign results. Press media played a vital role in covering all these functions giving publicity to the activities and results and people became aware of the outcome of the campaign.

10. Post-Campaign Review and Factors that Contributed to the Success of the Campaign

Review with other District managers and Medical Officers and field staff who were involved in the campaign provided opportunity to find out the positive features, problems encountered. Most of them came out with the difficulties experienced. They are:

I. Shortage of POL expenses and vehicles.

II. Money for incidental expenses.

III. Inadequate educational materials.

IV. Of course-time pressure.

The key factors contributed which contributed to the success are enlisted below:

- The "Political will" of the state is a major contributing factor which provide total support and strength to the campaign, in addition to giving due publicity and attention that campaign required. The participation of the Ministers and other elected representatives of people gave the camp a creditable visibility.

- The participation of bureaucrats and key officials provided encouragement and motivation to field staff.
- Co-ordination with various Govt. Health and Non-Health departments.
- Co-ordination with NGOs both working for leprosy and others.
- Orientation and involvement of Primary Health Care Staff and development of 'Micro Plan' by themselves.
- Involvement of local Panchayat members.
- Initiating and leadership of District level Leprosy Officials.
- A well designed IEC before and during the campaign and involvement of Public.
- Coverage of the entire project area within a short and specific time.
- The following media were used appropriately and effectively:
    - Video show/film show with cable TV
    - Loud speakers,
    - Posters and stickers,
    - Cine slides,
    - All India Radio—Announcements of Jingles.
    - Press—Leading Daily,
    - Hand bills,
    - Banners, Placards.
    - Processions, Rally,
    - Group meetings.
    - Interpersonal Communications and Individual counselling.

All these efforts have led to identify 2379 new cases during October 1991 in South Arcot District as detailed below:

	MB	PB	TOTAL
1) Cuddalore	19	353	372
2) Panruti	5	182	87
3) Vridhachalam	6	172	178
4) Chidambaram	4	161	165
5) Ulundurpet	10	142	152
6) Tindivanam	1	180	181
7) Villupuram	3	448	451
8) G.L.T and S.C -Trikoilur	1	197	198
9) Arakandanallur	6	178	184
10) Kallakurichi	5	177	182
11) Kalrayan Hills	6	113	119
	66	**2303**	**2369**

Because of the success of the campaign, similar campaigns were conducted during Jan-Mar. 1992 in all the areas of the five voluntary agencies doing leprosy work in South Arcot District. The strategies and action plans were similar to that of Phase-I campaign, keeping the post-campaign review in mind. During this period, ICDC was done in Neyveli Township area with the help and support of Neyveli Lignite Corporation. The NSS/NCC Volunteers of colleges and schools and the workers were involved in this venture. The results of the campaign Phase II are given below:

	MB	PB	TOTAL
1. Cases newly detected in the Vol. Agencies areas	30	407	437
2. Cases detected in Neyveli Township area	14	108	122
	44	**515**	**559**

In the rest of the half of the GLCU areas, ICDC was conducted during Jan-Mar. 1993. Experiences gained during

Phase I and II ICDC were kept in view while planning phase III of ICDC in terms of mobilisation of manpower, materials and logistics and their utilisation 1527 cases were detected of which 82 were MB cases and 1445 were PB cases.

To sum up,

a) Opportunities were given for the staff to plan, implement and monitor field based community sponsored health education and case finding programmes.

b) In a brief campaign period, the entire district was covered and awareness was created to a very great extent and a record no.of cases was found.

c) The response from the community, service clubs, banks, village based welfare organizations, youth and women groups and other voluntary agencies was highly encouraging. They provided tea/coffee, snacks, refreshments and breakfast to volunteers in addition to their participation in the campaign was very much encouraging.

d) Help, support and co-operation received from the Education, Public Health, Development, Information and Public Relations, Field Publicity and other departments were appreciable.

11. Visit of Independent Evaluation Team (IET)

Incidentally, an Independent Evaluation Team consisting of the representatives of World Health Organisation (WHO), Government of India (GoI) visited South Arcot District for evaluation of NLEP immediately after the campaign. They listened to the strategy of the campaign narrated by the Officials and staff and visited the field and assessed the information level of people and interacted with them. Based on their observations and finding, they appreciated the campaign and recommended this strategy to GoI as a replicable model throughout the country.

12. Efforts for Replication—State and National Level

The experience of ICDC was shared at the state level forum with other district officials. Few of the district officials carried out this campaign in small scale in their district as well.

When a state level review was conducted by the Health Secretary, the experiences were shared. He appreciated the initiatives taken by the South Arcof District Officials and came forward to replicate the whole exercise throughout Tamil Nadu. As such, ICDC was conducted all over Tamil Nadu in February in 1997.

The results were encouraging with the involvement of Primary Health Care system. The outcome of the campaign conducted all over Tamil Nadu lead to increase the leprosy awareness of people through multi-media mix to detect a total number of 12,796 leprosy cases which includes 1,045 Multi Bacillary (MB) and 11,751 Pauci Bacillary (PB) cases.

GoI were keenly observing Tamil Nadu's efforts in the context of the campaign and sent representatives to observe in the field. WHO deputed an expert in leprosy to study the campaign in depth. These observers after interacting with Government Officials, Non-Government Organisations, Vounteers and people and highly appreciated the work done during the campaign and recommended to GoI to replicate this all over the country.

As the campaign had all the elements and nuances of Leprosy Elimination Campaign (LEC), promulgated by WHO in order to bring this exercise in global parlance, the external observers named it as Modified Leprosy Elimination Campaign (MLEC). As per the recommendations of experts who visited Tamil Nadu, MLEC was conducted all over the country with World Bank support four times so far.

In Tamil Nadu alone, by these innovative exercises so far 31,548 leprosy patients were detected. These efforts have created very good awareness among people and brought out the so-called hidden cases. This has helped to accelerate the process of elimination of leprosy from Tamil Nadu as well. If a state reaches a level of one or less than one leprosy case per 10,000 population, then leprosy is considered as eliminated as per WHO's norms. Thus, the experiment initiatived at South Arcot District had helped to accelerate the process of reaching the goal of elimination of leprosy not only at the state level but also at the national.

The author of this paper is gratified in sharing this exciting experience to which he was instrumental right from its conceptualisation.

20

Social Action for Health

Saroj S. Jha

Introduction

Biomedical technologies employed for curing diseases and prolonging lives have achieved some remarkable successes in the world today. High potency drugs, nuclear medicine, laser surgery and other fast developments, are making it possible for people to live longer and more productively. Those who can afford the benefits of such development are not unduly concerned about its high cost. If organs can be transplanted, blood vessels re-channelled and joints replaced, a good life can be assured.

But good health, as we are often reminded, is not merely the absence of disease. It is a state of physical, mental and social well-being. Technologies may help people live longer, but not necessarily better. What is important is to enable people to increase control over and to improve their health. This means addressing the determinants of health through health promotion strategies that make government accountable and people empowered for health.

This means addressing the determinants of health through health promotion strategies that make government accountable and people empowered for health. In India where millions live below the poverty line, in homes that are crowded, ill ventilated and pest-ridden, work in sub-human conditions, exposed to infection, injuries and occupational diseases, the urgent need to promote health has never been greater.

The silent killers like poverty, ignorance, malnutrition and environmental pollution unobtrusively continue to attack vulnerable population. Health and poverty retain the poor in poverty and poverty retains them in poor health. Millions of people, the poor especially, are also illierate. Women are particularly disadvantaged with high rate of illiteracy, sexual exploitation. oppressive discrimination in the labour market, and in general low social status. The challenges are enormous.

- Diarrhoeas and acute respiratory infections are still killing hundreds of infants and children every year.
- TB is a major killer and there is increasing resistance to drugs that cure TB.
- Malaria cases may have dropped but more malignant forms of the disease are spreading.
- HIV infection has hit nearly 4 million people.
- Under-nourishment is common in children under 5 years.
- 50% of women live on subsistence diets and anaemia is a serious problem leading to high maternal mortality.

Health for all is still a distant dream. Despite concerted efforts to strengthen all the elements of primary health care, the philosophy underlying the HFA movement, viz., equity and social justice, is yet to translate into action. For example, the nexus between health and poverty, health and employment, health and social disintegration, has rarely been addressed.

At Alma Ata in 1978, it was re-iterated very strongly that health is a social goal and a fundamental human right. To secure this right for every individual, it was important that all social sectors, not merely the health sector, got involved in addressing issues related to equity and social justice—the key to attaining the HFA targets. A fundamental principle is that while the government have the responsibility of providing health to the people, it is the right and duty of the people individually and collectively to participate in the development of their health. While governments have been responsible, they have however largely focused upon technology centred health advances.

They have to a large extent, failed to address issues of social structures and their implications for health, especially in evolving strategies for mobilizing communities for social action and especially mobilizing the poor who are the most health deprived.

Inadequate access to quality health care will remain a formidable challenge to achieving health for all. In fact there are indicators that health inequalities may indeed widen with increasing privatization of health care, their concentrations in urban areas, and their high costs. A movement to seek peoples right to health must begin to spread across the country, involving not merely the health sector but all other sectors and groups that are concerned with social development. This clearly means that strategies must be evolved for mobilizing communities for social action.

Social action in health can only take place when reliable information on what makes or breaks health is available and disseminated to the widest audiences in the country. This involves all stakeholders including the ordinary citizen, whose voice unfortunately is rarely heard or heeded.

Social Action for Health

Social action for health is action taken to address the multidimensional determinants of health, especially the political, economic, social, and environmental forces that bring to people a level of health, to make it possible for people to lead a socially and economically productive life.

The need to involving communities in planning and implementing health programmes had been felt for a long time, long before the Alma Ata Conference, 1978. However, it was at Alma Ata that a major statement of the Declaration affirmed that people not only have the right to participate individually and collectively in the planning and implementation of health care programme but they also have a duty to do so. In emphasizing this importance of full and organized community participation and ultimate self-reliance with individuals, families and communities assuming more responsibility for their own health was recognized.

Ten years later at Riga, it was declared: Involvements of communities in PHC is not just an ethical nicety. It is a technical and social necessity. It is now well recognized that science and technology have come to a point where their contribution to further improvement of health standards can make a real impact only if the people themselves become full partners in health protection and promotion.

A few years later after Riga, there was some fresh thinking on development practices which led to the emergence of the concept of community involvement in health. The term, 'involvement' was preferred to 'participation' as it implied a deeper and more personal identification of members of the community with primary health care. It implied a partnership being established between individuals, community groups and organizations, both government and non-governments, in planning, operation and control of health activities, using local, national and other resources. From this emerged, 'community action for health', an area of special interest to WHO in the nineteen nineties.

Several benefits of such an approach are identified:

- It is a cost-effective way of extending a health care system to the geographical and social periphery of a country.
- The programme becomes more effective and also more efficient with greater coordination of resources, activities and efforts.
- It promotes equity, solidarity and sharing of resources.
- It promotes self-reliance and increases people's control over issues.
- It promotes sustainability.

Within the rigid boundaries that traditionally exist between the various development sectors in the government, it is obvious that soical action for health must rely heavily on community action to set priorities, make decision, plan and implement strategies to achieve better health for themselves. Community action is also central to fostering healthy public policy.

More often than not, confusion still prevails among health are providers and others in their understanding of the differences between the various terminologies used to indicate community participation. To many people, community participation has meant getting people to come forward to accept services, as for example, immunization or family planning services. Whether these were coerced or not was not an issue. Few really studied whether the community was galvanized into action to demand services, which it needed. There are also examples of cummunity participation with community members donating land or other resources or even exercising some degree of control through local self-governing bodies. Such efforts have unfortunately not succeeded in minimizing distribution distortions because, by and large, only the richer classes are able to donate or even get on to village committees, and thus become part of the control agencies. The poor who are the worst hit do not have any control on how or who would manage the resources. For this reason, many social scientists prefer to use the term community involvement, rather than community participation.

Community involvement reflects a process wherein individuals and communities identify with a movement and take responsibility along with health professional and others for making decisions and undertaking social action. Social action in health is now seen as an essential factor in a democratic health promotion approach and the driving force for self-reliance and development. It recognizes the community as an essential voice in matters of its health, living conditions and wellbeing. At the third international conference on health promotion in Dundsval, social action was identified as a key strategy in creating supportive environments of health. Several examples from many parts of the world showed that it had been done. Social action is indeed possible and works!

What does social action mean in operational terms? It means bringing together various sectors of the society, like youth organizations, trade unions, women's groups, social and political institutions, business, industry, etc., and using these groups to form networks, coalitions and alliances to address specific health issues faced by communities.

These issues cover a wide range depending upon what are considered priorities by communities. There are some good examples of social action in India addressing problems of alcoholism, violence against women and discrimination against HIV infected people. Social action also means promoting intersectoral action and building alliances with public authorities making accessible information and knowledge to all citizens not as a privilege but as a right and empowering people to take decisions and to act on them.

Facilitating Social Action

Social action has to be facilitated. It is in very rare instances that it springs overnight. A few examples however do come to mind such as during the plague threat in Surat in 1994 when people rallied together to make the city a cleaner and safer place. However, by and large, social action usually results through a series of democratization process that empowers individuals and communities to decide, plan, implement and evaluate their actions. Paramount for success is the need to educate communities through a continuous flow of information.

Information and Education for Health

Social action in health can only take place when reliable information on what makes or breaks health is available and disseminated to the widest audiences in the country. This involves all stakeholders including the ordinary citizen whose voice unfortunately is rarely heard or heeded. In India for example with its millions of illiterates living in conditions far removed from information highways, access to knowledge based on scientific evidence is dismally lacking. Women especially remain cocooned within the shells of ignorance, obscurantism and irrational beliefs.

Education is the key element in bringing about the political, economic and social changes needed to bring health to all. A cornerstone to effective action to promote health is education of the population and its leaders. At one level this will involve health education using various methods including the mass media to inform people and raise their awareness about health, nutrition and environmental issues, at another level this will involve assisting people in the development of skills that will enable them to become effective advocates for health, for themselves, their families, their communities and their co-workers and also to provide social support for health in their local communities.

For example, persons with HIV and AIDS have successfully formed such groups, some of which have been extremely powerful in impacting policies and services. There are also now small women's groups dialoguing between themselves for improving access to health care. Such support groups can well become the precursors of larger community organizations that will work through a socio-political alliance to get their voices heard at the top political decision making level.

In South East Asia there are good examples of how the poor have been mobilized by the NGOs to improve the quality of their lives. The Grameen Bank in Bangladesh, SEWA in India and Sarvodaya in Sri Lanka have made outstanding contributions in this area. Other smaller NGOs too have played a most credible role. They have generated in people a need to change and have equipped communities with the skills to make the right choices to improve and take control over their health.

Capacity Building

Facilitating Social Action also means building capacities in communities to identify, manage and solve their prioritised problems. This implies that they must learn to analyse the health effects of various development projects and how to influence public policy relating to development and allocation of resources.

Encouragement of self-reliance, based on the use of local skills and resources and the transfer and application of appropriate technology are critical to achieving sustainable solutions and for avoiding unnecessary reliance on outside support. Improving knowledge and skills especially in women for creating supportive environment for health is critical. This will involve raising awareness of both the reproductive and productive role of women in society and the allocation of resources to improve women's education and health status. Capacity building also involves training for political advocacy. Politicians and decision makers have to recognize the inextricable link between health, environment and sustainable development and that health is a valuable resource for economic and social development. This will require strong advocacy by communities, professional groups and relevant NGOs.

Empowering people for health

To meet the moral imperatives for social justice, the need to empower people is paramount. Empowering individuals demands a consistant and reliable access to decision making processes together with the skills and knowledge that are essential to effect change. First and foremost, is to facilitate people to articulate their opinions and aspirations. This is not easy particularly in areas where long years of oppression have crippled the minds of people who are afraid to ventilate their feelings in case of a backlash.

But from experiences reported from many parts of the world, this can be overcome through more sustained efforts and participatory approaches to develop in people capacities.

Building Partnership

Since health determinant are complex, influenced by political, economic, social, environmental and other forces, the need to look beyond the traditional activities of the health care agencies and promote the cause of health with others whose policies and activities impact on people's health, is urgent.

In short all talk about social action is meaningless without securing to all people, irrespective of culture, social class and gender the right to information.

Social action must forge such partnership between sectors, organizations and groups to place community concern high on the political agenda and to mobilize a very large constituency of decision makers and implementers along with other stake holders including community leaders in addressing their health problems.

Partnerships can be multiple and built at various levels through the sharing of expertise, skills and resources. It is most important that they be based on agreed principles, mutual understanding and trust. Effective partnerships between NGOs have greatly facilitated social action. This has generated new power which has made it possible for people to voice their demands through public pressures as well as to sustain problem solving process.

Success Stories

Several success stories from various parts of the world have been reported to produce the evidence needed that social action in health has been successful. Some inspiring initiatives have come from the women's sector to demonstrate that when women work together on particular causes, they can be powerful force for social action. In South East Asia, women's action groups in Bangladesh, India, Indonesia, Nepal and Thailand have made some significant contributions to empower women to focus on critical issues that affect them. Even though many of these issues may not have a direct bearing on health, dealing as they do with issues such as access to credits or assets, ability to market goods or raising female literacy, nevertheless the indirect benefit to health through raising the social status of women has been most significant. SEWA (Self-Employed Women's Association) in India is a shining example of this. Founded in 1972, SEWA's mission is to organize self-employed workers particularly women for full employment which would ensure for themselves work, income, food and social security. The latter includes health care, child care, insurance and shelter. SEWA's mission is also to organize women for self-reliance through several small self-help groups, cooperatives and district level associations. SEWA's health approach is based on the philosophy that women's needs must be approached holistically and that women themselves must take care of their own health as well as that of their families. The innovative element of this approach is to link health security to work security. In other words, all of SEWA's economic activities have a health component and, in turn, all health action is linked to economic activities.

Social action of a different kind and for a different purpose was exhibited in Surat in 1994 with the outbreak of plague. The people of Surat demanded a more efficient administration to deal with the outbreak and cleanse the city. Owing to the combined effort of the Surat Municipal Corporation and the local people, the city was transformed automatically into a clean and green city. In Sri Lanka, the Sarvodaya Shramadana Movement founded in 1958 demonstrated to the world that a process of social awakening and mobilizing communities for integrated rural development efforts was possible. Given the proper guidance and tools, communities, however, poor they may be capable of managing their own health programmes.

The BRAC (Bangladesh Rural Advancement Committee) which began its activities as a rehabilitation assistance committee after the war of liberation in Bangladesh, has spread its activities over the years in search of long-term solutions that would lead to sustainable development. Through its experience the BRAC learnt that for a lasting impact on health and nutrition, the villages themselves must participate in developing a level of health awareness to look after their own health needs, utilize services provided and increase their income generating capacities. The BRACs outstanding performances in diarrhoeal control programmes as well as in the TB control programmes have been extensively documented.

These are only some examples. There are several other inspirational stories that prove the point. Social action in health works. It must be seen as one of the important health promotion strategies to bring health to all. The challenges are enormous. And for health educators in the traditional health systems, with a long history of top-down approaches, telling communities what to do and what not to do, to prevent and manage illness rather than mobilizing communities for health action.

Developing community leadership, learning the skill of advocacy and above all fostering partnership with groups and institutions and working intersectorally to empower people and promote social action in health are even more difficult. But these are challenges that must be faced. It can be done because it has been done.

Part - V

POPULATION DYNAMICS

21

Ecology, Population and Health: Perspectives on Quality of Life

K. Mahadevan, Lory Laing, Iqbal Shah, K.A. Pisharoti, K.V. Ranganathan, M.S.R. Murthy, P. Mangesh, V.M. Sandeep, V.K.R. Kumar, C. Deepak & P. Ganesh

Introduction

The focus of this chapter centres on tripartite linkages among the three major concepts of ecology, population and health in our society. Generally these concepts have been hitherto discussed individually and not holistically and together, although they jointly affect overall quality of life of human beings, fauna and flora. In addition, they were not together deliberated in academic field because of neglect in the holistic and inter-disciplinary approach. However, now in modern context need arose to discuss them together on account of their enhanced scientific understanding on their certain reciprocal influence that affects the quality of life of people in particular. Out of these three concepts, ecology is the foundation on which population live. In fact health of the people, morbidity, mortality and survival chances are individually and jointly being affected by ecological conditions and characteristics of population. Under these assumptions the present chapter has been conceptualized and presented in a synergic manner focusing on their importance, conceptual issues, followed by their linkages and implications affecting quality of life of human beings in general. A conceptual model on linkages among them has been presented below for their deeper understanding.

Human Ecology

The relevance of ecological problem for human beings assumed importance initially after industrial revolution towards the end of 18th century. Industrial revolution followed by technological innovations contributed revolutionary changes in our society. They are manifold and diverse in nature. For instance, during the beginning of the 19th century exploitation of natural resources for human comfort using improved sophisticated technology became a reality. As a result balanced environment particularly air, water, land, fauna and flora were increasingly disturbed for the benefit and comfort of human beings. Further such explanation of nature steadily increased from 19th through 20th centuries, when population steadily grew. Hence environment was exploited by human beings in an increased magnitude all over the world without caring the consequences till late 20th century.

Importance of ecology and knowledge of inter-dependence of human beings with environment steadily grew only after the middle of 20th century. How did it happen? As stated by Amos Hawley (1992: 314) the ecological problems form a "*multi-factorial phenomena*" which has been realized, when global climate started changing. In fact through observation and experiences we have realized very lately that thinning of the atmospheric ozone layer, which protects all living beings from destructive cosmic rays, resulted out of defective exploitation of environment and technology. When volume of carbon dioxide in the air increased through industrialization and parallel destruction of forest, world climate started warming up and adversely started affecting our health and happiness. In fact, till a few decades ago forest was cut in a big way for export of timber, manufacturing furniture and for massive requirements of railway for laying tracks. When our forest cover in every country was over fifty per cent of the land surface, the so called "*green house effect*" resulting out of depletion of ozone layer of the atmosphere, was not a major threat. Today in several states in India forest cover has reduced to less than 20 per cent. Hence forest depletion is the major ecological crisis today in most regions of the world. In the light of these illustrations, we have to understand the concepts of ecology in relation to human beings.

Concepts of Ecology

"Human ecology deals with the spatial aspects of symbiotic relations of human beings and human Institutions" (McKenzie, 1925). "Ecology, in other words, is a study of the morphology of collective life in both it's static and it's dynamic aspects. It attempts to determine the nature of community structure in general, the types of communities that appear in different habitats, and the specific sequence of change in community development" (Hawley, 1950). Hawely also further stressed that human ecology is an attempt to deal holistically with the phenomenon of organization. In other words, life according to ecological viewpoint is not a separate or individual entity but an aggregate phenomenon. Of course human ecology is somewhat different from the other related disciplines like geography, since ecology makes a detailed analysis of the process and organization of relations involved in adjustment to environment. It deals with the development and man's adjustment to his habitat (Hawley, 1950). Nevertheless, human ecology has close affinity with population sciences, public health, sociology, anthropology, geography civil engineering and development in general.

Empirically under different disciplines, several ecological variables have been adopted for holistically understanding different problems. In this context rural-urban dichotomy has been extensively used by Population Scientists, Health educators, Geographers and all the other Development scientists. In fact, universally it has been confirmed that there is need to study development differentially in both rural and urban areas because of their manifold differences in the society. Similarly for understanding the magnitude of diverse characteristics, problems and impact of development, stratified sample procedure has been followed for the study of coastal, midland

and hinterland regions of a given geographical area. In addition, for studying the differential impact of development and demographic perspectives, infrastructural variables like road and rail length have been extensively considered in modern research. For instance, in a national study on differential determinants of the poor, moderate and good performance of family planning among the Indian states, infrastructure variable (road length) has been thoroughly studied which emerged as the Principal causal factor for success in family planning. It was identified by using path analysis method. The details can be seen in chapter 19th of the book on "Differential Development and Demographic Dilemma" (Mahadevan *et al.*, 1994). This finding of a major national study amply conforms the paramount importance of ecological variables for effective and appropriate development of diverse regions of a country. Further, based on the density of population and eco-cultural background of the habitat, ecological variables can be suitably and relevantly applied in empirical research.

Human Ecology and Health

Out of all the factors that affect human health, ecological factors constitute the root cause of the principal and extensive number of variables. However sufficient importance is not given to this reality, largely due to ignorance, fatalistic attitude, political apathy and resource crunch. Epidemiological studies have confirmed that 3,000 children die daily in Sub-Saharan region of Africa due to malaria and 250 people died out of "SARS" till April 25th, 2003 in south-east Asian countries and Canada (B.B.C. news 25th, April). In addition, people dying out of cholera and other communicable diseases there is no reliable statistics. In general it has been estimated that nearly 60 per cent of diseases are caused through water and poor environmental hazards.

Who creates ecological hazards in our society leading to health problems? Human beings are the main culprit. Absence of effective national/state policy to prevent deforestation, freely allow businessmen to denude forest leading to drought, erosion of land and increase in carbon dioxide in the atmosphere leading to several health hazards. For instance, industrialists freely allow the effluents to flow into rivers and streams and pollute them, which causes many diseases for common people. Further illiteracy of people, absence of personal and/or public latrines, make open air defecation a general feature in most of the developing countries leading to chronic, cholera, diarrhoea, dysentery, hookworm infection, amoebiasis and several other diseases.

Severe Acute Respiratory Syndrome (SARS) Evolved from Filthy Environment

In November 2002 in Guangdong province of China, SARS was first reported in the name of atypical pneumonia. It spread through environment and virus and they together were responsible for this deadly disease. It spread like a hurricane in and around the infected regions. Never in the history of the world such diseases scared the humanity everywhere. Latest statistics confirmed by BBC (August, 2003) is that in China alone 2422 cases of SARS have been reported and among them 110 died so far. As a result of tourism, business travel and migration of people it has recently and quickly spread to most of the south-east Asian countries, Toronto in Canada and through visitors from Hongkong and Singapore to India carried SARS virus to half dozen persons in Mumbai, Delhi, Kolkata and Trivandrum. Now out of panic all the south-east Asian Foreign Ministers are meeting during the last week of April in Malaysia to chalkout an emergency strategy to control the spread of SARS in south-east Asian countries. Hence on a war footing basis efforts have been made in all the countries to prevent its spread. Never in the past such panic has engulfed all over the world through any other disease.

The root cause of SARS was filthy environment, that caused the spread of virulent virus first to cattle and the other animals in Guangdong province in China, near Hong Kong, which later on affected human beings. In other words, filthy environment, facilitated the growth of virulent virus, which affected first animals and subsequently infected human beings. It is a typical example of the multi-factorial genesis and spread of a deadly disease through medium of environment. Here environment, animals, virus and human beings formed holistically a web of society and environment, which together formed the principal causal factor for this greatest threat of human survival in 21st century.

A CONCEPTUAL SCHEME

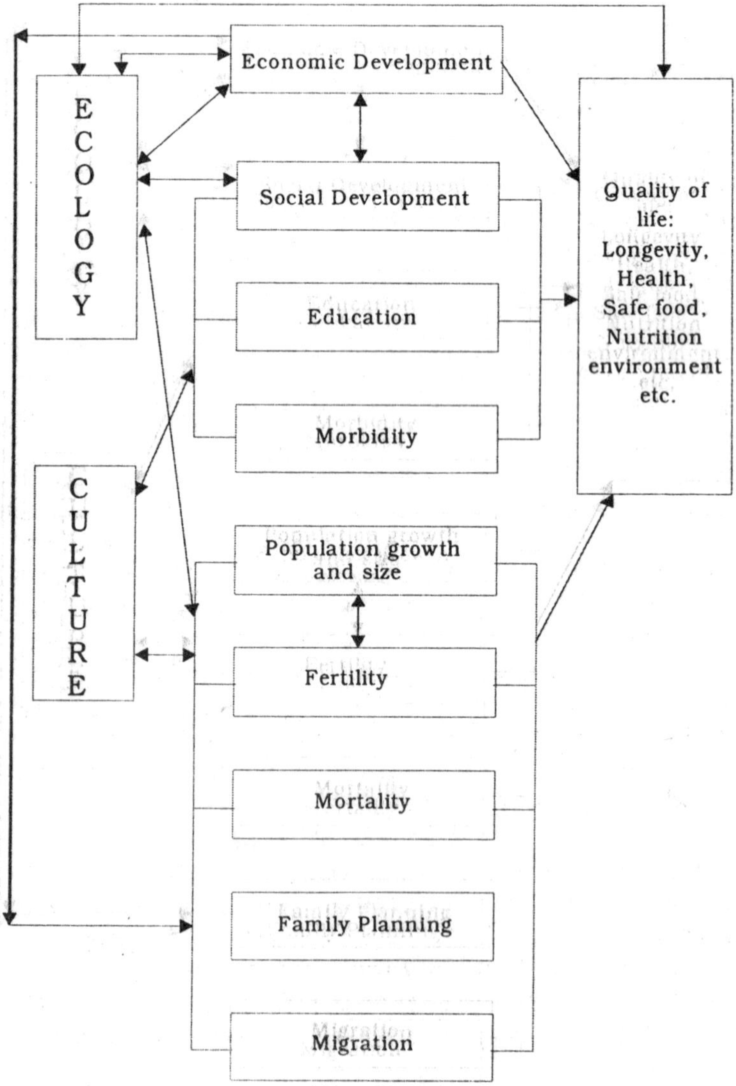

In order to contain this deadly disease on war footing environmental cleaning has been initiated all over the world for the first time in world history. Unfortunately information technology and mass media are not effectively used, so far in India to spread health education to prevent this disease. Added to such lapse, strict quarantine procedure and isolation of patients are not strictly followed. In addition, we should have discouraged the movement of people from infected country to non-infected nations.

However it is encouraging to hear that Canadians have succeeded in isolating the genetic features of this virus that inflict SARS, but it will take several months and years to develop appropriate measures to eradicate this epidemic. Meanwhile the role of health education must have been effectively used to prevent its spread all over the world.

Ecology and the Other Morbidity

There are several other diseases causing out of filthy environment. Of course they vary according to the nature of environment, extend of pollution, the scope for the vector to thrive and in difference-cum-apathy of the health workers, bureaucrats and politicians. Among such disease, malaria is a major disease followed by cholera, dengue fever, cancer and so on. In fact WHO reported that in August 2002 for every second 30 babies are dying in Sub-Saharan Africa out of Malaria. Since there is separate chapter on communicable disease and health education presented in this book, they are not elaborated here. However cancer causing out of chemical pollution from agriculture is specially highlighted here in view of their great risk and ignorance existing among most of the people.

Ecology, Agriculture and Cancer

Agricultural revolution became a necessity, largely due to repaid growth of population. For feeding ever growing population, conventional agriculture using bio-fertilizer could not meet the optimum requirements. Therefore, scientists discovered fertilizer to multiply the per hectare yield of cereals, fruits and vegetables. When forest was denuded the pest that normally confined to the forest started encroaching in to the agricultural field. In order to save the crops from pests, pesticides had to be developed. Thus, we succeeded in green revolution. However till recently we did not realize that chemical fertilizer and pesticides have deleterious consequences to cause cancer. When it was confirmed in Europe and Scandinavian countries they stopped using chemical fertilizer and pesticides in agriculture. Of course they can afford it because they have a limited size of population to feed. For thickly populated countries of India and China, they cannot altogether stop using chemical fertilizer at least in the near future. Interestingly in hundreds of areas near Theni and southern districts of Tamil Nadu, Netherland, Norway and Sweden are promoting Mango trees using Bio-fertilizer and neem as pesticides for exporting it to their countries. They also import several medical plants for preparation of laxatives, curing cancer and the other diseases. However, Indian policy makers have not opened their eyes to save Indians from the on going damages of defective agricultural revolution. Is it possible to adopt safe and new agricultural development in India without chemical manure and pesticides considering our 102 crores of population. Of course we can adopt neem to substitute chemical pesticide but cow dung alone cannot produce sufficient cereals to feed 102 crores of population. Therefore, India and China are forced to use chemical fertilizer for years to come and face rapid spread of cancer on a helpless situation because of over population of these two countries. Even India has not initiated any effort, so far, to use the safe neem as pesticide instead of risking with chemical pesticides.

When chemical pesticides are sprayed on to the paddy or wheat leaves the residues stay there and animals eat them and through animal meat and milk they enter human beings including children and become susceptible for cancer. When they spray pesticides to cauliflower vegetable and grapes, the residues of chemical pesticides fully do not go away with ordinary wash and in small quantities it enters in to our body. In India negligible people are aware of this risk. No preventive measure has been taken by any body in India so far. Of course, if health educators frequently disseminate these risk of using chemical pesticides, there is scope to save people from this man made tragedy. Parallelly our agricultural scientists, managers and politicians must be educated expeditiously to switch over to neem products as pesticides all over India, since India has the largest number of neem trees in the world. Why no action has been initiated by anyone to prevent the deadly disease of cancer slowly growing all over India through agricultural products is a characteristic of general apathy in our country. The conceptual model given here on the linkage of ecology and agriculture with morbidity and quality of life can help to understand it on a correct perspective.

TECHNOLOGY, AGRICULTURE, ECOLOGY AND CANCER: A CONCEPTUAL SCHEME

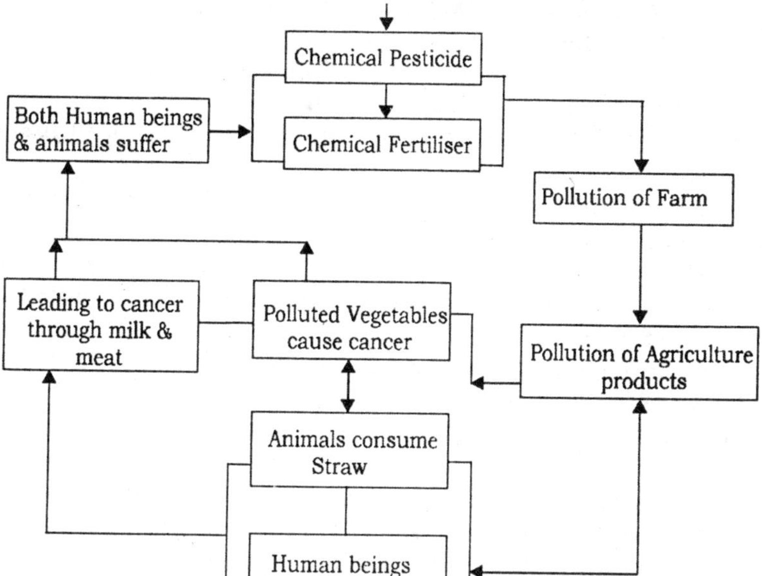

Medicinal Plants for Safe Medicine

In several developed countries during the last four decades, policy makers and scientists developed serious rethinking to substitute certain allopathic medicines with bio-medicines to avoid side effects and complications. As a result several European countries started importing a number of medicinal plant products from India and China to produce safe bio-medicine without complications and side effects. According to the report of WHO, now a large population of the developing countries also started using, bio-medicine like in developing countries. In India traditionally Ayurveda was the most popular medicine till the middle of 20th century however allopathy steadily replaced it after independence and also after the arrival of British India company. Nevertheless, India by 2000 AD exports herbal materials and medicine to the tune Rs. 446 crores while it has been estimated that this figure can be raised to Rs. 3000 crores by 2003. However Chinese export, based on plants including raw drugs therapeutics and other items estimated to be around Rs.18,000-22,000 crores. In view of the innate India's historical tradition of Ayurveda, ecologic systems, technical and farming facilities and strong manufacturing sector, the medicinal plants, can become a huge indigenous service and export opportunity for the common good of all human beings. It is ecofriendly and free from side effects.

Experiences have proved beyond doubt that for certain degenerative diseases and the other selected diseases like jaundice, retinopathy, spondylosis, arthritis, bio-medicine that is Indian Ayurveda is eminently suitable. However, adequate recognition has not yet been given by common people and allopathic doctors about the selective importance of bio-medicine. Since there is no side effect for bio-medicine and it is eco-friendly, health education must popularize it without prejudice. Interestingly in several European countries senna plant's leaves and seeds are extensively imported from India to manufacture safe laxatives. They also import Ocimum Sanctum (Thulasi), Neem and several other medicinal plants to prepare chemical free drugs to avoid side effects.

Population, Ecology and Health

The population science being an interdisciplinary subject, it has one of its roots embedded ecology, like the other roots linking with Health, Sociology, Economics,

Psychology, Statistics and Methodology. They are inseparable and complementary to each other. According to empirical evidence, they have reciprocal relationship, which is very rare in social phenomenon. Their complementary relationship can be vividly noticed when we present here the conceptual clarity of population science/demography. According to Namboodiri (1992) ".....demography is the scientific study of population structure and dynamics and their determinants and consequences. Population structure means population size, composition and distribution; population dynamics means change in population structure, with special attention to fertility, mortality, migration and social mobility, which are the components of population change." Several of these variables of demography, have linkage with ecology and health. Therefore it is appropriate to focus now on a selected demographic concepts, which have linkages with ecology and health per se. For want of space population growth and density alone are discussed here now.

Population Growth and Ecological Crisis

Population growth is the principal catastrophe of ecological crisis. The rate of growth of population is alarming, when we examine it from the last one century alone. The population growth is highest in developing countries compared to developed regions. Even among the former countries, it is very high in Africa, Muslim countries, followed by Asia and Latin America with certain minor exceptions. The total number of the population of developing countries grew from 1.7 billion in the 1950 to 4.1 billion in the 1990. According to the UN estimation it reached 5 billion by the year 2000 and expected to cross 7 billion by 2025. However, population of developed countries manifested only a moderate level of growth. In fact the total percentage of population of developing countries out of global population increased from 67 per cent to 77 per cent during 1950 to 1990 (UN 1991). As a result the pressure of population on ecology and infrastructure for health care increased by leaps and bounds in developing countries.

How did population growth affect ecology? First of all rapid urbanization deteriorated the housing, institutional, and service facilities and degraded the environment. In addition, demand for necessities of life like wood and wood products increased resulting into extra denudation of forest. Other demands for eatables like cereals, vegetables and fruits necessitated the cultivation of even forest land and deprived the scope for afforestation. Increased need for employment, necessitated massive industrialization, resulting in to air water and soil pollutions. Unmanageable population growth adversely affected the welfare programmes like education, health availability of nutritious food, childcare, security for the elderly and so on which seriously affected all human beings. They will have several adverse consequences for the sustained living and happiness of human race in future.

Population Density, Ecology and Morbidity

Population density is based on the rate of growth of population migration and the availability of vacant land. In this context in Asia, Bangladesh has one of the very high density of population due to high growth rate of population and availability of limited geographical area. While Bangladesh has 2401 population per square mile, China has only 344, India 814, Srilanka 771 and Pakistan 472 persons. It is an eye opener for future policy makers, planners and politicians. Correspondingly Bangladesh has the lowest GNP of US $ 370 followed by India $ 450, Pakistan $ 470, China $ 780 and Srilanka $ 820. Srilanka is the only exception country with high density of population and highest level of GNP in South Asia. This is the scenario in developing countries. Of course density of population is very less in most of the developed countries, except Japan, where geography has constrained the dispersal of population. Of course migration is yet another major factor that regulates density of population. In this context China's relatively low density of population compared to South Asia is due to migration of Chinese more than the Indians and also availability of more geographical area in mainland China.

High density of population equally affects the ecology and health of population. First of all density leads of over crowding in habitations leading to traffic problems, accidents and pollution. Density of population leads to constraints in creation of infrastructure facilities, like gardens, play grounds, and future expansion of all welfare and development programmes. Psychologically, population density inhibits the proper personality development. Physiologically, density may restrict the growth and functioning of human beings and adversely affect early degeneration of several organs of body. More than all these problems, high density of population will have the catastrophic spread of epidemics among very large population like the SARS now spreading in China. Air pollution and climatic change are the other hazards that may affect the general health of densely population regions of the developing countries. Of course more research has to be carried out to identify the unknown many other health hazards of high density population in developing and developed countries.

In conclusion, it has been scientifically proved that linkage between ecology, population and health constitute the most important root causal factor that adversely affect the quality of life of people all over the world. However, the seriousness of their threat has not been perceived and understood, so far, by policy makers, educationists, managers and politicians and common people in general. In order to understand the gravity of their danger, they must be holistically considered and suitable health education must be expeditiously promoted using all the interpersonal and mass media on a war footing.

For the posterity the successful longevity of Kurichia tribe, with negligible morbidity will be a valuable lesson to save ecology and promote health. They live on Wayanad Plateau at the Trijunction of Tamil Nadu, Kerala and Karnataka. Their longevity is far ahead of Japan and Scandinavian countries, however, they are mostly illiterate and do not follow allopathic medicine. They are not diabetic, and devoid of STD, tuberculosis and cancer. What are secrets of their better quality of life? The details can be seen in our paper and book referred under this paper.

We have studied them epidemiologically and identified the following major determinants of their successful living. First of all their life style is very appropriate, they take finger millet (Ragi) as staple diet, use forest based leaves (Indian

Ginseng), fowles, roots, fruits, etc. with diet. Daily they work with spade in their own coffee farms. In the evening they sit around fire wood and sing songs and enjoy. They have no individual property and joint property enjoyed by one and all. They have full social security and no worry for needs, facilities and comforts. They have no insecurity and tension. There are many more things, which can be seen in our paper. Lastly, they live in an ecologically healthy place without pollution and sanitation problems. The case study of Kurichia Tribe is a valuable lesson for health educators and the entire humanity all over the world to promote good ecological surroundings for health and longevity in life.

References

1. Amos, Hawley, H. 1950. Human Ecology: A theory of community Structure. The Ronald Press, New York.
2. Mckenzie, R.D. 1950. "Human Ecology", Encyclopeadia of the Social Sciences, V, 314. Quoted in Howley.
3. Guzevatyi, Y.N. 1992. Demographic Aspects of Ecological Problems (See Krishnan *et al.*, 1992).
4. Namboodiri, N.K. 1992. Ecological Demography: Its place in sociology (See in Krishnan *et al.*, 1992).
5. Krishnan, P., Chi Hsien Tuan and Mahadevan, K. 1992. Readings in population Research, BRPC, New Delhi.
6. Mahadevan, K. and Subramanyam, G. 1991. Life style, Health and Longevity of Kurichia Tribe: An Epidemiological study, Presented at World Gerentological Conference, in Sweden in 1992.
7. UN, 1991. World population prospects. No. 120 New York.
8. ESCAP, 2002. Population Data sheet.

22

Impact of Family Planning Management Education and Service Providing on Emergency Contraception Knowledge, Attitude, and Practice among Married Female Migrants at Reproductive Age

Wu Junqing, Li Wenying, Tao Jianguo, Zheng Ling, Chen Tikuwan, Chen Aimin, Zhang Zibao, Huang Weidong, Gao Ersheng, Pan Jiazeng, Zhang Meixing

Abstract

A "present-residence based" family planning intervention among married female migrants at reproductive age was carried out in 1998 in Shanghai, China, in order to probe an effective way to improve their reproductive health. According to the results, prior to intervention, only 9.46 per cent of subjects in the experiment group and 7.74 per cent in the control group knew about EC (emergency contraceptive), while after intervention, this proportion was 44.77 per cent and 12.93 per cent respectively. Multiple logistic regression analysis showed that after intervention, the experiment group had a higher awareness of EC, higher tendency to utilize EC and higher inclination to expand EC utilization. This study suggested that the "present-residence based" intervention integrated family planning management education and service could largely improve the awareness of EC, the tendency to utilize EC and the inclination to expand EC utilization in the urban migrants. It may be helpful to decrease the unintended pregnancy and the induced abortion in migrants.

With the development of socialism marketing economics in China, the proportion of migrants in urban has been increased. In this process, Shanghai has also restored its position as one of the central magnet cities attracting a large number of migrants (Wang, Zuo, and Ruan, forthcoming). The migrants have been dramatically increased. The migrant population increased from 750,000 in 1984 to 1,400,000 in 1988, to 2,510,000 in 1993, to 3,500,000 in 1997. Although, among these migrants, women have constituted an increasingly larger proportion (Wang, 2000). Approximately, one-third of migrants were women at reproductive age. There are some difficulties to improve family planning program and reproduction health service among migrants because of its floating characteristics.

To improve the family planning management and reproductive health service, we carried out a trial of "present resident-based" population and family planning management education and service. The trial was expected to decrease the rate of unplanned birth as well as that of unintended pregnancy. In this article, we analyzed the impacts of family planning management, education, and service on married female migrants knowledge of EC and attitude towards EC to evaluate the trial's effects, which could provide scientific suggestions to improve reproductive health of migrants and to ameliorate the family planning service among migrants.

Methods

Sample and Questionnaire

The project was designed as a community-based intervention study. Two towns of Minhang District, which accommodated much more migrants, were selected as field sites. The two selected towns were similar in terms of the amount of migrants, the profile of women at reproductive age, and the family planning service and management. One town (Hongqiao) was randomly allocated as the experiment group, the other (Meilong) as the control group.

Women at reproductive age who had lived at the study sites for at least three months and had no registered permanent residency in Shanghai were enrolled in the study. In the baseline survey, 518 and 336 were recruited in the experiment and the control group respectively, while in the post-intervention survey, the number of subjects in two groups was 440 and 263 respectively.

The experiment town's intervention included the following: (1) checking and registering the family planning service card, providing family planning information card and migrants bearing relation card, requesting migrants to show family planning certificate, when they applied for temporary residence card and work licence; (2) at 1st, 3rd, 6th, and 9th month of the intervention, family planning information, knowledge, and communication were provided to the subjects through diverse channels, such as manual, poster and counselling; (3) training family planning staff and service providers of the nuts and bolts of family planning policy, law, management and service, and the knowledge of usage, indication, effectiveness and side-effects of different contraceptives; (4) providing routine contraceptive, emergency contraception and counselling. During that year, routine family planning services were provided to the control town. The evaluation survey was conducted in January 1999, when we randomly sampled female migrants in two towns.

Investigation was conducted by trained investigators with the structured questionnaire in both baseline survey and the post-intervention survey. The information collected in the questionnaire included: age, husband's age, the nature of registered permanent residence, educational level, occupation, personal annual income, marital status, reproductive history, contraceptive history, induced abortion history, the knowledge, source and practice of contraceptive, the knowledge, attitude, and practice of EC, etc.

As to each specific contraceptive of nine, score was calculated according to the following principles: 2, if knowing about this method; 1, if knowing it after being reminded, otherwise, 0. The total score would be divided into three levels: the first level (0~5), the second level (6~11), and the third level (12~18), which served as the dependent variable in the multivariate statistical analysis.

Statistical Analysis

All the completed questionnaires were checked and coded twice by different individuals prior to being entered into database with Epi.Info 6.04. SAS 6.12 software was employed in data analysis on Pentium computer. Analysis emphasized on the effects of intervention to the knowledge, attitude, and practice among married female migrants at reproductive age.

Firstly, through $\chi 2$ test, general background information and EC knowledge, attitude, and practice prior to and after intervention in the experiment and the control group were compared.

Then, multiple logistic regression analysis was employed to analyze KAP of EC. It was conducted with the following variables as dependent variable respectively: whether knowing EC, whether willing to utilize EC if necessary, whether regarding it reasonable to expand EC and whether ever using EC. Independent variables were as follows: group, age, the type of permanent register, educational level, occupation in hometown, husband's age, husband's educational level, husband's occupation in hometown, personal annual income, years of living in Shanghai, satisfaction degree of marriage, frequency of sexual intercourse, number of live births, number of induced abortions, number of parities, whether ever receiving family planning education in hometown and in Shanghai, the sources and level of contraceptive knowledge, types of contraceptive method ever utilized, contraceptive method utilized now, whether wanting to change contraceptive method, whether selecting methods on their own, etc. After those independent variables entered model, back-step method was utilized to fit the model.

Results

Demographic Characteristics

A total of 1557 subjects, 94 per cent of whom came from rural area, were recruited in this study, aged from 18 to 45 with the average age of 27.8. Subjects' educational conditions were as follows: primary school or lower accounted for 39.5 per cent, junior high school accounted for 54.8 per cent, and the others were senior high school or higher. Their personal annual income was RBM 6,767.

EC Knowledge, Attitude, and Practice

As shown in Table 1, in the baseline survey, KAP of EC between the experiment and the control group had no statistical significance. While after intervention, there was statistically significant difference. The results indicated that the awareness of EC, the tendency to utilize EC if necessary, and the inclination to expand EC in the experiment group were higher than those of the control group.

Further analysis was conducted to understand the sources of EC knowledge of 306 subjects who knew EC. We found that prior to and after intervention, there was significant difference in the source of EC knowledge in the experiment group. After intervention, the proportion of EC knowledge coming from family planning cadres was higher. While in the control group, there was no statistically significant difference (p=0.884). After intervention, there were 26.40 per cent of subjects knew two types of EC. And 13.71 per cent knew three or more types. Prior to intervention, they only knew No. 53 contraceptive. While after intervention, many of them also knew "liuting" or "xiyin", and IUD (see Table 1).

Among 306 subjects knowing EC, 66.34 per cent of them were willing to utilize EC. And after explanation of the advantage of EC to those who didn't know EC, there were only 34.33 per cent of subjects willing to utilize EC. The difference between them had statistical significance. (p=0.001).

Moreover, there were 89.2 per cent of subjects who knew EC and 66.83 per cent of those who didn't know regarded it reasonable to expand the utilization of EC. The difference had statistical significance (p=0.001). Among subjects willing to utilize EC, there were 92.29 per cent of them who had the inclination to expand EC utilization. While among those unwilling to utilize EC, only 56.7 per cent regarded it reasonable to expand it. In the same way, 52.84 per cent of subjects who regarded it needed to expand EC were willing to utilize EC. Otherwise, there were only 10.94 per cent willing to utilize EC among those disapproved to expand EC utilization (see Table 2).

Multiple Logistic Regression Analysis

Whether Knowing EC

The results showed that the awareness of EC in the experiment group after intervention was higher than that of the control group prior to intervention. Compared with those using IUD, subjects using condom or oral contraceptive had higher awareness of EC. Compared with those coming from rural area, subjects coming from city had higher awareness of EC. Subjects with high educational level, having received family planning education in hometown, with high contraceptive knowledge, or having ability to select contraceptive method had higher awareness of EC. While compared with subjects using IUD, sterilization women had lower awareness of EC (see Table 3).

Whether Willing to Utilize EC

In the experiment group after intervention, subjects had higher tendency to utilize EC than that of control group prior to intervention. Compared with those whose husband was farmer, women whose husband was worker or others had higher tendency to utilize EC. Women experiencing more induced abortion, with high contraceptive knowledge, wanting to change method, or being able to choose contraceptive method on their own had higher tendency to utilize EC. In contrast, women with more surviving children had lower tendency to utilize EC (see Table 4).

Whether Regarding it Reasonable to Expand EC

Compared with those in the control group prior to

intervention, women in the experiment group after intervention were more likely to expand EC utilize. Women with higher education, with higher contraceptive knowledge, wanting to change methods, or being able to choose contraceptive method had higher inclination to expand EC utilization respectively. While women having more children had lower inclination to expand EC utilization (see Table 5).

Whether Having Ever Utilized EC

Compared with those using IUD, subjects using condom or oral contraceptive were more likely to utilize EC. Subjects whoever were worker in hometown had higher EC utilization than those ever were farmer. The ratio of ever using EC of women with more frequency of induced abortion, with higher contraceptive knowledge was higher respectively. While compared with that of control group prior to intervention, the ratio in the other three groups had no statistical significance (see Table 6).

Discussion

With increasing number of migrants gradually, migrants' reproductive health has gained more and more people's concerns. Induced abortion rate of female migrants was higher than that of residents. It's necessary to take effective efforts to reduce migrants' unintended pregnancy and induced abortion rate. Under this condition, it's imperative to improve family planning education management and service for migrants. Through this, migrants at reproductive age can choose suitable contraceptive methods and take emergency contraception after contraceptive failure or non-protective sexual intercourse. In this case, both of unintended pregnancy and induced abortion rate might be reduced. Through simple and further analyses, it's been found that intervention had enhanced the awareness of EC, the tendency to EC utilization and the inclination to expand EC utilization. Moreover, after intervention, subjects in the experiment group knew more types of EC. It showed that we could increase migrants' EC knowledge through taking appropriate family planning management education and service, and that it's feasible

Table 1: Comparison of Emergency Contraception Knowledge, Attitude and Utilization between the Experiment and the Control Group Prior to and after Intervention in Shanghai, China

	Baseline survey (per cent)			Post-intervention survey (per cent)				
	(1) Experiment group (n=518)	(2) Control group (n=336)	P_1	(3) Experiment group (n=440)	(4) Control group (n=263)	P_2	P_3	P_4
Know about EC#								
Yes	9.46	7.74	0.385	44.77	12.93	0.001	0.001	0.034
No	90.54	92.26		55.23	87.07			
Be willing to utilize EC if necessary*								
Yes	33.78	37.20	0.307	55.91	33.84	0.001	0.001	0.394
No	66.22	62.80		44.09	66.16			
Regard it reasonable to expand EC								
Yes	63.90	69.64	0.083	83.18	67.68	0.001	0.001	0.607
No	36.10	30.36		16.82	32.32			
Have utilized EC								
Yes	1.35	1.19	0.839	3.18	0.76	0.037	0.054	0.600
No	98.65	98.81		96.82	99.24			

P_1: P value of comparison of group 1 with group 2; P_2: P value of comparison of group 3 with group 4; P_3: P value of comparison of group 1 with group 3; P_4: P value of comparison of group 2 with group 4;

Emergency contraception;

* Asked after explaining emergency contraception.

Table 2: Source and Types Known of Emergency Contraception in the Experiment and the Control Group Prior to and after Intervention in Shanghai, China

	Baseline survey (per cent)			Post-intervention survey (per cent)				
	(1)	(2)		(3)	(4)			
	Experiment group (n=49)	Control group (n=26)	P_1	Experiment group (n=197)	Control group (n=34)	P_2	P_3	P_4
Source of EC knowledge								
Doctors	24.49	38.46	0.323	13.20	32.35	0.002	0.022	0.884
Family Planning cards	34.69	19.23		58.88	26.47			
Relatives or friends	8.16	15.38		5.08	11.76			
Others	32.65	26.92		22.84	29.41			
Types of EC known								
One	100.00	100.00		59.90	88.24	0.001	0.001	0.073
Two	0.00	0.00		26.40	11.76			
Three or more	0.00	0.00		13.71	0.00			

P_1: P value of comparison of group 1 with group 2; P_2: P value of comparison of group 3 with group 4; P_3: P value of comparison of group 1 with group 3; P_4: P value of comparison of group 2 with group 4.

Table 3: Multiple Logistic Regression Analysis of Whether Knowing EC

Variable	Reference	Comparison	Regression coefficient	Standard error	P value	OR	95 per cent CL Lower	Upper
Group¤	CGBI	EGBI	0.1945	0.2642	0.4616	1.215	0.724	2.038
		EGAI	2.2811	0.2380	0.0001	9.788	6.139	15.606
		CGAI	0.5043	0.2867	0.0786	1.656	0.944	2.905
Current contraceptive utilization	IUD	Male sterilization	-0.6314	0.7708	0.4127	0.532	0.117	2.409
	IUD	Female sterilization	-0.5300	0.2157	0.0140	0.589	0.386	0.898
	IUD	Condom	1.3488	0.3899	0.0005	3.853	1.794	8.273
	IUD	Pill	0.9513	0.3341	0.0044	2.589	1.345	4.983
	IUD	Others	-0.1641	0.7103	0.8173	0.849	0.211	3.414
Area of houtilizehold register	Village	Town	0.5356	0.2690	0.0465	1.708	1.008	2.895
Educational level*			0.2628	0.1322	0.0467	1.301	1.004	1.685
Family planning education in hometown	No	Yes	0.4419	0.1945	0.0231	1.556	1.063	2.277
Contraception knowledge level#			0.7094	0.1148	0.0001	2.033	1.623	2.546
Ability to choose contraceptive	Not have	Have	0.5134	0.2530	0.0424	1.671	1.018	2.743

¤ Group: CGBI: Control group prior to intervention, EGBI: Experiment group prior to intervention, CGAI: Control group after intervention, EGAI: Experiment group after intervention;

* Educational level: 1: Primary school and lower, 2: Junior high school, 3: Senior high school or higher;

Contraception knowledge level: 1: Contraception knowledge mark 0-5, 2: Contraception knowledge mark 6-11, 3: Contraception knowledge mark 12-18.

Table 4: Multiple Logistic Regression Analysis of whether Willing to Utilize EC if Necessary

Variable	Reference	Comparison	Regression coefficient	Standard error	P value	OR	95 per cent CL	
							Lower	Upper
Group¤	CGBI	EGBI	-0.1370	0.1523	0.3682	0.872	0.647	1.175
		EGAI	0.7390	0.1564	0.0001	2.094	1.541	2.845
		CGAI	-0.1368	0.1792	0.4452	0.872	0.614	1.239
Husband's occupation in hometown	Farmer	Worker	0.3153	0.1383	0.0226	1.371	1.045	1.797
		Others	0.5484	0.1665	0.0010	1.731	1.249	2.398
Frequency of live birth			-0.4764	0.0969	0.0001	0.621	0.514	0.751
Frequency of induced abortion			0.3029	0.0991	0.0022	1.354	1.115	1.644
Contraception knowledge level#			0.3031	0.0820	0.0002	1.354	1.153	1.590
Having intention to change contraceptive	No	Yes	0.5870	0.2045	0.0041	1.799	1.205	2.685
Ability to choose contraceptive	Not have	Have	0.5927	0.1655	0.0003	1.809	1.308	2.502

¤ Group: CGBI: Control group prior to intervention, EGBI: Experiment group prior to intervention, CGAI: Control group after intervention, EGAI: Experiment group after intervention;

Contraception knowledge level: 1: Contraception knowledge mark 0-5, 2: Contraception knowledge mark 6-11, 3 Contraception knowledge mark 12-18.

Table 5: Multiple Logistic Regression Analysis of whether Regarding it Reasonable to Expand EC Utilization

Variable	Reference	Comparison	Regression coefficient	Standard error	P value	OR	95 per cent CL	
							Lower	Upper
Group¤	CGBI	EGBI	-0.3491	0.1573	0.0265	0.705	0.518	0.960
		EGAI	0.6262	0.1829	0.0006	1.871	1.307	2.677
		CGAI	-0.2211	0.1867	0.2364	0.802	0.556	1.156
Educational level*			0.3863	0.1074	0.0003	1.471	1.192	1.816
Number of parity			-0.2860	0.1014	0.0048	0.751	0.616	0.917
Contraception knowledge level#			0.4847	0.0923	0.0001	1.624	1.355	1.946
Having intention to change contraceptive	No	Yes	0.5303	0.2634	0.0441	1.699	1.014	2.848
Ability to choose contraceptive	Not have	Have	0.8535	0.1528	0.0001	2.348	1.740	3.168

¤ Group: CGBI: Control group prior to intervention, EGBI: Experiment group prior to intervention, CGAI: Control group after intervention, EGAI: Experiment group after intervention;

* Educational level: 1: Primary school and lower, 2: Junior high school, 3: Senior high school or higher;

Contraception knowledge level: 1: Contraception knowledge mark 0-5, 2: Contraception knowledge mark 6-11, 3 Contraception knowledge mark 12-18.

Table 6: Multiple Logistic Regression Analysis of whether having ever Utilized EC

Variable	Reference	Comparison	Regression coefficient	Standard error	P value	OR	95 per cent CL Lower	95 per cent CL Upper
Group¤	CGBI	EGBI	0.0900	0.6870	0.8958	1.094	0.285	4.205
		EGAI	1.0255	0.6426	0.1105	2.789	0.791	9.826
		CGAI	-0.3894	0.9080	0.6680	0.677	0.114	4.016
Current contraceptive utilization	IUD	Female sterilization	0.5552	0.6011	0.3556	1.742	0.536	5.660
	IUD	Condom	2.0674	0.6232	0.0009	7.904	2.330	26.813
	IUD	Pill	2.2016	0.5966	0.0002	9.039	2.807	29.107
	IUD	Others	1.1445	1.0851	0.2915	3.141	0.374	26.345
Occupation in hometown	Farmer	Worker	1.3291	0.4877	0.0064	3.778	1.453	9.825
		Others	0.6967	0.5533	0.2080	2.007	0.679	5.937
Frequency of induced abortion			0.5201	0.2275	0.0222	1.682	1.077	2.627
Contraception knowledge level#			0.8228	0.3319	0.0132	2.277	1.188	4.363

¤ Group: CGBI: Control group prior to intervention, EGBI: Experiment group prior to intervention, CGAI: Control group after intervention, EGAI: Experiment group after intervention;

Contraception knowledge level: 1: Contraception knowledge mark 0-5, 2: Contraception knowledge mark 6-11, 3 Contraception knowledge mark 12-18.

to expand EC and utilize EC to decrease unintended pregnancy rate.

From March to May 1998, a study was conducted in Shanghai which results showed that 36.8 per cent of 3100 subjects knew about EC. While in this study, no more than 10 per cent of subjects prior to intervention were aware of EC. It only reached 44.7 per cent in the experiment group after intervention, which was much lower than the proportion found in similar studies in other country. This trial was a community-based intervention study and was difficult to implement, on the other hand, it showed that there was still much room for implementing communication and education among migrants. We should take efforts to expand the range of family planning management, education, and service and to promote EC awareness and utilization. In this study, after intervention, there were only 34.53 per cent of subjects willing to utilize EC if necessary among those who didn't know EC. The results indicated the need of a process from knowledge to attitude. The goal wouldn't be accomplished through once or twice simple education. This illustrated the necessary of comprehensive intervention package.

In multiple logistic regression analysis, we found out some other factors that had influence to EC knowledge and practice. The awareness of EC of subjects using condom or oral contraceptive was higher than that of those using IUD. Their EC utilization was also higher than those using IUD. It's more important to provide better education, service, and information about EC to those using condom or oral contraceptive. The awareness of EC, EC utilization, tendency of EC utilization and inclination to expand EC utilization of women with high EC knowledge were higher. It showed that EC education integrated with routine contraceptive education could achieve more effects.

Women with more induced abortion were much willing to utilize EC. In fact, their EC utilization rate was higher. It's consistent with the results of previous studies. The result reflected that induced abortion could have an impact on women's psyche. It also reflected the necessary of expanding EC objectively. The rate of induced abortion could be decreased through expanding EC.

General speaking, the intervention had obvious effects to improve the awareness of EC, the tendency to utilize EC and the inclination to expand EC of female migrants at reproductive age in this study. We suggested that in the future, we should strengthen to popularize EC knowledge, to integrate routine contraceptive education with EC, to improve the service of EC and to urge women at reproductive age to select contraceptive method on their own. We could bring down the occurrence of unintended pregnancy and induced abortion, and therefore improve the reproductive health of migrants through those measures.

Acknowledgements

We thank for the help by Minhang District Family Planning Committee and Hongaqiao District Family Planning Committee. And we also thank for the financial support by Chinese State Family Planning Committee.

References

1. 1992. "China State Family Planning Commission measures for the management of family planning of the floating population", China Population Today, 9(1):2-5.
2. Dong Chenxi, 1998. "The assessment of impact of migration to family planning and new management framework", China population science, (4): 54-60.
3. Qiu Shuhua, *et al.*, 1994. "Dynamics of contraceptive utilization", Publishing of population of China.
4. Rozelle, Scott, J. Edward Taylor and Alan deBrauw, 1999. "Migration, remittances, and agricultural productivity in China", American Economic Review, 89(2): 287-291.
5. Wang Feng, 2000. "Gendered migration and the migration of genders in contemporary China." In Re-drawing boundaries: work, houtilizeholds, and gender in China, edited by Barbara Entwisle and Gail E. Henderson. Berkeley: University of California Press, pp. 231-242.
6. Wang Feng, Xuejin Zuo and Danching Ruan, Forthcoming. "Rural migrants in Shanghai: living under the shadow of socialism", International Migration Review.
7. Wu Junqing, Gao Ersheng and Tao Jianguo, 2001. "Analysis of family planning management of migrants", Medicine and Society, 14(1): 19-23.
8. Wu Junqing, Tao Jianguo and Gao Ersheng, 2001. "The evaluation of family planning integrated intervention among migrants." Population information, (1): 20-23.
9. Zhang Henian, 1998. "Analysis of economic of migrants in Shanghai". Population, 2: 71-76.

23

Use of Emergency Contraception could have the Induced Abortion Rate in Shanghai, China

Lou Chaohua, Gao Ersheng, Zhao Shuangling

The aim of the study is to investigate women's knowledge, attitude, acceptability of emergency contraception, and to estimate the proportion of the induced abortion that could have been prevented by using emergency contraception in Shanghai. Structured interviews were conducted with a sample of 606 women (413 married and 193 unmarried) aged 18-50 years, attending three health care centres in Shanghai for termination of first trimester pregnancy. The results showed 98.2% of the pregnancies were unwanted, and 63.7% of women recognized that they were at risk of pregnancy soon after the intercourse. It is estimated that 52.2% of the induced abortion could have been prevented if the women had used levonorgestrel-only emergency contraception. However, only 28.5% of the respondents were aware of emergency contraception. Respondents who were younger, better educated, wealthier, and more knowledgeable about contraceptives in general were more likely to be aware of emergency contraception. The most important sources of information about emergency contraception identified by respondents were books, newspapers, and periodicals (38.2%), and relatives and friends (30.6%). Family planning educational campaigns on emergency contraception were noted by 28.9% of married women but only by 5.8% of unmarried women. 85.5% of all respondents reported they would be willing to use emergency contraception when needed. Those more willing to use emergency contraception included younger, better educated, and unmarried women experiencing their first pregnancy. Women preferred drugstores (60.1%) to hospitals (30.2%) for obtaining emergency contraception and drugstores were preferred for "convenience" (87.1%) even though hospitals were recognized for "reliability" (85.8%). The study indicated that promotion of emergency contraception by family planning programmes in Shanghai could have a substantial impact on reducing the rate of induced abortion.

Keywords: Emergency contraception; Unwanted pregnancy; Induced abortion

Induced abortion among both married and unmarried women in China is an important reproductive health concern. Statistics show the prevalence of induced abortion in the country is about 10 million in each year [Huang Runlong *et al.*, 2000]. Emergency contraception is a effective method used to prevent unwanted pregnancy within several hours or days when women find the contraceptive failure or without use of contraception in sexual intercourse. However, for many reasons, emergency contraception is not widely used in China. After the 1995 Bellagio Conference on emergency contraception [South to South Cooperation in Reproductive Health, 1995], scientists and health practitioners in China began to recognize the important role of emergency contraception in decreasing induced abortion rate. In 1996, Reproductive Medicine editorial panel held a workshop on emergency contraception in Beijing. The representatives agreed emergency contraception could be as a supplement and consummation of the birth control methods and the policy of "informed choice". Some institutions and hospitals carried out the studies of the efficacy of various emergency contraceptives [Han Xuejun *et al.*, 1996; Zhang Yan *et al.*, 1998; Xie Xi *et al.*, 1998; Hu Jing *et al.*, 1998; Fan Aihua *et al.*, 1998; Duan Wei *et al.*, 1997; Yang Yan *et al.*, 1997; Zhang Yan *et al.*, 1996; Hu Jing *et al.*, 1996]. There are two studies showing fewer women knew the method and far fewer women had ever used it in

China as compared with that in developed countries [Cheng Yimin *et al.*, 1996; Gan Shixiu *et al.*, 1998]. Studies surveying women's knowledge, attitude and acceptance to emergency contraception in Shanghai was not available however, where induced abortion rate was higher than those in other provinces or cities in China.

Using an emergency contraceptive method soon after unprotected intercourse is critical to its effectiveness; therefore, women must know in advance about emergency contraception and where to obtain it, be willing to use it, and emergency services and methods must be widely available. Under these considerations, understanding women's knowledge of emergency contraception, attitudes toward the method, and its acceptability will help to assess its potential for use and appropriate ways to deliver the method in China.

Methodology

Three Maternal and Child Health (MCH) centres in Shanghai were selected as study sites, located in high, middle, and low socio-economic level districts respectively. Study subjects were those aged 18-50 years who attended the three MCH centres to seek termination of first trimester pregnancy and had Shanghai household registration in 1998. They were voluntarily to participate in the study and face-to-face interviewed based on the structured questionnaire in the MCH centres. Totally, 606 subjects were recruited, 204, 201 and 201 in each MCH centre respectively. The interviewer was a female medical doctor, who was well trained on the methodology of the study and skills for the interview and did all interviews for the study. Before the survey, pilot interviews with 30 subjects were carried out, to revise questionnaire and determine procedures for data collection.

The interviews took about 30 minutes, and information concerning subjects' background, contraceptive use, pregnancy, and knowledge, attitude and practice of emergency contraception were collected. Questions referring to reasons for non-use of contraception, use or non-use of emergency contraception, and induced abortion were open-ended.

Results

Characteristics of the Subjects

The age range of the 606 subjects was from 17.7 to 46.8 years, with a median age of 25.8 years. Most subjects finished education in senior high school (61.6%), some in junior high school (19.5%) and college or higher (19.0%). The commercial and service workers accounted for 31.2%, the administrative personnel or managers 24.9%, and the jobless 10.7%. The median of subjects' yearly income was 12,000 yuan (RMB), and the low and high quartile was 8,000 and 20,000 yuan respectively. About 1/3 (31.8%) of subjects were unmarried. 59.1% of subjects had one or more times of induced abortion before this pregnancy (Table 1).

Table 1: Percentage Distribution of the Subjects with different Demographic Characteristics (n=606)

Characteristics	%	Characteristics	%
Age		Ownership of work unit	
<25	44.1	State	50.4
25~	24.8	Collective	6.5
30~	12.4	Joint venture/foreign capital enterprise	32.5
>=35	18.8	Self-employed	10.7
Education		Income (yuan, RMB)	
Junior high school	19.5	<12000	40.3
Senior high school	61.6	12000~	37.8
College or higher	19.0	24000~	12.5
Occupation		36000~	9.4
Worker	16.7	Marriage status	
Commercial & service worker	31.2	Married & had child	44.6
M.T.P*	5.5	Married & no child	23.6
Administrative personnel/manager	24.9	Unmarried	31.9
Self-employed	5.0	Times of induced abortion	
Unemployed	10.7	1st time	40.9
Others	6.1	2nd time	40.4
		3rd time	18.7

* including medical staff, teachers and other professionals.

The Reasons for Unwanted Pregnancy

Among 606 subjects, 595 (98.2%) were unwanted pregnancy, of which, 380 (63.9%) resulted from contraceptive failure, 67 (11.3%) from discrete use of contraceptives and 148 (24.9%) from non-use of contraception during the cycle. The main reasons for the unwanted pregnancy among the unmarried were non-use and discrete use of contraception (55.4%), while among the married was contraceptive failure (73.1%). The main failure methods were rhythm, withdrawal and condom. The proportion of IUD failure was only high among the married women with a child (Table 2). Among 380 contraceptive failures, 164 (43.2%) were recognized by subjects soon after the failure. Therefore, there were 379 (148+67+164) pregnancies which were suitable to use emergency contraception to be prevented. These 379 pregnancies accounted for 63.7% of all unwanted pregnancy.

Table 2: The Percentage of Contraceptive Failure Types by Marital Status and Family Structure

Type of failure	Marital status/family structure		
	Unmarried (n=86)	Married & no child (n=88)	Married & had a child (n=206)
Broken/shed condom	7.0	12.5	12.6
Missed O.C.	1.2	4.6	1.0
Withdrawal failure	26.7	12.5	17.5
Rhythm failure	62.8	64.8	45.2
IUD failure*	0.0	1.1	16.5
Spermicide failure	0.0	4.5	5.3
Other	2.3	0.0	1.9

* including expelled IUD and conceived with IUD.

The Knowledge of Emergency Contraception

Among the total of 606 subjects, 173 (28.5%) were aware of emergency contraception, in which, only 4.0% knew that the IUD could act as an emergency contraceptive. The proportion of awareness was not statistically different between married and unmarried subjects (29.3% vs. 26.9%) (χ^2=0.258, P>0.05).

Subjects who were younger, better educated, wealthier, and more knowledgeable about contraceptives in general were more likely to be aware of emergency contraception. The proportion of the awareness of emergency contraception was highest among medical staff, teachers, and other professionals, and lowest in workers. Married subjects without children were more likely to know emergency contraception than unmarried subjects and the married with a child. Subjects with more pregnancy and induced abortion were less likely to know emergency contraception (Table 3).

The most important sources of the knowledge of emergency contraception identified by respondents included books/newspapers/magazines (38.2%), relatives/friends/ parents (30.6%), family planning publicity (22.0%) and others (9.2%). More married subjects got the knowledge from family planning publicity than unmarried subjects (28.9% vs. 5.8%).

The Attitude to Emergency Contraception

The proportion of being willing to use emergency contraception

After the subjects were informed about the effects, the usage and the possible side-effects of emergency pill and emergency IUD, they were asked whether they would be willing to use them when needed. Among 606 subjects, 518 (85.5%) subjects answered they would use emergency contraception when needed, 79 (13.0%) subjects gave the negative response and 9 (1.5%) subjects gave the uncertain reply. The difference of the proportion of willingness between the subjects with unwanted pregnancy and with intended pregnancy was not statistic significant (85.2% vs.72.7%, $P>0.05$).

The proportion of the willingness was different among the women with different characteristics. Young, healthy, better educated and professional women were more willing to use emergency contraception when needed. Both the unmarried and the married without children were more willing to use emergency contraception than the married with children. Subjects in the first induced abortion had the higher proportion of willingness (Table 4). Subjects who had known emergency contraception before were more willing to use emergency contraception than those who just knew it from the study (χ^2 =8.062, $P>0.005$).

Table 3: The Proportions of Awareness of Emergency Contraception by Subjects' Characteristics

Characteristics	n	%	Characteristics	n	%
Age (years) #***			Age at menarche (year)#***		
<25	267	31.5	11-12	95	42.1
25	150	32.7	13-14	319	28.2
30	75	28.0	15-16	162	24.1
35	114	16.7	16-	30	13.3
Level of education#***			Marriage and family structure*		
Junior high school	118	9.3	Unmarried	193	26.9
Senior high school	373	26.3	Married with child	270	24.8
College or higher	115	55.7	Married without child	143	37.8
Occupation**			Frequency of pregnancy#**		
Worker	101	17.8	1	158	33.5
Commercial & service worker	189	21.7	2	208	29.3
M.T.P.[D]	33	57.6	3	140	28.6
Administrative personnel/manager	151	39.7	>=4	100	19.0
Self-employed	30	26.7	Times of induced abortion#		
Unemployed	65	29.2	1st time	248	30.7
Others	37	21.6	2nd time	245	29.0
Ownership of work unit			3rd time	113	23.0
State	265	30.2	Contraceptive knowledge scores#***		
Collective	34	35.3	<=25	43	14.0
Joint venture/ foreign capital enterprises	171	26.3	26 50	333	21.9
Private	56	21.4	51~ 75	204	39.7
Yearly income (yuan RMB)#*			76~100	26	50.6
<12000	244	23.4			
12000~	229	31.0			
24000~	76	32.9			
36000~	57	35.1			

D including medical staff, teachers and other professionals;
trend test;
*: Chi-square test, $p<0.05$; **: $p<0.01$.

Table 4: The percentage of Being Willing to Use Emergency Contraception by Subjects' Characteristics

Characteristics	n	% of willingness	Characteristics	n	% of willingness
Age (Years)#*			Occupation*		
<25	267	90.6	Worker	101	84.2
25~	150	86.7	Commercial & service worker	189	82.0
30~	75	81.3	M.T.P.[D]	33	90.9
>=35	114	74.6	Administration personnel/manager	151	93.4
Education#*			Self-employed	30	83.3
Junior high school	118	79.7	Unemployed	65	81.5
Senior high school	373	86.1	Others	37	78.4
College or higher	115	89.6	Times of induce abortion **		
Marital status/family structure **			1st time	248	90.3
Unmarried	193	90.2	2nd or more	358	82.1
Married & had a child	143	90.2	Chronic disease *		
Married & no child	270	79.6	Have	49	73.5
			Have not	557	86.5

D including medical staff, teachers and other professionals;
trend test;
*: Chi-square test, $p<0.05$; **: $p<0.01$.

The types of preferred emergency contraceptive

Among 518 women who were willing to use emergency contraception when needed, 428 (82.6%) women wanted to use emergency pill, 42 (8.1%) women wanted to use IUD as emergency contraceptive and 48 (9.3%) women had no preference. The main reasons for selecting the pill were its convenience (40.0%) and painless (21.0%). The main reasons for selecting IUD were its high efficacy (33.3%), less side effects (31.0%) and it could be used as a regular contraceptive method.

The ideal place for obtaining emergency contraceptive

Among subjects who were aware of emergency contraception, 74.6% noted that emergency contraception was available in Shanghai. Subjects preferred drugstores (60.1%) to hospitals (30.2%) for obtaining emergency contraception. Drugstores were preferred for "convenience" (87.1%) even though hospitals were recognized for "reliability" (85.8%).

Use of Emergency Contraception

The proportion of subjects using emergency contraception before and within this cycle

Both the percentages of the subjects whoever used emergency contraception before and used in this pregnancy were very low. The total of 32 subjects had used emergency contraception before, being 5.3% of all subjects and 18.5% of these who were aware of emergency contraception respectively. Thirteen subjects had used emergency contraception in this pregnant, being 2.1% of all subjects and 7.5% of the subjects who knew emergency contraception respectively. All users used the same regimen, anordrin-locally known as visiting pill No 53. Most of them got the medicine from drugstores.

The events for which emergency contraception should be used but not

Among 606 subjects, 57.9% subjects had experienced the events for which they should use emergency contraception but not before this pregnancy. Thirty per cent of the vaginal loop users had ever suffered the recognized dropping, 20.4% of the OC users had ever missed the pill sometimes, and 17.5% of the IUD users had ever experienced IUD expelling. Though the proportion of the subjects who ever experienced the breakage of condom was not very high (13.8%), the person times were the highest (Table 5). There were also 76 (12.5%) subjects who had suffered other recognized contraceptive failure before. There were also 226 (37.3%) subjects whoever had intercourse without use of any contraception.

Table 5: The Events where Emergency Contraception should be used but not

Events	N	%*	Person times 1-5	Person times 6-10	Person times >10
Broken/shed condom	55	13.8	33	5	3
Missed OC	21	20.4	8	0	9
Expelled IUD	25	17.5	18	0	0
Dropped vaginal loop	3	30.0	3	0	0

* referred to the ratio of subjects who had experienced the event among all who had used the method.

The reason for non-use of emergency contraception was variety, but the most common reason was that the subjects did not know about or not familiar with the method (78.1%). Other reason included the subjects thought they would not be pregnant (14.6%) and others (7.3%).

Among the unwanted pregnancy, there were 157 subjects who had heard of emergency contraception but not used it in this pregnant. The reason for their non-use included they "didn't find contraceptive failure" (46.6%), "were not familiar with emergency contraception" (31.2%), "thought the pregnancy wouldn't happen" (7.0%), "were careless" (6.4%), "had no emergency contraception pills at hand" (3.8%), "were afraid of the side effects" (2.5%) and others (2.5%).

The proportion of induced abortion which could have been prevented if emergency contraception was used

As mentioned above, 98.2% (595/606) of the pregnancies were unwanted, and 63.7% (379/595) of subjects recognized they were at risk of pregnancy soon after the intercourse, the duration which emergency contraception has the best chance of being effective. Based on these findings, and using a 85% efficacy rate [Task force on Post-ovulatory Methods of Fertility Regulation 1998] for levonorgestrel-only emergency contraception (when used within 12 hours of unprotected intercourse), it is estimated that if levonorgestrel-only regimen had been accessible and used correctly by subjects in the study, 52.20% of induced abortions could have been prevented according to the formula as follow:

P = Proportion of unintended pregnancy × Proportion of the pregnancies being appropriate to use of emergency contraception × Efficacy of emergency contraception

$= (595 \div 606) \times (379 \div 595) \times 0.8500 = 0.5220$

Discussion

Women's knowledge on emergency contraception

There were only 28.5% of subjects who knew of emergency contraception in the study. Among them, 97.1%

knew of emergency contraceptive pill and only 4.1% knew of IUD as an emergency contraception. Compared with the similar studies conducted in other countries, the proportion was lower, especially for emergency contraceptive pill. For example, in New Zealand, 76% of women who seek induced abortion knew of emergency contraception and 4% knew of IUD as emergency contraception [Young L *et al.*, 1995]; in Finland, 73% were familiar with emergency contraceptive pill, 11% knew IUD could be used for emergency contraception [Savonius H *et al.*, 1995]. The results implied that emergency contraception had not been paid enough attention and women's knowledge on emergency contraception was lack in China.

Similar with the results from the studies in England [George J *et al.*, 1994; Smith B H *et al.*, 1996], this study showed that books, newspapers, magazines and friends/ relatives were the main sources where subjects got the knowledge on emergency contraception. Only 20.0% of subjects got the knowledge from family planning materials. So, education on emergency contraception by family planning agencies in China should be strengthened. As books, newspapers and magazines were an important source for women to get the knowledge, especially for the unmarried, it is important for them to provide new, correct and scientific knowledge to public.

Women's attitude to emergency contraception

Previous studies showed that there was high proportion of women who had the intention to use emergency contraception [Gan Shixiu *et al.*, 1998; George J *et al.*, 1994; Harper C C and Ellertson C E, 1995]. In this study, 85.5% of subjects were willing to use emergency contraception when needed, indicated women's positive attitude to and high potential demand for the method. Subjects who had known of emergency contraception were more willing to use it, which implied that subjects' knowledge was closely related to the attitude.

Among women who were willing to use emergency contraception, the ideal place which most subjects chose was drugstores, followed by hospitals, suggesting that drugstore played an important role on the provision of emergency contraceptive pills. With the development of economics in China and the increase of women's role in society, women's leisure time became much less than before and only convenient service could meet their needs. Though a lot of women thought hospital was the reliable place to get contraceptive service, most of them actually got contraceptive service from drugstores for its "convenience" and other reasons. As most of drugstore could not provide necessary counselling and medical examination, the emergency contraceptives provided by drugstores should be those with less side-effects and of high effectiveness, and labelled with the exact description of use, indication, contraindication and notice items.

Women's needs on emergency contraception

Among unwanted pregnancy of the study, 63.7% were predictable, which proved that there were great potential users of emergency contraception in Shanghai, China. The analysis on the situation subjects should have used emergency but did not give the evidence also. Among the ever users, the proportion of having the situation of condom breaking or shedding, usual oral contraceptive pills miss-taking, IUD expelling, and diaphragm expelling were from 13.8% to 30.0%. There were also 37.3% of subjects whoever had at least one intercourse without use of contraceptive. These situations could result in pregnancies, which could be prevented by emergency contraception. One of the important reasons for women not to use emergency contraception was they didn't know emergency conception or lack the knowledge on emergency contraception. It indicated therefore that if emergency contraception were well known and generally available, many women who experienced unprotected intercourse would use it rather than resort to abortion.

Women's use status of emergency contraception

The proportion of women who had used emergency contraception was obviously lower in Shanghai, China as compared with those in other countries [Glasier A *et al.*, 1996; Percival-Smith R K and Abercrombie B, 1988]. One main reason for women not to use emergency contraception, which should have been used, was they didn't find contraceptive failure, had no enough knowledge on emergency contraception and thought they would not get pregnant. The results suggested that it was also important to inform women the knowledge on the recognition of observable contraceptive failure and other situations for which emergency contraception would be appropriate at the family planning education.

Though there were no detail data on emergency contraceptive use status in China, from available data, it still could be seen that women in Shanghai had higher use rate of emergency contraception if compared with other places of China. A study conducted in Zheng Zhou city showed, among 938 predictable pregnancies, only 10 subjects used emergency contraception in last circle, while among 379 predictable pregnancies in this study, 13 used it. Therefore, use of emergency contraception would have much more impact on the decrease of induced abortion on national level if widely used in whole country. In this study, if all women who were appropriate to using emergency contraception had used it, 59.4% of induced abortion could have been reduced. So, the advocacy and promotion of emergency contraceptive use would be meaningful for the decrease of induced abortion in China.

Conclusions and Policy Recommendations

- Over half (52.2%) of the induced abortion in Shanghai could have been avoided by using levonorgestrel-only emergency contraception. Promotion of emergency contraception by family planning programs could have a substantial impact on reducing the rate of induced abortion.
- Policy-makers should focus on improving women's awareness and knowledge of emergency contraception, placing particular emphasis on reaching less educated women. Women in the study were generally poorly informed about emergency contraception. However, attitudes toward emergency contraception were positive, indicating potential demand for the method.

- Women expressed a preference for drugstores for obtaining emergency contraception. Policy-makers should, therefore, focus on improving the quality of service offered by drugstores since they may play a potentially important role on the provision of emergency contraception.
- Family planning education should include recognition of observable contraception failure and instructions for prompt use of emergency contraception after failure since women's use of emergency contraception depends upon their ability to recognize situations for which emergency contraception would be appropriate.

Acknowledgement

The authors thank RHR/WHO for its financial and technical supports, which enables the study to be conducted.

References

1. Huang Runlong and Yu Shenguan, 2000. "Induced abortion and its influencing factors among married reproductive age women in China". In *Theses Collection of 1997 National Population and Reproductive Health Survey*. Ed. State Family Planning Committee and Chinese Population Information Research Centre. Chinese Population Publishing House: Beijing, pp. 267-275.
2. South to South Cooperation in Reproductive Health, 1995. "Consensus Statement on Emergency Contraception". *Contraception* 52: 211.
3. Han Xuejun, Weng Liju and Xiao Bilian, 1996. "Emergency contraception with mifepristone and anordrin". *Chinese Journal of Obstetrics and Gynaecology* 31: 526.
4. Zhang Yan, Qiao Genmei and Zhu Pengdi, *et al.*, 1998. "Clinical observation of three doses of mifepriston for emergency contraception." *Chinese Journal of Family Planning* 8: 343.
5. Xie Xi, Liu Yiping and Lin Xiaoling, 1998. "A clinical study on 600 cases of mifepristone for emergency contraception." *Reproduction and Contraception* 18: 223.
6. Hu Jing, Wu Shangchun and Sun Hongzhu, *et al.*, 1998. "The effectiveness of 50mg mifepristone (one dose) for emergency contraception." *Chinese Journal of Family Planning* 2: 80.
7. Fan Aihua, Wang Yinghong and Wang Zhanbiao, 1998. "The effectiveness of emergency postcoital contraception among 518 cases." *Chinese Journal of Family Planning* 9: 408.

8. Duan Wei, Wu Minghui and Li Shuxiu, 1997. "Postcoital contraception with anordrin." *Chinese Journal of Family Planning* 3:165.
9. Yang Yan, Zhang Xiaomei and Wei Dianying, *et al.*, 1997. "Clinical study of mifepristone, anordrin and intrauterine device used for emergency contraception." *Journal of Reproductive Medicine* 6: 171.
10. Zhang Yan, Qiao Genmei and Zhu Pengdi, *et al.*, 1996. "The clinical observation of mifepristone administered postcoitally during the period of ovulation." *Chinese Journal of Family Planning* 1: 29.
11. Hu Jing, Wu Shangchun and Sun Hongzhu, *et al.*, 1996. "Clinical trial of a single dose of mifepristone 25 mg for emergency contraception." *Chinese Journal of Family Planning* 6: 326.
12. Cheng Yimin, Zhu Wei and Zhang Yang, *et al.*, 1996. "Evaluation of emergency contraception knowledge among abortion seekers." *Journal of Reproductive Medicine* 5: 246.
13. Gan Shixiu, Xu Xiao and Cheng Yimin, *et al.*, 1998. "The attitude and aspiration on emergency contraception of the 20-30 years old fecund women in Zheng Zhou." *Chinese Journal of Family planning* 6: 266.
14. Task force on Post-ovulatory Methods of Fertility Regulation, 1998. "Randomised controlled trial of levonorgestrel versus the Yuzpe regimen of combined oral contraceptives for emergency contraception." *Lancet* 352: 428-33.
15. Young, L., Me McCowan, L. and FRCOG, *et al.*, 1995. "Emergency contraception—why women don't use it." *N Z Med J* 108: 145.
16. Savonius, H., Pakarinen, P. and Sjoberg, L. 1995. "Reason for pregnancy termination: negligence or failure of contraception?" *Acta Obstet Gynecol Scand,* 74: 818.
17. George, J., Turner, J. and Cooke, E. 1994. Women's knowledge of emergency contraception. Br J Gen Pract, 44: 451.
18. Smith, B.H., Gurney, E.M. and Aboulela, L. *et al.*, 1996. "Emergency contraception: a survey of women's knowledge and attitudes." *Br J Obstet Gynaecol,* 103: 1109.
19. George, J., Turner, J. and Cooke, E. 1994. "Women's knowledge of emergency contraception." *Br J Gen Pract,* 44: 451.
20. Harper, C.C. and Ellertson, C.E. 1995. "The emergency contraception pill: a survey of knowledge and attitudes among students at Princeton University." *Am J Obstet Gynecol,* 173: 1438.
21. Glasier, A., Ketting, E. and Palan, V.T. *et al.*, 1996. "Case studies in emergency contraception from six countries." *Intern Fam Plan Perspect,* 22: 57.
22. Percival-Smith, R.K. and Abercrombie, B. 1988. "Post-coital contraception: some characteristic of women who use this method." *Contraception,* 37: 425.

Part - VI

AYURVEDA AND HEALTH PROMOTION

24

Retinal Care and Prevention of Blindness: Successful Ayurvedic Therapies

Dr. P.K. Ravindranath

Introduction

The human eye and particularly the Retina is a vital organ for a successful and productive life. Any major defect or disease of the eye will deprive human beings of a successful life. People seldom realise its importance, in the absence of any eye problem. When people get eye problems some of them use self-medication or rush to a general Allopathic doctor depending upon the seriousness of the problem. If the problem is an infection like conjunctivitis due to bacterial infection of the eye very often an antibiotic helps to cure the disease. When the problem is deep rooted and associated with the retina, allopathic therapies have limitation in treating most retinal problems. In fact several patients with retinal problems after unsuccessful treatment by allopathic eye specialist, approached this author for treatment, which this author carried out during the past three decades and the same tradition perpetuated by my father Sri Konniyoor K.N. Kesava Pillai, former Professor and honorary consultant of Ophthalmology in Government Ayurveda college, Trivandrum prior to my initiation in to this specialised medical care. Although I have the background of Allopathic surgery and parallel specialisation in Ayurveda, I have been practising Ayurveda treatment only for retinal and the other eye problems, so far.

The focus of this paper is on different retinal problems and their successful Ayurvedic treatment. The discussion that follows begins with the different problems experienced in the retina the general allopathic treatments given like cryo therapy, Laser therapy and their implications for the patients. The subsequent section discuss suitable Ayurvedic therapies used for retinal care, their merits and advantages over other systems of medicine. In conclusion three case studies of retinal problems are discussed which were unsuccessfully treated by allopathic doctors from London, Nethralaya at Chennai, Aravind Eye hospital Madurai and the Christian Medical College hospital, Vellore. These cases were later successfully cured using Ayurvedic therapies without any recurrence.

Brief Summary of the Anatomy and Physiology of the Eye

The Eye ball may be considered to be a highly differentiated end organ of the optic nerve which is a sensory nerve. The eye ball is a rounded structure formed of an inelastic wall with a cavity inside. The wall is formed of three coats.

1. **Outer Fibrous Coat:** It is composed of a dense, slightly elastic supporting membrane. The Anterior part (1/6) is transparent called the Cornea and the posterior (5/6) is opaque—the sclera.
2. **Middle Vascular Coat:** It is highly vascular layer which is mainly responsible for supplying nutrition to the inner nervous layer—Retina. The layer is known as the uveal tract. This again consists of three parts.
   (a) Anterior part is called the Iris which rests on the lens. It has a central perforation called the Pupil, the average diameter of which is 3 mm. It contains two muscles—the Constrictor and dilator Pupillae.
   (b) Middle part is called the Ciliary Body. It contains a muscle called the ciliary muscle responsible for accommodation. On the inner surface of the Ciliary body, there are about 60 to 70 radially placed projections known as ciliary processes which secrete aqueous humour in to the posterior chamber of the eye ball.

(c) Posterior part:—the choroid which lies in opposition with the sclera. The function of the choroid is to supply nourishment to the Retina which lies on its inner surface.

3. **Inner Nervous Coat:** It is known as the Retina. This is the layer by means of which one can see objects. It consists of an outer single layer of pigmented cells and inner Retina proper which is made up of multiple layers of nerve cells and pluxuses. The nerve fibres arising from the Retina proper, come out of the eye ball posteriorly as the optic nerve. The optic nerve passes backwards along the base of the brain and ultimately reaches the posterior part of the brain known as the occipital lobe.

The cavity of the eye ball contains several structures. In the anterior part, there is a biconvex transparent structure called the Crystalline Lens. It is suspended from the ciliary body by fine delicate fibres called the Suspensory Ligament of lens. The lens together with its suspensory ligament divide the cavity into two compartments—a small Anterior and a large Posterior. The posterior compartment contains a transparent jelly like structure known as Vitreous Humour. The Anterior compartment is further subdivided by the iris in to Anterior and Posterior chambers, both of which contain Aqueous Humour. The chambers communicate each other through the pupil.

The Aqueous Humour, secreted by the ciliary processes, is first poured in to the posterior chamber. From the posterior chamber it passes through the pupil into the anterior chamber. From the angle of the anterior chamber the aqueous passes into the canal of Schlem from where it is drained by aqueous veins into the episcleral veins.

The blood supply of the eye ball comes from the branches of the ophthalmic artery which is a branch of the internal carotid artery.

The nerve supply of the eye comes from the ophthalmic branch of Vth cranial (Trigiminal) nerve.

Diseases of Retina

1. Haemorrhage of the Retina

   It may be due to

   (a) Vascular conditions, such as arterio sclerosis, Diabetes Mellitus, Nephritis

   (b) Blood diseases—Purpura, Haemophelia, Leukaemia

   (c) Traumatic

   (d) Unknown causes

2. Occlusion of Central Retinal Artery
3. Retinal Arteriosclerosis
4. Thrombosis of Retinal Vein
5. Retinopathies
6. Retinitis pigmentosa
7. Detachment of Retina

In my practice I have treated almost every type of cases and got a good result in Modern medicine there are some limitation for the treatment. I got good result in Retinitis Pigmentosa. But it needs prolonged treatment. Oral medicines, Tharpanam, Sirovasthi are essential treatment for Retinitis Pigmentosa. In modern medicine they are treating with Vitamins, changing of glasses for R.P. In cases of haemorrage Laser treatment and cauterisation etc. are the treatment. In Ayurveda these type of cases can be treated with oral medines and Tharpanam.

Successful case studies of Retinal care using Ayurveda

Although the present author has treated hundreds of eye patients successfully three cases are important for critical discussion for the benefit of future treatment by concerned physicians. Further these three case studies will throw more light on prevention of such cases, Mr. Ramesh, Dr. Devan and Mr. Ambaram belong to the states of Kerala, Andhra Pradesh and Tamil Nadu and professed the avocations of business, academic research and stenography respectively. All of them are educated, married and are serious persons. Genetically none of them have any predisposition eye problems. In spite of following diverse professions all of them had common retinal problems.

Case Study I

Mr. Ramesh's Retinal problem—Retinitis Pigmentosa—treatment in London and later Ayurvedic cure.

Mr. Ramesh aged 25 owns his own publishing company have ever faced any retinal problem. There was no known reason for developing Retinitis for Mr. Ramesh, however he slowly developed Retinitis Pigmentosa in the form of black dots on the retina from the age of 19. This became serious over the next five years. At that time they approached Ophthalmic specialist in their city. When this did not help, they went to London to seek the experts in Ophthalmology.

Experience in London—In London Mr. Ramesh sought the help of a senior Eye Specialist in one of the best Ophthalmic Hospitals. After a careful examination the doctor in London carried out several treatments. After three months there was no improvement for the sight. The doctor ultimately said that there is no treatment for this disease. Mr. Ramesh returned to Kerala and started searching for Ayurvedic remedies.

Ayurvedic Cure

The patient reported the history of the illness and treatment in detail to this author. The patient and his family members were dejected, frustrated and seriously worried. They believed that Mr. Ramesh was doomed to absolute blindness and that Ayurvedic treatment could save him. When assured him of a cure of the retinitis of Mr. Ramesh, they initially did not fully believe it. However they gave me full freedom to treat this patient. After psychologically consoling the patient and parents, the following therapies were given for the patient initially over a period of one month as an inpatient.

Ayurveda Treatment

According to the Ayurvedic procedure; the first three days were the preparatory period for the therapies commencing from the fourth day. Therefore, he was given oil bath, the restriction of food and medicines like "Gandharva Hasthadi Kashayam, Erndasukumaram, for bowel cleaning and Anu Tailam Nasal drops for cleaning the nostrils and sinuses. After cleaning the system, one after the other therapies were provided to Ramesh for improvement of health, rejuvenation and retinal care.

Initially oil massage was given daily for one hour for physical health and fitness. Subsequently retina focused specific treatment namely THARPANAM was arranged for seven days at 5.00 p.m. The medicine is prepared in the medium of refined ghee and saturated through repeated refinements. It was poured into both eyes after preparing a ridge below the eye using black gram paste prepared under sterilized conditions. The medicines was kept in the eye for a few minutes and then removed. After removal of the medicine and for seven days the patient is kept in a protected room without exposure to bright sun light or electrical bulbs. This is one of the major treatment for the cure of the disease.

After the completion of Tharpanam the patient is subjected to SHIROVASTHI, which was continued for another seven days. According to shirovasthi one litre of medicated oil (Dhanwantharam) to be kept on the head in a cap like leather material for half an hour daily for seven days. This medicated oil generally rejuvanates and strengthens the central nervous system including optic nerves. It will supplement the Tharpanam therapy. In addition oral medicines like Mahathribhala Ghritham, Jeevanthyadi Ghritham, Yashtivara Choornam were given to strengthen the nerves for six months. Mr. Ramesh has undergone the therapies for three consecutive years. After taking the first course of medicines Mr. Ramesh started experiencing improvement in his vision. Ultimately after repeating the same therapies for three years Mr. Ramesh regained his vision. The successful cure of Retinitis Pigmentosa of Mr. Ramesh by Ayurveda treatment is a lesson for the medical community and patients all over the world.

Case Study II

Dr. Devan is a well known university professor. He developed one black spot initially on his right eye. It was noticed after one year of hectic Library reference work in the USA. He then approached the well known Ophthalmic

Institute, Sankar Nethralaya at Chennai. There he was given cryo surgery to the black spot. As a result the transparent nature of the eye on the spot of cryo surgery was lost. One year later he had a similar problem in the left eye. He approached the Aravind Eye Hospital, Madurai and they too followed similar procedure. Fearing a recurrence of the problem Dr. Devan approached me for a permanent remedy. A similar course of treatment was administered. Now 28 years have passed since he took the first Ayurveda eye therapy and so far no problem has occurred. As a reputed scientist, he continued his Ayurveda therapies for rejuvenation viz., Oil massage Tharpanam periodically for 12 times. After his initial Ayurveda treatment, he carried out 25 major research projects and published 30 valuable books. He has become a reputed social scientist in the world. Thus despite heavy and continuous research work which has strained his eyes for the past 28 years, his eyes have remained healthy and normal after taking Ayurveda treatment. It is another success story of Ayurveda eye treatment.

Case Study III

Mr. Ambaram has been working as a stenographer for the past 20 years in a university. He has passed certificate courses in Homoeo medicine and Yoga. When ever he gets minor health problems he takes Homoeo medicine only. He is a vegetarian and no other habits like drinking or smoking.

Eye Problem

Three years ago he developed different vision problem such as mild discomfort and occasional pain. He experienced difficulty in typing due to his eye problem. Under pressure he falls a sleep after two or three hours work involuntarily. He has used certain Homoeo medicines to improve his health. However, he could not get any relief. Two years ago Mr. Ambaram approached the ophthalmology department of Christian Medical College Hospital at Vellore for diagnosis and treatment. They took a scan and conducted thorough examinations. They also used laser treatment. However, the Laser therapy and other examinations continued for six months. Finally he did not get any relief for his eye problems.

Ayurveda Treatment

Mr. Ambaram contacted me on 16-6-2003 and reported his prolonged allopathic trial and treatment. According to Ayurvedic procedure he was given three days Nasyam to clean his sense organs particularly Throat, Nose and Ear supplemented by oral medicines. Subsequently he was given oil bath and massage for a day. On the fourth day onwards he was given Tharpanam to treat his eye problem. Tharpanam continued for seven days. After that for his body rejuvenation oil massage was given for few more days. Simultaneously he was given oral medicines like Mahathribhala Ghritham, Yashtivarachoornam and Sahacharadi Thailam for external application and Dasamoola Rasayanam for strengthening nerves in general. After 14 days he was discharged and given oral medicines namely Mahathribhala Ghritham, Nayanachandra Louham and Dasamoolahareethaki, for strengthening nerves in general, for two more months. They included Dasamoolahareethaki, Vidaryadi Ghritham for rejuvenate his health especially his nervous system. When he was discharged he did not face fatigue and any discomfort of the eye. For further therapy of Sirovasthy to rejuvenate his nerves he will be again reporting to me after a month. The present indication is that a complete cure is possible after completing the pending Sirivasthy therapy and repeating all these courses of therapy for one more time after an year. After 2-3 months, the benefit of all these therapies and oral medicines will enable him to overcome his major problems and he can overcome all his eye problems.

Discussion and Recommendations

According to the Ayurveda philosophy of medical care, treatment is given to strengthen the weak and affected parts of body. In addition rejuvenation of entire body is also provided. When the body is strengthened against existing problems, it overcomes defects or diseases. In addition, symptomatic treatment for the affected part is also given. Since medicines given are all organic products, and useful for strengthening the physical system, no side effect will be there through Ayurveda treatment. When the entire body is treated for rejuvenation, it coordinates naturally and successfully to overcome the problems in different organs. Thus promotion of health and normal functioning of every system of body and the whole body through Ayurveda is attempted.

Relapse will not take place. However, Shirovasthy and Tharpanam are organ specific and problem centered therapies. Of course massage and oral medicines are for strengthening the entire body action to cure the localised problems. Ayurveda therapy like panchakarma chikitsa can be taken periodically to prevent diseases. When they are periodically taken degenerative problems like Arthritis, back ache, Cervical spondylitis, weakness of limbs, sexual problems and many other such problems can be avoided. Thus preventive care against possible diseases during old age can be successfully ensured through Ayurvedic therapies. Further more, many Ayurvedic therapies promote immunity against infections and diseases. Therefore, Ayurveda is more of a protective measure against diseases and degeneration. In fact it is a total rejuvenation therapy for the entire body without any side effect. Therefore, selected periodic use of Ayurveda therapies based on the need of the organs of the body will be a life promoting habit which will promote health, longevity and better quality of life.

25

Pioneer and Great Health Educator in India

Iqbal Shah, K.A. Pisharoti, K.V. Ranganathan, Gao Ersheng, R. Kausalya Devi, V.M. Sandeep and P. Krishnamoorthy

Non-agenarian Dr. V. Ramakrishna, after several decades of successful and productive life, now lives peacefully in the city of Bangalore. He is hale and healthy, true to his profession of Health Education. He is a man of humility, erudition and compassion and incessantly concerned with the welfare of common people, particularly their health and well being.

Dr. V. Ramakrishna has had a brilliant academic career in the best Medical institutions in Mysore, Calcutta and California Universities, which has enabled him to render valuable service in the field of health for all. Affectionately referred to as Dr. Ram by his friends and admires he is considered to be a legendary health educator who has occupied all the categories of positions with distinction right from Medical Officer through all the other positions in the medical hierarchy of state, national and international levels.

Brilliant Academic Achievements

Dr. Ram was fortunate in getting the best education from the medical colleges located in Mysore city from which he graduated. It was followed by his obtaining D.PH. from the well known Hygiene and Public Health Institute in Kolkata (Calcutta) in India. After a decade, he enrolled for

M.PH. in the best school of public health in California, USA. Even as a student he made a mark and won the following awards.

- Surgery prize in MBBS from Mysore University, 1938.
- Delta Omega Society award for Distinction in Masters in Public Health, University of California, Berkeley the USA, 1955.

Thereafter during his active life he was honoured with the following:

- National merit award of the Delta Omega Society for outstanding achievements in Public Health, Oct. 1978.
- Alumnus award in Recognition of Distinguished Service, School of Public Health, University of California, Berkeley (8th July, 1980).
- Jacques Parisot Award for Outstanding contributions to the Development of Health Education, Dublin, Ireland (1985).
- The Elise and Walter A. Haas International award, University of California, Berkely (1996).

His brilliant career will be an inspiration for posterity to emulate and achieve similar academic excellence. In addition to distinguishing himself on medical education, specialised in a variety of applied training programmes, which made in a unique and successful practitioner of Health Administration and Education. They include the following specialisations:

- Development Administration
- Personal Management and Training
- Public Health Administration
- Health Education planning, programming and management and
- Health manpower, planning and development in the USA, USSR, UK, Philippines and Japan

His expertise in all these human resource development programmes focusing on all essential, valuable and diverse aspects of human development made him an institution in public health and health education at the national and international level.

Health Administrator

Dr. Ram began his career as early as 1938 as house surgeon, in the premier Victoria Hospital in Bangalore. After one year, he moved out to the Department of Public Health as a Probationary Officer. It was a turning point in his career to pursue health education. Thereafter he assumed diverse professional responsibilities which enriched his career, such as Health Officer in Public Health Institute, Bangalore, District Health Officer, Asstt. Health Administrator at the state level, Superintendent of Bureau of Health Education and Training and so on.

At the national level, Dr. Ram began his career as Director of Central Health Education Bureau, New Delhi. Subsequently, he joined as a faculty member of National Institute of Health Administration and Education and National Institute of Family Planning, New Delhi. All these academic assignments, he completed by 1967. However, from 1968 onwards for two years he served as Deputy Commissioner for Family Planning, in-charge of IEC, Research and Training followed by Deputy Director General of Health Services of Government of India. After successfully completing all these assignments he moved out of India to assume an International role in WHO in 1969.

International Services

In 1969, he assumed charge as Regional Advisor of World Health Organisation for Health Education in South East Asia region. In 1975, for two years, he served as a country representative of WHO for Health Manpower Development of Bangladesh, Indonesia and Mongolia. Later on for a year, he was entrusted with the task of drafting the Asian Charter for health development by WHO. Subsequently for five years, he was Professor of Public Health in the University of Hawaii, USA. Here he was also Chairman of the International Health Programme of the School of Public Health. After retirement form this assignment, for 15 years, he was Regional Director of the South East Asia Regional Bureau of the International Union for Health Promotion and Education. Parallelly he was serving as Consultant to several institutions for the development of health promotion programmes and health education, notably in the Gandhigram Institute of Rural Health and Family Planning and the other institutions in India.

Internationally Dr. Ramakrishna extended consultancy services to WHO, UNICEF, ESCAP, UNESCO, World Bank, USAID, DANIDA, Ford and Rockfeller Foundation, Red Cross and several other national organizations like ICMR, FPAI, and so on. His valuable and diverse experiences in human resource development in health its promotion and education programmes benefited internationally, nationally and at the regional levels. Thus, he became a legendary figure in Health Education in the world at large.

Recognitions

In his Yeoman services rendered in the field of health in general and his contributions to health education, it is not at all surprising that he is given a number of awards at international and national levels. A few major awards he has received, so far, are the following:

- Honorary fellow of the Society of Public Health Education of the USA (1970).
- Honorary Fellow of the Indian Public Health Association for meritorious services to the Science of Public Health (1975).
- Alumnus Award in Recognition of Distinguished Service, School of Public Health, University of California, Berkeley (8 July, 1980).
- Jacques Parisot Award for Outstanding contributions to the Development of Health Education in South East Asia, International Union of Health Education, Dublin, Ireland (1985).
- The Elise and Walter A. Haas International Award, University of California, Berkeley (1996).

Academic Contributions

Despite his busy administrative assignments Dr. Ram has considerable time to produce valuable academic work. They are listed here for the benefit of the academic community in its teaching, research and education programmes.

- Scientific papers and Technical Articles on Different Aspects of Health Education and Health Development.
- "Health Education in South East Asia—Meeting the Challenges", Paper presented at the WHO consultative meeting held in New Delhi, 10-15 December, 1990, and published by WHO/SEARO.
- "Health Education in Family Welfare Programmes", Keynote speech delivered at the seminar on reviewing and strengthening of National Family Welfare Programme.
- "Health Education is the Essential Component of Effective Water Supply and Sanitation Management", Discussion paper presented at the workshop on Management of Water Supply and Sanitation projects for Executive Engineers.
- "Role of Urban Health Organisation in achieving health for all", paper presented at the First National Conference of Health Officers of Municipal Corporations and Major Municipalities, 1987.
- "Basics of Effective eye health education programmes", paper presented at the Inter-state eye care education workshop held in Bangalore.
- "The real challenge: A self-health system with Genuine Commitment", International Journal of Health Education, 20(1): 19-28, 1977.
- "Health education as a self-health system in primary health care", paper presented at the WHO workshop on Health education services in family health, December 13-23, 1976, SEA/HE/WS 105.
- Manpower development for health education, paper presented at the WHO/PAHO inter-regional consultation on health education manpower for family health and health aspects of human reproduction, Berkeley, California, September 19-26, 1971. Published in the International Journal of Health Education.
- Strategy for development of health education in south east Asia during the VI General program of work of the WHO, 1978-1983, Discussion paper. SEARO, 1974.

- A review of health education in the South East Asia region, paper presented for the gobal review at WHO, Geneva, 1973.
- Education for effective family welfare planning programmes, paper presented at the fifth Central Family Planning Council, Nainital, India, April 17-18, 1968.
- Role of National Health Programs in Bringing about social change since independence, paper presented at the seminar on planning for social change, Council for Social Development, New Delhi, March, 1968.
- Problem of patient motivation for family planning, paper presented at the national hospital administration seminar, New Delhi, 1968.
- Planning, implementation, and evaluation of health education services, background paper for the WHO expert committee, Geneva, 1966.
- Role of voluntary agencies in health education, paper presented at the national health seminar on role of voluntary agencies in the five-year plans, New Delhi, 1966.
- Building national health education services, English Annual Dorothy B. Nyswander, Lecture April 1964, SOPHE Health Education Monograph No. 18, 1964.
- Educational Diagnosis and implementation, paper presented at the international conference on health education of IUHE, Philadelphia, 1962, Published by IUHE.
- Towards effective nutrition education, paper presented at the All India applied nutrition seminar, Lucknow, India, October, 17-23, 1963.
- Papers published in Swasth Hind, the monthly journal of the Ministry of Health and Family planning, Government of India:

    School Health Education: Role of Teachers
    Health Education in Tuberculosis programme
    Medical practitioners and health education
    Health education and environmental sanitation

Bridging the gap

Scheme for the establishment of health education bureaux in states

Health education in the program of employees state insurance corporation

Extension education as a process in family planning

Better health through education

Importance of health education and social sciences in the training of medical students

Papers presented to the planning commission's task force on health, Government of India:

- What needs to be done for developing health education in India, 1957
- Health education past, present and future
- Health education in India
- Training needs for the development of health education in the IV five-year plan.

There is little exaggeration in saying that Dr. V. Ramakrishna is an international model on health promotion and education for inspiring posterity to achieve excellence in health programmes for promoting the quality of life of people all over the world. In such times as ours, complex and bewildering countless problem, such person as Dr. Ramakrishna, rare though they may be, are living examples whose great ideas, devotion and commitment, and hard work have to be emulated by all. This festschrift to Dr. Ram is only a token gesture to express our profound regard for him and deep appreciation of his achievement.

About the Book

This book focuses on contemporary and international perspectives on high priority themes of development particularly on the neglected health education to prevent health hazards, population control to prevent poverty and poor quality of life and to promote reproductive health. In order to promote these high priority themes of development, appropriate policies and strategies have been evolved through several chapters. The classical and holistic systems approach provided in certain chapters can help planners, policy makers and promoters of these programmes to revitalize them with vision and efficiency. There are several valuable and successful experiences presented here, which have been pooled from many countries for the benefit of all the developing regions.

Dr. K. Mahadevan, has consolidated all the valuable chapters with the active collaboration of co-editors and chapter writers for the fast development of these programmes.

This book is a valuable text for students of health education, population, sociology, social work, management, home science, ecology and policy makers and professionals interested in holistic development. It will be valuable for both developed and developing countries alike. This classical and applied book deserves to get several awards from international agencies very soon.

About the Editors

Prof. Dr. K. Mahadevan is an internationally reputed academician in the field of health education, population sciences, communication, women development studies and perspectives on holistic development. He is the author of the holistic development model for Third World countries and theories of life affecting variables of children, variables affecting reproductive health, status affecting variables women (empowerment) and produced 35 valuable books and guided over three dozens of Ph.D. holders from all over India, Africa and west Asia.

Currently he is professor of health education in Addis Ababa University in Africa, and previously he was the Principal, Dean and Professor in Sri Venkateswara University. He was Visiting Professor in the University of Alberta Canada and Fullbright Professor in Columbia, Michigan and Eastwest American Universities. He edited 7 books on all the Asian countries and 3 books on China and India in collaboration with several Asian scholars.

Dr. Iqbal Shah works in WHO, and he is a specialist on reproductive health and also a behavioural scientist. He has promoted research programmes on preventive aspects of health through the funding by WHO in several countries.

Dr. GAO Ersheng is an epidemiologist, population expert and Director of SIPPR, Shanghai. He is a leading scholar in China and contributed several valuable and original papers. He is also a consultant to WHO. He collaborated with the chief editor and produced several books on China and India on a comparative basis.

Vijayan K. Pillai is Professor at the School of Social Work, University of Texas at Arlington, USA. He is a demographer with several research publications. His current interest includes adolescent reproductive health in Sub-Saharan Africa. Currently he is engaged in writing a book on Cross-National Reproductive Rights among Women. He is widely travelled all over the world and has presented research papers at International Seminars. He has authored/co-edited many books.

Dr. K.A. Pisharoti is a public health expert and was the former Director of Gandhigram School of Public Health. He was Visiting Professor in North Carolina University, USA. He was an architect of the Ponnamali Health Project, Chennai. He is a practical and eminent health-cum-population consultant now.

Dr. K.V. Ranganathan is a well-known health educator and former Director of GIRH and FP and was a World Bank employee in Washington for several years. He developed the Gandhigram Institute to the international level before joining the World Bank.

Dr. V.M. Sandeep is a medical graduate and associated with Prof. Mahadevan in doing research and writing several papers. He is a co-editor in a few books related to health, population and fast development perspectives of Andhra Pradesh, India.